SOURCES
Notable Selections
in *Mass Media*

Edited by

JARICE HANSON

University of Massachusetts–Amherst

DAVID J. MAXCY

University of New Hampshire

Dushkin Publishing Group / Brown & Benchmark Publishers

A TIMES MIRROR HIGHER EDUCATION GROUP COMPANY

© 1996 by Dushkin Publishing Group/Brown & Benchmark Publishers,
A Times Mirror Higher Education Group Company, Guilford, Connecticut 06437

Manufactured in the United States of America

First Edition

10 9 8 7 6 5 4 3 2 1

Library of Congress Cataloging-in-Publication Data
  Main entry under title:
    Sources: notable selections in mass media/edited by Jarice Hanson and David J.
  Maxcy.
    Includes bibliographical references and index.
    1. Mass media. I. Hanson, Jarice, *comp.* II. Maxcy, David J., *comp.*

                                                                    302.23
    1-56134-764-7   95-83882

Printed on Recycled Paper

ACKNOWLEDGMENTS

1.1 From Herbert Blumer and Philip M. Hauser, *Movies, Delinquency, and Crime* (Macmillan, 1933). Copyright © 1933 by Macmillan. Reprinted by permission. Notes omitted.

Acknowledgments and copyrights are continued at the back of the book on pages 375–377, which constitute an extension of the copyright page.

Preface

The study of mass communication has followed trends similar to those of other social science disciplines, such as sociology, psychology, and anthropology. What makes communication research different—and what makes it a distinct discipline—is that it involves the study of a unique social phenomenon: human communication as an elemental process of human social formation. In the case of mass media, this fundamental process is mediated not only by language and the dynamics of interpersonal interactions but also by the institutions and technologies that distribute messages to broad, often heterogeneous groups of people. Despite the rich variety of conceptual and methodological research perspectives, the 40 selections contained in this book do not simply represent a babble of conflicting opinions concerning the impact of mass media on society. Rather, we have selected key texts that illuminate the development of specific research questions and theoretical perspectives that have animated the field throughout its history. In each case we have chosen the selection because it represents the scope and explanatory power of its particular "brand" of media research. We do not evaluate any of these perspectives; instead, we attempt to show how they have developed internally and how they have responded to each other within the scientific field of mass media scholarship.

As we began our search for the original selections included in this text, we found that, like popular stories and mythology, the retelling of these seminal works has undergone some embellishment, some broad interpretation, and some distortion. Surprisingly, we found that many of the references later writers made to primary works were inadvertently inaccurate, drawing instead on later revisions of the original works. We hope that *Sources* will serve to remind students and teachers of the real evolution in mass media research and how history has played a role in shaping the questions, methods, and interpretations of the studies.

The relatively few women authors in the early years of mass media study is worth noting. In more recent research, we find a greater variety of perspectives discussed by both women and minorities. As a result, the field of research in media and society has broadened, and with it, the number of perspectives has grown.

We hope that these selections help focus students' attention on the growth and development of the field of research in mass media and society, and that theories and methodologies will be considered more closely for the way they shape and define a research agenda.

Organization of the book In each of the 15 chapters of this book, we have attempted to trace the evolution of a research question, perspective, or theory. In some cases, later selections draw from some of the early writings in an area, defining and redefining original concepts. Chapters 1 and 2 present early effects research that helped influence the growth of media research in the United States. Chapters 3, 4, and 5 explore different aspects of effects research. Chapters 6 and 7 incorporate an approach to thinking about media from the perspective of sense extension and a philosophical approach to media logic. Chapter 8 includes issues of power and ideology that influence media content. Chapter 9 explores topics that subtly influence the way we look at culture through media artifacts. Chapters 10 (cultural process), 11 (cultural criticism), 12 (feminist criticism), and 13 (media and race) explore a variety of interpretive approaches toward the relationship of media, society, and culture. Chapters 14 and 15 broaden the framework of research to international and intercultural issues. Each selection is preceded by a short introductory headnote that establishes the relevance of the selection and that provides biographical information on the author.

Suggestions for reading the selections Students are encouraged to read the introductory headnotes prior to reading the selections. The headnotes will give you a way of thinking about the selections as you read them. Keep in mind that the language used in some early selections is undoubtedly sexist and, in some cases, racist. While we are more sensitive to the impact of certain words today, some of these selections were written at a time in which different values and standards were the norm. Although the selections have been edited for brevity, they have not been altered with regard to the authors' original style and use of speech. Therefore, such usages as the masculine pronoun *he* to refer to everyone may not be acceptable today, but it does reflect a certain sense of history.

A word to the instructor An *Instructor's Manual With Test Questions* (multiple-choice and essay) is available through the publisher for instructors using *Sources: Notable Selections in Mass Media* in the classroom.

Acknowledgments We were very happy to have the opportunity to work together on this project, and we would like to thank Mimi Egan, publisher for the Sources series, for her enthusiastic support. Each of us has worked with Dushkin Publishing Group/Brown & Benchmark Publishers prior to our collaboration on this volume, and we have developed an enormous respect for the care and expertise that all of the Dushkin personnel devote to producing fine products. In particular, Mimi Egan, publisher for the Sources series; David

Dean, list manager; and David Brackley, developmental editor, are a powerful trio of publishing talent. Many thanks!

If readers have any comments or suggestions for other selections to be considered for inclusion in future editions of *Sources,* please write to us in care of SOURCES, Dushkin Publishing Group/Brown & Benchmark Publishers, Sluice Dock, Guilford, CT 06437.

Jarice Hanson
University of Massachusetts–Amherst

David J. Maxcy
University of New Hampshire

SOURCES

Contents

"The traditional press conference has given way to the presidential town hall; the scathing broadside has been supplanted by the fifteen-second spot; campaign oratory has been replaced by the emotional pastiche of the convention film. . . . Television has changed politics itself."

CHAPTER 5   Cultivation Research   103

"The 'mainstream' can be thought of as a relative commonality of outlooks that television tends to cultivate. By 'mainstreaming' we mean the sharing of that commonality among heavy viewers in those demographic groups whose light viewers hold divergent views."

"As mass media become more centralized and homogeneous, the cultural currents become narrower, more standardized, and more sharply defined, and mass communication becomes a more effective mechanism of social control."

PART TWO   *Media of Communication*   125

CHAPTER 6   Media Bias and Sense Extension   127

" 'The medium is the message' means, in terms of the electronic age, that a totally new environment has been created."

"Television does not extend or amplify literate culture. It attacks it. If television is a continuation of anything, it is of a tradition begun by the telegraph and photograph in the mid-nineteenth century, not by the printing press in the fifteenth."

"The homogenized information networks fostered by electronic media offer individuals a comparatively holistic view of society and a wider field within which to measure their relative lot."

"As it became obvious that rap was here to stay, a permanent fixture in black ghetto youths' musical landscape, the reactions changed from dismissal to denigration, and rap music came under attack from both black and white quarters. Is rap really as dangerous as many critics argue? Or are there redeeming characterisitcs to rap music that warrant our critical attention?"

"Before *Boyz N the Hood*, there were two kinds of black female characters in film—whores and good girls. Following 'race' film conventions set in the days of *Cabin in the Sky* and *Stormy Weather*, these women were all portrayed as lightweight (and more often than not, light-skinned) cartoon characters."

PART FIVE   *Media and the Global Order   323*

CHAPTER 14   Perspectives on Development   325

"Where Europeanization once penetrated only the upper level of Middle East society, affecting mainly leisure-class fashions, modernization today diffuses among a wider population and touches public institutions as well as private aspirations with its disquieting 'positivist spirit.' "

"Theoretical writings about modernization in this period after World War II generally followed an 'individual-blame' logic and may have been overly narrow and ethnocentric in a cultural sense."

"The explosion of a great diversity of information technologies and their diffusion around the world during the past two decades have given rise to hopes for accelerating global development and democratization. However, what some liberal theorists have considered as the dawn of a new post-industrial, information society, Marxist theorists have generally viewed as the increasing commodification and privatization of information in the worldwide expansion of monopoly capitalism."

CHAPTER 15 Cultural Imperialism and National Identity 355

PART ONE

Media Effects

CHAPTER 1 Early Approaches

1.1 HERBERT BLUMER AND PHILIP M. HAUSER

Movies, Delinquency, and Crime

In the early 1930s, children made up a large proportion of the movie audience, and there was widespread concern about the impact of film on young people. *Movies, Delinquency, and Crime* (MacMillan, 1933), from which the following selection is excerpted, was one volume in the 12 studies of the influence of motion pictures upon children and youth commissioned by the Payne Fund, a private foundation concerned with issues of mass media and education, at the request of the Motion Picture Research Council. The Payne Fund Studies were the most thorough investigations of film undertaken to that date; the researchers used a variety of methods—including laboratory testing of physical responses to movie images, survey questionnaires, and extensive interview questionnaires—to determine how movies influenced young people. In the following selection, Herbert Blumer (1900–1987) and Philip M. Hauser (b.1909), both professors of sociology at the University of Chicago, discuss their studies of the relationship between movie viewing and criminal and delinquent behavior in young people.

During the early decades of the twentieth century, one prominent psychological theory held that humans are primarily irrational beings whose behaviors are determined by the stimulation of deep, emotional impulses. This "Stimulus-Response" (S-R) theory was carried over into the first quasi-theory of mass communication, later referred to as the "hypodermic nee-dle," or "magic-bullet," model. The magic-bullet concept presumed that media messages emanate from the institutions of mass communication as powerful stimuli, which act directly to shape and manipulate human behavior (as in propaganda or advertising).

Although the Payne Fund Studies were based upon the stimulus-response psychological model and the magic-bullet notion of mass media process, they indicated that the effects of movie viewing are not as immediate and direct as these models predicted. Rather, a number of factors, including prior attitudes and interests, social background, and education of the viewers, influence the impact of the movies on viewer behavior and attitudes. The studies concluded that there may be negative effects of film viewership for *some* "at-risk" individuals.

Only a brief example of Blumer and Hauser's interview transcripts are included in the following selection, though they constituted much of the content of *Movies, Delinquency, and Crime.* Blumer also edited the Payne Fund volume titled *Movies and Conduct* (1933). He went on to become an important name in the field of communication primarily for his work in symbolic interactionism—the study of the dynamics of influence and inter-personal behavior. Hauser, who continued his work in sociology, has conducted several studies on population and demographics.

Key Concept: effects of film on youth

CHAIRMAN'S PREFACE

Motion pictures are not understood by the present generation of adults. They . . . make an enormous appeal to children; and they present ideas and situations which parents may not like. Consequently when parents think of the welfare of their children who are exposed to these compelling situations, they wonder about the effect of the pictures upon the ideals and behavior of the children. Do the pictures really influence children in any direction? Are their conduct, ideals, and attitudes affected by the movies? Are the scenes which are objectionable to adults understood by children, or at least by very young children? Do children eventually become sophisticated and grow superior to pictures? Are the emotions of children harmfully excited? In short, just what effect do motion pictures have upon children of different ages?

. . . [S]tudies were designed to form a series to answer the following questions: What sorts of scenes do the children of America see when they attend the theaters? How do the mores depicted in these scenes compare with those of the community? How often do children attend? How much of what they see do they remember? What effect does what they witness have upon their ideals and attitudes? Upon their sleep and health? Upon their emotions? Do motion pictures directly or indirectly affect the conduct of children? Are they related to delinquency and crime, and, finally, how can we teach children to discriminate between movies that are artistically and morally good and bad? . . .

PROBLEM AND PROCEDURE

Many people believe that current commercial motion pictures are responsible in considerable measure for present-day crime and delinquency. Official censorship, state and municipal, as well as the denunciation by some groups of the showing of crime pictures are expressions of this belief. Many of these people decry the production of "crime" or "gangster" pictures, as fraught with dangerous possibilities of disposing youth to crime.

Opposed to this belief is the assertion of many people, particularly of the partisans of the movies, that motion pictures in general and crime pictures in particular do not dispose to crime; that quite the contrary is true, for by stressing the inevitable punishment of the criminal, motion pictures discourage crime and incidentally deter many who have criminal tendencies.

This disagreement in belief has set the problem of the present study—it is indicative of the absence of adequate information on the effects of motion pictures. Specifically the object of the investigation is to consider (1) the rôle of motion pictures in the lives of delinquents and criminals of both sexes; (2) the effects on the inmates of motion pictures shown at correctional schools, reformatories, and penitentiaries; and (3) some effects of crime pictures on nondelinquent boys and girls. . . .

DIRECT INFLUENCE ON DELINQUENCY AND CRIME

The materials secured in this investigation show that motion pictures may contribute either directly or indirectly to delinquency and crime. . . .

First let us consider the direct influence of motion pictures on the behavior of delinquent boys. Of a group of 139 truant and behavior cases in a special school in Chicago (most of them from 13 to 15 years of age), 17 per cent indicated in response to a questionnaire that the movies have led them "to do something wrong." Nine per cent of a group of 184 boys (most of them from 12 to 15) in areas where the rate of delinquency is high, nine per cent of a group of 181 boys in medium-rate delinquency areas (age concentration from 11 to 14 years), and 3 per cent of the 75 boys (age concentration from 11 to 13) in low-rate delinquency areas indicated a similar influence.

These groups seem representative of the respective classes of which they are samples. These figures give us some information on the number of boys, from different backgrounds, who feel that motion pictures have influenced them "to do something wrong." Of course, many of them may have had in mind forms of questionable conduct suggested by motion pictures, which still were not serious enough to be classed as "delinquent." The figures should be regarded, then, merely as suggestive. They will serve, however, to introduce us to the problem of the influence of motion pictures on delinquency.

5

Let us begin with a few autobiographical accounts of some minor forms of delinquency, attributed by their writers to suggestions from motion pictures. These represent some of the kinds of experiences referred to as "doing something wrong." The first account comes from a high-school student, the other two from two young criminals serving prison sentences.

Male, white, Jewish, 17, high school senior.—I remember I saw a picture that gave me a yearning to steal. Once I wanted to go to a show and I didn't have any money. I went to our register and took out a quarter and went to a show. I did this taking in a sly manner just as in the show.

Male, white, Polish, sentenced for burglary, inmate of reformatory.—I don't remember the name of the picture but one time I saw a picture where a bunch of boys turned over an apple cart and ran away with a bunch of apples. A few days later our gang tried the same thing. We succeeded in turning over the cart and grabbing a bunch of apples. Everybody got away except me. The "wop" who owned the cart caught me and kicked me.

The writer of the account given continues with a statement of further experiences which, while of minor significance, show the direct influence of motion pictures.

After seeing a gangster picture all of our gang would get together and plan what we would do when we got older. How tough we would be, and always carry a couple of guns. And if anybody got hard with us how we would pull out one of our guns and boom! shoot 'em dead. Then after talking all about what we were going to do, we'd go around different neighborhoods and act tough. We'd break windows and put horse manure in bags and throw it at people. If any boy said anything to us, we would all jump on him and give him a good beating, but if some man would come after us, boy! how we'd run. After we did this for awhile it got tiresome and then we would waylay some boy from a different neighborhood. We would stop and if he would show any signs of reluctance we would give him a severe pummelling. Then we would proceed to give him a "general shakedown" and if he had any money on him we would take it away from him, and split it amongst our bunch. If he was unfortunate enough not to have any cash in his pockets we would proceed to strip him until he stood in his birthday suit and then we would tie all kinds of knots in his clothes, give him a couple of swift kicks, and call it a day. . . .

Male, white, 24, sentenced for robbery, inmate of reformatory.—In some ways we learn a few things about crime from the movies and we get pretty good ideas of how we should act and the things we should and could do in an emergency. They use their guns a lot—mostly machine guns now (anyone that craves excitement in crime likes to have automatic and shot guns and if they are big enough or up in the bucks he will want a machine gun). We get an idea of how to use these weapons and blackjacks, brass knuckles, and bombs too.

Ideas for eluding the police as depicted in the movies are also imitated. Following is an account written by an inmate of a school for delinquent boys:

> *Male, white, 19, sentenced for robbery, inmate of state training school.*—We were in a robbed car while being chased by the police. We pulled into an alley as shown in the movies and waited until they passed us; then backed out, turned around, and went in the opposite direction.

These accounts should convey some understanding of how gangster and crime pictures may suggest "techniques" or ways of committing crimes. . . .

Significance of the Accounts

. . . It has been given to show how the witnessing of certain kinds of motion pictures has contributed directly to criminal or delinquent behavior in the case of certain individuals. The skill and cleverness with which a form of crime may be carried out in a picture; the adventure and the thrill surrounding the act; the power and importance of the criminal or gang leader; the enjoyment of money and of high and fast life, frequently shown as an integral part of criminal life—these, separately or in combination, it seems from the accounts may incite certain individuals to criminal or delinquent behavior. Such motion-picture experiences are, of course, not the sole factors. (It is scarcely conceivable that any instance of criminal behavior could be traced to a single factor.) Yet they take their place alongside of other influences, being sometimes of minor importance, and occasionally of major importance. Frequently they have a different importance in different periods of the same criminal career. . . .

In response to questioning, 49 per cent of the sample of 110 inmates of a penal institution indicated that movies give one the desire to carry a gun; forty-three per cent think that movies do not exert such an influence; while 8 per cent did not express an opinion. Twenty-eight per cent of the sample indicate that the movies give one the desire to practice stick-ups; 42 per cent think that they do not exert such an influence; while 30 per cent did not express an opinion on this point. Twenty per cent indicated that the movies have taught them ways of stealing; 34 per cent declared that the movies did not have such an influence; while 46 per cent did not respond to the question. Twenty-one per cent stated that the movies have taught them how to fool the police; 32 per cent indicated no such influence; while 47 per cent did not respond to the question. Twelve per cent of the group stated that they planned to hold up someone or to pull a job when they saw an adventuresome, bandit, burglar, or gangster picture. . . .

INDIRECT INFLUENCE ON DELINQUENCY AND CRIME

. . . We wish to call attention . . . to the fact that the number of delinquents and criminals who speak of being influenced by motion pictures in certain ways which we might think of as associated with crime, exceeds those who admit that motion pictures have actually contributed to their delinquency or crime. While approximately 10 per cent of the male delinquents and criminals studied feel that motion pictures contributed to their wrongdoing, larger proportions (of the sample of 110 criminals) speak of these specific influences. Thus: 49 per cent say that the movies give one the desire to carry a gun, 28 per cent declare that they give one the desire to practice stick-ups, 20 per cent that the movies have taught them ways of stealing, 21 per cent that movies taught them ways of fooling the police, 12 per cent that they had planned to hold up someone or "pull a job" when they saw an adventuresome bandit or gangster picture, 45 per cent that the movies suggest ways of getting money easily, 26 per cent that the movies led them to be daring and to act "tough," 20 per cent that certain movies led them to daydream of being a gangster or burglar. . . .

FEMALE DELINQUENCY

. . . It is evident that the motion pictures play an important rôle in the lives of delinquent girls and young women. . . . Twenty-five per cent of [a] sample of 252 delinquent girls studied, mainly from 14 to 18 years of age, stated they had engaged in sexual relations with men following the arousing of sex impulses by a passionate love picture. Forty-one per cent admit that going to wild parties, cabarets, roadhouses, etc., "like they do in the movies," "got them into trouble." More specifically, 38 per cent of them say that they were led, in their attempts to live a wild, gay, fast life such as presented in the movies, to stay away from school; 33 per cent were led to run away from home; 23 per cent were led to sexual delinquencies. In their efforts to enjoy clothes, automobiles, lives of luxury and ease as depicted on the screen, 27 per cent have been led on occasion to run away from home. In their efforts to achieve a life of luxury easily through means suggested, at least in part, by motion pictures, 18 per cent say that they have lived with a man and let him support them; 12 per cent that they have engaged in other forms of sexual delinquency; 8 per cent that they have been led to "gold-dig" men; 8 per cent have been led to gamble; and 4 per cent that they have engaged in shoplifting. Fifty-four per cent of the girls declared they have stayed away from school to go to movies; and 17 per cent that they have run away from home after conflict with their parents over frequent motion picture attendance.

. . . Forty-eight per cent of the 252 girls studied admit feeling like having a man make love to them after they have seen a passionate love picture. Thirty-nine per cent stated that they invited men to make love to them and "pet" them after witnessing such pictures. Seventy-two per cent stated that they improved their attractiveness to men by imitation of clothes, hair-dress, make-up, etc.; and 30 per cent that they imitated techniques of flirting, kissing, or making love. Forty-nine per cent acknowledged that movies made them want to live a gay, fast life; 41 per cent admit that movies have instilled desires to go to wild parties, cabarets, and roadhouses. Seventy-one per cent reveal that motion pictures have made them want fine clothes, automobiles, wealth, servants, etc.;

and 43 per cent indicate pictures have made them want to make a lot of money easily. Thirty-nine per cent stated that they daydreamed of lives of luxury and ease; 26 per cent of gay, fast life, wild parties, cabarets, etc.; 32 per cent of having a man make love to them as they do in the motion pictures; and 7 per cent of being a vampire or "gold-digger." Finally, 35 per cent indicated that they had conflicts with their parents over motion picture attendance. . . .

THE DETERRENT AND REFORMATIVE INFLUENCE OF MOTION PICTURES

One of the most interesting problems of the relation of motion pictures to crime is that of deterrency. In most pictures which deal with crime, the criminal suffers ultimately some punishment or comes to some untimely end. In fact, it has been asserted frequently by representatives of the producers of motion pictures that crime pictures are consciously planned to show the eventual retribution which comes to the criminal as a result of his wrongdoing. Their claim has been that motion pictures discourage crime by stressing the eventual ill-fate suffered by the criminal. In view of what is ostensibly a conscious effort, it is interesting to study the extent of their success in accomplishing this purpose. This, of course, is just part of a larger setting, for there are other pictures besides those which treat crime which presumably may check criminal or delinquent tendencies.

Our materials show that motion pictures may play some part in the prevention of delinquency or crime chiefly in these ways: by playing on the sentiments of individuals, thereby arousing impulses "to be good"; by depicting criminal or delinquent careers as unattractive and dangerous; and by vivid portrayal of punishment of the offenders.

. . . If we rely upon the questionnaire responses of delinquents of both sexes, and of criminals, we see the admission by a substantial proportion that motion pictures may promote good conduct and discourage bad conduct. Yet there is much indication that these declarations refer to temporary effects. In addition there is considerable material showing how pictures supposedly exercising deterrent effects come to be discounted, ignored, and even reacted against in a hostile spirit. A short summary statement will help one to realize the inconsistency of the rôle of motion pictures as a deterrent agency.

The ways in which motion pictures seem to serve as a deterrent were found to be three: (1) playing upon the sentiments and arousing desires "to be good"; (2) showing delinquent or criminal conduct as unattractive and dangerous; (3) making a vivid portrayal of the punishment of the offenders. As over against this, we should notice the short life of the deterrent effect; the readiness to yield to temptation or to the injunctions of one's associates despite the movie experience (suggesting that the deterrent influence of motion pictures is not likely to be strong); the indifference to the punishment of the criminal as shown in motion pictures; the assertion by delinquents and criminals that motion pictures gloss over punishment as it is, and so do not make it vivid or keen; the tendency to discount pictures showing punishment of the criminal; the belief that one can outwit the law and thus escape punishment as it is shown; the sympathy for the criminal aroused by showing him being punished; and the feelings of resentment against society resulting from the punishment administered in the movies. Considerations such as these signify that the deterrent effects of motion pictures may be nullified, or that individuals may be immune to their influence. . . .

As we have tried to show, it seems clear from the expressions of experience given by high-school students that motion pictures have led many of them to a more lenient and tolerant view of crime and criminals. It is also clear that many of these students have been influenced in the opposite way by motion pictures. This contradiction in effect, while it seems to confuse the situation, is not unexpected. People may be influenced in different ways by the same pictures. . . .

THE SOCIAL MILIEU AND MOTION-PICTURE INFLUENCE

. . . The materials presented seem to throw some light on the two questions "Why are different groups affected by motion pictures differently?" and "What portion of the population seems to be most subject to influence by the movies?" It seems quite clear that the variety of influences which motion pictures may exercise arises from the wide range of themes and patterns of conduct which are shown, and the different backgrounds of experience of the observers. Because of their difference in experience, gained mainly from the groups in which they live, persons acquire attitudes which sensitize or immunize them to certain motion picture influences. The likelihood is for boys and girls reared in low-rate delinquency areas to be less susceptible to questionable patterns of conduct shown on the screen.

It should be noted as a further point that children living in high-rate delinquency areas have more opportunity and greater temptations to engaged in delinquency than children in better socially organized areas. Motion pictures may excite in boys in both areas thoughts and desires conducive to delinquency, yet the boys in the stable, well-organized community may not engage in delinquency, while those in the area of social disorganization may do so.

From our materials it would seem that persons living in high-rate delinquency areas are most subject to influence by the themes of life treated by motion pictures. In these areas of high social disorganization the family and school and church play a relatively minor rôle in the life of the child. Parents in all areas may be equally aware of possible dire consequences of some motion pictures, as is indicated by the fact that in response to the question, "Do your parents tell you some movies are bad?" 76 per cent of the truant and behavior-problem boys, 75 per cent of the high-rate delinquency area boys, 79 per cent of the medium-rate delinquency area boys, and 76 per cent of the low-rate delinquency area boys responded in the affirmative. In the areas of high delinquency and social disorganization, however, the parents as a rule tend to lose control over their children, as a result, apparently, of culture conflicts. In this situation motion pictures assume more importance as an educational agency for the boy and girl, and become a significant source of many ideas and schemes of life. It is to be expected perhaps that truant and behavior-problem boys and, in general, boys and girls in areas of high delinquency, would be influenced more by motion pictures, towards delinquency, than would boys living in stable areas of little delinquency.

The influence of motion pictures on the behavior of individuals may be regarded against the background of other institutions. The community and groups of which the child is a part transmit to him tradition and custom, forms of thought and behavior. Especially important in transmitting this social heritage have been the family, the school, the neighborhood, and the church. In recent years motion pictures seem to have become an important agency in transmitting patterns of thought and behavior. Yet peculiarly the influence that they exert in this respect seems to be in inverse proportion to the strength of family and neighborhood, school and church. Where these traditional institutions are relatively highly organized, motion pictures are seemingly of lesser influence, though nevertheless a factor in forming social attitudes and transmitting schemes of life.

. . . [M]ovies shown in institutions may have appreciable recreational, disciplinary, and reformatory value. Ninety-five per cent of the sample of delinquent girls in the girls' institution and 67 per cent of the boys and young men in the reformatory declare that pictures have to some extent made them feel more cheerful and contented. About 66 per cent of the institution heads feel motion pictures are helpful in maintaining discipline. Eighty-four per cent of the female delinquents and 61 per cent of the male convicts indicate that motion pictures make them feel to some extent like keeping out of trouble or going straight; and 29 per cent of the institutional heads regard movies as favorable to some degree to reformation. Nevertheless, motion pictures seem comparatively unimportant as a factor in reformation. Only 14 per cent of the male inmates, 15 per cent of the female, and 5 per cent of the institutional heads ranked motion pictures first, second, or third in order of their importance in reformation among a list of twelve activities.

Another picture is presented to us by the questionnaire responses. Motion pictures may contribute to disciplinary problems and to some extent they may embitter inmates rather than exert a reformative influence. About 75 per cent of the girls and young women, 68 per cent of the boys and young men, and 51 per cent of the ex-convicts admit being sexually aroused by motion pictures presented in the institutional situation which, in so far as it tends to autoerotic behavior and homosexual behavior, augments problems of sex conduct within the institutions. Certain types of pictures, it has been found, may embitter inmates and make them feel they have not been justly dealt with.

From the discussion it is reasonably clear that motion pictures shown to inmates of correctional or penal institutions may help to redirect the behavior of offenders along socially acceptable lines; yet they may also exercise the opposite influence. In the light of our earlier discussion this seeming contradiction is not strange. Motion pictures present a wide range of themes and forms of life which, added to the differences in personal inclination, may influence people to diverse and conflicting lines of conduct. . . .

SUMMARY

Rôle of motion pictures in the lives of delinquents and criminals.—It seems clear that the motion pictures were a factor of importance in the delinquent or criminal careers of about 10 per cent of the male and 25 per cent of the female offenders studied. These percentages are essentially conservative and represent the instances in which the contributors have been able to trace with confidence the influence of the movies in their own delinquent or criminal careers. In addition to these readily traced influences, motion pictures, by reason of subtle and often unconscious effects may unwittingly dispose or lead individuals to various forms of misconduct. At least two considerations justify this conclusion: first, the number of delinquents and criminals who admit having experienced motion-picture influences of a character obviously associated with crime far exceeds the number who detect a relationship between such influences and their own criminal behavior; second, there are always some offenders who can detect in their own experience such a relation. It is reasonable to assume that what presents itself to some as a conscious factor in delinquency may operate as an unconscious factor in the experience of others.

Several important indirect influences disposing or leading persons to delinquency or crime are discernible in the experience of male offenders. Through the display of crime techniques and criminal patterns of behavior; by arousing desires for easy money and luxury, and by suggesting questionable methods for their achievement; by inducing a spirit of bravado, toughness, and adventurousness; by arousing intense sexual desires; and by invoking daydreaming of criminal rôles, motion pictures may create attitudes and furnish techniques conducive, quite unwittingly, to delinquent or criminal behavior.

One may detect in the case of delinquent girls and young women influences similar to those spoken of in the case of young men. Motion pictures may play a major or minor rôle in female delinquency and crime by arousing sexual passion, by instilling the desire to live a gay, wild, fast life, by evoking longings for luxury and smart appearance, and by suggesting to some girls questionable methods of easily attaining them; by the display of modes of beautification and love techniques; by the depiction of various forms of crime readily imitated by girls and young women; and by competing with home and school for an important place in the life of the girls.

On the other hand, movies may redirect the behavior of delinquents and criminals along socially acceptable lines and make them hesitant about, and sometimes deter them from, the commission of offenses. Through instilling the impulse to "be good," in depicting the unattractive and dangerous aspects of criminal careers, and by vividly portraying the punishment and ill fate of the violators of the moral and legal code, motion pictures may produce attitudes and furnish insights which, consciously or unwittingly, may offer some check to a delinquent or criminal career.

Yet, pictures meant to be deterrent do not always have such a desired effect. There are a number of nullifying and immunizing factors which may effectively counteract the elements in the picture meant to guide behavior along conventional paths. Among these are: the short life of the deterrent effect;

yielding to temptation or group pressure; getting accustomed to the punishment shown; the lack of a sufficiently vivid portrayal of punishment; the discounting of the pictures showing the punishment of offenders; the feeling by observers that they can outwit the law; the feeling of sympathy for the criminals; or the feeling of resentment to their punishment. By reason of these attitudes and conditions the delinquent or criminal observer may not be affected by the deterrent lesson, presumably to be conveyed by a given picture. Because of the frequent inclusion in such pictures of entrancing scenes, such as those of a life of gayety, wild life, luxury, adventure, easy money, etc., the deterrent aspect may be overshadowed. The discrimination of the observer may be confused, and his subsequent difficulty in keeping apart the different "motifs" may end in a failure to get the deterrent import of the picture. . . .

Concluding Remarks

It is evident that motion pictures may exert influences in diametrically opposite directions. The movies may help to dispose or lead persons to delinquency and crime or they may fortify conventional behavior. Movies shown to inmates may cheer them and help make them contented or may make them blue and disconsolate; they may be of value in the maintenance of institutional discipline or they may create or augment problems of institutional misconduct; they may encourage reformation of the offender or they may make the inmate bitter and resentful against society. Motion pictures may create attitudes favorable to crime and the criminal or unfavorable to them.

How are these conflicting influences to be explained? As we have indicated, two conditions determine the nature and direction of the effects of motion pictures on the behavior of a given person: first, the diversity and wide range of themes depicted on the screen; and second, the social milieu, the attitudes and interests of the observer. On the one hand the social background of the person tends to be quite unconsciously the basis for the selection and interpretation of motion picture themes and patterns of behavior that in their immediate or cumulative effect may leave their imprint on him. The child in the high-rate delinquency area tends to be sensitized and the child in the low-rate delinquency area immunized to delinquent and criminal attitudes and forms of behavior depicted on the screen. On the other hand the forms of thought and behavior presented by the movies are such as to provide material and incentive to those sensitized to delinquent and criminal suggestion.

Motion pictures play an especially important part in the lives of children reared in socially disorganized areas. The influence of motion pictures seems to be proportionate to the weakness of the family, school, church, and neighborhood. Where the institutions which traditionally have transmitted social attitudes and forms of conduct have broken down, as is usually the case in high-rate delinquency areas, motion pictures assume a greater importance as a source of ideas and schemes of life.

Motion pictures are a relatively new factor in modern life. While primarily a form of recreation, they play an appreciably important rôle in developing conceptions of life and transmitting patterns of conduct. They may direct the behavior of persons along socially acceptable lines or they may lead, as has been indicated, to misconduct. They may be, therefore, an agency of social value or of social harm. As the former they raise no issue, as the latter they raise problems of social control.

1.2 KURT LANG AND GLADYS ENGEL LANG

The Mass Media and Voting

Research on political communication effects has undergone three major shifts. Initially, the mass media were regarded as having considerable power to shape opinion and belief. During the second stage (1945–1960), mass media were regarded primarily as forms that would reinforce existing beliefs, but they were thought to have little effect on initial attitudes or opinion change. The third stage, from 1960 to the present, involves the ways in which media shape the image of candidates and the way voters respond to the images and agendas set forth by the media.

The following selection is from "The Mass Media and Voting," in Eugene Burdick and Arthur J. Brodbeck, eds., *American Voting Behavior* (Free Press, 1959). In it, Kurt Lang and Gladys Engel Lang demonstrate a shift toward limited effects research and thus represent the second stage. The Langs' approach helped later researchers focus on how media contribute to the shaping of political images. As the Langs write in this selection, earlier voting studies tended to show weaknesses in the methodologies that were used rather than evaluating the impact of mass media on voters' beliefs or actions. The Langs discuss, among other key ideas regarding media impact and voting, the importance of audience selectivity in perceiving mediated messages and people's tendency to filter unwanted messages.

At the time this article was written, Kurt Lang was on the staff of the Canadian Broadcasting Corporation, and Gladys Engel Lang had been associated with Carlton University in Ottawa, Ontario. Both eventually moved to the University of Washington, where Kurt was director of the School of Communication and Gladys had a joint appointment in political science and sociology. The Langs have coauthored several research studies, including *Politics and Television* (1968), *Politics and Television Re-Viewed* (1984), and *The Battle for Public Opinion: The President, the Press, and the Polls During Watergate* (1983).

Key Concept: voting and indirect effects of the mass media

*A*fter each national election students of political behavior comment on how little effect the mass media appear to have had on the outcome. Franklin D. Roosevelt and Harry S. Truman won *in spite of* the press. The personal nature of the Eisenhower victory in 1952 showed that the campaign was so much shouting and tumult; the election was won before the campaign had even begun. Still, all of us—politicians, candidates, public servants, symbol manipulators, members of the Great Audience, and even students of political behavior in our private capacities as interested and partisan citizens—much as we may publicly belittle what the mass media do, act most of the time *as if* we believed in their potency. Republican members of the faculty pay for a newspaper ad supporting their candidate; the Democrats must counter with their own publicity. The vagaries of research lead us away from a principal concern with the impact of press, radio, television, and magazines, but nothing would seem to have banished our not yet empirically demonstrated beliefs that the mass media are more influential than we would sometimes wish. Outcries against certain political television shows during and between campaigns, as well as the enduring and enthusiastic acceptance accorded to George Orwell's [novel] *1984*, indicate vividly that our research may not tell us what our common sense reveals is there to be told.

At first glance recent research on voting behavior appears to go along with this emphasis on *how little* the mass media determine the vote. The reader's attention is called to influences that intervene between the content itself and the individual's voting decision. Emphasis also moves away from a concern with the power once attributed to mass communications to the personal dispositions and group influences that circumscribe it.

None of the three voting studies—Elmira, 1948; Bristol North-East, 1951; the U.S. national survey in 1952[1]—draw any explicit conclusions to the effect that mass communications are *not* an important influence in voting behavior. They all point to their own methodological inadequacies, and in the most recent of the three studies the problem of mass-media impact has actually been avoided.[2] At many points, the importance of the mass media is stressed; nowhere is their role in connection with the vote actually belittled. Yet there may be a difference between the author's own interpretations and more or less popular understandings of what their findings mean.

MASS COMMUNICATIONS DURING THE CAMPAIGN

Exactly what do we learn about the influence of mass communication on voting behavior by studying its effect within the scope of a single campaign?

Both the Elmira and the Bristol studies reiterate findings of earlier research. In Elmira the group who changed their voting intentions during the campaign, compared with those who followed through, included fewer people who were interested in the election. They were less "exposed" to the mass media, and they arrived at their decision later. Likewise in Bristol, "floaters [those inconsistent either in their intentions or in their vote], no matter what their final party, listened to fewer broadcasts and read fewer national newspapers than the regular voters."[3] These observations are consistent with the most widely accepted finding on mass-media impact: "Media exposure gets out the vote at the same time that it solidifies preferences. It crystallizes and reinforces more than it converts."[4]

Accordingly, then, the election period serves less as a force for change than as a period for reclarification. There are several concrete circumstances in a campaign which severely circumscribe opportunities for observing the influence of mass-media propaganda.

Most obvious in this connection is the observation, confirmed in different contexts and by different methods, that the minds of most voters are closed even before the campaign officially opens. At various places and at different times, this figure has been set at anywhere from 50 to 84 per cent of the voters.[5] But even if a voter arrives at his decision late in the campaign, he is not necessarily in a constant quandary, endlessly pulled in opposite directions by conflicting propaganda. Evidence from panel studies indicates that in most cases where the final decision comes late in the campaign, prior leanings are crystallized into a firm intent. The impregnability of voting intentions as a whole limits drastically the number of people who are, so to speak, potential converts.

Moreover, during a campaign, people cannot help but be aware, however unhappily, that they are the targets of deliberate propaganda. Neither side enjoys a monopoly of available space or time, and so propaganda is almost always exposed as such. Expecting attempts at persuasion, voters come prepared with stereotyped meanings. It is not altogether unusual to hear speeches discounted as so much campaign talk. People, being aware of the intent of the messages, tend to avoid views contrary to their own. They tend to believe their own side and to question the arguments of the other. As long as old loyalties are activated, selective perception will serve as an effective screen. . . .

At any rate, the number of people who have already "made up their minds" before the campaign begins, the overwhelming importance of "filtering" effects resulting from self-selection and selective perception of media content, and the awareness of the intent with which all campaign statements are phrased all work together to make "conversion" through any medium particularly difficult during an election. But, in addition, there is something in the way the problem is approached which may obscure certain ways in which the mass media are effective. . . .

PERSONAL INFLUENCE AND MASS INFLUENCE

The mass media, then, exert some of the influence they do because they are more than a channel through which national party policy is brought before the local electorate. In filtering, structuring, and spotlighting certain public activities, the media content is not confined to conveying what party spokesmen proclaim and what the candidates say. All news that bears on political activity and beliefs—and not only campaign speeches and campaign propaganda—is somehow relevant to the vote. Not only during the campaign but also in the periods between, the mass media provide perspectives, shape images of candidates and parties, help highlight issues around which a campaign will develop, and define the unique atmosphere and areas of sensitivity which mark any particular campaign. Any long-run view, therefore, reveals certain differences among elections which make clear that in each case voters, much as they may respond to traditional allegiances, also respond to a unique historical situation.

The scheme of analysis outlined in *Voting* barely touches upon the role of the mass media in creating a secondhand reality, through which public policy is elaborated and the effects of that policy on the voter clarified and made tangible. The "main concern," we are told, "is with the electorate itself. How many individuals pay *direct* attention to the campaign via the mass media?"[6] In this scheme the mass media act primarily as transmitters of content supplied by the national parties and by their candidates and subsequently consumed, in one way or another, by the electorate. The personal network of communications within the community hooks onto and makes use of the mass media. Opinion leaders usually pay more attention to the mass media than their peers, and they relay relevant information to those less firm in their partisan convictions. . . .

The persons generally designated by social scientists as "opinion leaders" prepare the ground for mass-media impact. They translate the mass-media reality into the experience of local groups. Some persons may enjoy informal status as opinion leaders precisely because they attend to the relevant mass-media content. Or it may be that in order to wield influence a man may have to be especially knowledgeable about what the mass media do and say. In either case, the opinion leaders exhibit greater responsiveness to the mass media, channeling for their peers—to whose dispositions they are particularly sensitive—that which the mass media have already made significant.

Theirs is essentially a transmission function and through them the views and interests of persons not directly exposed to the content of the mass media are involved. Yet these leaders select what they will transmit, and hence such influentials need not act only as a stabilizing influence. An emergent local leadership at odds with the official party may make use of whatever prestige or credibility the mass-media content has per se to subvert older loyalties.

The short-run frame of reference, with its primary concern with the electorate and how it lines up within the course of a single campaign, has perhaps exaggerated the dominant role of personal influences and the effectiveness of "normal" social pressures. For it puts the accent on the type of changer who is most susceptible—perhaps by a sort of default—to such influences, that is, it draws attention almost exclusively to changers who are converted or whose decision crystallizes only *during the campaign*. In the first place, such persons are, quite logically, those with a relatively low interest in politics and for whom political loyalties are not ordinarily salient; second, they are further characterized by low mass-media exposure. . . .

SECONDHAND REALITY AND THE MASS AUDIENCE

Persons in the mass society are, as we all know, members of many more or less formally organized groups. Some of these memberships are, of course, more politically relevant than others. Trade unionists in the United States tend to vote Democratic; in England they most often side with Labour. Some minority groups "stick together" politically, and some organizations formed to defend "majority" interests have their own characteristic voting patterns. We know a considerable amount about the political perspectives that derive from such memberships and about the cross-pressures exerted by multiple allegiances.

We are also aware that most of what people know about political life comes to them secondhand—or even thirdhand—through the mass media. The media do structure a very real political environment but one which, even in these days of TV, we can only know "at a distance." Because of the way people select from the political content of the mass media and interpret what they select, the political communication system serves to transmit materials peculiarly relevant to persons in various milieus. Beyond this, however, the mass media also structure a larger, nonlocal reality from which it is hard to escape. The content filters through, even though people are not directly exposed to it or do not claim to be paying a great deal of attention.[7] There is something obtrusive about what the mass media present, something that makes their influence cumulative.

The mass media have, then, another function. They not only transmit materials that feed into the political perspectives of relevant groups; they leave an impress of their own. There are political perspectives that rise out of an individual's position as a member of a mass, as the object of direct and indirect stimuli coming from the mass media. The relationships between voting behavior and the perspectives developed by virtue of one's position in the mass have as yet been inadequately investigated, perhaps because of the very real methodological difficulties involved, perhaps because we overestimate the difficulties or fear to risk criticism of our results.

The subsections that follow outline briefly *some* ways in which the media shape the perspectives of voters, so to say, en masse. Whether individuals accept the media content as "authentic" or discount it as "propaganda," they nonetheless respond to it. The relationship of the following three areas of mass-media impact to voting, however, apparent their relevance to politics, has so far not been systematically investigated. . . .

CONCLUSION

. . . Studies in voting behavior have dealt with both long-run trends and short-run changes. In either case, since voting rates and voting decisions can be determined with a high degree of validity, we seek inferences about antecedent conditions influencing these end products of political activity. Such influences as age differences, regional locations, and traditional political affiliations which may affect voting habits can with relative ease be isolated for examination. When we come to deal with mass-media influences, however, these are much more difficult to single out. They operate among a multitude of other factors and their effects do not always take tangible shape. Consequently, the measures of mass-media exposure are usually crude and the effects looked for are relatively specific and short run.

Quite naturally, campaign studies such as we have been considering, have focused on the short-range influences operating during the period of active electioneering and on how these culminate in a final voting decision. It so happens, as we have tried to point out, that this approach to the problem, with its emphasis on individual conversion during the "official" campaign, minimizes the important cumulative influences of the mass media and emphasizes instead how political communications are transmitted through personal networks and how latent tendencies are activated. In this way, attention has been focused on the limits to mass-media influence.

Where the question for study is "What makes the electorate tick?" research is naturally shaped to fit the problem; the mass media become just one among many concerns. On the other hand, experts in mass communications have not in recent years distinguished themselves by probing the long-range influence of mass media on political life—and more particularly on voting behavior. The cumulative and society-wide effects about which we often talk vaguely as shifts in public moods or drifts in political opinion are hard to demonstrate; yet, if we would further our knowledge of political behavior, such effects are much in need of clarification. And they can only be clarified through research specifically designed to get at them.

In turning attention to the continuous, and not only the intermittent, aspects of mass-media influence, we must deal, first, with the role of *mass* communications as such, focusing not only on the communicator's job as a transmitting agent for party propagandists but on the direct impress the communications have on what individuals in the mass society know of the larger political world. We have to get at the political perspectives that rise out of the individual's remote participation in politics as a member of the mass and at the relationships between voting behavior and these perspectives.

Moreover, we must develop a more apt definition of relevant changes and "changers." In place of turnover during a campaign, changes in party allegiances between one election and the next, together with discrepancies between "fundamental dispositions" and voting decisions, ticket splitting, and the like, are suggested.

A few specific problems for study have been directly outlined or indicated. The imagery made especially relevant by the mass media—the imagery of the "public imagination," of public personalities, of what politics is really like—and the relationship of such imagery to party alignments seem noteworthy. Among other subjects, the specific role of television, its authenticity and the exploitation of that authenticity by public officials and publicity directors, and the impact of such exploitation on voting participation constitute important areas for inquiry.

NOTES

1. B. R. Berelson, P. F. Lazarsfeld, and W. N. McPhee, *Voting* (Chicago: University of Chicago Press, 1954); R. S. Milne and H. C. Mackenzie, *Straight Fight* (London: the

Hansard Society, 1954); and Angus Campbell, Gerald Gurin, and W. E. Miller, *The Voter Decides* (Evanston, Ill.: Row, Peterson, 1954).

2. In a separate article, the authors have discussed the role of television but qualify their data in stating that they had "no clear evidence" on how it affected the voting. Cf. Angus Campbell and Others, "Television and the Elections," *Scientific American*, 188 (1953), 46–48.

3. Milne and Mackenzie, *op. cit.,* pp. 96 ff.

4. Berelson, Lazarsfeld, and McPhee, *op. cit.,* p. 248.

5. In Erie County, Ohio (1940), roughly one half were pre-campaign deciders. Cf. P. F. Lazarsfeld, B. R. Berleson, and Hazel Gaudet, *The People's Choice* (2d ed.; New York: Columbia University Press, 1948), p. 53. According to a "Gallup" poll before nomination day, 84 per cent of the British electorate were already decided. Cited by R. B. McCallum and A. Readman, *The British General Election of 1945* (London: Oxford University Press, 1947), p. 201. British figures seem to over around the 80 per cent mark, with American figures, perhaps because of the more protracted campaign period, on the whole closer to two-thirds.

6. Berelson, Lazarsfeld, and McPhee, *op. cit.* p. 235. Italics supplied.

7. Berelson, Lazarsfeld, and McPhee, *op. cit.,* report this "unexpected" finding: "More people showed signs of exposure than claimed to be paying 'attention.' "

CHAPTER 2

Media Effects

The Structure and Function of Communication in Society

Much of the media research in the United States has attempted to study the impact of media on the individual's psychological makeup. But after the Payne Fund Studies on the influence of motion pictures on children, conducted in the 1930s, some scholars turned their attention to the effects of mass media within larger social structures. This required not only a psychological model of the individual consumer of media messages but also a model of social structure.

Harold D. Lasswell's influential article "The Structure and Function of Communication in Society," in Lyman Bryson, ed., *The Communication of Ideas* (Institute for Religious & Social Studies, 1948), from which the following selection has been taken, provides an important refinement to the "magic-bullet" model. In the article's summary, Lasswell states, "The communication process in society performs three functions: (a) *surveillance* of the environment . . . ; (b) *correlation* of the components of society . . . ; and (c) *transmission* of the social inheritance." Later, other scholars added the function of "entertainment" to Lasswell's original description. Lasswell's concept of media function compares both individual and society to biological organisms. Just as different types of cells work together in the body, mass media "functions" only when they work smoothly together with other parts, thereby contributing to the integrity of the whole organism, either individual or social. And, as when cells proliferate erratically, causing cancer and the breakdown of an organism, mass media can *dysfunction* if they fail to meet social and individual needs for information, explanation, cultural transmission, and release from drudgery.

Lasswell (1902–1978) continued his propaganda research with the Experimental Division for the Study of War-Time Communications during World War II, where he worked with Paul F. Lazarsfeld, Kurt Lewin, and Wilbur Schramm. All participated in the Rockefeller Communication Seminar, which met monthly from September 1939 to June 1940. In 1948 papers from these meetings were published in *The Communication of Ideas.*

Key Concept: media functions

THE ACT OF COMMUNICATION

A convenient way to describe an act of communication is to answer the following questions:

> Who
> Says What
> In Which Channel
> To Whom
> With What Effect?

The scientific study of the process of communication tends to concentrate upon one or another of these questions. Scholars who study the "who," the communicator, look into the factors that initiate and guide the act of communication. We call this subdivision of the field of research *control analysis.* Specialists who focus upon the "says what" engage in *content analysis.* Those who look primarily at the radio, press, film and other channels of communication are doing *media analysis.* When the principal concern is with the persons reached by the media, we speak of *audience analysis.* If the question is the impact upon audiences, the problem is *effect analysis.*[1]

Whether such distinctions are useful depends entirely upon the degree of refinement which is regarded as appropriate to a given scientific and managerial objective. Often it is simpler to combine audience and effect analysis, for instance, than to keep them apart. On the other hand, we may want to concentrate on the analysis of content, and for this purpose subdivide the field into the study of purport and style, the first referring to the message, and the second to the arrangement of the elements of which the message is composed.

STRUCTURE AND FUNCTION

Enticing as it is to work out these categories in more detail, the present discussion has a different scope. We are less interested in dividing up the act of communication than in viewing the act as a whole in relation to the entire social process. Any process can be examined in two frames of reference, namely, structure and function; and our analysis of communication will deal with the specializations that carry on certain functions, of which the following may be clearly distinguished: (1) The surveillance of the environment; (2) the correlation of the parts of society in responding to the environment; (3) the transmission of the social heritage from one generation to the next.

BIOLOGICAL EQUIVALENCIES

At the risk of calling up false analogies, we can gain perspective on human societies when we note the degree to which communication is a feature of life at every level. A vital entity, whether relatively isolated or in association, has specialized ways of receiving stimuli from the environment. The single-celled organism or the many-membered group tends to maintain an internal equilibrium and to respond to changes in the environment in a way that maintains this equilibrium. The responding process calls for specialized ways of bringing the parts of the whole into harmonious action. Multi-celled animals specialize cells to the function of external contact and internal correlation. Thus, among the primates, specialization is exemplified by organs such as the ear and eye, and the nervous system itself. When the stimuli receiving and disseminating patterns operate smoothly, the several parts of the animal act in concert in reference to the environment ("feeding," "fleeing," "attacking").[2]

In some animal societies certain members perform specialized roles, and survey the environment. Individuals act as "sentinels," standing apart from the herd or flock and creating a disturbance whenever an alarming change occurs in the surroundings. The trumpeting, cackling or shrilling of the sentinel is enough to set the herd in motion. Among the activities engaged in by specialized "leaders" is the internal stimulation of "followers" to adapt in an orderly manner to the circumstances heralded by the sentinels.[3]

Within a single, highly differentiated organism, incoming nervous impulses and outgoing impulses are transmitted along fibers that make synaptic junction with other fibers. The critical points in the process occur at the relay stations, where the arriving impulse may be too weak to reach the threshold which stirs the next link into action. At the higher centers, separate currents modify one another, producing results that differ in many ways from the outcome when each is allowed to continue a separate path. At any relay station there is no conductance, total conductance or intermediate conductance. The same categories apply to what goes on among members of an animal society. The sly fox may approach the barnyard in a way that supplies too meager stimuli for the sentinel to sound the alarm. Or the attacking animal may eliminate the sentinel before he makes more than a feeble outcry. Obviously there is every gradation possible between total conductance and no conductance.

ATTENTION IN WORLD SOCIETY

When we examine the process of communication of any state in the world community, we note three categories of specialists. One group surveys the political environment of the state as a whole, another correlates the response of the whole state to the environment, and the third transmits certain patterns of response from the old to the young. Diplomats, attachés, and foreign correspondents are representative of those who specialize on the environment. Editors, journalists, and speakers are correlators of the internal response. Educators in family and school transmit the social inheritance.

Communications which originate abroad pass through sequences in which various senders and receivers are linked with one another. Subject to modification at each relay point in the chain, messages originating with a diplomat or foreign correspondent may pass through editorial desks and eventually reach large audiences.

If we think of the world attention process as a series of *attention frames*, it is possible to describe the rate at which comparable content is brought to the notice of individuals and groups. We can inquire into the point at which "conductance" no longer occurs; and we can look into the range between "total conductance" and "minimum conductance." The metropolitan and political centers of the world have much in common with the interdependence, differentiation, and activity of the cortical or subcortical centers of an individual organism. Hence the attention frames found in these spots are the most variable, refined, and interactive of all frames in the world community.

At the other extreme are the attention frames of primitive inhabitants of isolated areas. Not that folk cultures are wholly untouched by industrial civilization. Whether we parachute into the interior of New Guinea, or land on the slopes of the Himalayas, we find no tribe wholly out of contact with the world. The long threads of trade, of missionary zeal, of adventurous exploration and scientific field study, and of global war, reach the far distant places. No one is entirely out of this world.

Among primitives the final shape taken by communication is the ballad or tale. Remote happenings in the great world of affairs, happenings that come to the notice of metropolitan audiences, are reflected, however dimly, in the thematic material of ballad singers and reciters. In these creations far away political leaders may be shown supplying land to the peasants or restoring an abundance of game to the hills.[4]

When we push upstream of the flow of communication, we note that the immediate relay function for nomadic and remote tribesmen is sometimes performed by the inhabitants of settled villages with whom they come in occasional contact. The relayer can be the school teacher, doctor, judge, tax collector, policeman, soldier, peddler, salesman, missionary, student; in any case he is an assembly point of news and comment.

MORE DETAILED EQUIVALENCIES

The communication processes of human society, when examined in detail, reveal many equivalencies to the specializations found in the physical organism, and in the lower animal societies. The diplomats, for instance, of a single state are stationed all over the world and send messages to a few focal points.

Obviously, these incoming reports move from the many to the few, where they interact upon one another. Later on, the sequence spreads fanwise according to a few to many pattern, as when a foreign secretary gives a speech in public, an article is put out in the press, or a news film is distributed to the theaters. The lines leading from the outer environment of the state are functionally equivalent to the afferent channels that convey incoming nervous impulses to the central nervous system of a single animal, and to the means by which alarm is spread among a flock. Outgoing, or efferent impulses, display corresponding parallels.

The central nervous system of the body is only partly involved in the entire flow of afferent-efferent impulses. There are automatic systems that can act on one another without involving the "higher" centers at all. The stability of the internal environment is maintained principally through the mediation of the vegetive or autonomic specializations of the nervous system. Similarly, most of the messages within any state do not involve the central channels of communication. They take place within families, neighborhoods, shops, field gangs, and other local contexts. Most of the educational process is carried on the same way.

A further set of significant equivalencies is related to the circuits of communication, which are predominantly one-way or two-way, depending upon the degree of reciprocity between communicators and audience. Or, to express it differently, two-way communication occurs when the sending and receiving functions are performed with equal frequency by two or more persons. A conversation is usually assumed to be a pattern of two-way communication (although monologues are hardly unknown). The modern instruments of mass communication give an enormous advantage to the controllers of printing plants, broadcasting equipment, and other forms of fixed and specialized capital. But it should be noted that audiences do "talk back," after some delay; and many controllers of mass media use scientific methods of sampling in order to expedite this closing of the circuit.

Circuits of two-way contact are particularly in evidence among the great metropolitan, political and cultural centers in the world. New York, Moscow, London and Paris, for example, are in intense two-way contact, even when the flow is severely curtailed in volume (as between Moscow and New York). Even insignificant sites become world centers when they are transformed into capital cities (Canberra in Australia, Ankara in Turkey, the District of Columbia, U.S.A.). A cultural center like Vatican City is in intense two-way relationship with the dominant centers throughout the world. Even specialized production centers like Hollywood, despite their preponderance of outgoing material, receive an enormous volume of messages.

A further distinction can be made between message controlling and message handling centers and social formations. The message center in the vast Pentagon Building of the War Department in Washington, D.C., transmits with no more than accidental change incoming messages to addressees. This is the role of the printers and distributors of books; of dispatchers, linemen, and messengers connected with telegraphic communication; of radio engineers, and other technicians associated with broadcasting. Such message handlers may be contrasted with those who affect the content of what is said, which is the function of editors, censors, and propagandists. Speaking of the symbol specialists as a whole, therefore, we separate them into the manipulators (controllers) and the handlers; the first group typically modifies content, while the second does not.

NEEDS AND VALUES

Though we have noted a number of functional and structural equivalencies between communication in human societies and other living entities, it is not implied that we can most fruitfully investigate the process of communication in America or the world by the methods most appropriate to research on the lower animals or on single physical organisms. In comparative psychology when we describe some part of the surroundings of a rat, cat, or monkey as a stimulus (that is, as part of the environment reaching the attention of the animal), we cannot ask the rat; we use other means of inferring perception. When human beings are our objects of investigation, we can interview the great "talking animal." (This is not that we take everything at face value. Sometimes we forecast the opposite of what the person says he intends to do. In this case, we depend on other indications, both verbal and non-verbal.)

In the study of living forms, it is rewarding, as we have said, to look at them as modifiers of the environment in the process of gratifying needs, and hence of maintaining a steady state of internal equilibrium. Food, sex, and other activities which involve the environment can be examined on a comparative basis. Since human beings exhibit speech reactions, we can investigate many more relationships than in the non-human species.[5] Allowing for the data furnished by speech (and other communicative acts), we can investigate human society in terms of values; that is, in reference to categories of relationships that are recognized objects of gratification. In America, for example, it requires no elaborate technique of study to discern that power and respect are values. We can demonstrate this by listening to testimony, and by watching what is done when opportunity is afforded.

It is possible to establish a list of values current in any group chosen for investigation. Further than this, we can discover the rank order in which these values are sought. We can rank the members of the group according to their position in relation to the values. So far as industrial civilization is concerned, we have no hesitation in saying that power, wealth, respect, well being, and enlightenment are among the values. If we stop with this list, which is not exhaustive, we can describe on the basis of available knowledge (fragmentary though it may often be), the social structure of most of the world. Since values are not equally distributed, the social structure reveals more or less concentration of relatively abundant shares of power, wealth and other values in a few hands. In some places this concentration is passed on from generation to generation, forming castes rather than a mobile society.

In every society the values are shaped and distributed according to more or less distinctive patterns (*institutions*). The institutions include communications which are invoked in support of the network as a whole. Such communications are the ideology; and in relation to power we can differentiate the political *doctrine,* the political *formula* and the *miranda.*[6] These are illustrated in the United States by the doctrine of individualism, the paragraphs of the Constitution, which are the formula, and the ceremonies and legends of public life, which comprise the miranda. The ideology is communicated to the rising generation through such specialized agencies as the home and school.

Ideology is only part of the myths of any given society. There may be counter ideologies directed against the dominant doctrine, formula, and miranda. Today the power structure of world politics is deeply affected by ideological conflict, and by the role of two giant powers, the United States and Russia.[7] The ruling elites view one another as potential enemies, not only in the sense that interstate differences may be settled by war, but in the more urgent sense that the ideology of the other may appeal to disaffected elements at home and weaken the internal power position of each ruling class. . . .

EFFICIENT COMMUNICATION

. . . One task of a rationally organized society is to discover and control any factors that interfere with efficient communication. . . .

But even technical insufficiencies can be overcome by knowledge. In recent years shortwave broadcasting has been interfered with by disturbances which will either be surmounted, or will eventually lead to the abandonment of this mode of broadcasting. During the past few years advances have been made toward providing satisfactory substitutes for defective hearing and seeing. A less dramatic, though no less important, development has been the discovery of how inadequate reading habits can be corrected. . . .

Some of the most serious threats to efficient communication for the community as a whole relate to the values of power, wealth and respect. Perhaps the most striking examples of power distortion occur when the content of communication is deliberately adjusted to fit an ideology or counter ideology. Distortions related to wealth not only arise from attempts to influence the market, for instance, but from rigid conceptions of economic interest. A typical instance of inefficiencies connected with respect (social class) occurs when an upper class person mixes only with persons of his own stratum and forgets to correct his perspective by being exposed to members of other classes. . . .

SUMMARY

The communication process in society performs three functions: (a) *surveillance* of the environment, disclosing threats and opportunities affecting the value position of the community and of the component parts within it; (b) *correlation* of the components of society in making a response to the environment; (c) *transmission* of the social inheritance. In general, biological equivalents can be found in human and animal associations, and within the economy of a single organism.

In society, the communication process reveals special characteristics when the ruling element is afraid of the internal as well as the external environment. In gauging the efficiency of communication in any given context, it is necessary to take into account the values at stake, and the identity of the group whose position is being examined. In democratic societies, rational choices depend on enlightenment, which in turn depends upon communication; and especially upon the equivalence of attention among leaders, experts and rank and file.

NOTES

1. For more detail, consult the introductory matter in Bruce L. Smith, Harold D. Lasswell and Ralph D. Casey, *Propaganda, Communication, and Public Opinion: A Comprehensive Reference Guide,* Princeton University Press, Princeton, 1946.
2. To the extent that behavior patterns are transmitted in the structures inherited by the single animal, a function is performed parallel to the transmission of the "social heritage" by means of education.
3. On animal sociology see: Warder C. Allee, *Animal Aggregations,* University of Chicago Press, Chicago, 1931; *The Social Life of Animals,* Norton, New York, 1935.
4. Excellent examples are given in Robert Redfield's account of *Tepoztlan, A Mexican Village: A Study of Folk Life,* University of Chicago Press, Chicago, 1930.
5. Properly handled, the speech event can be described with as much reliability and validity as many non-speech events which are more conventionally used as data in scientific investigations.
6. These distinctions are derived and adapted from the writings of Charles E. Merriam, Gaetano Mosca, Karl Mannheim, and others. For a systematic exposition see the forthcoming volume by Harold D. Lasswell and Abraham Kaplan.
7. See William T. R. Fox, *The Super-Powers,* Harcourt, Brace, New York. 1944, and Harold D. Lasswell, *World Politics Faces Economics,* McGraw-Hill, New York, 1945.

The Invasion from Mars: A Study in the Psychology of Panic

When Orson Welles's radio show *Mercury Theatre on the Air* broadcast an adaptation of H.G. Wells's *War of the Worlds* the night before Halloween in 1938, approximately 1 million people were panicked by this fictional account of a Martian invasion of Earth. During the program, some people even fled the New Jersey area where the Martian invaders were said to have landed. Even though most scientific studies of media effects prior to this time indicated that the power of mass media to change people's behavior was very limited, *The War of the Worlds* broadcast resurrected public concern about media messages as "magic bullets" that could directly stimulate irrational and dangerous responses in audience members.

In the aftermath of the broadcast and panic, Hadley Cantril (1906–1969), a psychologist at Princeton University and a leading authority on the persuasiveness of the media under stressful conditions, quickly organized a research project to study and evaluate the means by which some people were frightened. This quick follow-up allowed Cantril and his colleagues, Hazel Gaudet and Herta Herzog, to pull together data from radio ratings, public polls, and other "immediate" forms of response to the program. The team formulated two research questions for study: (1) Why did *this* broadcast trigger such a powerful response? (2) Why did some people panic while others did not? The following excerpt from Cantril's study *The Invasion from Mars: A Study in the Psychology of Panic* (Harper Torchbooks, 1966) focuses on the second question, describing the condition of psychological "suggestibility" that caused many listeners to respond irrationally to the fictional broadcast.

Both the research questions and the study's conclusions criticize the assumptions of magic-bullet thinking about mass media. Cantril concluded that not all media messages have the power to directly shape human behavior; that is, not all listeners are psychologically vulnerable to media stimuli.

Instead, various mediating factors, described here as "suggestibility," moderate the power of media influence. Many media effects studies in the United States have attempted to uncover and elaborate other such intervening variables.

Key Concept: suggestibility

THE BROADCAST

At eight P.M. eastern standard time on the evening of October 30, 1938, Orson Welles with an innocent little group of actors took his place before the microphone in a New York studio of the Columbia Broadcasting System. He carried with him Howard Koch's freely adapted version of H. G. Wells's imaginative novel, *War of the Worlds.* He also brought to the scene his unusual dramatic talent. With script and talent the actors hoped to entertain their listeners for an hour with an incredible, old-fashioned story appropriate for Hallowe'en.

Much to their surprise the actors learned that the series of news bulletins they had issued describing an invasion from Mars had been believed by thousands of people throughout the country. For a few horrible hours people from Maine to California thought that hideous monsters armed with death rays were destroying all armed resistance sent against them; that there was simply no escape from disaster; that the end of the world was near. Newspapers the following morning spoke of the "tidal wave of terror that swept the nation." It was clear that a panic of national proportions had occurred. The chairman of the Federal Communications Commission called the program "regrettable." . . .

THE NATURE AND EXTENT OF THE PANIC

Long before the broadcast had ended, people all over the United States were praying, crying, fleeing frantically to escape death from the Martians. Some ran to rescue loved ones. Others telephoned farewells or warnings, hurried to inform neighbors, sought information from newspapers or radio stations, summoned ambulances and police cars. At least six million people heard the broadcast. At least a million of them were frightened or disturbed.

For weeks after the broadcast, newspapers carried human-interest stories relating the shock and terror of local citizens. Men and women throughout the country could have described their feelings and reactions on that fateful evening. . . . [I]nterviewers and correspondents gathered hundreds of accounts. . . .

Who Listened?

The best direct evidence upon which to base an estimate of the number of people who listened to this broadcast is obtained from a poll made by the

American Institute of Public Opinion (AIPO) about six weeks after the broadcast.[1] In a nation-wide sample of several thousand adults, 12 per cent answered "Yes" to the question "Did you listen to the Orson Welles broadcast of the invasion from Mars?" The representativeness of the sample used by the Gallup survey is based on the characteristics of the "voting public." It therefore contains more men, fewer young people, and, probably fewer southern Negroes than the actual radio-listening public.[2] According to the 1930 census there are 75,000,000 persons of voting age in the country. Twelve per cent of this number would indicate that about 9,000,000 adults heard the broadcast. If we consider all persons over ten years of age, then, according to the 1930 census we shall have 12 per cent of 99,000,000 people or, almost 12,000,000. It is undoubtedly true that many children even under ten years of age listen to the radio after eight o'clock on Sunday evening, especially when we remember that for more than half of the country this broadcast was at least an hour earlier than eight p.m. In addition to these young listeners, a large number of youngsters must have been wakened by frightened parents preparing to flee for their lives.

The AIPO figure is over 100 per cent higher than any other known measure of this audience. However, since the Institute reaches many small communities and non-telephone homes not regularly sampled by radio research organizations, its result is probably the most accurate.[3] C. E. Hooper, Inc., a commercial research organization making continuous checks on program popularity, indicates a listening audience of about 4,000,000 to the Mercury Theatre broadcast on October 30, 1938.[4] If we pool the AIPO and Hooper results, a final estimate of 6,000,000 listeners is conservative. Had the program enjoyed greater popularity, the panic might have been more widespread. . . .

How Many Were Frightened?

In answer to the AIPO question, "At the time you were listening, did you think this broadcast was a play or a real news report?" 28 per cent indicated that they believed the broadcast was a news bulletin. Seventy per cent of those who thought they were listening to a news report were frightened or disturbed. This would mean that about 1,700,000 heard the broadcast as a news bulletin and that about 1,200,000 were excited by it.

In spite of the attempt to word the question concerning the individual's reaction in a casual way, it must be remembered that the number of persons who admitted their fright to the AIPO interviewers is probably the very minimum of the total number actually frightened. Many persons were probably too ashamed of their gullibility to confess it in a cursory interview. On the other hand, people would not be so likely to prevaricate when asked whether or not they had heard the broadcast or whether or not they regarded it as news. But there is the possibility that some people heard so much about the broadcast that they reported actually hearing it. . . .

Telephone volume. Accounts of frantic telephone calls flooding switchboards of radio stations, newspapers and police stations are confirmed by figures secured from the American Telephone Company.[5] An increase of 39 per cent was reported in the telephone volume in metropolitan northern New Jersey during the hour of the broadcast as compared to the usual volume of that hour of the evening. A 25 per cent increase over normal in the same area occurred the succeeding hour. Increases for several suburban exchanges on Long Island for the same hours ranged from 5 to 19 per cent. In six suburban exchanges surrounding Philadelphia, traffic increased 9.6 per cent for the entire day of October 30 and for the entire New York metropolitan area traffic was above normal. Telephone officials see no other way to account for the increased volume than assigning responsibility to the broadcast.

The managers of the 92 radio stations that carried the broadcast were questioned by mail about their telephone during and immediately following the program. Of the 52 who replied, 50 reported an increase. Thirty-seven per cent noted increases of at least 500 per cent over the usual Sunday night volume; 31 per cent reported increases below 500 per cent. The others had no figures available. There seems little doubt then that a public reaction of unusual proportions occurred.

Mail volume. The interest the broadcast aroused is further shown by the number of letters written when it was over. Three-quarters of the station managers reported that their mail volume exceeded 100 per cent of the normal number of letters received. Several instances were reported of increases of over 500 per cent. Station WABC, Columbia's key station, was flooded with 1770 pieces of mail on this one subject, 1086 favorable, 684 unfavorable. The Mercury Theatre itself received 1450 letters concerning the program; 91 per cent congratulating them, 9 per cent condemning them. The Federal Communications Commission received 644 pieces of mail. Sixty per cent of the letters were unfavorable to the broadcast; 40 per cent favorable. These differences in the nature of the letters sent to the federal "watch dog of broadcasting" and to the producers are not surprising. They clearly indicate that those who wanted their protests taken seriously did not hesitate to communicate with the proper authorities, while those who appreciated good drama gave praise where praise was due.

Newspaper clippings. The opinion was frequently encountered the day after the broadcast that the general state of hysteria reported in the newspapers was merely an attempt to find good copy for papers on Monday morning when news is notoriously at low ebb. Even if we assume that less than 5 per cent of the population contributed to the reaction, this is hardly a legitimate suspicion. If something can excite 5 per cent of the population it *is* news. However, the figures above confirm the theory that there actually was something unusual and significant to report. Furthermore, the amount of newspaper space devoted to the episode for two weeks after the broadcast indicates a lingering fascination, although it cannot, of course, refute the charge that many accounts were embroidered to make good stories.

An analysis of 12,500 newspaper clippings appearing in papers throughout the country during the three weeks following the broadcast, reveals that, although the volume of press notices took the usual sharp decline the second and third days, considerable interest was maintained for five days and had not fallen below 30 per cent of the original volume by the end of the first week.[6]

WHY THE PANIC? . . .

✳ Why the Suggestion Was or Was Not Believed

What is most inconceivable and therefore especially interesting psychologically is why so many people did not do something to verify the information they were receiving from their loudspeakers. The failure to do this accounts for the persistence of the fright. To understand any panic—whether the cause is a legitimate one or not—it is necessary to see precisely what happens to an individual's mental processes that prevents him from making an adequate check-up.

The persons who were frightened by the broadcast were, for this occasion at least, highly suggestible, that is, they believed what they heard without making sufficient checks to prove to themselves that the broadcast was only a story. Those who were not frightened and those who believed the broadcast for only a short time were not suggestible—they were able to display what psychologists once called a "critical faculty." The problem is, then, to determine why some people are suggestible, or to state the problem differently, why some people lack critical ability.

There are essentially four psychological conditions that create in an individual the particular state of mind we know as suggestibility. All these may be described in terms of the concept of standard of judgment.

In the first place, individuals may refer a given stimulus to a standard or to several standards of judgment which they think are relevant for interpretation. The mental context into which the stimulus enters in this case is of such a character that it is welcomed as thoroughly consistent and without contradiction. A person with standards of judgment that enable him to "place" or "give meaning to" a stimulus in an almost automatic way finds nothing incongruous about such acceptance, his standards have led him to "expect" the possibility of such an occurrence. Thus a reactionary citizen will believe almost any rumor he hears that casts aspersions at political liberals; the communist will believe nearly all stories regarding progress in the Soviet Union; ideas or occurrences which contradict a rigidly established standard of judgment will be discarded, or overlooked.

We have found that many of the persons who did not even try to check the broadcast had preexisting mental sets that made the stimulus so understandable to them that they immediately accepted it as true. Highly religious people who believed that God willed and controlled the destinies of man were already furnished with a particular standard of judgment that would make an invasion of our planet and a destruction of its members merely an "act of God." This was particularly true if the religious frame of reference was of the eschatological variety providing the individual with definite attitudes or beliefs regarding the end of the world. Other people we found had been so influenced by the recent war scare that they believed an attack by a foreign power was imminent and an invasion—whether it was due to the Japanese, Hitler, or Martians—was not unlikely. Some persons had built up such fanciful notions of the possibilities of science that they could easily believe the powers of strange superscientists were being turned against them, perhaps merely for experimental purposes.

Whatever the cause for the genesis of the standards of judgment providing ready acceptance of the event, the fact remains that many persons already possessed a context within which they immediately placed the stimulus. None of their other existing standards of judgment was sufficiently relevant to engender disbelief. We found this to be particularly true of persons whose lack of opportunities or abilities to acquire information or training had insufficiently fortified them with pertinent standards of judgment that would make the interpretation of the broadcast as a play seem plausible. More highly educated people, we found, were better able to relate a given event to a standard of judgment they *knew* was an *appropriate* referrent. In such instances, the knowledge itself was used as a standard of judgment to discount the information received in the broadcast. These listeners, then, had the ability to refer to relevant standards of judgment which they could rely on for checking purposes and therefore had no need of further orientation.

A second condition of suggestibility exists when an individual is not sure of the interpretation he should place on a given stimulus and when he lacks adequate standards of judgment to make a reliable check on his interpretation. In this situation the individual attempts to check on his information but fails for one of three reasons: (1) he may check his original information against unreliable data which may themselves be affected by the situation he is checking. We found that persons who checked unsuccessfully tended to check against information obtained from friends or neighbors. Obviously, such people were apt themselves to be tinged with doubt and hesitation which would only confirm early suspicions. (b) A person may rationalize his checking information according to the original hypothesis he is checking and which he thinks he has only tentatively checked. Many listeners made hasty mental or behavioral checks but the false standard of judgment they had already accepted was so pervasive that their checkups were rationalized as confirmatory evidence. For example, one woman said that the announcer's charred body was found too quickly but she "figured the announcer was excited and had made a mistake." A man noticed the incredible speeds but thought "they were relaying reports or something." Others turned to different stations but thought the broadcasters were deliberately trying to calm the people. A woman looked out of her window and saw a greenish eerie light which she thought was from the Martians. (c) In contrast to those who believe almost any check they make are the people who earnestly try to verify their information but do not have sufficiently well grounded standards of judgment to determine whether or not their new sources of information are reliable.

A third and perhaps more general condition of suggestibility exists when an individual is confronted with a stimulus which he must interpret or which he would like to interpret and when *none* of his existing standards of judgment is adequate to the task. On such occasions the individual's mental context is unstructured, the stimulus does not fit any of his established categories and he seeks a standard that will suffice him. The less well structured is his mental context, the fewer meanings he is able to call forth, the less able will he be to understand the relationship between himself and the stimulus, and the greater will become his anxiety. And the more desperate his need for interpretation, the more likely will he be to accept the first interpretation given him. Many conditions existed to create in the individuals who listened to the invasion from Mars a chaotic mental universe that contained no stable standards of judgment by means of which the strange event reported could be evaluated. A lack of information and formal educational training had left many persons without any generalized standards of judgment applicable to this novel situation. And even if they did have a few such standards these were vague and tenuously held because they had not proved sufficient in the past to interpret other phenomena. This was especially true of those persons who had been most adversely affected by the conditions of the times.

The prolonged economic unrest and the consequent insecurity felt by many of the listeners was another cause for bewilderment. The depression had already lasted nearly ten years. People were still out of work. Why didn't somebody do something about it? Why didn't the experts find a solution? What was the cause of it anyway? Again, what would happen, no one could tell. Again, a mysterious invasion fitted the pattern of the mysterious events of the decade. The lack of a sophisticated, relatively stable economic or political frame of reference created in many persons a psychological disequilibrium which made them seek a standard of judgment for this particular event. It was another phenomenon in the outside world beyond their control and comprehension. Other people possessed certain economic security and social status but wondered how long this would last with "things in such a turmoil." They, too, sought a stable interpretation, one that would at least give this new occurrence meaning. The war scare had left many persons in a state of complete bewilderment. They did not know what the trouble was all about or why the United States should be so concerned. The complex ideological, class, and national antagonisms responsible for the crisis were by no means fully comprehended. The situation was painfully serious and distressingly confused. What would happen, nobody could foresee. The Martian invasion was just another event reported over the radio. It was even more personally dangerous and no more enigmatic. No existing standards were available to judge its meaning or significance. But there was quick need for judgment and it was provided by the announcers, scientists, and authorities.

Persons with higher education, on the other hand, we found had acquired more generalized standards of judgment which they could put their faith in. The result was that many of them "knew" the broadcast was a play as soon as the monsters began crawling out of the cylinder. It was too fantastic to be real as judged by their knowledge of the known world which they had always relied on. Others "knew" that the phenomenal speeds with which the announcers and soldiers moved was impossible even in this day and age. The greater the possibility of checking against a variety of reliable standards of judgment, the less suggestible will a person be. We found that some persons who in more normal circumstances might have had critical ability were so overwhelmed by their particular listening situation that their better judgment was suspended. This indicates that a highly consistent structuration of the external stimulus world may, at times, be experienced with sufficient intensity because of its personal implications to inhibit the operation of usually applicable internal structurations or standards of judgment. Other persons who may normally have exhibited critical ability were unable to do so in this situation because their own emotional insecurities and anxieties made them susceptible to suggestion when confronted with a personally dangerous circumstance. In such instances, the behavioral consequence is the same as for a person who has no standards of judgment to begin with but the psychological processes underlying the behavior are different.

A fourth condition of suggestibility results when an individual not only lacks standards of judgment by means of which he may orient himself but lacks even the realization that any interpretations are possible other than the one originally presented. He accepts as truth whatever he hears or reads without even thinking to compare it to other information. Perhaps the clearest index of critical ability is a person's readiness to reevaluate interpretations he first receives, to look for new standards of judgment and juxtapose them against others. One of the outstanding indices of suggestibility is the complete absence of the awareness that things might be otherwise than they are made out to be. This final psychological condition of suggestibility is essentially an extreme instance of the third one mentioned. But with the important difference that in this case the problem of *selecting* and *seeking* a standard of judgment never arises.

Psychologically, then, most persons who tuned in to the broadcast as a news report were unable to verify the interpretation they heard because (1) they possessed standards of judgment that adequately accounted for the events and made them consistent with latent expectancies, (2) because they did not have adequate standards of judgment to distinguish between a reliable and an unreliable source of confirmation, (3) they had no standard of judgment and felt the need of one by means of which they could interpret the reports, thus accepting the interpretations provided by the "observers" of the events and by the prestige of radio, and (4) they had no standard of judgment and unhesitatingly accepted the one provided.

Why Such Extreme Behavior?

Granted that some people believed the broadcast to be true, why did they become so hysterical? Why did they pray, telephone relatives, drive at dangerous speeds, cry, awaken sleeping children and flee? Of all the possible modes of reaction they may have followed, why did these particular patterns emerge? The obvious answer is that this was a serious affair. As in all other panics, the individual believed his well being, his safety, or his life was at stake. The situation was a real threat to him. Just what constitutes a personal threat to an individual must be briefly examined.

When an individual believes that a situation threatens him he means that it threatens not only his physical self but all of those things and people which he somehow regards as a part of him. This Ego of an individual is essentially composed of the many social and personal values *he* has accepted.[7] *He* feels threatened if his investments are threatened, *he* feels insulted if his children or parents are insulted, *he* feels elated if his alma mater wins the sectional football cup. The particular pattern of values that have been introcepted by an individual will give him, then, a particular Ego. For some individuals this is expanded to include broad ideals and ambitions. *They* will be disturbed if a particular race is persecuted in a distant country because that persecution runs counter to their ideal of human justice and democracy, *they* will be flattered if someone admires an idea of theirs or a painting they have completed.

Different values are accepted by a person with different degrees of conviction or felt-significance. Two people may each value democracy but one may be willing to die for it while another person would do nothing more than vote in a particular way and then sacrifice the value if it meant sacrificing other values more closely involved in his Ego. The particular pattern of values that constitutes a given individual's Ego will be due to the particular norms to which he has been exposed and which his temperament and previous experience have led him to select. People living in a given culture will tend by and large to accept similar values.

These values that become a part of the Ego, together with certain basic needs, may be considered as the source of an individual's motivation. The values correspond to derived needs which are often of just as dynamic a nature as the needs for sex, food and shelter.[8] The individual strives to preserve or to achieve the values he has acquired. More broadly speaking, he tries to maintain or reach a status he has learned to value and he tries to express himself.

One of the most universal of all values is, of course, life itself. Almost equally ubiquitous is the value of life for one's immediate relatives. To be sure, certain cultures teach the value of sacrificing life for an ideal and all cultures instill this value in times of national crisis. But by and large most individuals through the experience of living and the context of their culture value life.

A panic occurs when some highly cherished, rather commonly accepted value is threatened and when no certain elimination of the threat is in sight. The individual feels that he will be ruined, physically, financially or socially. The invasion of the Martians was a direct threat to life, to other lives that one loved, as well as to all other cherished values. The Martians were destroying practically everything. The situation was, then, indeed a serious affair. Frustration resulted when no directed behavior seemed possible. One was faced with the alternative of resigning oneself and all of one's values to complete annihilation or of making a desperate effort to escape from the field of danger, or of appealing to some higher power or stronger person whom one vaguely thought could destroy the oncoming enemy.

If one assumed that destruction was inevitable, then certain limited behavior was possible: one could cry, make peace with one's Maker, gather one's loved ones around and perish. If one attempted escape, one could run to the house of friends, speed away in a car or train, or hide in some gas-proof, bomb-proof, out-of-the-way shelter. If one still believed that something or someone might repulse the enemy, one could appeal to God or seek protection from those who had protected one in the past. Obviously none of these modes of behavior was a direct attack on the problem at hand, nothing was done to remove the causes of the crisis. The behavior in a panic is characteristically undirected and, from the point of view of the situation at hand, functionally useless.

The desire to be near loved ones was very common. As we have already implied this behavior was due to the fact that immediate relatives have become, for most persons, a part of the Ego. One wants to help them or be helped by them. In either case, psychologically, one is doing something for oneself, one is gaining emotional security. And if the most highly prized values are to be destroyed, then the individual feels that there is no use for him to live longer since so much of him will disappear with the values that are part of him. The patriot will die rather than have his country destroyed, the martyr will be burned at the stake rather than separate himself from his ideal, the revolutionist will suffer any hardship rather than forego his dream of a new social order.

In short, the extreme behavior evoked by the broadcast was due to the enormous felt ego-involvement the situation created and to the complete inability of the individual to alleviate or control the consequences of the invasion. The coming of the Martians did not present a situation where the individual could preserve one value if he sacrificed another. It was not a matter of saving one's country by giving one's life, of helping to usher in a new religion by self-denial, of risking the thief's bullet to save the family silver. In this situation the individual stood to lose *all* his values at once. Nothing could be done to save *any* of them. Panic was inescapable. The false standard of judgment used by the individual to interpret the broadcast was not itself the motivational cause of the behavior but it was absolutely essential in arousing the needs and values which may be regarded as the sources of the actions exhibited. A false standard of judgment aroused by the broadcast and causing the individual to be disturbed had its roots in values which were a part of the Ego.

When the broadcast was over and the truth had been learned, the evidence indicates that many persons wanted to make some relatively pertinent response to the horrifying stimulus they had experienced. They had a desire for "closure." The tremendous volume of fan mail and the many telephone calls after the broadcast indicate that people were satisfying a need to relieve the strain through which they had passed. As one letter-writer said in a postscript, "this is the first fan letter I have ever written. But I felt that I just had to do something about this. So I sat down and wrote this immediately." Others talked the event over with their friends or relatives. The interest in the experience, as reflected by newspaper accounts, lasted for several days.

✳ Social Significance

The particular incident we have analyzed was of interest to many persons other than psychologists. Since its roots were so deeply imbedded in both culture and personality and since its fruits so clearly reflected apparent cultural maladjustments, our account would be incomplete if we did not at least speculate on the social significance of the panic. The panic was a specific ailment in the social body, one from which it rapidly recovered. The diagnosis we have so far made should be concluded with a report on this type of case in general together with suggestions as to how such panics may be prevented. The educator and the social scientist who is a citizen as well as a scholar will ask "So what?"

Observers who took the incident casually might agree with the sociologist who believed that only unintelligent people were listening to this anyway and that the chances were slight any others would be disturbed. All our evidence seems to indicate, however, that many more persons might have been panicky had they happened to listen under what we might call optimum panic-producing conditions. There seems no reason to expect that relatively poor and uneducated persons should have been tuned to this program in any significantly great proportion. There is every reason to believe that the anxiety and fear revealed by the panic were latent in the general population, not specific to the persons who happened to participate in it.

In his column on November 2, 1938, the late Heywood Broun said, "I doubt if anything of the sort would have happened four or five months ago. The course of world history has affected national psychology. Jitters have come to roost. We have just gone through a laboratory demonstration of the fact that the peace of Munich hangs heavy over our heads, like a thundercloud.[9] Our data have indicated the rôle which the war scare of the last summer and early fall of 1938 played in producing the panic. But they also show that for many persons, the fear of war played only a secondary rôle if it indeed played any rôle at all. To imply that specific events that recently occurred in Europe and were broadcast to the United States served as the chief cause of the panic would be to disregard the multitude of other factors we have found so important.

That "the course of world history" has affected us is a truism. But this course of history contains more than war crises. Just what has happened is too familiar to be recited here. Probably more important than anything else, the highly disturbed economic conditions many Americans have experienced for the past decade, the consequent unemployment, the prolonged discrepancies between family incomes, the inability of both young and old to plan for the future have engendered a widespread feeling of insecurity. And persons underprivileged financially are underprivileged educationally, not to mention the many other personal consequences of a low and insecure income.

Prolonged bewilderment combined with lack of training to seek the basic causes of maladjustment are precisely the conditions most conducive to frustration and anxiety. Individuals sooner or later are likely to rebel at a situation which is far from satisfactory and which they cannot understand. They neither have the opportunity nor the training to see the complex and contradictory bases creating their maladjustments. Yet they desire an understanding and their desire increases with their perplexity. They become highly suggestible to some simple and sovereign formula provided by a demagogue. The whole tactics of Hitler show the importance he places on providing directed relief to bewildered souls. If they are not already sufficiently bewildered, bewilderment can be manufactured by sufficient propaganda.

Just as there is little possibility that people will be wholly impervious to propaganda for war or for dictatorship until the basic economic and ideological conflicts causing wars and dictatorships are removed, so it would seem that there is little reason to expect people would be wholly insulated from panic-creating situations until the basic causes for panic are removed. It is not the radio, the movies, the press or "propaganda" which, in themselves, really create wars and panics. It is the discrepancy between the whole superstructure of economic, social, and political practices and beliefs, and the basic and derived needs of individuals that creates wars, panics or mass movements of any kind. And human needs can only be curbed by the deliberate and forceful cultivation of ignorance, intolerance, and abstention. Such practices all adherent to democracy abhor.

But the latent anxieties conducive to panic may nevertheless be minimized if the critical abilities of people can be increased. . . . Thus while objective conditions may be slow to change, there is encouragement in the fact that our subjective reactions to these conditions may be made to change somewhat more rapidly by education. (And education, we discovered, was one of the greatest preventives of panic behavior. A greater critical ability would not only enable people to distinguish between reality and fiction but it would also enable them to make more appropriate adjustments if they ever were caught in a genuinely critical situation.) Just as a knowledge of hygiene and the rudiments of medicine help to prevent illness, they also help to restore the individual who is actually sick.

(Our study of the common man of our times has shown us that his ability to orient himself appropriately in critical situations will be increased if he can be taught to adopt an attitude of readiness to question the interpretations he hears. But when he achieves this healthy skepticism he must have sufficient and relevant knowledge to be able to evaluate different interpretations. If he is to judge these interpretations intelligently, his knowledge must be grounded in evidence or tested experience. If this skepticism and knowledge are to be spread more widely among common men, they must be provided extensive educational opportunities.) And if this final critical ability is to be used more generally by common men, they must be less harassed by the emotional insecurities which stem from underprivileged environments.

NOTES

1. This delay was unavoidable due to the fact that sufficient funds were available for the survey only after this time had elapsed. The writer is indebted to Mr. Lawrence Benson and Mr. Edward Benson of the American Institute of Public Opinion for their cooperation during this survey; also to Dr. George Gallup for permitting the facilities of the Institute to be used for this study.
2. For a discussion of public opinion polls and the techniques of measurement, see D. Katz and H. Cantril, "Public Opinion Polls," *Sociometry*, 1937, Vol. I, pp. 155–179.
3. A critical discussion of methods of measuring the listening audience, by Frank Stanton, *Measuring the Listening Audience*, is scheduled to be published by Princeton University Press, 1940.
4. The Cooperative Analysis of Broadcasting report (CAB) did not survey Oct. 30. The Oct. 23 figure is 4 per cent of radio homes; the Nov. 6 figure 7.4 per cent of radio homes. It is not without significance that the program's popularity increased almost 100 per cent in these two weeks and it seems probable that almost this entire jump was due to the excitement and publicity aroused by the Oct. 30 broadcast.

5. The writer wishes to acknowledge the assistance of members of the Traffic Department in the New York office of the company for their assistance in gathering the data.

6. These clippings were collected from newspapers of every state by a reputable clipping bureau. The writer is indebted to the Mercury Theatre for generous permission to make full use of its files.

7. M. Sherif, *Psychology of Social Norms,* New York: Harpers, 1936, Chap. IX.

8. G. W. Allport, *Personality,* New York: Holt, 1937, Chap. VII.

9. *New York World-Telegram,* Nov. 2, 1938.

The Two-Step Flow of Communication: An Up-to-Date Report on an Hypothesis

Elihu Katz was a member of the Bureau of Applied Social Research at Columbia University. Much of his work there was influenced by prominent market researcher Paul F. Lazarsfeld, coauthor of the marketing study *The People's Choice: How the Voter Makes Up His Mind in a Presidential Campaign.* In commenting on this study's conclusions, Katz wrote, "Of all the ideas in *The People's Choice,* . . . the two-step flow hypothesis is probably the one that was least well documented by empirical data."

In the following excerpt from his article "The Two-Step Flow of Communication: An Up-to-Date Report on an Hypothesis," *Public Opinion Quarterly* (Spring 1957), Katz compares some of the studies that followed *The People's Choice* to analyze interpersonal influence and its impact on voter behavior. Three studies—*The Rovere Study, The Decatur Study,* and *The Elmira Study*—each further examined the role of opinion leaders in influencing attitudes and behaviors. Katz also applies the two-step flow hypothesis to what became known as *The Drug Study* to determine interpersonal influence in diffusion research.

By further exploring the applications of the two-step flow hypothesis, Katz attempted to explain how and under what circumstances ameliorating factors in interpersonal influence might occur. His comparative research on the role of personal influence had a great impact on many subsequent studies.

Katz received his Ph.D. from Columbia University. He was an assistant professor at the University of Chicago and a lecturer in sociology at the Hebrew University in Jerusalem. He is now with the Communication Institute at the Hebrew University. He has authored or coauthored many books on the study of media, including *Broadcasting in the Third World: Promise and Performance* (Harvard University Press, 1977), with George Wedell; *The Export of Meaning: Cross-Cultural Readings of Dallas* (Oxford University Press, 1990), with Tamar Liebes; and *Media Events: The Live Broadcasting of History* (Harvard University Press, 1992), with Daniel Dayan.

Key Concept: personal influence and two-step flow

Analysis of the process of decision-making during the course of an election campaign led the authors of *The People's Choice* to suggest that the flow of mass communications may be less direct than was commonly supposed. It may be, they proposed, that influences stemming from the mass media first reach "opinion leaders" who, in turn, pass on what they read and hear to those of their every-day associates for whom they are influential. This hypothesis was called "the two-step flow of communication."[1]

The hypothesis aroused considerable interest. The authors themselves were intrigued by its implications for democratic society. It was a healthy sign, they felt, that people were still most successfully persuaded by give-and-take with other people and that the influence of the mass media was less automatic and less potent than had been assumed. For social theory, and for the design of communications research, the hypothesis suggested that the image of modern urban society needed revision. The image of the audience as a mass of disconnected individuals hooked up to the media but not to each other could not be reconciled with the idea of a two-step flow of communication implying, as it did, networks of interconnected individuals through which mass communications are channeled.

Of all the ideas in *The People's Choice*, however, the two-step flow hypothesis is probably the one that was least well documented by empirical data. And the reason for this is clear: the design of the study did not anticipate the importance which interpersonal relations would assume in the analysis of the data. Given the image of the atomized audience which characterized so much of mass media research, the surprising thing is that interpersonal influence attracted the attention of the researchers at all.[2]

In the almost seventeen years since the voting study was undertaken, several studies at the Bureau of Applied Social Research of Columbia University have attempted to examine the hypothesis and to build upon it. Four such studies will be singled out for review. These are Merton's study of interpersonal influence and communications behavior in Rovere;[3] the Decatur study of decision-making in marketing, fashions, movie-going and public affairs, reported by Katz and Lazarsfeld;[4] the Elmira study of the 1948 election campaign reported by Berelson, Lazarsfeld and McPhee;[5] and, finally, a very recent study by Coleman, Katz and Menzel on the diffusion of a new drug among doctors.[6] . . .

DESIGNS OF THREE SUBSEQUENT STUDIES

. . . 1. *The Rovere Study.* Undertaken just as the 1940 voting study was being completed, the earliest of the three studies was conducted in a small town in

New Jersey. It began by asking a sample of 86 respondents to name the people to whom they turned for information and advice regarding a variety of matters. Hundreds of names were mentioned in response, and those who were designated four times or more were considered opinion leaders. These influentials were then sought out and interviewed.[7] . . .

2. *The Decatur Study*, carried out in 1945–46, tried to go a step further.[8] Like the voting study, but unlike Rovere, it tried to account for decisions—specific instances in which the effect of various influences could be discerned and assessed. Like Rovere, but unlike the voting study, it provided for interviews with the persons whom individuals in the initial sample had credited as influential in the making of recent decisions (in the realms of marketing, movie-going, and public affairs). The focus of the study this time was not on the opinion leaders alone, but (1) on the relative importance of personal influence and (2) on the person who named the leader as well as the leader—the advisor-advisee dyad. . . .

The authors of *The People's Choice* had said that "asking people to whom they turn and then investigating the interaction between advisers and advisees . . . would be extremely difficult if not impossible." And, in fact, it proved to be extremely difficult. Many problems were encountered in the field work, the result of which was that not all the "snowball" interviews could be completed.[9] In many parts of the analysis of the data, therefore, it was necessary to revert to comparisons of leaders and non-leaders, imputing greater influence to groups with higher concentrations of self-designated leadership. Yet, in principle, it was demonstrated that a study design taking account of interpersonal relations was both possible an profitable to execute.

But about the time it became evident that this goal was within reach, the goal itself began to change. It began to seem desirable to take account of chains of influence longer than those involved in the dyad; and hence to view the adviser-advisee dyad as one component of a more elaborately structured social group.

These changes came about gradually and for a variety of reasons. First of all, findings from the Decatur study and from the later Elmira study revealed that the opinion leaders themselves often reported that their own decisions were influenced by still other people.[10] It began to seem desirable, therefore, to think in terms of the opinion leaders of opinion leaders.[11] Secondly, it became clear that opinion leadership could not be viewed as a "trait" which some people possess and others do not, although the voting study sometimes implied this view. Instead, it seemed quite apparent that the opinion leader is influential at certain times and with respect to certain substantive areas by virtue of the fact that he is "empowered" to be so by other members of his group. Why certain people are chosen must be accounted for not only in demographic terms (social status, sex, age, etc.) but also in terms of the structure and values of the groups of which both adviser and advisee are members. Thus, the unexpected rise of young men to opinion leadership in traditional groups, when these groups faced the new situations of urbanization and industrialization, can be understood only against the background of old and new patterns of social relations within the group and of old and new patterns of orientation to the world outside the group.[12] Reviewing the literature of small group research hastened the formulation of this conception.[13]

One other factor shaped the direction of the new program as well. Reflecting upon the Decatur study, it became clear that while one could talk about the role of various influences in the making of fashion *decisions by individuals,* the study design was not adequate for the study of fashion in the aggregate—*fashion as a process of diffusion*—as long as it did not take account of either the content of the decision or the time factor involved. The decisions of the "fashion changers" studied in Decatur might have cancelled each other out: while Mrs. X reported a change from Fashion A to Fashion B, Mrs. Y might have been reporting a change from B to A. What is true for fashion is true for any other diffusion phenomenon: to study it, one must trace the flow of some specific item over time. Combining this interest in diffusion with that of studying the role of more elaborate social networks of communication gave birth to a new study which focused on (1) a specific item, (2) diffusion over time, (3) through the social structure of an entire community.

3. *The Drug Study.* This study was conducted to determine the way in which doctors make decisions to adopt new drugs. This time, when it came to designing a study which would take account of the possible role of interpersonal influence among physicians, it became clear that there were so few physicians (less than one and one-half per 1000 population) that it was feasible to interview all members of the medical profession in several cities. If all doctors (or all doctors in specialties concerned with the issue at hand) could be interviewed, then there would be no doubt that all adviser-advisee pairs would fall within the sample. All such pairs could then be located within the context of larger social groupings of doctors, which could be measured by sociometric methods. . . .

In addition to the opportunity of mapping the networks of interpersonal relations, the drug study also provided for the two other factors necessary for a true diffusion study: attention to a specific item in the course of gaining acceptance, and a record of this diffusion over time. This was accomplished by means of an audit of prescriptions on file in the local pharmacies of the cities studied, which made it possible to date each doctor's earliest use of a particular new drug—a drug which had gained widespread acceptance a few months before the study had begun. Each doctor could thus be classified in terms of the promptness of his decision to respond to the innovation, and in terms of other information provided by the prescription audit. . . .

THE IMPACT OF PERSONAL INFLUENCE

Personal and the Mass Media Influence

The 1940 study indicated that personal influence affected voting decisions more than the mass media did, particularly in the case of those who changed their minds during the course of the campaign. The Decatur study went on to explore the relative impact of personal influences and the mass media in three other realms: marketing, fashions and movie-going. Basing its conclusions on the testimony of the decision-makers themselves, and using an instrument for evaluating the relative effectiveness of the various media which entered into the decisions, the Decatur study again found that personal influence figured both more frequently and more effectively than any of the mass media.[14]

In the analysis to date, the drug study has not approached the problem of the relative effectiveness of the various media from the point of view of the doctor's own reconstruction of what went into the making of his decision. Comparing mere frequency of mention of different media, it is clear that colleagues are by no means the most frequently mentioned source. Nevertheless, exploration of the factors related to whether the doctor's decision to adopt the drug came early or late indicates that the factor most strongly associated with the time of adoption of the new drug is the extent of the doctor's integration in the medical community. That is, the more frequently a doctor is named by his colleagues as a friend or a discussion partner, the more likely he is to be an innovator with respect to the new drug. Extent of integration proves to be a more important factor than any background factor (such as age, medical school, or income of patients), or any other source of influence (such as readership of medical journals) that was examined. . . .

THE FLOW OF PERSONAL INFLUENCE

The 1940 voting study found that opinion leaders were not concentrated in the upper brackets of the population but were located in almost equal proportions in every social group and stratum. This finding led to efforts in subsequent studies to establish the extent to which this was true in areas other than election campaigns and also to ascertain what it is that *does* distinguish opinion leaders from those whom they influence.

The first thing that is clear from the series of studies under review is that the subject matter concerning which influence is transmitted has a lot to do with determining who will lead and who follow. Thus, the Rovere study suggests that within the broad sphere of public affairs one set of influentials is occupied with "local" affairs and another with "cosmopolitan" affairs.[15] The Decatur study suggests that in marketing, for example, there is a concentration of opinion leadership among older women with larger families, while in fashions and movie-going it is the young, unmarried girl who has a disproportionate chance of being turned to for advice. There is very little overlap of leadership: a leader in one sphere is not likely to be influential in another unrelated sphere as well.[16]

Yet, even when leadership in one or another sphere is heavily concentrated among the members of a particular group—as was the case with marketing leadership in Decatur—the evidence suggests that people still talk, most of all, to others like themselves. Thus, while the marketing leaders among the older "large-family wives" also influenced other kinds of women, most of their influence was directed to women of their own age with equally large families. In marketing, fashions, and movie-going, furthermore, there was no appreciable concentration of influentials in any of the three socio-economic levels. Only in public affairs was there a concentration of leadership in the highest status, and there was some slight evidence that influence flows from this group to individuals of lower status. The Elmira study also found opinion-leaders in similar proportions on every socio-economic and occupational level and found that conversations concerning the campaign went on, typically, between people of similar age, occupation, and political opinion.

What makes for the concentration of certain kinds of opinion leadership within certain groups? And when influential and influencee are outwardly alike—as they so often seem to be—what, if anything, distinguishes one from the other? Broadly, it appears that influence is related (1) to the *personification of certain values* (who one is); (2) to *competence* (what one knows); and (3) to *strategic social location* (whom one knows). Social location, in turn, divides into whom one knows within a group; and "outside."

Influence is often successfully transmitted because the influencee wants to be as much like the influential as possible.[17] That the young, unmarried girls are fashion leaders can be understood easily in a culture where youth and youthfulness are supreme values. This is an example where "who one is" counts very heavily.

But "what one knows" is no less important.[18] The fact is that older women, by virtue of their greater experience, are looked to as marketing advisers and that specialists in internal medicine—the most "scientific" of the practicing physicians—are the most frequently mentioned opinion leaders among the doctors. The influence of young people in the realm of movie-going can also be understood best in terms of their familiarity with the motion picture world. The Elmira study found slightly greater concentrations of opinion leadership among the more educated people on each socioeconomic level, again implying the importance of competence. Finally, the influence of the "cosmopolitans" in Rovere rested on the presumption that they had large amounts of information.

It is, however, not enough to be a person whom others want to emulate, or to be competent. One must also be accessible. Thus, the Decatur study finds gregariousness—"whom one knows"—related to every kind of leadership. The Rovere study reports that the leadership of the "local" influentials is based on their central location in the web of interpersonal contacts. Similarly, studies of rumor transmission have singled out those who are "socially active" as agents of rumor.[19]

Of course, the importance of whom one knows is not simply a matter of the number of people with whom an opinion leader is in contact. It is also a question of whether the people with whom he is in touch happen to be interested in the area in which his leadership is likely to be sought. For this reason, it is quite clear that the greater interest of opinion leaders in the subjects over which they exert influence is not a sufficient explanation of their influence. While the voting studies as well as the Decatur study show leaders to be more interested, the Decatur study goes on to show that interest alone is not the determining factor.[20] In fashion, for example, a young unmarried girl is considerably more likely to be influential than a matron with an equally great interest in clothes. The reason, it is suggested, is that a girl who is interested in fashion is much more likely than a matron with an equally high interest to know other people who share her preoccupation, and thus is more likely than the matron to have followers who are interested enough to ask for her advice. In other words, it takes two to be a leader—a leader and a follower.

Finally, there is the second aspect of "whom one knows." An individual may be influential not only because people within his group look to him for advice but also because of whom he knows outside his group.[21] Both the Elmira and Decatur studies found that men are more likely than women to be opinion leaders in the realm of public affairs and this, it is suggested, is because they have more of a chance to get outside the home to meet people and talk politics. Similarly, the Elmira study indicated that opinion leaders belonged to more organizations, more often knew workers for the political parties, and so on, than did others. The drug study found that influential doctors could be characterized in terms of such things as their more frequent attendance at out-of-town meetings and the diversity of places with which they maintained contact, particularly far-away places. It is interesting that a study of the farmer-innovators responsible for the diffusion of hybrid seed-corn in Iowa concluded that these leaders also could be characterized in terms of the relative frequency of their trips out of town.[22]

THE OPINION LEADERS AND THE MASS MEDIA

The third aspect of the hypothesis of the two-step flow of communication states that opinion leaders are more exposed to the mass media than are those whom they influence. In *The People's Choice* this is supported by reference to the media behavior of leaders and non-leaders.

The Decatur study corroborated this finding, and went on to explore two additional aspects of the same idea.[23] First of all, it was shown that leaders in a given sphere (fashions, public affairs, etc.) were particularly likely to be exposed to the media appropriate to that sphere. This is essentially a corroboration of the Rovere finding that those who proved influential with regard to "cosmopolitan" matters were more likely to be readers of national news magazines, but that this was not at all the case for those influential with regard to "local" matters. Secondly, the Decatur study shows that at least in the realm of fashions, the leaders are not only more exposed to the mass media, but are also more affected by them in their own decisions. This did not appear to be the case in other realms, where opinion leaders, though more exposed to the media than non-leaders, nevertheless reported personal influence as the major factor in their decisions. This suggests that in some spheres considerably longer chains of person-to-person influence than the dyad may have to be traced back before one encounters any decisive influence by the mass media, even though their contributory influence may be perceived at many points. This was suggested by the Elmira study too. It found that the leaders, though more exposed to the media, also more often reported that they sought information and advice from other persons.[24]

Similarly, the drug study showed that the influential doctors were more likely to be readers of a large number of professional journals and valued them more highly than did doctors of lesser influence. But at the same time, they were as likely as other doctors to say that local colleagues were an important source of information and advice in their reaching particular decisions.

Finally, the drug study demonstrated that the more influential doctors could be characterized by their greater attention not only to medical journals, but to out-of-town meetings and contacts was well. This finding has already been discussed in the previous section treating the *strategic location* of the opinion leader with respect to "the world outside" his group. Considering it again under the present heading suggests that the greater exposure of the opinion leader to the mass media may only be a special case of the more general proposition.that opinion leaders serve to relate their groups to relevant parts of the environment through whatever media happen to be appropriate. This more general statement makes clear the similar functions of big city newspapers for the Decatur fashion leader; of national news magazines for the "cosmopolitan" influentials of Rovere; of out-of-town medical meetings for the influential doctor; and of contact with the city for the farmer-innovator in Iowa as well as for the newly-risen, young opinion leaders in underdeveloped areas throughout the world.[25]

CONCLUSIONS

. . . Opinion leaders and the people whom they influence are very much alike and typically belong to the same primary groups of family, friends and co-workers. While the opinion leader may be more interested in the particular sphere in which he is influential, it is highly unlikely that the persons influenced will be very far behind the leader in their level of interest. Influentials and influencees may exchange roles in different spheres of influence. Most spheres focus the group's attention on some related part of the world outside the group, and it is the opinion leader's function to bring the group into touch with this relevant part of its environment through whatever media are appropriate. In every case, influentials have been found to be more exposed to these points of contact with the outside world. Nevertheless, it is also true that, despite their greater exposure to the media, most opinion leaders are primarily affected not by the communication media but by still other people.

The main emphasis of the two-step flow hypothesis appears to be on only one aspect of interpersonal relations—interpersonal relations as channels of communication. But from the several studies reviewed, it is clear that these very same interpersonal relations influence the making of decisions in at least two additional ways. In addition to serving as networks of communication, interpersonal relations are also sources of pressure to conform to the group's way of thinking and acting, as well as sources of social support. The workings of group pressure are clearly evident in the homogeneity of opinion and action observed among voters and among doctors in situations of unclarity or uncertainty. The social support that comes from being integrated in the medical community may give a doctor the confidence required to carry out a resolution to adopt a new drug. Thus, interpersonal relations are (1) channels of information, (2) sources of social pressure, and (3) sources of social support, and each relates interpersonal relations to decision-making in a some-what different way.[26]

NOTES

1. Paul F. Lazarsfeld, Bernard Berelson and Hazel Gaudet, *The People's Choice*, New York: Columbia University Press, 1948 (2nd edition), p. 151.
2. For the discussion of the image of the atomized audience and the contravening empirical evidence, see Elihu Katz and Paul F. Lazarsfeld, *Personal Influence: The Part Played by People in the Flow of Mass Communications*, Glencoe, Illinois: The Free Press, 1955, pp. 15–42; Eliot Friedson, "Communications Research and the Concept of the Mass," *American Sociological Review*, Vol. 18, (1953), pp. 313–317; and Morris Janowitz, *The Urban Press in a Community Setting*, Glencoe, Illinois: The Free Press, 1952.
3. Robert K. Merton, "Patterns of Influence: A Study of Interpersonal Influence and Communications Behavior in a Local Community," in Paul F. Lazarsfeld and Frank N. Stanton, eds., *Communications Research, 1948–9*, New York: Harper and Brothers, 1949, pp. 180–219.
4. Elihu Katz and Paul F. Lazarsfeld, *op. cit.*, Part Two.
5. Bernard R. Berelson, Paul F. Lazarsfeld and William N. McPhee, *Voting: A Study of Opinion Formation in a Presidential Campaign*, Chicago: University of Chicago Press, 1954.
6. A report on the pilot phase of this study is to be found in Herbert Menzel and Elihu Katz, "Social Relations and Innovation in the Medical Profession," *Public Opinion Quarterly*, Vol. 19, (1955), pp. 337–52; a volume and various articles on the full study are now in preparation.
7. Merton, *op. cit.*, 184–185.
8. Katz and Lazarsfeld, *op. cit.*, Part Two.
9. Partly this was due to inability to locate the designated people, but partly, too, to the fact that original respondents did not always know the person who had influenced them as is obvious, for example, in the case of a woman copying another woman's hat style, etc. See *Ibid.* pp. 362–363
10. *Ibid.*, p. 318; Berelson, Lazarsfeld and McPhee, *op. cit.*, p. 110.
11. This was actually tried at one point in the Decatur study. See Katz and Lazarsfeld, *op. cit.* pp. 283–287.
12. See, for example, the articles by Eisenstadt, *op. cit.*, and Glock, *op. cit.*; the Rovere study, too, takes careful account of the structure of social relations and values in which influentials are embedded, and discusses the various avenues to influentiality open to different kinds of people.
13. Reported in Part I of Katz and Lazarsfeld, *op. cit.*
14. Katz and Lazarsfeld, *op. cit.*, pp. 169–186.
15. Merton, *op. cit.*, pp. 187–188.
16. For a summary of the Decatur findings on the flow of interpersonal influence, see Katz and Lazarsfeld, *op. cit.*, pp. 327–334.
17. That leaders are, in a certain sense, the most conformist members of their groups—upholding whatever norms and values are central to the group—is a proposition which further illustrates this point. For an empirical illustration from a highly relevant study, see C. Paul Marsh and A. Lee Coleman, "Farmers' Practice Adoption Rates in Relation to Adoption Rates of Leaders," *Rural Sociology*, Vol. 19 (1954), pp. 180–183.
18. The distinction between "what" and "whom" one knows is used by Merton, *op. cit.*, p. 197.
19. Gordon W. Allport and Leo J. Postman, *The Psychology of Rumor*, New York: Henry Holt, 1943, p. 183.

20. Katz and Lazarsfeld, *op. cit.,* pp. 249–252.

21. It is interesting that a number of studies have found that the most integrated persons within a group are also likely to have more contacts outside the group than others. One might have expected the more marginal members to have more contacts outside. For example, see Blau, *op. cit.,* p. 128.

22. Bryce Ryan and Neal Gross, *Acceptance and Diffusion of Hybrid See Corn in Two Iowa Communities,* Ames, Iowa: Iowa State College of Agriculture and Mechanic Arts, Research Bulletin, 372, pp. 706–707. For a general summary, see Ryan and Gross, "The Diffusion of Hybrid Seed Corn in Two Iowa Communities," *Rural Sociology,* Vol. 8 (1942), pp. 15–24. An article, now in preparation, will point out some of the parallels in research design and in findings between this study and the drug study.

23. Katz and Lazarsfeld, *op. cit.,* pp. 309–320.

24. Berelson, Lazarsfeld and McPhee, *op. cit.,* p. 110.

25. See the forthcoming book by Lerner, *et. al* cited above.

26. These different dimensions of interpersonal relations can be further illustrated by reference to studies which represent the "pure type" of each dimension. Studies of rumor flow illustrate the "channels" dimension; see, for example, Jacob L. Moreno, *Who Shall Survive,* Beacon, N.Y.: Beacon House, 1953, pp. 440–450. The study by Leon Festinger, Stanley Schachter and Kurt Back, *Social Pressures in Informal Groups,* New York: Harper and Bros., 1950, illustrates the second dimension. Blau, *op. cit.,* pp. 126–129, illustrates the "social support" dimension.

2.4 ALBERT BANDURA, DOROTHEA ROSS, AND SHEILA A. ROSS

Imitation of Film-Mediated Aggressive Models

Psychologist Albert Bandura (b. 1925) has long been considered one of the most influential experimental psychologists in the area of social learning. His coauthors for the following selection, Dorothea Ross and Sheila A. Ross, were researchers at Stanford University, where most of Bandura's studies on children and imitative behavior were conducted.

"Imitation of Film-Mediated Aggressive Models," *Journal of Abnormal and Social Psychology* (vol. 66, no. 1, 1963), from which the following selection is taken, is the well-known "Bobo Doll" study. For this study, young children were shown a film depicting aggressive behavior and then observed to see whether or not they would repeat the aggressive act viewed on the film and whether or not their behavior would be tempered by the presence of a positive adult role model. The hypothesis and methodology in this study are consistent with the stimulus-response (S-R) belief about children's modeling behavior. The article gave credence to the belief that media violence encourages children to act aggressively or violently.

Although effects research was moving away from the direct effects models at the time that Bandura performed his research, children were still thought to be impressionable and were therefore regarded as different types of media users than adults. Even today, many studies support or seek to prove that children are more susceptible to the images presented by the media than are adults.

Key Concept: media and imitative behavior

Most of the research on the possible effects of film-mediated stimulation upon subsequent aggressive behavior has focused primarily on the drive reducing function of fantasy. While the experimental evidence for the catharsis or drive reduction theory is equivocal (Albert, 1957; Berkowitz, 1962; Emery,

1959; Feshbach, 1955, 1958; Kenny, 1952; Lövaas, 1961; Siegel, 1956), the modeling influence of pictorial stimuli has received little research attention.

A recent incident (San Francisco Chronicle, 1961) in which a boy was seriously knifed during a re-enactment of a switchblade knife fight the boys had seen the previous evening on a televised rerun of the James Dean movie, *Rebel Without a Cause*, is a dramatic illustration of the possible imitative influence of film stimulation. Indeed, anecdotal data suggest that portrayal of aggression through pictorial media may be more influential in shaping the form aggression will take when a person is instigated on later occasions, than in altering the level of instigation to aggression.

In an earlier experiment (Bandura & Huston, 1961), it was shown that children readily imitated aggressive behavior exhibited by a model in the presence of the model. A succeeding investigation (Bandura, Ross, & Ross, 1961), demonstrated that children exposed to aggressive models generalized aggressive responses to a new setting in which the model was absent. The present study sought to determine the extent to which film-mediated aggressive models may serve as an important source of imitative behavior.

Aggressive models can be ordered on a reality-fictional stimulus dimension with real-life models located at the reality end of the continuum, nonhuman cartoon characters at the fictional end, and films portraying human models occupying an intermediate position. It was predicted, on the basis of saliency and similarity of cues, that the more remote the model was from reality, the weaker would be the tendency for subjects to imitate the behavior of the model.

Of the various interpretations of imitative learning, the sensory feedback theory of imitation recently proposed by Mowrer (1960) is elaborated in greatest detail. According to this theory, if certain responses have been repeatedly positively reinforced, proprioceptive stimuli associated with these responses acquire secondary reinforcing properties and thus the individual is predisposed to perform the behavior for the positive feedback. Similarly, if responses have been negatively reinforced, response correlated stimuli acquire the capacity to arouse anxiety which, in turn, inhibit the occurrence of the negatively valenced behavior. On the basis of these considerations, it was predicted subjects who manifest high aggression anxiety would perform significantly less imitative and nonimitative aggression than subjects who display little anxiety over aggression. Since aggression is generally considered female inappropriate behavior, and therefore likely to be negatively reinforced in girls (Sears, Maccoby, & Levin, 1957), it was also predicted that male subjects would be more imitative of aggression than females.

To the extent that observation of adults displaying aggression conveys a certain degree of permissiveness for aggressive behavior, it may be assumed that such exposure not only facilitates the learning of new aggressive responses but also weakens competing inhibitory responses in subjects and thereby increases the probability of occurrence of previously learned patterns of aggression. It was predicted, therefore, that subjects who observed aggressive models would display significantly more aggression when subsequently frustrated than subjects who were equally frustrated but who had no prior exposure to models exhibiting aggression.

Subjects

The subjects were 48 boys and 48 girls enrolled in the Stanford University Nursery School. They ranged in age from 35 to 69 months, with a mean age of 52 months.

Two adults, a male and a female, served in the role of models both in the real-life and the human film-aggression condition, and one female experimenter conducted the study for all 96 children.

General Procedure

Subjects were divided into three experimental groups and one control group of 24 subjects each. One group of experimental subjects observed real-life aggressive models, a second group observed these same models portraying aggression on film, while a third group viewed a film depicting an aggressive cartoon character. The experimental groups were further subdivided into male and female subjects so that half the subjects in the two conditions involving human models were exposed to same-sex models, while the remaining subjects viewed models of the opposite sex.

Following the exposure experience, subjects were tested for the amount of imitative and nonimitative aggression in a different experimental setting in the absence of the models.

The control group subjects had no exposure to the aggressive models and were tested only in the generalization situation.

Subjects in the experimental and control groups were matched individually on the basis of ratings of their aggressive behavior in social interactions in the nursery school. The experimenter and a nursery school teacher rated the subjects on four five-point rating scales which measured the extent to which subjects displayed physical aggression, verbal aggression, aggression toward inanimate objects, and aggression inhibition. The latter scale, which dealt with the subjects' tendency to inhibit aggressive reactions in the face of high instigation, provided the measure of aggression anxiety. Seventy-one percent of the subjects were rated independently by both judges so as to permit an assessment of interrater agreement. The reliability of the composite aggression score, estimated by means of the Pearson product-moment correlation, was .80. . . .

Experimental Conditions

Subjects in the Real-Life Aggressive condition were brought individually by the experimenter to the experimental room and the model, who was in the hallway outside the room, was invited by the experimenter to come and join in the game. The subject was then escorted to one corner of the room and seated at a small table which contained potato prints, multicolor picture stickers, and colored paper. After demonstrating how the subject could design pictures with the materials provided, the experimenter escorted the model to the opposite corner of the room which contained a small table and chair, a tinker toy set, a mallet, and a 5-foot inflated Bobo doll. The experimenter explained that this was the model's play area and after the model was seated, the experimenter left the experimental room.

The model began the session by assembling the tinker toys but after approximately a minute had elapsed, the model turned to the Bobo doll and spent the remainder of the period aggressing toward it with highly novel responses which are unlikely to be performed by children independently of the observation of the model's behavior. Thus, in addition to punching the Bobo doll, the model exhibited the following distinctive aggressive acts which were to be scored as imitative responses:

The model sat on the Bobo doll and punched it repeatedly in the nose.

The model then raised the Bobo doll and pommeled it on the head with a mallet.

Following the mallet aggression, the model tossed the doll up in the air aggressively and kicked it about the room. This sequence of physically aggressive acts was repeated approximately three times, interspersed with verbally aggressive responses such as, "Sock him in the nose..," "Hit him down . . . ," "Throw him in the air . . . ," "Kick him . . . ," and "Pow."

Subjects in the Human Film-Aggression condition were brought by the experimenter to the semidarkened experimental room, introduced to the picture materials, and informed that while the subjects worked on potato prints, a movie would be shown on a screen, positioned approximately 6 feet from the subject's table. The movie projector was located in a distant corner of the room and was screened from the subject's view by large wooden panels.

The color movie and a tape recording of the sound track was begun by a male projectionist as soon as the experimenter left the experimental room and was shown for a duration of 10 minutes. The models in the film presentations were the same adult males and females who participated in the Real-Life condition of the experiment. Similarly, the aggressive behavior they portrayed in the film was identical with their real-life performances.

For subjects in the Cartoon Film-Aggression condition, after seating the subject at the table with the picture construction material, the experimenter walked over to a television console approximately 3 feet in front of the subject's table, remarked, "I guess I'll turn on the color TV," and ostensibly tuned in a cartoon program. The experimenter then left the experimental room. The cartoon was shown on a glass lens screen in the television set by means of a rear projection arrangement screened from the subject's view by large panels.

The sequence of aggressive acts in the cartoon was performed by the female model costumed as a black cat similar to the many cartoon cats. In order to heighten the level of irreality of the cartoon, the floor area was covered with artificial grass and the walls forming the backdrop were adorned with brightly colored trees, birds, and butterflies creating a fantasyland setting. The cartoon began with a close-up of a stage on which the curtains were slowly drawn revealing a picture of a cartoon cat along with the title, *Herman the Cat.* The remainder of the film showed the cat pommeling the Bobo doll on the head with a mallet, sitting on the doll and punching it in the nose, tossing the doll in the air, and kicking it about the room in a manner identical with the performance in the other experimental conditions except that the cat's movements were characteristically feline. To induce further a cartoon set, the program was introduced and concluded with appropriate cartoon music, and the cat's verbal aggression was repeated in a high-pitched, animated voice.

*Albert Bandura
et al.*

In both film conditions, at the conclusion of the movie the experimenter entered the room and then escorted the subject to the test room.

Aggression Instigation

In order to differentiate clearly the exposure and test situations subjects were tested for the amount of imitative learning in a different experimental room which was set off from the main nursery school building.

The degree to which a child has learned aggressive patterns of behavior through imitation becomes most evident when the child is instigated to aggression on later occasions. Thus, for example, the effects of viewing the movie, *Rebel Without a Cause*, were not evident until the boys were instigated to aggression the following day, at which time they re-enacted the televised switchblade knife fight in considerable detail. For this reason, the children in the experiment, both those in the control group, and those who were exposed to the aggressive models, were mildly frustrated before they were brought to the test room.

Following the exposure experience, the experimenter brought the subject to an anteroom which contained a varied array of highly attractive toys. The experimenter explained that the toys were for the subject to play with, but, as soon as the subject became sufficiently involved with the play material, the experimenter remarked that these were her very best toys, that she did not let just anyone play with them, and that she had decided to reserve these toys for some other children. However, the subject could play with any of the toys in the next room. The experimenter and the subject then entered the adjoining experimental room.

It was necessary for the experimenter to remain in the room during the experimental session; otherwise, a number of the children would either refuse to remain alone or would leave before the termination of the session. In order to minimize any influence her presence might have on the subject's behavior, the experimenter remained as inconspicuous as possible by busying herself with paper work at a desk in the far corner of the room and avoiding any interaction with the child.

Test for Delayed Imitation

The experimental room contained a variety of toys, some of which could be used in imitative or nonimitative aggression, and others which tended to elicit predominantly nonaggressive forms of behavior. The aggressive toys included a 3-foot Bobo doll, a mallet and peg board, two dart guns, and a tether ball with a face painted on it which hung from the ceiling. The nonaggressive toys, on the other hand, included a tea set, crayons and coloring paper, a ball, two dolls, three bears, cars and trucks, and plastic farm animals.

In order to eliminate any variation in behavior due to mere placement of the toys in the room, the play material was arranged in a fixed order for each of the sessions.

The subject spent 20 minutes in the experimental room during which time his behavior was rated in terms of predetermined response categories by judges who observed the session through a one-way mirror in an adjoining observation room. . . .

RESULTS

. . . The results of the analysis . . . reveal that the main effect of treatment conditions is significant . . . , confirming the prediction that exposure of subjects to aggressive models increases the probability that subjects will respond aggressively when instigated on later occasions. Further analyses . . . show that subjects who viewed the real-life models and the film-mediated models do not differ from each other in total aggressiveness but all three experimental groups expressed significantly more aggressive behavior than the control subjects. . . .

The Freidman analysis reveals that exposure of subjects to aggressive models is also a highly effective method for shaping subjects' aggressive responses. . . . Comparisons of treatment conditions by the Wilcoxon test reveal that subjects who observed the real-life models and the film-mediated models, relative to subjects in the control group, performed considerably more imitative physical and verbal aggression. . . .

The prediction that imitation is positively related to the reality cues of the model was only partially supported. While subjects who observed the real-life aggressive models exhibited significantly more imitative aggression than subjects who viewed the cartoon model, no significant differences were found between the live and film, and the film and cartoon conditions, nor did the three experimental groups differ significantly in total aggression or in the performances of partially imitative behavior. Indeed, the available data suggest that, of the three experimental conditions, exposure to humans on film portraying aggression was the most influential in eliciting and shaping aggressive behavior. Subjects in this condition, in relation to the control subjects, exhibited more total aggression, more imitative aggression, more partially imitative behavior, such as sitting on the Bobo doll and mallet aggression, and they engaged in significantly more aggressive gun play. In addition, they performed significantly more aggressive gun play than did subjects who were exposed to the real-life aggressive models. . . .

Sex of subjects had a highly significant effect on both the learning and the performance of aggression. Boys, in relation to girls, exhibited significantly more total aggression . . . , more imitative aggression . . . , more aggressive gun play . . . , and more nonimitative aggressive behavior. . . . Girls, on the other hand, were more inclined than boys to sit on the Bobo doll but refrained from punching it. . . .

The results of the present study provide strong evidence that exposure to filmed aggression heightens aggressive reactions in children. Subjects who viewed the aggressive human and cartoon models on film exhibited nearly twice as much aggression than did subjects in the control group who were not exposed to the aggressive film content.

In the experimental design typically employed for testing the possible cathartic function of vicarious aggression, subjects are first frustrated, then provided with an opportunity to view an aggressive film following which their overt or fantasy aggression is measured. While this procedure yields some information on the immediate influence of film-mediated aggression, the full effects of such exposure may not be revealed until subjects are instigated to aggression on a later occasion. Thus, the present study, and one recently reported by Lövaas (1961), both utilizing a design in which subjects first observed filmed aggression and then were frustrated, clearly reveal that observation of models portraying aggression on film substantially increases rather than decreases the probability of aggressive reactions to subsequent frustrations.

Filmed aggression, not only facilitated the expression of aggression, but also effectively shaped the form of the subjects' aggressive behavior. The finding that children modeled their behavior to some extent after the film characters suggests that pictorial mass media, particularly television, may serve as an important source of social behavior. In fact, a possible generalization of responses originally learned in the television situation to the experimental film may account for the significantly greater amount of aggressive gun play displayed by subjects in the film condition as compared to subjects in the real-life and control groups. It is unfortunate that the qualitative features of the gun behavior were not scored since subjects in the film condition, unlike those in the other two groups, developed interesting elaborations in gun play (for example, stalking the imaginary opponent, quick drawing, and rapid firing), characteristic of the Western gun fighter.

The view that the social learning of aggression through exposure to aggressive film content is confined to deviant children (Schramm, Lyle, & Parker, 1961), finds little support in our data. The children who participated in the experiment are by no means a deviant sample, nevertheless, 88% of the subjects in the Real-Life and in the Human Film condition, and 79% of the subjects in the Cartoon Film condition, exhibited varying degrees of imitative aggression. In assessing the possible influence of televised stimulation on viewers' behavior, however, it is important to distinguish between learning and overt performance. Although the results of the present experiment demonstrate that the vast majority of children *learn* patterns of social behavior through pictorial stimulation, nevertheless, informal observation suggests that children do not, as a rule, *perform* indiscriminately the behavior of televised characters, even those they regard as highly attractive models. The replies of parents whose children participated in the present study to an open-end questionnaire item concerning their handling of imitative behavior suggest that this may be in part a function of negative reinforcement, as most parents were quick to discourage their children's overt imitation of television characters by prohibiting certain programs or by labeling the imitative behavior in a disapproving manner. From our knowledge of the effects of punishment on behavior, the responses in question would be expected to retain their original strength and could reappear on later occasions in the presence of appropriate eliciting stimuli, particularly if instigation is high, the instruments for aggression are available, and the threat of noxious consequences is reduced. . . .

A question may be raised as to whether the aggressive acts studied in the present experiment constitute "genuine" aggressive responses. Aggression is typically defined as behavior, the goal or intent of which is injury to a person, or destruction of an object (Bandura & Walters, 1959; Dollard, Doob, Miller, Mowrer, & Sears, 1939; Sears, Maccoby, & Levin, 1957). Since intentionality is not a property of behavior but primarily an inference concerning antecedent events, the categorization of an act as "aggressive" involves a consideration of both stimulus and mediating or terminal response events.

According to a social learning theory of aggression recently proposed by Bandura and Walters (in press), most of the responses utilized to hurt or to injure others (for example, striking, kicking, and other responses of high magnitude), are probably learned for prosocial purposes under nonfrustration conditions. Since frustration generally elicits responses of high magnitude, the latter classes of responses, once acquired, may be called out in social interactions for the purpose of injuring others. On the basis of this theory it would be predicted that the aggressive responses acquired imitatively, while not necessarily mediating aggressive goals in the experimental situation, would be utilized to serve such purposes in other social settings with higher frequency by children in the experimental conditions than by children in the control group.

The present study involved primarily vicarious or empathic learning (Mowrer, 1960) in that subjects acquired a relatively complex repertoire of aggressive responses by the mere sight of a model's behavior. It has been generally assumed that the necessary conditions for the occurrence of such learning is that the model perform certain responses followed by positive reinforcement to the model (Hill, 1960; Mowrer, 1960). According to this theory, to the extent that the observer experiences the model's reinforcement vicariously, the observer will be prone to reproduce the model's behavior. While there is some evidence from experiments involving both human (Lewis & Duncan, 1958; McBrearty, Marston, & Kanfer, 1961; Sechrest, 1961) and animal subjects (Darby & Riopelle, 1959; Warden, Fjeld, & Koch, 1940), that vicarious reinforcement may in fact increase the probability of the behavior in question, it is apparent from the results of the experiment reported in this paper that a good deal of human imitative learning can occur without any reinforcers delivered either to the model or to the observer.

REFERENCES

Albert, R. S. The role of mass media and the effect of aggressive film content upon children's aggressive responses and identification choices. *Genet. psychol. Monogr.*, 1957, **55**, 221–285.

Bandura, A., & Huston, Aletha C. Identification as a process of incidental learning. *J. abnorm. soc. Psychol.*, 1961, **63**, 311–318.

Bandura, A., Ross, Dorothea, & Ross, Sheila A. Transmission of aggression through imitation of aggressive models. *J. abnorm. soc. Psychol.*, 1961, **63**, 575–582.

Bandura, A., & Walters, R. H. *Adolescent aggression.* New York: Ronald, 1959.

Bandura, A., & Walters, R. H. *The social learning of deviant behavior: A behavioristic approach to socialization.* New York: Holt, Rinehart, & Winston, in press.

Berkowitz, L. *Aggression: A social psychological analysis.* New York: McGraw-Hill, 1962.

Darby, C. L., & Riopelle, A. J. Observational learning in the Rhesus monkey. *J. comp. physiol. Psychol.*, 1959, **52**, 94–98.

Dollard, J., Doob, L. W., Miller, N. E., Mowrer, O. H., & Sears, R. R. *Frustration and aggression.* New Haven: Yale Univer. Press, 1939.

Emery, F. E. Psychological effects of the Western film: A study in television viewing: II. The experimental study. *Hum. Relat.*, 1959, **12**, 215–232.

Feshbach, S. The drive-reducing function of fantasy behavior. *J. abnorm. soc. Psychol.*, 1955, **50**, 3–11.

Feshbach, S. The stimulating versus cathartic effects of a vicarious aggressive activity. Paper read at the Eastern Psychological Association, 1958.

Hill, W. F. Learning theory and the acquisition of values. *Psychol. Rev.*, 1960, **67**, 317–331.

Kenny, D. T. An experimental test of the catharsis theory of aggression. Unpublished doctoral dissertation, University of Washington, 1952.

Lewis, D. J., & Duncan, C. P. Vicarious experience and partial reinforcement. *J. abnorm. soc. Psychol.*, 1958, **57**, 321–326.

Lövaas, O. J. Effect of exposure to symbolic aggression on aggressive behavior. *Child Develpm.*, 1961, **32**, 37–44.

McBrearty, J. F., Marston, A. R., & Kanfer, F. H. Conditioning a verbal operant in a group setting: Direct vs. vicarious reinforcement. *Amer. Psychologist*, 1961, **16**, 425. (Abstract)

Mowrer, O. H. *Learning theory and the symbolic processes.* New York: Wiley, 1960.

San Francisco Chronicle. "James Dean" knifing in South city. *San Francisco Chron.*, March 1, 1961, 6.

Schramm, W., Lyle, J., & Parker, E. B. *Television in the lives of our children.* Stanford: Stanford Univer. Press, 1961.

Sears, R. R., Maccoby, Eleanor E., & Levin, H. *Patterns of child rearing.* Evanston: Row, Peterson, 1957.

Sechrest, L. Vicarious reinforcement of responses. *Amer. psychologist*, 1961, **16**, 356. (Abstract)

Siegel, Alberta E. Film-mediated fantasy aggression and strength of aggressive drive. *Child Develpm.*, 1956, **27**, 365–378.

Warden, C. J., Fjeld, H. A., & Koch, A. M. Imitative behavior in cebus and Rhesus monkeys. *J. genet. Psychol.*, 1940, **56**, 311–322.

CHAPTER 3 Functionalism, Uses, and Gratifications

3.1 CHARLES R. WRIGHT

The Nature and Functions of Mass Communication

Many studies in communication have been influenced by social science theories and methods from the fields of anthropology, psychology, and political science. Another discipline that has influenced media studies is sociology, which treats mass communication as a social phenomenon. In the following selection from *Mass Communication: A Sociological Perspective,* 3rd ed. (Random House, 1986), Charles R. Wright, a professor at the Annenberg School of Communications, investigates the way in which media functions in society.

Functionalism is a theoretical approach that has been criticized for its apolitical stance and for the way it seems to confirm that what exists in the social/media relationship is positive. It assumes no ideological impact, and it supports a commonsense approach toward understanding the complex relationship. Functionalism offers both a language and concepts for relations between media and society that are generally not found in other theories.

In particular, the following selection explains the social consequences of mass communication and makes clear distinctions between functions and dysfunctions, as well as how manifest and latent content influence media users within the social context. In addition, the fourth function of mass communication, entertainment, has been added as a significant topic for analysis and study.

Key Concept: social aspects of mass media and functionalism

As a social process, communication is essential to society and to human survival. Every human society—so-called primitive or modern—depends on communication to enable its members to live together, to maintain and modify working arrangements about the social order and social regulation, and to cope with the environment. Participation in the communication process establishes a person as a social being and as a functioning member of society.

It is not surprising that a matter so basic to human life has been a topic for study and speculation throughout history. From antiquity to modern times, the subject of human communication has attracted the attention of a long line of authors representing a rich variety of intellectual orientations, and including artistic, humanistic, and political approaches. Only relatively recently, however, has it become a popular topic for investigation by social scientists. Communication has been studied by social scientists trained in anthropology, political science, psychology, social psychology, sociology, and other disciplines, in addition to those specializing in the study of communication itself. . . .

FOUR MAJOR COMMUNICATION ACTIVITIES

Harold Lasswell, a political scientist who was a pioneer in mass communication research, once distinguished three major communication operations: (1) surveillance of the environment, (2) correlation of the parts of society in responding to the environment, and (3) transmission of the social heritage from one generation to the next.[1] Modifying Lasswell's categories somewhat and adding a fourth, entertainment, gives us the classification of the major communication activities with which we will be concerned. . . .

Surveillance refers to the collection and distribution of information concerning events in the environment, both within a particular society and outside it. Coverage of events during a presidential election campaign is an example. To some extent, surveillance corresponds to what is commonly thought of as the handling of news. The news process, however, as we shall see later involves much more than "collecting" and distributing "facts" about self-evident events. There is a complex social process that produces what is accepted as news in a society.

Correlation includes interpretation of the information presented about the environment, prescriptions about what to do about it, and attempts to influence such interpretations, attitudes, and conduct. These operations are usually seen as editorial activity, propaganda, or attempts at persuasion.

Although it is useful here to distinguish surveillance from correlation, in practice this may be difficult to do. Surveillance itself incorporates editorial judgments that determine what items qualify as news or information to be disbursed. Interpretation and value judgments are often implicit, sometimes explicit, in the "news" that is reported by mass media and by word of mouth. Linda Lannus, for example, reports that surveillance and correlation activities tended to be indistinguishable to the reporters, editors, and readers of two daily metropolitan newspapers that she studied in 1977.[2] True, the newspapers had special sections regarded as mainly editorial, such as the editorial page and signed columns of opinion or commentary. But the news people found it difficult and unrealistic to separate certain kinds of editorial judgments, such as the significance of an event and how much coverage to give it, from the surveillance process. Nevertheless, the distinction between surveillance and correlation is useful to our discussion—and easier to see in certain kinds of communication ventures, such as propaganda campaigns and mass persuasion. So we will keep it.

The third communication activity, transmission of the social heritage, focuses on the assimilation of people in society. It concerns the communicative processes by which society's store (or part of its store) of values, social norms, knowledge, and other cultural components is made known to and instilled in members and potential members. Our meaning goes beyond Lasswell's specification of transmission of the social heritage from one generation to the next and includes concern with communication relevant to the assimilation of children and adults into various social roles, immigrants into a new (new to them, that is) society, and related matters. This activity sometimes is called education or *socialization,* the term we will use.

Finally, *entertainment* refers here to communication activities primarily (even if arbitrarily) considered as amusement, irrespective of any other features they may seem to have. A television situation comedy, for example, may be regarded as an entertainment activity, even though it may contain some information.

It is good to remember that our four major communication activities are abstractions, useful for purposes of discussion and analysis. Clearly any specific case may be seen in terms of any or all four activities. A television news story, for example, may play a part in surveillance of events (A hurricane is coming this way!), evaluation of what to do (board up the windows), reflect social norms (people are responsible for protecting themselves and their property), and still be entertaining (It's a thrilling drama of humanity versus the elements!). Or a choice piece of gossip passed along to a friend may be informative, judgmental, reinforcing of some shared values, and titillating. (That's what makes gossip so much fun!) People may use the same materials in different ways—for entertainment or instruction. Life doesn't follow theory. Nonetheless our distinctions serve a useful purpose so long as we treat them as abstractions—convenient ways of looking at certain aspects of communication. . . .

SOME FUNCTIONS OF MASS COMMUNICATION: AN OVERVIEW

The first lesson we can learn from functional theory is not to infer the social consequences of mass communication from its apparent or stated purposes. [Contemporary sociologist Robert K.] Merton stresses the need to distinguish between the significant consequences (functions) of a social activity and the apparent goals or aims given for it. The two matters need not be, and often are not, identical. This means that the functions of mass communication are not necessarily what is intended by the communicators.

Public health programs, for example, sometimes use mass communication in order to persuade people to get physical checkups, to get immunization shots against the flu, to stop smoking, and so on. This is the explicit purpose of regular local health campaigns. In pursuing these goals, the campaigns also may have important side effects. For example, as some research suggests, they could improve the social prestige and the morale of local public health workers, whose formerly unrecognized work now receives attention from the mass media and hence from the public. If this improvement in prestige and boost in morale leads to better community cooperation in public health efforts, that would be an important, but unexpected, consequence of the mass communication campaigns.

Merton labels significant intended consequences *manifest* and those that are unintended *latent*. Functional interpretation also distinguishes between those consequences that seem significantly useful to the maintenance and well-being of a system and those that seem harmful to it. Positive consequences are called *functions* and negative ones *dysfunctions*. (Those that seem irrelevant to the system under study are considered nonfunctions.) Any regular social activity, such as mass communication campaigns, can be analyzed in terms of what seem to be manifest or latent functions and dysfunctions for the society, its members, or its culture.

To return to our example of public health campaigns, we might look for such manifest functions as reductions in the risk of an epidemic, and for latent functions such as the boosts in prestige given to public health workers (thereby improving their occupational effectiveness in the community). We also might look for possible dysfunctions, such as frightening away potential health clients who fear they may learn that they have some incurable disease. Clearly the interpretation of social consequences as functional or dysfunctional involves judgment by the researcher. Are there some guidelines?

It seems important, to me, to avoid two problems if possible.[3] First, we should avoid trying to classify *every* possible effect of mass communication as functional or dysfunctional. It is more useful to limit functional analysis to those consequences that seem important to the maintenance and/or change of society, its members, or culture. For example, movie or television stories set in contemporary places might lead some viewers to learn a few new facts about the story's locale, such as some street names. But unless we can see how that minor effect is significant for the maintenance or change of society, its members, or culture, then simply calling it functional or dysfunctional does not increase our understanding of mass communication. Suppose, on the other hand, that movie and television settings influenced viewers' ideas about how attractive (or unattractive) a place is and thereby affected how many people sought to migrate to it. That could be a matter of considerable social significance and a potential topic for functional interpretation.

Second, it is important to avoid equating the terms functional and dysfunctional with our personal ideas of good and bad. We need not personally approve of some aspect of mass communication that we interpret as functional for a society. It does not have to fit our ideological preference. To call it functional means only that the practice seems to contribute to the strength and continuing operation of the society under study. . . .

Surveillance by Mass Communication

Consider what it means to a society for its members to have a constant stream of public information about events in the world. One positive consequence (function) of such surveillance is that it provides warnings about imminent threats of danger—a hurricane, earthquake, or military attack. Forewarned, the population can mobilize and protect itself from destruction. Furthermore, insofar as the information is available to all, rather than to a select few, warnings through mass communication may have the additional function of supporting feelings of egalitarianism within the society—everyone has had fair warning to escape from danger.[4] Such warnings also can be interpreted as functional for individual members of the society . . . insofar as personal (and family) safety is at stake.

A second social consequence of such communication is that it contributes to the everyday institutional operations of the society: it is instrumental in stock market activities, sales navigation, and recreation plans. The instrumental functions of news also apply to the individual. For instance, a group of social scientists took advantage of a local newspaper strike in New York City to study what people "missed" when they did not receive their regular newspaper. One clearly identifiable role of the newspaper for these urbanites was providing information about routine events: local radio programs and movie schedules, sales by local stores, weather forecasts, and so on. When people "missed" their daily newspapers, they were missing a multipurpose tool for daily living.[5]

Two important functions of mass-communicated news, suggested by sociologists Paul Lazarsfeld and Robert Merton are (1) status conferral and (2) ethicizing or the enforcement of social norms.[6] *Status conferral* means that news reports about persons, groups, or social issues increase their importance in the public's view by the very fact that they receive such attention. Presumably this is beneficial to society, in the case of certain social issues which thereby get put on the public agenda for consideration, discussion, and social action. Status conferral also benefits individuals and groups who receive the media's attention, since it certifies their importance and even may legitimize their real or aspired status as celebrities, leaders, and spokespersons for particular groups or about certain topics.

Mass-communicated news has an *ethicizing* effect when it strengthens social control by exposing deviant behavior to public view and possible censure. Newspaper crusades, for instance, publicize wrongdoings that might already have been known about privately by some people and silently borne, if not condoned, by them. Public disclosure of these wrongdoings makes them now a matter of public, not private, knowledge. Under these conditions, most people are obliged to condemn the misbehavior and to support public standards of morality. In this way, mass-communicated news strengthens social control, complementing other formal and informal methods for community detection and control of deviant behavior.

Mass-communicated surveillance can be dysfunctional for society and its members in a variety of ways. For example, the flow of world news could threaten the stability of a particular society or nation. Information about better living conditions elsewhere or about different ideologies might lead to invidious contrasts with conditions at home and to pressures for social change. Or, as another example, some people fear that mass-communicated news about impending danger, broadcast to the general public without local mediation and interpretation by someone, may lead to widespread panic (although contemporary sociological and social psychological research on disasters suggests that mass panic such as this rarely, if ever, happens.)[7]

Mass-communicated news may heighten an individual's anxieties, some say, especially concerning dangerous conditions in the world. What used to be called "war nerves" is an example. Perhaps "nuclear nerves" is the contemporary equivalent. Too much news—an information overload, as some call it—may lead to privatization. The individual overwhelmed by matters brought to his or her attention by mass communication, escapes to private concerns over which there seems to be more control—family or hobbies, cultivating one's own garden, so to speak. Mass-communicated news may lead to individual apathy about civic activity, it is said, because people spend so much time following the news that they have little time or energy left to try to solve social problems. They become so intent on keeping informed, mesmerized by the newscasts and newspapers, that they equate being an informed citizen with being an active citizen.

Lazarsfeld and Merton call this *narcotization.* Thus, for example, the person—feeling compelled to watch an hour or more of daily news (network or local) on television, read through the newspaper (maybe also the Sunday edition), several newsmagazines—ends up so numbed or self-satisfied by it all that he or she misses the local township meeting for public action to clean up toxic waste dumps in the neighborhood!

One also can analyze functions and dysfunctions of mass-communicated news for specific populations or subgroups, such as ethnic groups, minorities, workers, children, elderly people, or political elites. To illustrate . . . , news attention given to political leaders can confer status on them and legitimize their position. Mass-communicated news also may be instrumental for them by providing information that is useful for governance, by exposing subversive activities, and by gauging public opinion. On the other hand, one can think of some dysfunctions too. Uncensored mass-communicated news can threaten the political elite's power by presenting news that contradicts the leaders' claims about some situation (wartime victories, economic prosperity), or allows opponents (domestic or foreign) to present their message, or exposes wrongdoings (taking bribes).

Finally, one can consider possible consequences of mass communication surveillance for a society's cultural system—its body of social values, norms, folkways, beliefs, and other cultural features. Mass-communicated news and information about other societies and their cultures might enrich and add variety to one's own culture, and encourage cultural growth and adaptability. On the other hand, some people fear that the host culture will lose some or all its distinctiveness and integrity as a result of such open cultural "invasion."

Correlation by Mass Communication

Many of the functions of the correlation activity in mass communication seem to prevent or limit some of the undesirable consequences of the mass communication of news. Correlation—including the selection, evaluation, and interpretation of events—imposes order on the surveillance activity and signifies the relative importance of what is reported. This helps to prevent an even greater flood of mass-communicated news than we already have, one that could overwhelm and confuse the public. Editorial activity also packages the news into categories (international news, sports, business) and signals a story's importance through the conventions of headlines, placement in the paper or newscast, and other devices.

We become more aware of such taken-for-granted management of the news when it is not provided. For example, in the study of what "missing" the newspaper means to readers, people said that they not only missed information about events, but also the evaluation and interpretation that the papers ordinarily provided. Some journalists believe it is their responsibility to evaluate and interpret events for the reader or listener—that is, to set events within their larger historical and social context, to evaluate the sources from which the "facts" came, and to suggest what the reader or listener may make of the facts reported. This could have the function, for example, of preventing undue public anxiety about news of impending danger.

One possible dysfunction of editorial-type activities through mass communication is that needed social changes may not get media support while social conformism does. Because of the public nature of mass communication, communicators risk sanctions if they publicly express social criticism or take an unpopular stand on issues. There may be political sanctions, economic ones, consumer boycotts, or other repercussions. Discretion may lead some mass communicators to avoid controversial topics and social criticism.[8] Certain practices associated with news reporting and interpretation may also work against social change, as for example when the mass media heavily rely on government, business, or other institutional sources for interpretations of events.

Another possible dysfunction would be the weakening of peoples' critical ability to find, sift, sort, interpret, and evaluate news for themselves. It can be argued that dependence on mass-communicated, prepackaged news, ideas, opinions, and views lessens people's effectiveness as citizens and makes them less capable of thinking for themselves. (It should be noted here, however, that people rarely, if ever, depend solely on mass communication, and frequently talk with one another in forming their opinions.)[9] . . .

Socialization

In this section we simply note some possible functions and dysfunctions of handling socialization activities by mass communication. Such activities may help unify the society and increase social cohesion by providing a broad base of common social norms, values, and collective experiences to be shared by its members. That would be functional. Individuals too might be helped in their integration into the society through exposure to common social norms and other cultural matters. That could be especially functional for immigrants or other socially mobile persons. Mass communication also may contribute to the socialization of adults into new social values and changing social norms.

On the other hand, the presentation of a more or less standardized view of culture through mass communication could result in a loss of regional, ethnic, and other subcultural variety and could discourage cultural diversity and creativity. That would be dysfunctional. It can also be argued that mass communication makes the process of socialization seem less humane in some respects. David Riesman, for example, suggests that the moral lessons of tales told by mass media cannot be tailored to fit the capacity of the individual child hearing or seeing the story, as they might have been in traditional face-to-face storytelling. Hence some children might make unduly harsh demands on themselves if they try to internalize cultural lessons from movies, television, and other mass media.[10]

Entertainment

Mass entertainment offers some diversion and amusement for everybody, and relaxation and respite can be functional for people and beneficial to society. But too much escapism, too many TV circuses at one's fingertips, may distract people from important social issues and divert them from useful social participation and action. That would be dysfunctional. It would also be dysfunctional if people became so dependent on mass communication for entertainment that they no longer were able to entertain themselves and became permanent mass media spectators.

Some critics suggest that entertainment changes its nature and quality when mass-communicated. Mass entertainment, it is argued, lowers, or at least fails to raise, public taste to the level that might be achieved by less extensive forms of entertainment such as the theater, books, or opera.[11] There also may be significant changes in the social institutions of entertainment. Change in organized sports provides a case in point.

Mass communication, if nothing else, has vastly increased the number of people who witness a sports event (or, more accurately, the version of the event as presented by television, radio, or some other medium). Some 105 million television viewers saw the 1984 Super Bowl XVIII football game.[12] By comparison, personal attendance at professional football games usually averages in the thousands. Television, perhaps more than any other mass medium of communication, has affected this area of popular entertainment and its institutions.

Sociologists John Talamini and Charles Page remark that "the most spectacular rise of sport as mass entertainment, a post World War II development, has been largely the product of . . . television."[13] Commenting on the functional and dysfunctional results of the increasing dependence of organized sports on the technology of television and on advertising funds, Talamini and Page see these consequences as including

> . . . on the one hand, higher salaries and pensions for professional athletes geographical expansion, dividends for spectators such as instant replay and visibility of errors by officials, and improved quality of play; and, on the other hand, ruthless schedule manipulation, the conversion of athletes into ad men and salesman, and, in boxing and baseball, the undermining of local clubs and minor league teams—with tragic effects for apprentice players and journeyman fighters.[14]

These observations illustrate some of the potential consequences of mass-communicated sports for the sport itself as well as for individuals and society. How socially significant these effects seem depends on one's viewpoint. Certainly they are important to those directly involved (professional athletes, businessmen, amateurs).

The symbolic value of mass-communicated sports also should not be overlooked. For example, consider the political significance of the Olympics, which are televised throughout the world. The study of these and other social implications of mass-communicated sports presents a relatively unexplored but interesting area for research in the sociology of mass communication.

NOTES

1. Harold D. Lasswell, "The Structure and Function of Communication in Society," in Lyman Bryson, ed., *The Communication of Ideas* (New York: Harper & Brothers, 1948), pp. 37–51. Lasswell calls these operations "functions," a term we reserve for a different meaning later in this [selection.]
2. Linda Rush Lannus, "The News Organization and News Operations of the Urban Press: A Sociological Analysis based on Two Case Studies" (Ph. D. dissertation, University of Pennsylvania, 1977).
3. For a further brief discussion of these problems and other experiences in applying functional analysis to mass communication, see my "Commentary" on functional analysis in *The New Communications*, ed. Frederick Williams (Belmont, CA: Wadsworth, 1983), pp, 89–90
4. I am indebted to Herbert H. Hyman for this suggestion.
5. Bernard Berelson, "What 'Missing the Newspaper' Means," in *Communications Research 1948–1949*, eds. Paul F. Lazarsfeld and Frank Stanton (New York: Harper & Brothers, 1949), pp. 111–129.
6. Several ideas about the functions of mass communication that we discuss here stem from this classic essay. Paul F. Lazarsfeld and Robert K. Merton, "Mass Communication, Popular Taste and Organized Social Action," in Bryson, *The Communication of Ideas*, pp. 95–118.
7. For a classic study, see Hadley Cantril, Hazel Gaudet, and Herta Herzog, *Invasion from Mars* (Princeton, NY: Princeton University Press, 1940). For discussions of current research that questions earlier interpretations, see John F. Lofland, "Collec-

tive Behavior," in Morris Rosenberg and Ralph Turner, eds., *Social Psychology: Socio-logical Perspectives* (New York: Basic Books, 1981), and Joseph B. Perry, Jr., and Meredith D. Pugh, *Collective Behavior: Response to Social Stress* (St. Paul, MN: West Publishing, 1978).

8. On the other hand, playing down socially divisive news and criticism may be interpreted as functional for keeping the society together. For an example, see Warren Breed, "Mass Communication and Socio-cultural Integration," *Social Forces* 37 (1958), pp. 109–116.

9. For a recently articulated theory of mass media dependency on the individual level, some of the conditions leading to it, and some functional and dysfunctional conse-quences, see Sandra J. Ball-Rokeach and Melvin De Fleur, "A Dependency Model of Mass Media Effects," *Communication Research,* 3 (1976), pp. 3–21. See also *Theories of Mass Communication,* 4th ed., by De Fleur and Ball-Rokeach (New York: Longman, 1982), pp. 236–251.

10. David Riesman et al., *The Lonely Crowd* (Garden City, NY: Doubleday, 1953), chap. 4.

11. For an examination of the mass culture critique and an alternative to it presenting a sociological analysis of the qualities of mass entertainment, see Herbert J. Gans, *Popular Culture and High Culture* (New York: Basic Books, 1974). For a sociological analysis of mass entertainment and its functions, see Harold Mendelsohn's *Mass Entertainment* (New Haven, CT: College and University Press, 1966), especially chapter II; and Harold Mendelsohn and H. T. Spetnagel, "Entertainment as a Socio-logical Enterprise," in *The Entertainment Functions of Television,* ed. Percy H. Tannen-baum (Hillsdale, NJ: Lawrence Erlbaum, 1980), pp. 13–29.

12. *Broadcasting,* January 14, 1985, p. 70.

13. John T. Talamini and Charles H. Page, *Sport and Society: An Anthology* (Boston: Little, Brown, 1973), p. 417.

14. Ibid., p. 418.

3.2 ELIHU KATZ, JAY G. BLUMLER, AND MICHAEL GUREVITCH

Utilization of Mass Communication by the Individual

Within the paradigm of functionalism is an approach loosely called "uses and gratifications" research. The following selection is from "Utilization of Mass Communication by the Individual," in Jay G. Blumler and Elihu Katz, eds., *The Uses of Mass Communications* (Sage Publications, 1974). In it, Elihu Katz, Jay G. Blumler, and Michael Gurevitch discuss how empirical research in uses and gratifications evolved. One of the important features about the uses and gratifications approach is that it examines the process of communication starting from the audience members' individual perceptions.

The uses and gratifications perspective investigates *why* individuals choose to use media. The areas of greatest difficulty for researchers following this approach is to understand and account for the audience's selective behavior: Why do they choose to watch a videotape rather than read a book? Is it the humor in a comedy they like, or is it an identification with the characters? Are people turning to media for reasons other than habit?

The coauthors of this selection are scholars in the field of mass communication research. Katz is currently a professor at the Hebrew University in Jerusalem and director of its Communications Institute. Blumler, a British researcher, is director of the Centre for Television Research and Reader in Mass Communications at the University of Leeds, England, where Gurevitch is a senior research fellow.

Key Concept: uses and gratifications

*S*uppose that we were studying not broadcasting-and-society in mid-twentieth-century America but opera-and-society in mid-nineteenth-century Italy. After all, opera in Italy, during that period, was a "mass" medium. What would we be studying? It seems likely, for one thing, that we would find interest in the attributes of the medium—what might today be called its "grammar"—for example, the curious convention that makes it possible to sign contradictory emotions simultaneously. For another, we would be interested in the functions of the medium for the individual and society: perceptions of the values expressed and underlined; the phenomena of stardom, fanship, and connoisseurship; the festive ambience which the medium created; and so on. It seems quite unlikely that we would be studying the effects of the singing of a particular opera on opinions and attitudes, even though some operas were written with explicit political, social, and moral aims in mind. The study of short-run effects, in other words, would not have had a high priority, although it might have had a place. But the emphasis, by and large, would have been on the medium as a cultural institution with its own social and psychological functions and perhaps long-run effects.

We have all been over the reasons why much of mass communication research took a different turn, preferring to look at specific programs as specific messages with, possibly, specific effects. We were social psychologists interested in persuasion and attitude change. We were political scientists interested in new forms of social control. We were commissioned to measure message effectiveness for marketing organizations, or public health agencies, or churches, or political organizations, or for the broadcasting organizations themselves. And we were asked whether the media were not causes of violent and criminal behavior.

Yet even in the early days of empirical mass communication research this preoccupation with short-term effects was supplemented by the growth of an interest in the gratifications that the mass media provide their audiences. Such studies were well represented in the Lazarsfeld-Stanton collections (1942, 1944, 1949); Herzog (1942) on quiz programs and the gratifications derived from listening to soap operas; Suchman (1942) on the motives for getting interested in serious music on radio; Wolfe and Fiske (1949) on the development of children's interest in comics; Berelson (1949) on the functions of newspaper reading; and so on. Each of these investigations came up with a list of functions served either by some specific contents or by the medium in question: to match one's wits against others, to get information or advice for daily living, to provide a framework for one's day, to prepare oneself culturally for the demands of upward mobility, or to be reassured about the dignity and usefulness of one's role.

What these early studies had in common was, first, a basically similar methodological approach whereby statements about media functions were elicited from the respondents in an essentially open-ended way. Second, they shared a qualitative approach in their attempt to group gratification statements into labelled categories, largely ignoring the distribution of their frequency in the population. Third, they did not attempt to explore the links between the gratifications thus detected and the psychological or sociological origins of the needs that were so satisfied. Fourth, they failed to search for the interrelationships among the various media functions, either quantitatively or conceptually, in a manner that might have led to the detection of the latent structure of media gratifications. Consequently, these studies did not result in a cumulatively more detailed picture of media gratifications conducive to the eventual formulation of theoretical statements.

The last few years have witnessed something of a revival of direct empirical investigations of audience uses and gratifications, not only in the United States but also in Britain, Sweden, Finland, Japan, and Israel. These ... studies have a number of differing starting points, but each attempts to press toward a greater systematization of what is involved in conducting research in this field. Taken together, they make operational many of the logical steps that were only implicit in the earlier work. They are concerned with (1) the social and psychological origins of (2) needs, which generate (3) expectations of (4) the mass media or other sources, which lead to (5) differential patterns of media exposure (or engagement in other activities), resulting in (6) need gratifications and (7) other consequences, perhaps mostly unintended ones. Some of these investigations begin by specifying needs and then attempt to trace the extent to which they are gratified by the media or other sources. Others take observed gratifications as a starting point and attempt to reconstruct the needs that are being gratified. Yet others focus on the social origins of audience expectations and gratifications. But however varied their individual points of departure, they all strive toward an assessment of media consumption in audience-related terms, rather than in technological, aesthetic, ideological, or other more or less "elitist" terms. The convergence of their foci, as well as of their findings, indicates that there is a clear agenda here—part methodological and part theoretical—for a discussion of the future directions of this approach.

SOME BASIC ASSUMPTIONS OF THEORY, METHOD AND VALUE

Perhaps the place of "theory" and "method" in the study of audience uses and gratifications is not immediately apparent. The common tendency to attach the label "uses and gratifications approach" to work in this field appears to virtually disclaim any theoretical pretensions or methodological commitment. From this point of view the approach simply represents an attempt to explain something of the way in which individuals use communications, among other resources in their environment, to satisfy their needs and to achieve their goals, and to do so by simply asking them. Nevertheless, this effort does rest on a body of assumptions, explicit or implicit, that have some degree of internal coherence and that are arguable in the sense that not everyone contemplating them would find them self-evident. Lundberg and Hultén (1968) refer to them as jointly constituting a "uses and gratifications model." Five elements of this model in particular may be singled out for comment:

1. The audience is conceived of as active, that is, an important part of mass media use is assumed to be goal directed (McQuail, Blumler and Brown, 1972). This assumption may be contrasted with Bogart's (1965) thesis to the effect that "most mass media experiences represent pastime rather than purposeful activity, very often [reflecting] chance cir-

cumstances within the range of availabilities rather than the expression of psychological motivation or need." Of course, it cannot be denied that media exposure often has a casual origin; the issue is whether, in addition, patterns of media use are shaped by more or less definite expectations of what certain kinds of content have to offer the audience member.

2. In the mass communication process much initiative in linking need gratification and media choice lies with the audience member. This places a strong limitation on theorizing about any form of straight-line effect of media content on attitudes and behavior. As Schramm, Lyle and Parker (1961) said:

   In a sense the term "effect" is misleading because it suggests that television "does something" to children. . . . Nothing can be further from the fact. . . .

3. The media compete with other sources of need satisfaction. The needs served by mass communication constitute but a segment of the wider range of human needs, and the degree to which they can be adequately met through mass media consumption certainly varies. Consequently, a proper view of the role of the media in need satisfaction should take into account other functional alternatives—including different, more conventional, and "older" ways of fulfilling needs.

4. Methodologically speaking, many of the goals of mass media use can be derived from data supplied by individual audience members themselves—that is, people are sufficiently self-aware to be able to report their interests and motives in particular cases, or at least to recognize them when confronted with them in an intelligible and familiar verbal formulation.

5. Value judgments about the cultural significance of mass communication should be suspended while audience orientations are explored on their own terms. It is from the perspective of this assumption that certain affinities and contrasts between the uses and gratifications approach and much speculative writing about popular culture may be considered.

STATE OF THE ART: THEORETICAL ISSUES

From the few postulates outlined above, it is evident that further development of a theory of media gratification depends, first, on the clarification of its relationship to the theoretical traditions on which it so obviously draws and, second, on systematic efforts toward conceptual integration of empirical findings. Given the present state of the art, the following are priority issues in the development of an adequate theoretical basis.

Each major piece of uses and gratification research has yielded its own classification scheme of audience functions. When placed side by side, they reveal a mixture of shared gratification categories and notions peculiar to individual research teams. The differences are due in part to the fact that investigators have focused on different levels of study (e.g., medium or content) and different materials (e.g., different programs or program types on, say, television) in different cultures (e.g., Finland, Israel, Japan, Sweden, the United Kingdom, the United States, and Yugoslavia).

Unifunctional conceptions of audience interests have been expressed in various forms. Popular culture writers have often based their criticisms of the media on the ground that, in primarily serving the escapist desires of the audience, they deprived it of the more beneficial uses that might be made of communication (McDonald, 1957). Stephenson's analysis (1967) of mass communication exclusively in terms of "play" may be interpreted as an extension, albeit in a transformed and expanded expression, of this same notion. A more recent example has been provided by Nordenstreng (1970), who, while breaking away from conventional formulations, still opts for a unifunctional view when he claims that, "It has often been documented (e.g., during television and newspaper strikes in Finland in 1966–67) that perhaps the basic motivation for media use is just an unarticulated need for social contact."

The wide currency secured for a bifunctional view of audience concerns is reflected in Weiss' (1971) summary, which states that, "When . . . studies of uses and gratifications are carried out, the media or media content are usually viewed dichotomously as predominantly fantasist-escapist or informational-educational in significance." This dichotomy appears, for example, in Schramm's (1949) work (adopted subsequently by Schramm, Lyle and Parker, 1961: Pietila, 1969; and Furu, 1971), which distinguishes between sets of "immediate" and "deferred" gratifications, and in the distinction between informational and entertainment materials. In terms of audience gratifications specifically, it emerges in the distinction between surveillance and escape uses of the media.

The four-functional interpretation of the media was first proposed by Lasswell (1948) on a macro-sociological level and later developed by Wright (1960) on both the macro- and the micro-sociological levels. It postulated that the media served the functions of surveillance, correlation, entertainment, and cultural transmission (or socialization) for society as a whole, as well as for individuals and subgroups within society. An extension of the four-function approach can also be found in Wright's suggestive exploration of the potential dysfunctional equivalents of Lasswell's typology.

None of these statements, however, adequately reflects the full range of functions, which has been disclosed by the more recent investigations. McQuail, Blumler and Brown (1972) have put forward a typology consisting of the following categories: diversion (including escape from the constraints of routine and the burdens of problems, and emotional release); personal relationships (including substitute companionship as well as social utility); personal

identity (including personal reference, reality exploration, and value reinforcement); and surveillance.

An effort to encompass the large variety of specific functions that have
been proposed is made in the elaborate scheme of Katz, Gurevitch and Haas
(1973). Their central notion is that mass communication is used by individuals
to connect (or sometimes to disconnect) themselves—via instrumental, affective, or integrative relations—with different kinds of others (self, family,
friends, nation, etc.). The scheme attempts to comprehend the whole range of
individual gratifications of the many facets of the need "to be connected." And
it finds empirical regularities in the preference for different media for different
kinds of connections.

Gratification and Needs

The study of mass media use suffers at present from the absence of a
relevant theory of social and psychological needs. It is not so much a catalogue
of needs that is missing as a clustering of groups of needs, a sorting out of
different levels of need, and a specification of hypotheses linking particular
needs with particular media gratifications. It is true that the work of Schramm,
Lyle and Parker (1961) draws on the distinction between the reality and pleasure principles in the socialization theories of Freud and others, but more recent
studies suggest that those categories are too broad to be serviceable. Maslow's
(1954) proposed hierarchy of human needs may hold more promise, but the
relevance of his categories to expectations of communication has not yet been
explored in detail. Lasswell's (1948) scheme to specify the needs that media
satisfy has proven useful, and it may be helpful to examine Lasswell and
Kaplan's (1950) broader classification of values as well.

Alternatively, students of uses and gratifications could try to work back-
wards, as it were, from gratifications to needs. In the informational field, for
example, the surveillance function may be traced to a desire for security or the
satisfaction of curiosity and the exploratory drive; seeking reinforcement of
one's attitudes and values may derive from a need for reassurance that one is
right; and attempts to correlate informational elements may stem from a more
basic need to develop one's cognitive mastery of the environment. Similarly,
the use of fictional (and other) media materials for "personal reference" may
spring from a need for self-esteem; social utility functions may be traced to the
need for affiliation; and escape functions may be related to the need to release
tension and reduce anxiety. But whichever way one proceeds, it is inescapable
that what is at issue here is the long-standing problem of social and psychological science: how to (and whether to bother to) systematize the long lists of
human and societal needs. Thus far, gratifications research has stayed close to
what we have been calling media-related needs (in the sense that the media
have been observed to satisfy them, at least in part), but one wonders whether
all this should not be put in the broader context of systematic studies of needs.

Studies have shown that audience gratifications can be derived from at least three distinct sources: media content, exposure to the media per se, and the social context that typifies the situation of exposure to different media. Although recognition of media content as a source of gratifications has provided the basis for research in this area from its inception, less attention has been paid to the other sources. Nevertheless, it is clear that the need to relax or to kill time can be satisfied by the act of watching television, that the need to feel that one is spending one's time in a worthwhile way may be associated with the act of reading (Waples, Berelson and Bradshaw, 1940; Berelson, 1949), and that the need to structure one's day may be satisfied merely by having the radio "on" (Mendelsohn, 1964). Similarly, a wish to spend time with one's family or friends can be served by watching television at home with the family or by going to the cinema with one's friends.

Each medium seems to offer a unique combination of (a) characteristic contents (at least stereotypically perceived in that way); (b) typical attributes (print vs. broadcasting modes of transmission, iconic vs. symbolic representation, reading vs. audio or audio-visual modes of reception); and (c) typical exposure situations (at home vs. out-of-home, alone vs. with others, control over the temporal aspects of exposure vs. absence of such control). The issue, then, is what combinations of attributes may render different media more or less adequate for the satisfaction of different needs (Katz, Gurevitch and Haas, 1973).

Gratification and Media Attributes

Much uses and gratifications research has still barely advanced beyond a sort of charting and profiling activity: findings are still typically presented to show that certain bodies of content serve certain functions or that one medium is deemed better at satisfying certain needs than another. The further step, which has hardly been ventured, is one of explanation. At issue here is the relationship between the unique "grammar" of different media—that is, their specific technological and aesthetic attributes—and the particular requirements of audience members that they are then capable, or incapable, of satisfying. Which, indeed, are the attributes that render some media more conducive than others to satisfying specific needs? And which elements of content help to attract the expectations for which they apparently cater?

It is possible to postulate the operation of some kind of division of labor among the media for the satisfaction of audience needs. This may be elaborated in two ways: taking media attributes as the starting point, the suggestion is that those media that differ (or are similar) in their attributes are more likely to serve different (or similar) needs; or, utilizing the latent structure of needs as a point of departure, the implication is that needs that are psychologically related or conceptually similar will be equally well served by the same media (or by media with similar attributes).

To illustrate the first approach, Robinson (1972) has demonstrated the interchangeability of television and print media for learning purposes. In the Israeli study, Katz, Gurevitch and Haas (1973) found five media ordered in a circumplex with respect to their functional similarities: books-newspapers-radio-television-cinema-books. In other words, books functioned most like newspapers, on the one hand, and like cinema, on the other. Radio was most similar in its usage to newspapers, on the one hand, and to television, on the other. The explanation would seem to lie not only with certain technological attributes that they have in common, but with similar aesthetic qualities as well. Thus, books share a technology and an informational function with newspapers, but are similar to films in their aesthetic function. Radio shares a technology, as well as informational and entertainment content, with television, but it is also very much like newspapers—providing a heavy dose of information and an orientation to reality.

An illustration of the second aspect of this division of labor may also be drawn from the same study. Here, the argument is that structurally related needs will tend to be serviced by certain media more often than by others. Thus, books and cinema have been found to cater to needs concerned with self-fulfilment and self-gratification: they help to "connect" individuals to themselves. Newspapers, radio, and television all seem to connect individuals to society. In fact, the function of newspapers for those interested in following what is going on in the world may have been grossly underestimated in the past (Edelstein, 1973; Lundberg and Hultén, 1968). Television, however, was found to be less frequently used as a medium of escape by Israeli respondents than were books and films. And a Swedish study of the "functional specialities of the respective media" reported that, "A retreat from the immediate environment and its demands—probably mainly by the act of reading itself—was characteristic of audience usage of weekly magazines" (Lundberg and Hultén, 1968).

REFERENCES

BERELSON, B. (1949) "What 'missing the newspaper' means," in P. F. Lazarsfeld and F. N. Stanton (eds.) Communications Research, 1948–9. New York: Duell, Sloan & Pearce.

BOGART, L. (1965) "The mass media and the blue-collar worker," in A. Bennett and W. Gomberg (eds.) Blue-Collar World: Studies of the American Worker. Englewood Cliffs, N.J.: Prentice-Hall.

EDELSTEIN, A. (1973) "An alternative approach to the study of source effects in mass communication." Studies of Broadcasting 9.

FURU, T. (1971) The Function of Television for Children and Adolescents. Tokyo: Sophia University.

HERZOG, H. (1942) Professor quiz: a gratification study," in P. F. Lazarsfeld and F. N. Stanton (eds.) Radio Research, 1941. New York: Duell, Sloan & Pearce.

KATZ, E., M. GUREVITCH, and H. HAAS (1973) "On the use of mass media for important things." American Sociological Review 38.

LASSWELL, H. (1948) "The structure and function of communications in society," in L. Bryson (ed.) The Communication of Ideas. New York: Harper.

_____ and A. KAPLAN (1950) Power and Society. New Haven: Yale Univ. Press.

LAZARSFELD P. F. and F. N. STANTON [eds.] (1949) Communications Research, 1948–9. New York: Harper.

_____ (1944) Radio Research, 1942–3. New York: Duell, Sloan & Pearce.

_____ (1942) Radio Research, 1941. New York: Duell, Sloan & Pearce.

LUNDBERG, D. and O. HULTEN (1968) Individen och Massmedia. Stockholm: EFI.

McDONALD, D. (1957) "A theory of mass culture," in D. M. White and B. Rosenberg (eds.) Mass Culture: the Popular Arts in America. Glencoe: Free Press.

McQUAIL, D., J. G. BLUMLER, and J. R. BROWN (1972) "The television audience: a revised perspective," in D. McQuail (ed.) Sociology of Mass Communications. Harmondsworth: Penguin.

MASLOW, A. H. (1954) Motivation and Personality. New York: Harper.

MENDELSOHN, H. (1964) "Listening to radio," in L. A. Dexter and D. M. White (eds.) People, Society and Mass Communications. Glencoe: Free Press.

NORDENSTRENG, K. (1970) "Comments on 'gratifications research' in broadcasting." Public Opinion Quarterly 34.

PIETILA, V. (1969) "Immediate versus delayed reward in newspaper reading." Acta Sociologica 12.

ROBINSON, J. P. (1972) "Toward defining the functions of television," in Television and Social Behavior, Vol. 4. Rockville, Md.: National Institute of Mental Health.

SCHRAMM, W. (1949) "The nature of news." Journalism Quarterly 26.

_____ J. LYLE, and E. B. PARKER (1961) Television in the Lives of Our Children. Stanford: Stanford Univ. Press.

STEPHENSON, W. (1967) The Play Theory of Mass Communication. Chicago: Univ. of Chicago Press.

SUCHMAN, E. (1942) "An invitation to music," In P. F. Lazarsfeld and F. N. Stanton (eds.) Radio Research, 1941. new York: Duell, Sloan & Pearce.

WAPLES, D., B. BERELSON, and F. R. BRADSHAW (1940) What Reading Does to People. Chicago: Univ. of Chicago Press.

WEISS, W. (1971) "Mass communication." Annual Review of Psychology 22.

WOLFE, K. M. and M. FISKE (1949) "Why children read comics," in P. F. Lazarsfeld and F. N. Stanton (eds.) Communications Research, 1948–9. New York: Harper.

WRIGHT, C. (1960) "Functional analysis and mass communication." Public Opinion Quarterly 24.

CHAPTER 4 Political Communication

4.1 MAXWELL E. McCOMBS AND DONALD L. SHAW

The Agenda-Setting Function of Mass Media

How people interpret and are affected by political messages has long been a part of public opinion research. When Maxwell E. McCombs and Donald L. Shaw conducted the study that is described in the following selection, they assumed that the producers of news (reporters, editors, and broadcasters) would contribute to the ways in which "reality" was shaped. The "agenda-setting function" the authors discuss has been considered invaluable for understanding that producers and consumers of messages each contribute to the media's impact.

In the following selection from "The Agenda-Setting Function of Mass Media," *Public Opinion Quarterly* (Spring 1972), McCombs and Shaw demonstrate how they drew from earlier research to better understand the mutual tensions in presenting and making sense of information that is distributed during an election campaign. Their combination of content analysis and audience surveys involves a rigorous methodology that encouraged future researchers to ask questions related to their agenda, such as "What constitutes news?" and "How can something get on the agenda?"

McCombs is currently a professor in the Department of Journalism at the University of Texas at Austin, and Shaw is a professor in the School of Journalism at the University of North Carolina, Chapel Hill.

Key Concept: agenda setting

In choosing and displaying news, editors, newsroom staff, and broadcasters play an important part in shaping political reality. Readers learn not only about a given issue, but also how much importance to attach to that issue from the amount of information in a news story and its position. In reflecting what candidates are saying during a campaign, the mass media may well determine the important issues—that is, the media may set the "agenda" of the campaign. . . .

In our day, more than ever before, candidates go before the people through the mass media rather than in person.[1] The information in the mass media becomes the only contact many have with politics. The pledges, promises, and rhetoric encapsulated in news stories, columns, and editorials constitute much of the information upon which a voting decision has to be made. Most of what people know comes to them "second" or "third" hand from the mass media or from other people.[2]

Although the evidence that mass media deeply change attitudes in a campaign is far from conclusive,[3] the evidence is much stronger that voters learn from the immense quantity of information available during each campaign.[4] People, of course, vary greatly in their attention to mass media political information. Some, normally the better educated and most politically interested (and those least likely to change political beliefs), actively seek information; but most seem to acquire it, if at all, without much effort. It just comes in. As Berelson succinctly puts it: "On any single subject many 'hear' but few 'listen'." But Berelson also found that those with the greatest mass media exposure are most likely to know where the candidates stand on different issues.[5] Trenaman and McQuail found the same thing in a study of the 1959 General Election in England.[6] Voters do learn.

They apparently learn, furthermore, in direct proportion to the emphasis placed on the campaign issues by the mass media. Specifically focusing on the agenda-setting function of the media, Lang and Lang observe:

> The mass media force attention to certain issues. They build up public images of political figures. They are constantly presenting objects suggesting what individuals in the mass should think about, know about, have feelings about.[7]

Perhaps this hypothesized agenda-setting function of the mass media is most succinctly stated by Cohen, who noted that the press "may not be successful much of the time in telling people what to think, but it is stunningly successful in telling its readers what to think *about*."[8] While the mass media may have little influence on the direction or intensity of attitudes, it is hypothesized that *the mass media set the agenda for each political campaign, influencing the salience of attitudes toward the political issues.*

METHOD

To investigate the agenda-setting capacity of the mass media in the 1968 presidential campaign, this study attempted to match what Chapel Hill voters *said* were key issues of the campaign with the *actual content* of the mass media used by them during the campaign. Respondents were selected randomly from lists of registered voters in five Chapel Hill precincts economically, socially, and racially representative of the community. By restricting this study to one community, numerous other sources of variation—for example, regional differences or variations in media performance—were controlled.

Between September 18 and October 6, 100 interviews were completed. To select these 100 respondents a filter question was used to identify those who had not yet definitely decided how to vote—presumably those most open or susceptible to campaign information. Only those not yet fully committed to a particular candidate were interviewed. Borrowing from the Trenaman and McQuail strategy, this study asked each respondent to outline the key issues as he saw them regardless of what the candidates might be saying at the moment.[9] Interviewers recorded the answers as exactly as possible.

Concurrently with the voter interviews, the mass media serving these voters were collected and content analyzed. A pretest in spring 1968 found that for the Chapel Hill community almost all the mass media political information was provided by the following sources: Durham *Morning Herald*, Durham *Sun*, Raleigh *News and Observer*, Raleigh *Times*, New York *Times*, *Time*, *Newsweek*, and NBC and CBS evening news broadcasts.

The answers of respondents regarding major problems as they saw them and the news and editorial comment appearing between September 12 and October 6 in the sampled newspapers, magazines, and news broadcasts were coded into 15 categories representing the key issues and other kinds of campaign news. Media news content also was divided into "major" and "minor" levels to see whether there was any substantial difference in mass media emphasis across topics.[10] For the print media, this major/minor division was in terms of space and position; for television, it was made in terms of position and time allowed. More specifically, *major* items were defined as follows:

1. Television: Any story 45 seconds or more in length and/or one of the three lead stories.
2. Newspapers: Any story which appeared as the lead on the front page or on any page under a three-column headline in which at least one-third of the story (a minimum of five paragraphs) was devoted to political news coverage.
3. News Magazines: Any story more than one column or any item which appeared in the lead at the beginning of the news section of the magazine.

4. Editorial Page Coverage of Newspapers and Magazines: Any item in the lead editorial position (the top left corner of the editorial page) plus all items in which one-third (at least five paragraphs) of an editorial or columnist comment was devoted to political campaign coverage.

Minor items are those stories which are political in nature and included in the study but which are smaller in terms of space, time, or display than major items.

FINDINGS

The over-all *major* item emphasis of the selected mass media on different topics and candidates during the campaign ... indicates that a considerable amount of campaign news was *not* devoted to discussion of the major political issues but rather to *analysis of the campaign itself.* This may give pause to those who think of campaign news as being primarily about the *issues.* . . .

The media appear to have exerted a considerable impact on voters' judgments of what they considered the major issues of the campaign (even though the questionnaire specifically asked them to make judgments without regard to what politicians might be saying at the moment). . . .

But while the three presidential candidates placed widely different emphasis upon different issues, the judgments of the voters seem to reflect the *composite* of the mass media coverage. . . . [V]oters pay some attention to all the political news *regardless* of whether it is from, or about, any particular favored candidate. . . . [I]t is possible that individual differences, reflected in party preferences and in a predisposition to look mainly at material favorable to one's own party, are lost by lumping all the voters together in the analysis. Therefore, answers of respondents who indicated a preference (but not commitment) for one of the candidates during the September-October period studied (45 of the respondents; the others were undecided) were analyzed separately. . . .

If one expected voters to pay more attention to the major and minor issues oriented to their own party—that is, to read or view *selectively*—the correlations between the voters and news/opinion about their own party should be strongest. This would be evidence of selective perception.[11] If, on the other hand, the voters attend reasonably well to *all* the news, *regardless* of which candidate or party issue is stressed, the correlations between the voter and total media content would be strongest. This would be evidence of the agenda-setting function. The crucial question is which set of correlations is stronger.

In general ... voters who were not firmly committed early in the campaign attended well to *all* the news. For major news items, correlations were more often higher between voter judgments of important issues and the issues reflected in all the news (including of course news about their favored candidate/party) than were voter judgments of issues reflected in news *only* about their candidate/party. For minor news items, again voters more often correlated highest with the emphasis reflected in all the news than with the emphasis reflected in news about a favored candidate. Considering both major and minor item coverage, 18 of 24 possible comparisons show voters more in agreement with all the news rather than with news only about their own party/candidate preference. This finding is better explained by the agenda-setting function of the mass media than by selective perception. . . .

*Maxwell E.
McCombs and
Donald L. Shaw*

Two sets of factors, at least, reduce consensus among the news media. First, the basic characteristics of newspapers, television, and newsmagazines differ. Newspapers appear daily and have lots of space. Television is daily but has a severe time constraint. Newsmagazines appear weekly; news therefore cannot be as "timely". . . .

Second, news media do have a point of view, sometimes extreme biases. However, the high correlations . . . (especially among like media) suggest consensus on news values, especially on major news items. Although there is no explicit, commonly agreed-upon definition of news, there is a professional norm regarding major news stories from day to day. These major-story norms doubtless are greatly influenced today by widespread use of the major wire services—especially by newspapers and television—for much political information.[12] But as we move from major events of the campaign, upon which nearly everyone agrees, there is more room for individual interpretation, reflected in the lower correlations for minor item agreement among media. . . . Since a newspaper, for example, uses only about 15 percent of the material available on any given day, there is considerable latitude for selection among minor items.

In short, the political world is reproduced imperfectly by individual news media. Yet the evidence in this study that voters tend to share the media's *composite* definition of what is important strongly suggests an agenda-setting function of the mass media.

DISCUSSION

The existence of an agenda-setting function of the mass media is not *proved* by the correlations reported here, of course, but the evidence is in line with the conditions that must exist if agenda-setting by the mass media does occur. This study has compared aggregate units—Chapel Hill voters as a group compared to the aggregate performance of several mass media. This is satisfactory as a first test of the agenda-setting hypothesis, but subsequent research must move from a broad societal level to the social psychological level, matching individual attitudes with individual use of the mass media. Yet even the present study refines the evidence in several respects. Efforts were made to match respondent attitudes only with media actually used by Chapel Hill voters. Further, the analysis includes a juxtaposition of the agenda-setting and selective perception hypotheses. Comparison of these correlations too supports the agenda-setting hypothesis.

Interpreting the evidence from this study as indicating mass media influence seems more plausible than alternative explanations. Any argument that the correlations between media and voter emphasis are spurious—that they are simply responding to the same events and not influencing each other one way or the other—assumes that voters have alternative means of observing the day-to-day changes in the political arena. This assumption is not plausible; since few directly participate in presidential election campaigns, and fewer still see presidential candidates in person, the information flowing in interpersonal communication channels is primarily relayed from, and based upon, mass media news coverage. The media are the major primary sources of national political information; for most, mass media provide the best—and only—easily available approximation of ever-changing political realities.

It might also be argued that the high correlations indicate that the media simply were successful in matching their messages to audience interests. Yet since numerous studies indicate a sharp divergence between the news values of professional journalists and their audiences, it would be remarkable to find a near perfect fit in this one case.[13] It seems more likely that the media have prevailed in this area of major coverage.

While this study is primarily a sociology of politics and mass communication, some psychological data were collected on each voter's personal cognitive representation of the issues. Shrauger has suggested that the salience of the evaluative dimension—not the sheer number of attributes—is the essential feature of cognitive differentiation.[14] So a content analysis classified respondents according to the *salience of affect* in their responses to open-ended questions about the candidates and issues.[15] Some voters described the issues and candidates in highly affective terms. Others were much more matter-of-fact. Each respondent's answers were classified by the coders as "all affect," "affect dominant," "some affect but not dominant," or "no affect at all."[16] Regarding each voter's salience of affect as his cognitive style of storing political information, the study hypothesized that cognitive style also influences patterns of information-seeking.

Eschewing causal language to discuss this relationship, the hypothesis states that salience of affect will index or locate differences in the communication behavior of voters. But a number of highly efficient locator variables for voter communication behavior already are well documented in the research literature. Among these are level of formal education and interest in politics generally. However, in terms of *The American Voter*'s model of a "funnel" stretching across time, education and political interest are located some distance back from the particular campaign being considered.[17] Cognitive style is located closer to the end of the funnel, closer to the time of actual participation in a campaign. It also would seem to have the advantage of a more functional relationship to voter behavior.

Examination of the relationship between salience of affect and this pair of traditional locators, education and political interest, showed no significant correlations. The independent effects of political interest and salience of affect on media use are demonstrated in Table 1. Also demonstrated is the efficacy of salience of affect as a locator or predictor of media use, especially among persons with high political interest.[18]

Both salience of affect and media use in Table 1 are based on the issue that respondents designated as the most important to them personally. Salience of affect was coded from their discussion of why the issue was important. Use of each communication medium is based on whether or not the respondent had seen or heard anything via that medium about that particular issue in the past twenty-four hours.

High salience of affect tends to block use of communication media to acquire further information about issues with high personal importance. At

TABLE 1

Proportion of Media Users by Political Interest and Salience of Affect

*Maxwell E.
McCombs and
Donald L. Shaw*

Media	Low Political Interest		High Political Interest	
	High Affect (N = 40)	Low Affect (N = 17)	High Affect (N = 25)	Low Affect (N = 12)
TV	15.0%	17.7%	20.0%	41.7%
Newspapers	27.5	35.4	36.0	58.3
News Magazines	7.5	11.8	24.0	33.3
Radio	12.5	11.8	8.0	33.3
Talk	20.0	17.7	64.0	75.0

least, survey respondents with high salience of affect do not recall acquiring recent information. This is true both for persons with low and high political interest, but especially among those with high political interest. For example, among respondents with high political interest *and* high salience of affect only 36 percent reported reading anything in the newspaper recently about the issue they believed to be most important. But among high political interest respondents with low salience of affect nearly six of ten (58.3 percent) said they acquired information from the newspaper. Similar patterns hold for all the communication media.

Future studies of communication behavior and political agenda-setting must consider both psychological and sociological variables; knowledge of both is crucial to establishment of sound theoretical constructs. Considered at both levels as a communication concept, agenda-setting seems useful for study of the process of political consensus.

NOTES

1. See Bernard R. Berelson, Paul F. Lazarsfeld, and William N. McPhee, *Voting*, Chicago, University of Chicago Press, 1954, p. 234. Of course to some degree candidates have always depended upon the mass media, bu radio and television brought a new intimacy into politics.
2. Kurt Lang and Gladys Engel Lang, "The Mass Media and Voting," in Bernard Berelson and Morris Janowitz, eds., *Reader in Public Opinion and Communication*, 2d ed., New York, Free Press, 1966, p. 466.
3. See Berelson *et al., op. cit.,* p. 223; Paul F. Lazarsfeld, Bernard Berelson, and Hazel Gaudet, *The People's Choice,* New York, Columbia University Press, 1948. p. xx; and Joseph Trenaman and Denis McQuail, *Television and the Political Image,* London, Methuen and Co., 1961, pp. 147, 191.
4. See Bernard C. Cohen, *The Press and Foreign Policy,* Princeton, Princeton University Press, 1963, p. 120.
5. Berelson *et al., op. cit.,* pp. 244, 228.
6. Trenaman and McQuail, *op. cit.,* p. 165.
7. Lang and Lang, *op. cit.,* p. 468. Trenaman and McQuail warn that there was little evidence in their study that television (or any other mass medium) did anything

other than provide information; there was little or no attitude change on significant issues. "People are aware of what is being said, and who is saying it, but they do not necessarily take it at face value." See *op. cit.* p. 168. In a more recent study, however, Blumler and McQuail found that high exposure to Liberal party television broadcasts in the British General Election of 1964 was positively related to a more favorable attitude toward the Liberal party for those with medium or weak motivation to follow the campaign. The more strongly motivated were much more stable in political attitude. See Jay G. Blumler and Denis McQuail, *Television in Politics: Its Uses and Influence*, Chicago, University of Chicago Press, 1969, p. 200.

8. Cohen, *op. cit.*, p. 13.
9. See Trenaman and McQuail, *op. cit.*, p. 172. The survey question was: "What are you *most* concerned about these days? That is, regardless of what politicians say, what are the two or three *main* things which you think the government *should* concentrate on doing something about?"
10. Intercoder reliability was above .90 for content analysis of both "major" and "minor" items. Details of categorization are described in the full report of this project. A small number of copies of the full report is available for distribution and may be obtained by writing the authors.
11. While recent reviews of the literature and new experiments have questioned the validity of the selective perception hypothesis, this has nevertheless been the focus of much communication research. For example, see Richard F. Carter, Ronald H. Pyszka, and Jose L. Guerrero, "Dissonance and Exposure to Arousive Information," *Journalism Quarterly*, Vol. 46, 1969, pp. 37–42; and David O. Sears and Jonathan L. Freedman, "Selective Exposure to Information: A Critical Review," *Public Opinion Quarterly*, Vol. 31, 1967, pp. 194–213.
12. A number of studies have focused on the influence of the wire services. For example, see David Gold and Jerry L. Simmons, "News Selection Patterns among Iowa Dailies," *Public Opinion Quarterly*, Vol. 29, 1965, pp. 425–430; Guido H. Stempel III, "How Newspapers Use the Associated Press Afternoon A-Wire." *Journalism Quarterly*, Vol. 41, 1964, pp. 380–384; Ralph D. Casey and Thomas H. Copeland Jr., "Use of Foreign News by 19 Minnesota Dailies," *Journalism Quarterly*, Vol. 35, 1958, pp. 87–89; Howard L. Lewis, "The Cuban Revolt Story: AP, UPI, and Three Papers," *Journalism Quarterly*, Vol. 37, 1960, pp. 573–578; George A. Van Horn, "Analysis of AP News on Trunk and Wisconsin State Wires," *Journalism Quarterly*, Vol. 29, 1952, pp. 426–432; and Scott M. Cutlip, "Content and Flow of AP News—From Trunk to TTS to Reader," *Journalism Quarterly*, Vol. 31, 1954, pp. 434–446.
13. Furthermore, five of the nine media studied here are national media and none of the remaining four originate in Chapel Hill. It is easier to argue that Chapel Hill voters fit their judgments of issue salience to the mass media than the reverse. An interesting study which discusses the problems of trying to fit day-to-day news judgments to reader interest is Guido H. Stempel III, "A Factor Analytic Study of Reader Interest in News," *Journalism Quarterly*, Vol. 44, 1967, pp. 326–330. An older study is Philip F. Griffin, "Reader Comprehension of News Stories: A Preliminary Study," *Journalism Quarterly*, Vol. 26, 1949, pp. 389–396.
14. Sid Shrauger, "Cognitive Differentiation and the Impression-Formation Process," *Journal of Personality*, Vol. 35, 1967, pp. 402–414.
15. Affect denotes a "pro/con" orientation, a feeling of liking or disliking something. Cognition, by contrast, denotes the individual's perception of the attitude object, his "image" or organized set of information and beliefs about a political object.
16. Coder reliability exceeded .90.
17. Angus Campbell, Philip Converse, Warren Miller, and Donald Stokes, *The American Voter*, New York, Wiley, 1960, chap. 2.
18. No statistical analysis is reported for the five separate three-way analyses in the Table because of small N's in some cells, but despite these small N's the pattern of results is consistent across all media.

4.2 KATHLEEN HALL JAMIESON

Packaging the Presidency

In the most recent phase of political communication research, many authors have moved beyond theories and methodologies that are closely aligned with psychology and sociology. In the current phase of political research, attention has become focused on how media influence the political process by using techniques that have become familiar to audiences over time. In particular, television has assumed a place in culture that allows researchers to investigate how real-world issues, like politics, become "packaged" like products.

Kathleen Hall Jamieson, professor and dean of the Annenberg School of Communications at the University of Southern California, Los Angeles, has produced a number of works on rhetorical style in the television age, including *Packaging the Presidency: A History and Criticism of Presidential Campaign Advertising*, 2d ed. (Oxford University Press, 1992), from which the following selection is taken, and *Dirty Politics: Deception, Distraction, and Democracy* (Oxford University Press, 1992). Her work examines the images and the words used by candidates and their managers to influence the public's perception of issues in the political world.

The following selection shows how television has become regarded as a central mediating technology in the political process. Jamieson's links between the content of advertising, political speeches, and the political process demonstrates an evolution in the media.

Key Concept: political advertising

*P*olitical advertising is now the major means by which candidates for the presidency communicate their messages to voters. As a conduit of this advertising, television attracts both more candidate dollars and more audience attention than radio or print. Unsurprisingly, the spot ad is the most used and the most viewed of the available forms of advertising. By 1980 the half hour broadcast speech—the norm in 1952—had been replaced by the 60 second spot.

Ads enable candidates to build name recognition, frame the questions they view as central to the election, and expose their temperaments, talents, and agendas for the future in a favorable light. In part because more voters attend to spot ads than to network news and in part because reporters are fixated with who's winning and losing instead of what the candidates are proposing, some scholars believe that ads provide the electorate with more information than network news. Still, ads more often successfully reinforce existing dispositions than create new ones.

Ads also argue the relevance of issues to our lives. In the 1950s the public at large did not find political matters salient to it. From the late 1950s to the early 1970s the perception of the relevance of political matters to one's day-to-day life increased at all educational levels. Citizens saw a greater connection between what occurred in the political world and what occurred in their lives.

TV ads' ability to personalize and the tendency of TV news to reduce issues to personal impact have, in my judgment, facilitated that change. Ads argued, for example, that a vote against nonproliferation could increase the Strontium 90 [a radioactive isotope present in fallout from nuclear explosions] in children's ice cream. As the salience of political issues increased so too did the consistency of the beliefs of individual voters. Dissonant views are less likely to be simultaneously held now than before. This tendency is also reinforced by political advertising, for politicians have increasingly argued the interconnection of issues of importance to them. In 1980 Reagan predicated a strong defense on a strong economy. In 1968 Nixon tied crime, lawlessness, and the war in Vietnam into a single bundle and laid it on Humphrey's doorstep.

Ads also define the nature of the presidency by stipulating the attributes a president should have. In the process they legitimize certain occupations. Ike polished the assumption that being a general was a suitable qualification. Carter argued that being an outsider plus an engineer, a farmer, a businessman but not a lawyer qualified him. Reagan contended that being the governor of a large state as well as a union leader were stronger qualifications than being an incumbent president. Eisenhower, Nixon, Johnson, Ford, and Carter argued that being the incumbent qualified one for the presidency.

... [A]dvertising provides an optic through which presidential campaigns can be productively viewed. In the ten campaigns I have focused on we have seen, for example, various styles of leadership reflected in the candidates' treatment of their advertisers and advertising. Where Nixon maintained tight control over advertising decisions in 1960, Kennedy delegated all responsibility for advertising to others. At the same time, ad campaigns that lurched uncertainly from one message form to another, from one set of strategists to another, as did Ford's, Mondale's, and Dukakis's, suggested perhaps that the candidate and his advisers were unable to provide a clear sense of the direction in which they wanted to take the country, an observation consistent with the failure of these campaigns to forecast their candidates' visions of the future.

Occasionally, a candidate's response to the requirements of advertising raises troublesome questions about his suitability for the office or, perhaps, about the intensity of his desire to hold it. Adlai Stevenson's perpetual quest for the perfect word or perfectly phrased argument and his apparent need to continue to perfect texts even as he was walking to the stage invite doubts about his ability to act decisively.

When the acceptance speech and the election eve telecasts are taken as the brackets bounding advertising, a focus on paid messages can reveal a campaign's fundamental coherence or incoherence. In a coherent campaign, the acceptance speech at the convention synopsizes and polishes the message the candidate has communicated in the primaries as a means of forecasting both the themes of the general election campaign and of this person's presidency. The message is then systematically developed in the advertising of the general election and placed in its final form on election eve where the candidate tries on the presidency by indicating for the country his vision of the next four years under his leadership. When from the first campaign advertising of January through the last on election eve in November, candidates offer consistent, coherent messages about themselves and the future as they envision it, they minimize the likelihood that their record or plans will be distorted effectively by opponents, and create a clear set of expectations to govern their conduct in office, expectations that may haunt them when they seek reelection.

Viewing campaign advertising as an extended message rather than a series of discrete message units also enables us to see how a candidate's response to attacks in the primaries can either strengthen or strangle the candidate's chances in the general election. When attacks are raised in the primaries and effectively neutralized, as were questions about Kennedy's age and religion in 1960, the issues can be effectively dispatched in the general election. Kennedy's widely aired speech to the Houston ministers builds on a structure of belief first cemented in Kennedy's speeches and ads in the West Virginia primary. Accordingly, those including NCPAC, Glenn, and Hart, whose ads in 1984 exploited Mondale's vulnerability to the charge that he was the captive of special interests, may have done Mondale a favor since the charges forced him to demonstrate that he had called and would continue to call for sacrifices from every segment of the electorate including those whose endorsements fueled his candidacy. At the same time, these charges against Mondale forced his natural constituencies to accept a fact they might otherwise have rejected—that if they demanded Mondale's public and total embrace of their agendas, that embrace would enfeeble his candidacy and the credibility of their endorsements.

Preventing candidates from using advertising to create a sense of themselves discrepant from who they are and what they have done is the vigilant presence of opponents and the potentially vigilant presence of the press. . . . [W]e have seen instances in which candidates' words and actions in settings they did not control undermined the crafted images of their ads. So, for example, the image of the sweating, gaunt, pale Nixon of the first debate in 1960 clashed with the polished presence in his ads. When ads lie, the vigilance of press and opponents can, but do not necessarily, protect the public.

In many ways televised political advertising is the direct descendant of the advertised messages carried in song and on banners, torches, bandannas, and broadsides. Ads continue to ally the candidate with the people, only now that takes the form of showing the candidate pressing the flesh or answering questions from groups of citizens. Candidates continue to digest their messages into slogans, yet these now appear at the end of broadcast ads rather than on banners and torches. Candidates continue to overstate their accomplishments and understate their failures. So, for example, as governor, despite his claims to the contrary, Ronald Reagan did not increase welfare benefits 43%, although he did increase them just as, contrary to his advertising, Andy Jackson had served in one, not two wars.

What differentiates the claims of Jackson's time from those aired today is the role the press has now assumed as monitor of presidential advertising. While the partisan papers controlled by his opponent revealed Jackson's actual war record and noted that this was not the hand that guided the plow, those papers were not a credible source of information for Jackson's likely supporters. By contrast, in the 1980 presidential and 1990 statewide races, articles and news stories—bearing the imprint of neither party—publicly scrutinized the adequacy of candidates' claims. The difficulty in relying on news to correct distortions in advertising is, of course, that comparatively few people consume news while many are exposed to ads.

One of the argumentative ploys born in the political and product advertising of the nineteenth century was refined by politicians in the age of television and then shunted aside by Watergate. By visually associating the favored candidate with pictures of well-fed cattle, happy families, large bundles of grain, and bulging factories, banners and broadsides argued to literate and illiterate alike that this candidate stood for prosperity. The opponent, on the other hand, was visually tied to drawings of starving cattle, poverty-ravished families, empty grain bins, and fireless factories. Some of the associations seemed to have no direct bearing on what sort of president the candidate would make.

Political argument by visual association flowered for the same reason it appeared in product advertising. Initially, advertising for products simply identified the existence, cost, function, and way to obtain the product. As success bred success, products performing the same function proliferated. Distinguishing attributes—some real, some fictional—were sought to persuade customers that one product rather than its twin should be purchased. Van Buren and Harrison were parity products, differentiated by the associations sculpted by their respective campaigns. Since the advertising of the early nineteenth century relied on drawings rather than photographs the range of possible associations was limited only by the artist's imagination.

The wizardry of videotape and film editing did not change the nature of argument from visual association—it simply increased its subtlety. In the process, the evidentiary burden that candidates should assume dropped. So, for example, Goldwater's ads juxtaposed a picture of Billie Sol Estes with scenes of street riots and then intercut a picture of Bobby Baker. Goldwater then appeared on screen to indict the Democrats for their disregard of law, order, and morality. Estes' relation to Baker, the relation of either to the street riots, or the relation among the three and Lyndon Johnson are not explicitly argued.

In 1968 this type of argument reached a new level of complexity in the Republican ad that intercut scenes from the Vietnam War and from the riots outside the Democratic convention with pictures of Hubert Humphrey, including one in which he appears to be smiling. The juxtaposition of highly evocative images invites the audience to impute causality.

The form of argument embodied in this ad is as powerful as it is irrational. It solicits a visceral and not an intellectual response. As a vehicle of attack, this type of ad was vanquished by Watergate because Watergate forced politicians and public to consider what is and is not fair attack in a political campaign. Lurking in the McGovern and Bush campaigns are the forms of attack that replace it: the personal witness, neutral reporter, and pseudo-documentary furlough ad. These mimic some of the features of news. The personal testimony ads consist of actual individuals reporting their opinions of the opposing candidate's performance. They resembled person-in-the-street interviews and are almost a survey; the opinions expressed are not scripted—indeed, their ungrammatical nature underscores their spontaneity. They do not appear to be unfair because, first, we are taught that everyone is entitled to express his or her opinion and, second, these people are voicing opinions that the electorate presumably is disposed to share. In 1976 Ford pioneered this form against Carter.

In the neutral reporter spot, an announcer whose delivery is deliberately low key details facts about the opponent. The ad itself rarely draws any conclusion from the data. That task is left to the audience. Ford did this in a 1976 ad comparing Carter's statements in the campaign with his actual record as governor of Georgia. An ad by Carter did the same to Reagan in 1980.

Pseudo-documentary ads dramatize supposedly real conditions. Here the "revolving door" ad is a prime illustration. As strange as it may seem since the independent PACs have been roundly criticized for their advertising against Democratic senators, the PAC presidential ads also fall, in the main, in 1980, into the neutral reporter category. A typical one simply quotes a promise by Carter and demonstrates that he had not kept it. The most cogent are those by the National Conservative Political Action Committee that edit from the Carter-Ford debates specific promises by Carter, show him making them, freeze the frame, and print across the screen the evidence establishing that the promise has been broken. . . .

By replacing attack ads that use visual not verbal means to prompt sweeping inferences with attack ads that verbally and visually invite judgments based on verifiable facts, Watergate temporarily transformed a form of presidential attack advertising from an exercise in the prompting of false inferences to an exercise in traditional argument. In 1988, invitations to false inference were back with a vengeance.

Just as political attack advertising survives, but in a circumscribed form, so too the political speech survives, albeit in shortened form, in televised advertising. Contrary to popular belief, the speech remains the staple of paid political broadcasting. There is not a presidential general election campaign in the televised age in which each candidate did not deliver at least two nationally broadcast speeches. In most campaigns far more are given and the candidates deliver short speeches in spot ads as well. Speeches and segments of speeches also recur in telecast campaign biographies. The rise of C-Span means that over 50% of viewing households can watch campaign speeches daily.

The reason we mistakenly think the broadcast speech is an object of antiquity is that half hour speeches tend to draw smaller, more highly partisan audiences than spots. Additionally, when a candidate such as Nixon or Ford delivers addresses by radio, he is speaking on a medium to which many of us do not routinely attend. Moreover, we tend not to think of five minute or 60 second statements by the candidate as speeches. Finally, a televised speech by a presidential candidate was more novel in the 1950s than it is now and so we are more likely to have noted and to long remember its occurrence then than now. Still, if judged by number of minutes on the air in which the candidate is speaking directly to the audience, Reagan's total exceeds Eisenhower's from either 1952 or 1956. If judged by the total number of televised appearances each made speaking directly to the audience, Reagan leads by a substantial margin.

The widespread perception that being able to present broadcast messages persuasively to a mass public would emerge as a criterion governing selection of presidential candidates is not convincingly confirmed from 1952 to 1980. Of the candidates to receive their party's nomination since 1952, Kennedy, Bush, and Dukakis were adequate speakers, Goldwater and Nixon often excellent, and only Reagan a master. In short, the ability to deliver televised messages artfully, while certainly an asset for those who possess it, has not become so central a qualification for the presidency that it has exiled candidates who lack it.

Another misconception about political advertising holds that spots and paid programming are somehow alien to the political speech, a thing apart, a bad dream, an aberration. An analysis of both the stock campaign speeches and the acceptance addresses of the presidential candidates suggests instead that the advertising is rarely anything but a digest of the speeches being delivered throughout the country. Occasionally, but not often, the candidate will say something important in a stump speech that does not appear in the paid broadcasting. But these things are usually strategic blunders such as Carter's assertion that Reagan will rend the country North from South.

. . . [T]he convention acceptance speeches are a highly reliable predictor of the content of the candidate's ads in the general election. For those who read the campaign's position papers, examine its brochures, and listen to its stump speeches, the ads function as reinforcement. Those who ignore the other campaign-produced materials receive a digest of them in the ads. This is true both of the advertising against the opponent and the advertising supporting the candidate.

The cost of reaching voters through broadcast advertising poses other problems. Since spot advertising is both costly and often the most cost efficient means of reaching a mass of voters, the contemporary reliance on spots means that those who cannot afford to purchase them, with rare exceptions, are denied the ability to have their ideas either heard or taken seriously in presidential primaries.

For these and related reasons, . . . public concern over the nature and influence of political advertising has been rising. Responding to this escalating public concern, legislators drafted or considered drafting bills that can be grouped into three broad categories. The first would have either the public or the radio and TV stations assume the burden of financing some or all of candidate advertising; the second would give candidates attacked by PACs free response time or—regardless of the origin of attack—would give the attacked candidate free response time; the third, still in the talking stage as this book goes to press, would promote changes in the form by offering free time to those agreeing to certain formats (e.g., mandate talking head ads) or lengths (e.g., specify a minimum length or make available free time in no less than five minute and half hour blocks).

Underlying the debate over these and like proposals is widening consensus that the electoral process would benefit if the candidates' cost of reaching a mass audience could be reduced; if all bona-fide candidates could be provided with sufficient access to communicate their basic ideas; if politicians made greater use of longer forms of communication and the electorate as a whole attended more readily to such forms; if candidates assumed or could be enticed to assume the obligation of being viewed by the public in forms such as debates that they do not control; if the advantage PACs can bring to a presidential candidate could be countered or muted.

Still, if political advertising did not exist we would have to invent it. Political advertising legitimizes our political institutions by affirming that change is possible within the political system, that the president can effect change, that votes can make a difference. As a result, advertising like campaigns in general channels discontent into the avenues provided by the government and acts as a safety valve for pressures that might otherwise turn against the system to demand its substantial modification or overthrow.

Political advertising does this, in part, by underscoring the power of the ballot. Your vote makes a difference, it says, at the same time as its carefully targeted messages imply that the votes that would go to the opponent are best left uncast.

Political ads affirm that the country is great, has a future, is respected. The contest they reflect is over who should be elected, not over whether there should be an election. The very existence of the contest suggests that there is a choice, that the voters' selection of one candidate over the other will make a difference.

Political Feelings

Roderick P. Hart's book *Seducing America: How Television Charms the Modern Voter* (Oxford University Press, 1994), from which the following selection has been taken, develops a unique strain of research by focusing on how the medium of television has altered viewers' sense of what constitutes public versus private life. Hart draws from a tradition of rhetorical studies and explores culture from a perspective that views television as an integral part of political (as well as other) social reality. He acknowledges that the presence of television in today's society has revolutionized some of society's most important institutions, including the political process and democracy.

Hart's research focuses on how television has propelled politics into a new arena in which earlier thoughts and beliefs about the inviolability of democracy is challenged. A way to think about his work is to consider whether your own worldviews have been altered or influenced by modern technologies, such as computers or television.

Hart is a professor in the speech communication department at the University of Texas at Austin. He is also the author of *The Sound of Leadership: Presidential Communication in the Modern Age* (University of Chicago Press, 1987).

Key Concept: television, image, and political processes

REEXAMINING POLITICS

Examining the electronic media raises special problems for those of us who grew up with it and who therefore see it but darkly. Yet the power of television cannot be denied, with its conflation of high and low culture, with its most surreal polyvocality, with its always-starting-never-stopping texts that chain together endlessly. Those of us who study such complexities are surely all blink, grabbing fitfully at the televisual elephant in an attempt to understand it. . . . The traditional press conference has given way to the presidential town hall; the scathing broadside has been supplanted by the fifteen-second spot;

campaign oratory has been replaced by the emotional pastiche of the convention film. . . . Television has changed politics itself.

That claim will be too sweeping for some. The essentialist, for example, would argue that no matter how different it may look from time to time and from place to place, politics is, ineluctably, politics. From such a perspective, politics is the story of how citizens deliberate when parceling out previous resources. As long as people choose to live together and as long as the world's resources remain finite, the essentialist would say, politics will do what it has always done: force cooperation, enforce regulations. Television can hardly change these brute facts of public life. But television can, and does, mystify such facts. Television can, and does, make the public sphere seem more private.

Television's revolution is therefore a perceptual revolution or, more accurately, a phenomenological revolution. Television makes us see politics in a certain way, but it also makes us see seeing in a certain way. Television tells us, incrementally and additively, today and once again tomorrow, that politics can be reduced to pictures. Television is thus not only a messenger but also, as Marshall McLuhan would say, a message. Television certifies a special way of seeing and hence a special way of knowing. Most important, television endorses a special set of feelings. . . .

Television, I shall argue, now tells us how to feel about politics, producing in us a postmodern swagger: We tower above politics by making it seem beneath us. Television produces what critic Raymond Williams has called a "structure of feeling" about politics, a complex of emotions that lies deeper than our individual attitudes about political parties or social issues or citizen referenda.[1] During the last fifty years, this structure of feeling has made the burdens of citizenship increasingly taxing for us, and it is, I believe, responsible for much of the alienation we now feel.

. . . Television, . . . fills an emotional void in modern life, a void perhaps created by modern life itself. Television has become a delivery system For intimacy, that luxuriant product of the sixties, and it delivers intimacy to us from dawn to dusk. If politics were suddenly obliterated from the television screen, if the United States suddenly enacted a more draconian version of the Israelis' draconian restrictions on election-year broadcasting, politics would instantly become less personal. In response, however, television would simply deliver its intimacies (and its peevishness and its loathings) in other, nonpolitical venues and viewers would continue to have relationships with the people they see on daily soap operas. They would continue to mourn, sometimes quite literally, when a favorite character is unexpectedly removed from *All My Children* because of stormy contract negotiations. They would do so because watching television is an oddly emotional business.

How could it be otherwise? Television is a people's medium, after all, and it celebrates that fact each day. It celebrates people's joys in its game shows, their strivings in its sports programs, their lusts via the Playboy Channel. But it is television's capacity to generate surprise that makes it especially attractive. Each time—each time—the set is turned on, new joys, new strivings, and new lusts await. Each of these emotional experiences is unanticipated and, yet, curiously anticipatable.

As an emotional medium, television performs both personal and cultural work for its viewers. It lets them learn about themselves, as when scenes from the Kennedy assassination and the Challenger explosion become synecdoches for two different generations of Americans. To remember such scenes is to be reminded of who we once were and of the people who shared those moments with us. In these ways and more, television expands time and enlarges the human family. It delivers Mother Theresa to us as well as the serial rapist. Even when watched alone, television reminds us that life need not be solitary.

Television has its detractors, of course, especially when it comes to politics. Social scientists have long noted, for example, that heavy television watchers know precious little about how they are governed, presumably because political programming is directed at the lowest common denominator. But being informed and *feeling* informed are different matters. Far too many Americans feel eminently knowledgeable about politics, and that is a danger of some consequence. A democracy, I will argue, becomes imperiled (1) when its people do not know what they think they know and (2) when they do not care about what they do not know. Television miseducates the citizenry but, worse, it makes that miseducation attractive. . . .

Capturing such feelings is the job of phenomenology, that branch of study designed to investigate "the content of consciousness."[2] Because television is essentially a technology of consciousness and because politics is little more than public consciousness made manifest, a new phenomenology of politics is needed. It is needed for both theoretical and practical reasons. More traditional approaches to politics—calculating voter demographics or tracking macroeconomic trends, for example often tell us much about the how of politics but not about the why. A good phenomenology, in contrast, tries to scratch an itch that is hard to find but that cannot be denied. It attaches words to perceptions that cannot be easily described. It examines taken-for-granted assumptions about politics and in that sense becomes an "investigation of appearances."[3]

Most important, phenomenology offers a language for the emotions. It captures what Hwa Yol Jung has called the perceiver's "natural attitude" toward the world, that "prereflective and naive point of view" that tells us what is intuitively true.[4] For Jung, "the ordinary language of political man precedes the objectified language of political science, and the second must be consistent with the first."[5] Alas, that is rarely the case. Too often, political study is reduced to abstract talk of political systems or to reifications of felt needs. Too often, human politics loses both its humanity and its politics when dissected.

Phenomenology tries to change that. It treats people as emotionally complicated, and it questions differences between "fact" and "perception."[6] Television does the same thing when it artfully obscures differences between the real and the fictive. A clever president like Ronald Reagan, for example, could borrow effortlessly from a celluloid hero like Dirty Harry Callaghan by challenging his political antagonists to "make his day" and oppose him legislatively. By aping Callaghan's bravado, Mr. Reagan undermined facile distinctions between the world of movies and the world of politics and, simultaneously, questioned distinction making itself.

George Bush tried the same thing but got caught. While he, too, used Callaghan's lexicon, the *New York Times* reported in June 1992 that the vast majority of Mr. Bush's supporters *actually believed* his pledge when he made it: " 'I'm disgusted with all politicians,' said Ron Purkhiser, a fifty-year-old welder in Akron, Ohio. 'They say one thing, then they go ahead and do the opposite. 'Read my lips: No new taxes.' Yeah, right.'"[7] The *Times'* writer seemed stunned that people like Mr. Purkhiser still existed in the ingenuous nineties.

Roderick P. Hart

Ingenuous or not, however, televised politics reaches out and grabs us in continually surprising ways. At the moment, we do not have an efficient way of talking about such influences. To discover one, we might take the lead of cultural critic Frederic Jameson, who says that to appreciate postmodern architecture one must retrain the viewing habits one acquired in an earlier, modernist era.[8] So too with television. To appreciate what it has done to politics' we must learn to speak television's language—the language of feelings.

. . . Television's theory of politics flatters the medium (as one might expect), and it flatters viewers too. It makes them feel close to their leaders, at least for a while. It makes them feel informed about public affairs, at least nominally. Television also gives certain Americans feelings of enterprise and influence, although these feelings come at a price. And this theory *is* a theory, a distinctive way of seeing the world. Its parts are integrated, and it produces a predictable set of emotional experiences. The feelings it creates within us are often pleasing initially, but they become more disturbing later on. This contrariety of emotions is what distinguishes and perpetuates the theory. . . .

Because television's theory of politics is genuinely a theory, a way of seeing the world, it operates in the part as well as the whole and therefore "precedes" any individual political event a citizen might witness. When watching George Bush and Dan Rather disembowel one another during the nightly news in 1988, American viewers didn't experience that confrontation newly born. They came equipped with a wealth of assumptions about reporters and presidents, about political propriety, about newsworthiness, about perfidy. Television itself had helped to create some of those assumptions. Its model therefore binds us tightly, although it is not monolithic and it affects some people more than others.

And yet it affects all of us in part. This is a phenomenological principle that philosopher Laurie Spurling calls "anchorage": "If, for example, I see a stone falling through the air, this means my gaze is anchored in the garden, so that it is in terms of the garden that the stone is seen as moving."[9] In other words, because we always stand *somewhere* when watching politics, it is good to know where we stand, especially if television is helping us stand there. . . .

REEXAMINING REMEDIES

Over the years, numerous commentators have suggested how televised politics might be fixed. Collectively, they define "political television" broadly . . . , including within it the news (local, national, and international), political advertising, campaign-based communications as well as office holders' pronouncements, interview shows, political documentaries, public service messages, lobbying by those in the private sector, and citizen-action agendas, as well as a variety of popular culture formats. The solutions for dealing with political television have been no less restricted:

1. *The Socratics.* Some observers, such as political scientist James Fishkin,[10] have called for a reinvigorated public interchange to rescue the nation from the political doldrums. The Socratics endorse deliberative opinion polls, the televising of House and Senate proceedings, and the regularizing of presidential press conferences. These solutions are clearly testosteronal in nature, designed to counteract the "soft politics" that produces excessive chumminess among the nation's elites. But can palliatives like these get at the sources of unbelief that threaten the polity? Can a new dialectic counteract the forces (of socialization that undergird people's attitudes? Are changes in media formats adequate solutions to the alienations that confront us? I argue that they are not.

2. *The Epicureans.* A more progressive set of observers argues that politics has fallen (on hard times because it is no longer emotionally available to the citizenry. Voters are alienated, this group holds, because politics is now gray and lifeless, drained of the human connectedness once found in the New England village. The Epicureans favor more sociable formats that draw people into the public realm by humanizing political options. They are therefore attracted to Ross Perot's electronic town halls, to Rush Limbaugh and Jim Hightower on talk radio, and to the ever-new forms of psychobiography found on television. Instead of improving things, however, these strategies merely usher in a distorting politics of intimacy. It seems to me that we need to become more abstemious, not more Dionysian, when imagining a politics for the future.

3. *The Deweyites.* A third school of thought stresses the need for a more informed electorate and looks to the nation's press for solutions. The Deweyites champion in-depth reporting, longer nightly news programs, less dependence on restrictive sources of information, and fewer lacerating political profiles but also less toadying by the White House press corps, and elimination of Washington's employment merry-go-round between the first and fourth estates.[11] "Drench the people with the right kind of information," the Deweyites promise, "and they will respond." Nobody can disagree with such good sense. But is it enough? Probably not. It seems to me that it is what people feel, not what they know, that must be dislodged before they will become politically involved. . . .

4. *The Bolsheviks.* This is the view from the left and it features, predictably enough, money.[12] By this perspective, the mass media are corporate captives, a fact that clouds each image projected onto viewers screens by the television networks. Political information is capitalized information, the Bolsheviks argue, and that makes both establishment politicians and establishment reporters dance to the same tune. The solution? Break up the economic cartels, the cross-ownership patterns, the centralized news bureaus, the privately owned satellites, the news-for-profit routines. Break up, too, the cozy relationships between political contributers and political candidates, between news personnel and their corporate rolodexes, between the Corporation for "Public" Broadcasting and its hegemonic overlords. Typically, the Bolsheviks leave one gasping for air, so totalistic is their critique. . . .

5. *The Hamiltonians.* Rarely explicated in serious commentaries about televised politics, this view underlies many of them nonetheless. The Hamiltoni-

ans acknowledge that television is a soporific but they find inevitability, not horror, in that fact. They argue that people want pleasure, not mindless wrangling, when relaxing before the television set in the evening and that that is why they ignore politics. Besides, argue the Hamiltonians, television educates everyone (obliquely at least), including nonvoters. The result of all this is clear: an electronic republicanism that keeps the best of us active and the rest of us quiet. Surely this is a dangerous attitude. Surely a sense of citizenship cannot be allowed to pass for the real thing in an enlightened democracy. Surely a society must find a way of getting all of its hands on deck.

6. *The Sentinels*. The Sentinels endorse a different kind of citizen's wisdom, a meta-wisdom, when encouraging the ongoing deconstruction of contemporary politics. The Sentinels consist of academic pundits who make the rounds, explaining politicians' advertising strategies; media critics who watch the press' political watchers; and social activists who publish monthly exposes of political journalism. Many of these Sentinels are well intentioned, but an equal number preen noxiously when exposing the expediencies of politics, thereby adding to an already ample supply of cultural cynicism. . . .

Each of the foregoing perspectives offers possibilities for political renewal but each suffers from an unblinking technocratic faith, from the belief that altering communication methodologies will alter political consciousness. To change politics, they suggest, one must change the political text, change how that text is formatted, or change how it is received by viewers. But will a new, less manipulative, breed of politician come of age overnight? Will media staffers ensnared in labyrinthine corporate cultures suddenly become more responsible? Will new systems for delivering political information come on line and make political thinking easier? I suspect not and I suspect, further, that any solution to political malaise must reckon, more fundamentally, with how people feel about democracy and not with what they know about it.

CONCLUSION

. . . While Americans have always had a healthy skepticism about politicians, they have not always distrusted politics itself. They do now. This change has been gradual but insistent. It has also been revolutionary and unfortunate. I believe that the very concept of politics—what government is for—is now threatening to slip away from us as a nation, that we as citizens are vaguely aware of this slippage, and, most disturbing of all, that we do not care about our loss. The reasons behind this eclipse, this deferral, of politics are many. Some of the reasons lie in the unremitting series of political debacles Americans have witnessed during the last forty years: Vietnam, Watergate, Iran-Contra, savings and loan scandals, the House bank. While these events have passed into history (some more quickly than others), they have left an aftertaste. Other reasons press upon us: An often sick economy exacerbates class divisions in the ostensibly classless United States; a growing cultural malaise has enveloped the citizenry; governmental leaders in the mold of Franklin Roosevelt, and even of Harry Truman, seem unavailable. These things, individually and collectively, have made Americans sad, later angry, now numb. Or so many have claimed.

NOTES

1. R. Williams, *Marxism and Literature* (New York: Oxford University Press, 1977). pp. 133–134.
2. D. Stewart and A. Mickunas, *Exploring Phenomenology: A Guide to the Field and Its Literature* (Chicago: American Library Association, 1974). p. 73.
3. L. Hinchman and S. Hinchman, "In Heidegger's Shadow: Hannah Arendt's Phenomenological Humanism," *The Review of Politics,* 46 (1984), p. 187.
4. H. Y. Jung, "Introduction," in H. Y. Jung (ed.), *Existential Phenomenology and Political Theory: A Reader* (Chicago: Henry Regnery, 1972), p. xxi.
5. Jung (1972), p. xxx.
6. For an example of an author who doesn't question this distinction, see D. Nesbit, *Viedestyle in Senate Campaigns* (Knoxville: University of Tennessee Press, 1988), pp. 21–22.
7. "Words on Bush's Lips in '88 Now Stick in Voters' Craw," *New York Times,* June 14, 1992, p. A1.
8. F. Jameson, "Postmodernism, or The Cultural Logic of Late Capitalism," *The New Left Review,* 146 (1984), p. 80.
9. L. Spurling, *Phenomenology and the Social World: The Philosophy of Merleau-Ponty and its Relations to the Social Sciences* (London: Routeledge, 1977), p. 38.
10. J. Fishkin, *Democracy and Deliberation: New Directions for Democratic Reform* (New York: Yale University Press, 1991).
11. For a thorough presentation of the ills currently afflicting political reporting, see L. Sabato, *Feeding Frenzy: How Attack Journalism Has Transformed American Politics* (New York: Free Press, 1991).
12. Because this viewpoint is so prevalent in the American academy, it has produced a corpulent bibliography. For an informed and accessible treatment see T. Luke, *Screens of Power: Ideology, Domination, and Resistance in Informational Society* (Urbana: University of Illinois Press, 1989).

CHAPTER 5 Cultivation Research

5.1 GEORGE GERBNER ET AL.

The "Mainstreaming" of America: Violence Profile No. 11

George Gerbner is considered one of the most respected scholars in the field of mass media studies today. Now retired from a long tenure as dean of the Annenberg School of Communications at the University of Pennsylvania, where he formed and directed the world-renowned Cultural Indicators project in the 1970s, he continues his mass media research and activism concerning the impact of mass media on everyday life. Gerbner has edited many books on such issues as media effects, government mass media policy, international communication, and media and education. The other members of the Cultural Indicators research team who worked with Gerbner on the study discussed in the following selection are Larry Gross, Michael Morgan, and Nancy Signorielli. Gross and Signorielli are both professors of communication, and all three carry on their own cultural indicators research.

Gerbner et al. argue that traditional media effects researchers err by focusing solely on the immediate "before and after" effects of exposure to media messages on people's behavior and attitudes. They suggest that in any culture it is the telling of stories that forms the *symbolic environment,* which gives order and meaning to human actions; growing up within a particular system of storytelling slowly but surely cultivates an individual's perceptions and judgments about society. Gerbner and his associates also argue that television provides a concentrated system of storytelling that rivals (and in modern societies supersedes) religion in its power to shape people's social perceptions.

Due to the unique nature of television, Gerbner et al. recommend what scientists term "longitudinal," or long-term, study of media effects. The Cultural Indicators project is itself a long-term study involving a three-pronged research effort: *institutional analysis,* which focuses on the structures of decision making that are involved in the production of media messages; *message system analysis,* which involves in-depth, quantitative content analysis aimed at discovering basic, social building blocks of TV content; and *cultivation analysis,* which focuses on TV viewers, correlating attitudes about the social world with, first, the amount of TV viewing and, second, the content of TV. Cultivation theory hypothesizes that perceptions of the social world on the part of heavy viewers will very closely resemble the structure of the "world of TV" content. In fact, Gerbner and his associates have gone on to posit a *mainstreaming effect* among heavy TV viewers.

The following selection is from "The 'Mainstreaming' of America: Violence Profile No. 11," *Journal of Communication* (vol. 30, no. 3, 1980). In it, Gerbner and his associates provide an annual report on their research and further expound the theory of cultivation.

Key Concept: theory of cultivation

*T*elevision makes specific and measurable contributions to viewers' conceptions of reality. These contributions relate both to the synthetic world television presents and to viewers' real life circumstances. These are the basic findings of our long-range research project called Cultural Indicators, and they have been supported, extended, and refined in a series of studies. Here we shall report new findings and introduce theoretical developments dealing with the dynamics of the cultivation of general concepts of social reality (which we shall call "mainstreaming") and of the amplification of issues particularly salient to certain groups of viewers (which we shall call "resonance").

The design of our research consists of two interrelated parts: message system analysis and cultivation analysis. Message system analysis is the annual monitoring of samples of prime-time and weekend daytime network dramatic programming (including series, other plays, comedies, movies, and cartoons). Cultivation analysis is the investigation of viewer conceptions of social reality associated with the most recurrent features of the world of television. Our studies since 1967–68 have traced some conceptual and behavioral correlates of growing up and living with a television world in which men outnumber women three to one, young people comprise one-third and old people one-fifth of their real numbers, professionals and law-enforcers dominate the occupations, and an average of five acts of violence per prime time hour (and four times that number per weekend daytime hour) involve more than half of all leading characters. . . .

For purposes of this analysis, we define violence as the overt expression of physical force (with or without a weapon, against self or others) compelling action against one's will on pain of being hurt and/or killed or threatened to be so victimized as part of the plot. Idle threats, verbal abuse, or gestures without credible violent consequences are not coded as violence. However, "accidental" and "natural" violence (always purposeful dramatic actions that do victimize certain characters) are, of course, included.

A violent act that fits the definition is recorded, whatever the context. This definition includes violence that occurs in a fantasy or "humorous" context as well as violence presented in a realistic or "serious" context. There is substantial evidence that fantasy and comedy are effective forms in which to convey serious lessons (1, 3, 11). Thus eliminating fantasy or comic violence, as well as violence of an "accidental" nature, would be a major analytical error.

All items are coded by pairs of trained coders (see 4 and 5) and are subjected to an extensive reliability analysis (see 10). Only those items meeting acceptable standards of reliability (.6 or above) are included in the analysis.

The Violence Index combines three sets of observations in order to provide a single indicator sensitive to a range of program characteristics. These observations measure the extent to which violence occurs at all in the programs sampled, the frequency and rate of violent episodes, and the number of roles calling for characterization as violents, victims, or both. These three measures have achieved high inter-coder reliability over the years we have been collecting these data. Although here we report only the Index, the component measures are always reported in our full technical reports (e.g., 5). . . .

The frequency of violence and the patterns of victimization in the world of dramatic television are remarkably stable from year to year. Overall, the Fall 1979 Violence Index shows some decline over the 1978 Index, much of which can be accounted for by a reduction of violence on ABC. Violence also declined after 9 p.m. but rose in the 1979 "family viewing" time (8:00 to 9:00 p.m. EST) (see Figure 1). Although still way above the level in prime time, violence in weekend-daytime (children's) programs also declined. The largest increase in violence in the 1979 sample was in new prime-time programs, especially in the former "family hour" and particularly on NBC. The largest reductions in violence were in the late evening by ABC and NBC and on weekend-daytime programs by all networks, but especially NBC.

In prime time, 70 percent of all programs still contained violence. The rate of violent episodes was 5.7 per hour, up from 4.5 in 1978. Nearly 54 percent of all leading characters were involved in some violence, about the same as in 1978. In weekend-daytime (children's) programs, 92 percent of all programs contained some violence, down from 98 percent in 1978. The rate of violent episodes was 17 per hour, down from 25 the year before. Nearly 75 percent of all leading characters were involved in violence, down from 86 percent in 1978.

Overall, the percent of characters involved in violence has remained fairly steady since 1969. About two-thirds of the males and nearly half of the females

FIGURE 1   *Violence Index in Children's and Prime-Time Programming, 1967–1979*

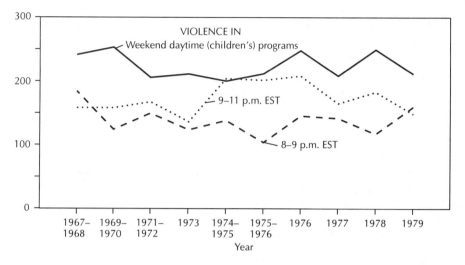

are involved. When involved, female characters are more likely than male characters to be the victims rather than the perpetrators of violence. Only one group of male characters—young boys—are among the ten groups who are most likely to be victimized. Women cast in minority roles (old women, upper-class women, non-white women, young women, and lower-class women) are especially more likely to suffer rather than to inflict violence. Only two groups of characters—old men and "bad" women—are more likely to hurt others than to be hurt themselves (for details of these and other message analysis findings, see 5).

We now turn to the theory of cultivation and to findings relating to conceptions of a mean world and its dangers.

Television is the central and most pervasive mass medium in American culture and it plays a distinctive and historically unprecedented role. Other media are accessible to the individual (usually at the point of literacy and mobility) only after the socializing functions of home and family life have begun. In the case of television, however, the individual is introduced virtually at birth into its powerful flow of messages and images. The television set has become a key member of the family, the one who tells most of the stories most of the time. Its massive flow of stories showing what things are, how things work, and what to do about them has become the common socializer of our times. These stories form a coherent if mythical "world" in every home. Television dominates the symbolic environment of modern life.

Cultivation analysis is the investigation of the consequences of this ongoing and pervasive system of cultural messages. Given our premise that television's images cultivate the dominant tendencies of our culture's beliefs, ideologies, and world views, the observable independent contributions of television can only be relatively small. But just as an average temperature shift of a few degrees can lead to an ice age or the outcomes of elections can be determined by slight margins, so too can a relatively small but pervasive influence make a crucial difference. The "size" of an "effect" is far less critical than the direction of its steady contribution.

We have found that amount of exposure to television is an important indicator of the strength of its contributions to ways of thinking and acting. For heavy viewers, television virtually monopolizes and subsumes other sources of information, ideas, and consciousness. Thus, we have suggested that the more time one spends "living" in the world of television, the more likely one is to report perceptions of social reality which can be traced to (or are congruent with) television's most persistent representations of life and society. Accordingly, we have examined the difference that amount of viewing makes in people's images, expectations, assumptions, and behaviors.[1]

In previous reports, we have stressed across-the-board consequences of television viewing. Thus, we expected heavier viewers to be more likely to give the "television answers" to a series of informational and opinion questions than lighter viewers. This theoretical perspective still holds and provides some of the most compelling evidence for the existence of television's contributions to conceptions of social reality. But further examination of previously analyzed and new data reveals there are substantially different patterns of associations for different social groups between amount of viewing and certain conceptions of social reality.

Television's cultivation of conceptions and behaviors is a consistent process but is integrated in different ways and with different results into different patterns of life. Therefore, a fuller understanding of television's contribution may be achieved by paying particular attention to differences across different subgroups.

Many differences between groups of viewers can be explained in terms of one of two systematic processes which we call "mainstreaming" and "resonance."

The "mainstream" can be thought of as a relative commonality of outlooks that television tends to cultivate. By "mainstreaming" we mean the sharing of that commonality among heavy viewers in those demographic groups whose light viewers hold divergent views. In other words, differences deriving from other factors and social forces may be diminished or even absent among heavy viewers. Thus, in some cases we should only find evidence for cultivation within those groups who are "out" of the mainstream. In other cases, we may find that viewing "moderates" attitudes in groups whose light viewers tend to hold extreme views. But in all cases, more viewing appears to signal a convergence of outlooks rather than absolute, across-the-board increments in all groups.

For example, it is well documented that more educated, higher income groups have the most diversified patterns of cultural opportunities and activities; therefore, they tend to be lighter viewers. We found that, when they are light viewers, they also tend to be the least imbued with the television view of the world. But the heavy viewers in the higher education/high income groups respond differently. Their responses to our questions are more like those of other heavy viewers, most of whom have less education and income. It is the college-educated, higher income light viewers who diverge from the "mainstream" cultivated by television; heavy viewers of all groups tend to share a relatively homogeneous outlook.

But the relationship of real life experience to television's cultivation of conceptions of reality entails not only this generalized notion of "mainstreaming" but also special cases of particular salience to specific issues. This is what we call "resonance." When what people see on television is most congruent with everyday reality (or even *perceived* reality), the combination may result in a coherent and powerful "double dose" of the television message and significantly boost cultivation. Thus, the congruence of the television world and real-life circumstances may "resonate" and lead to markedly amplified cultivation patterns.

These processes are not the only possible mechanisms which might explain variations in susceptibility to cultivation. For example, related analyses of children and adolescents suggest that cultivation may be most pronounced when parents are not involved in their children's viewing (7) or when children are less integrated into cohesive peer groups (13). Furthermore, the constructs of "mainstreaming" and "resonance" are still being developed and investigated. Although the number of empirical instances of each is rapidly growing, too few have been accumulated to allow for predictions of when one or the other—or neither—will occur. Nonetheless, we believe that the results we will report here suggest that these concepts merit serious consideration.

Before we present findings further illuminating the two phenomena, it may help to illustrate them graphically. The data for this illustration come from our most recent sample of adults, collected in March 1979 by the Opinion Research Corporation (ORC).[2] In this sample we found instances of "mainstreaming" and "resonance" in the differential patterns of responses to a single question which may tap some conceptions cultivated by the violent and dangerous world of television. Figure 2 presents two examples of each in terms of the relationship between amount of viewing and responding that "fear of crime is a very serious personal problem."

As shown in Figure 2 this relationship holds only for respondents with medium or high incomes; low-income respondents are more likely to agree, regardless of viewing. The proportion of light viewers giving the "television answer" is much lower in the higher income groups; yet the middle- and high-income heavy viewers are in the "mainstream." When we look at the responses by race we see a consistent but different pattern. The relationship between viewing and fear is positive for whites but slightly negative for non-whites. Non-white light viewers are especially likely to express the notion that fear of crime is a "very serious personal problem." Heavy viewing among non-whites may moderate this outlook; thus, they are closer to the "mainstream."

. . . Figure 2 also shows that the association is strongest among females and among those who live in cities. To a large extent, this fear may be most salient to such respondents. Accordingly, real-life circumstances and environmental factors may "resonate" with television's messages and augment them.

FIGURE 2 *Examples of Mainstreaming and Resonance in Terms of the Relationship between Amount of Viewing and Percent of Respondents Saying that "Fear of Crime Is a Very Serious Personal Problem"*

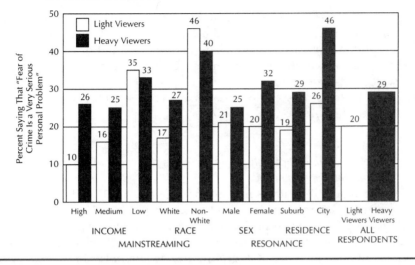

Data source: Opinion Research Corporation, March 1979.

We shall now examine both mainstreaming and resonance in light of new data and in response to critiques of our earlier analyses.

Examples of "mainstreaming" can be found in analyses of questions relating to what we have called the "mean world syndrome." We combined three items from the 1975 and 1978 National Opinion Research Center (NORC) General Social Surveys to form an index of interpersonal mistrust (alpha = .68) similar to Rosenberg's "faith in people" scale (12). The three items—which form the Mean World Index—measure the degree to which respondents agree that most people are just looking out for themselves, that you can't be too careful in dealing with people, and that most people would take advantage of you if they got a chance. . . . [T]elevision viewing overall is significantly associated with the tendency to express mistrust (r = .12, p < .001). This relationship is not fully accounted for by any individual control. Simultaneous controls greatly reduce its strength, but the relationship remains statistically significant.

Even more revealing than this small overall correlation is the relationship between television viewing and mistrust for specific groups of the population. The relationship is strongest for respondents who have had some college education—those who are also least likely to express interpersonal mistrust. (The correlation between education and the Mean World Index is −.28, p < .001.) The most striking specifications emerge for whites and non-whites. As a group, non-whites score higher on the Mean World Index (r = .23, p < .001). Yet, there is a significant *negative* association among non-whites between television and this index (r = −.10, p < .05). The relationship for whites, however, remains positive. Thus, those groups who in general are *least* likely to hold a television-related attitude are *most* likely to be influenced toward the "mainstream" television view; and those who are most likely to hold a view *more* extreme than the TV view may be "coaxed back" to the "mainstream" position.

Similar patterns can be found by examining the relationship between amount of viewing and feelings of alienation. In the 1977 NORC survey, alienation was measured by three of Srole's (14) anomie items—the lot of the average man is getting worse, it is hardly fair to bring a child into the world, and most public officials are not interested in the lot of the average man. We had previously reported (4) that the relationship between amount of viewing and the tendency to agree with these statements holds up in most groups. When these items were reanalyzed by Stevens (15), Hughes (9), and Hirsch (8), they all found that the overall association disappears when several demographic variables are controlled all at once.

But the lack of an overall relationship does not mean that the relationship does not hold for any specific group of respondents.

We combined these items into an index (alpha = .61) and found that the best predictor of anomie appeared to be education (r = −.31, p < .001). When the relationship between television viewing and endorsing statements of alienation is examined within educational subgroups, the relationship persists for those respondents who, as a group, are far less likely to express alienation—again, those with some college education. This relationship withstands the implementation of a large number of controls, either singly or simultaneously (r = .14, p < .01). For respondents with less education, who are relatively alienated to begin with, television viewing has no apparent relationship with anomie. Again, we see that television may influence a convergence of outlooks toward its "mainstream" rather than cultivating absolute across-the-board changes.

New data from a national probability sample of adults (ORC) provide numerous examples of this "mainstreaming" phenomenon with regard to people's conceptions about crime and violence. Using a question that replicates some of our earlier work, we asked respondents whether chances of being involved in violence in any given week are one in ten or one in a hundred. Our basic expectation is that relatively more heavy than light viewers will answer that their chances of encountering violence are higher.

Heavy viewers are indeed significantly more likely to give this response, overall and within most subgroups. Yet, there are important specifications. A large majority (84 percent) of both light and heavy viewers *with low incomes* give the higher risk response, and thus show no evidence of a relationship between amount of viewing and responses to this question. When we examine the middle- and upper-income groups, however, we find that the proportion of light viewers giving the "television answer" drops; "only" 62 percent of light viewers with higher incomes overestimate their chances of being involved in violence. Yet, the *difference* between light and heavy viewers rises sharply. Light viewers with middle and upper incomes are considerably less likely to express a high expectation of encountering violence, while heavy viewers with middle or high incomes exhibit almost the same level of perceived risk as the low-income group.

Such differences could be explained in terms of a ceiling effect. However, we think that the results we have found are a strong indication that television does contribute to the cultivation of common perspectives. In particular, heavy viewing may serve to cultivate beliefs of otherwise disparate and divergent groups toward a more homogeneous "mainstream" view.

The other important refinement of our theory suggests that cultivation will be most pronounced when other aspects of one's social environment are most congruent and thereby "resonate" with television's message.

Among Canadians, Doob and Macdonald (2) found the strongest positive associations between amount of television viewing and fear of crime among those who live in high crime centers. Although they interpreted this finding as evidence of spuriousness of the relationship between television viewing and fear of crime, clearly the concept of neighborhood does not "explain" the observed relationship. Rather, it points to an important specification. For those urban dwellers who live in high crime centers, television's violent imagery may be most congruent with their real-life perceptions. These people receive a "double dose" of messages that the world is violent, and consequently show the strongest associations between viewing and fear.

We have found parallel results in an analysis of data from our most recent national survey of adults (ORC). We asked people about how safe they felt walking around alone, at night, in their own neighborhoods, and assumed that those who lived in urban areas would also be most likely to express fear. We found, as would be expected, that those who live in large cities are much more likely to be afraid in their own neighborhoods at night, regardless of amount of viewing. But city dwellers also "resonate" most—they show the strongest association between amount of viewing and expressing this fear.

To provide further evidence we tried to approximate Doob and Macdonald's high crime/low crime distinction for respondents who live in cities. We assumed that respondents who live in larger cities *and* have lower incomes are likely to live in areas with relatively high crime rates, while high-income urban residents arguably live in less dangerous areas. We used the five questions from the 1979 ORC survey* to form a Perceptions of Danger Index-I.[3] When amount of television viewing was correlated with the Perceptions of Danger Index-I scores, the relationship was much stronger for residents in low-income (presumably high crime) urban areas ($r = .26$, $p < .001$) than for those in high-income (presumably low crime) urban areas ($r = .05$).

This relationship remains positive and significant ($r = .13$ $p < .001$) for urban dwellers with low incomes and falls to zero for high-income urban residents when within-group controls for demographic factors are imple-

*[The five questions from the 1979 ORC survey measured (1) the percentage of respondents overestimating their chances of being involved in violence; (2) percentage agreeing that women are more likely to be victims of crime; (3) percentage saying that their neighborhoods are only somewhat safe or not safe at all; (4) percentage saying that fear of crime is a very serious problem; and (5) percentage agreeing that cime is rising.—Eds.]

mented simultaneously. While the correspondence between income and neighborhood crime is ambiguous in suburban and non-metropolitan areas, it is worth noting that the association between amount of viewing and these images of danger, crime, and violence remains significant despite controls. Thus, the role of television in the cultivation of attitudes and fears may be most pronounced when an issue has direct relevance to the respondent's life.

A further example of "resonance" from the same survey focuses upon the assumption that older people are more likely than younger people to be victims of crime (an assumption contrary to the facts). Young and middle-aged respondents show no overall relationship between amount of viewing and the tendency to think that the elderly are most likely to be victimized. But, among older respondents, there is a significant positive association between television viewing and expressing this belief (gamma = .27, p < .001). In particular, this holds for older respondents in those demographic groups in which light viewers are less likely to respond this way.

We must stress that these specifications do not exhaust cultivation results. Amount of viewing remains significantly related to scores on the Perceptions of Danger Index-I, over and above the effects of education, income, sex, race, age, urban proximity, and newspaper reading (seventh order partial r = .11, p < .001). Although the amount of the variance in these scores explained by television viewing is small, with other things being held constant its predictive power is equal to or greater than that of age, race, urban proximity, income, or newspaper reading. But even where a relationship disappears for an entire sample, as Hirsch (8), Hughes (9), and Stevens (15) have found, it may quite clearly hold up in certain groups.

Thus, we have seen two distinct processes which help explain differential susceptibility to cultivation. "Resonance" may occur when a feature of the television world has special salience for a group, e.g., greater fear among city dwellers, or perceived over-victimization by the elderly. In these cases, the correlates of heavy viewing are most apparent among those for whom the topic holds considerable personal relevance. "Mainstreaming," on the other hand, may be related more to general and widespread images and norms of social reality.

Data from our three-year longitudinal study of adolescents also provide strong evidence for both an overall effect of viewing and important specification/interaction effects.

In the second and third years of this study we included two dependent measures—the Mean World Index (see above) and an index of Perceptions of Danger-II. The Perceptions of Danger Index-II was composed of four questions relating to estimates of the chances of encountering violence, aspects of murders and killings, and the importance of knowing self-defense. Agreement with these beliefs was interpreted as reflecting a strong image of the world as a dangerous place.

. . . Among boys, there is an interaction between second year viewing and second year scores on the Perceptions of Danger Index-II upon the third Perceptions of Danger Index-II scores. With IQ, SES, grade, early viewing, and early scores on the Perceptions of Danger Index-II already in a regression equation, there is still a negative and significant interaction (partial r = −.30, F = 6.26, d.f. = 1, 64, p < .05). This means that for those boys who had low Perceptions of Danger Index-II scores and watched more television in the second year, third year scores increased. But among those who were initially *more* afraid, heavy viewing led to less fear.

This is a dramatic and significant demonstration of the power of television to cultivate mainstream outlooks. There are, to be sure, significant "main effects," in a generally positive direction. But perhaps the more fundamental underlying process is that of convergence into a "mainstream" television view of the world, regardless of starting points. The ultimate homogenization of initially different perspectives may be the critical consequence of living with television.

The results reported here confirm, amplify, extend, and specify previous findings. The basic stability of the Violence Index and the apparent convergence of different programming parts (with the disappearance of the former "family hour" as a relatively low-violence zone) are the most noteworthy findings of message analysis. The cultivation analysis provides further strong support for the theory of pervasive cultivation of mistrust, apprehension, danger, and exaggerated "mean world" perceptions. Important specifications suggest that television viewing is associated with a cultural "mainstream" that tends to absorb or assimilate groups that otherwise diverge from it, and that the salience of certain real-life circumstances is likely to boost television's cultivating potential.

NOTES

1. We refer to this difference as the "cultivation differential" (CD) which is the spread between the percentages of light and heavy viewers who give a "television answer" to questions about social reality. The classification of respondents as relatively light, medium, and heavy viewers is determined by the distribution of amount of viewing in a given sample. Consequently, the actual proportions of lighter and heavier viewers will vary from one sample to another.
2. These data were collected as part of an Administration on Aging research grant (No. 90-A-1299) on "Aging with Television." George Gerbner, Larry Gross, and Nancy Signorielli were co-principal investigators (see 6).
3. These items essentially tap discrete dimensions; their conceptual link, however, is that they examine various aspects of television's portrayal of violence. Thus, it is not surprising that while these questions are all positively and significantly related to each other, their additive index has relatively low internal homogeneity (alpha = .34). At the same time, there is only one factor underlying the five items, indicating a high degree of unidimensionality. This index is called the Images of Violence Index in Violence Profile No. 11 (5).

REFERENCES

1. Bandura, Albert, Dorothea Ross, and Sheila Ross. "Transmission of Aggression through Imitation of Aggressive Models." *Journal of Abnormal and Social Psychology* 63, 1967, pp. 575–582.

2. Doob, Anthony N. and Glenn E. Macdonald. "Television Viewing and Fear of Victimization: Is the Relationship Causal?" *Journal of Personality and Social Psychology* 37(2), 1979, pp. 170–179.

3. Ellis, Glenn T. and Francis Sekura III. "The Effect of Aggressive Cartoons on the Behavior of First Grade Children." *Journal of Psychology* 81, 1972, pp. 7–43.

4. Gerbner, George, Larry Gross, Marilyn Jackson-Beeck, Suzanne Jeffries-Fox, and Nancy Signorielli. "Cultural Indicators: Violence Profile No. 9." *Journal of Communication* 28(3), Summer 1978, pp. 176–207.

5. Gerbner, George, Larry Gross, Michael Morgan, and Nancy Signorielli. "Violence Profile No. 11: Trends in Network Television Drama and Viewer Conceptions of Social Reality, 1967–1979." Technical Report, The Annenberg School of Communications, University of Pennsylvania, May 1980.

6. Gerbner, George, Larry Gross, Nancy Signorielli, and Michael Morgan. "Aging with Television: Images on Television Drama and Conceptions of Social Reality." *Journal of Communication* 30(1), Winter 1980, pp. 37–47.

7. Gross, Larry and Michael Morgan. "Television and Enculturation." In J. R. Dominick and J. Fletcher (Eds.) *Broadcasting Research Methods: A Reader.* Boston: Allyn and Bacon, in press.

8. Hirsch, Paul. "The 'Scary World' of the Nonviewer and Other Anomalies: A Reanalysis of Findings on the Cultivation Hypothesis, Part I." Paper presented at the 35th Annual Conference of the American Association for Public Opinion Research, Cincinnati, May 1980. Also, *Communication Research,* in press.

9. Hughes, Michael. "The Fruits of Cultivation Analysis: A Re-examination of the Effects of Television Watching on Fear of Victimization, Alienation, and the Approval of Violence." *Public Opinion Quarterly,* in press.

10. Krippendorff, Klaus. "Bivariate Agreement Coefficients for the Reliability of Data." In E. F. Borgatta and G. W. Bohrnstedt (Eds.) *Sociological Methodology 1970.* San Francisco: Jossey-Bass, 1970.

11. Lovas, O. I. "Effects of Exposure to Symbolic Aggression on Aggressive Behavior." *Child Development* 32, 1961, pp. 37–44.

12. Rosenberg, Morris. *Occupations and Values.* Glencoe, Ill.: Free Press, 1957.

13. Rothschild, Nancy F. "Group as a Mediating Factor in the Cultivation Process Among Young Children." Unpublished master's thesis, The Annenberg School of Communications, University of Pennsylvania, 1979.

14. Srole, Leo. "Social Integration and Certain Correlaries: An Exploratory Study." *American Sociological Review* 21, 1956, pp. 709–712.

15. Stevens, Geoffrey. "TV and Attitudes of Fear and Alienation." Unpublished master's thesis, The Annenberg School of Communications, University of Pennsylvania, 1980.

5.2 MICHAEL MORGAN

Television and Democracy

Michael Morgan has expanded the focus of cultivation research to include such issues as computers in the home, television and academic achievement, media and the family, and TV in the classroom. He is an associate professor of communication at the University of Massachusetts, Amherst, and he has published many scholarly articles.

In the following excerpt from his essay "Television and Democracy," in Ian Angus and Sut Jhally, eds., *Cultural Politics in Contemporary America* (Routledge, 1989), Morgan focuses on the relationship between television and the democratic process. His cultivation analysis shows that heavy TV viewers, no matter what their actual political party affiliation, tend to identify themselves as "middle of the road" or "moderate." Likewise, and perhaps more troubling, heavy TV viewers from all classes tend to describe themselves as middle class. These viewer perceptions closely resemble the world of TV content, which systematically avoids representing "extreme" or "deviant" viewpoints. Morgan argues that this convergence of viewpoints toward a mythical "middle" represents a narrowing-down and homogenization of the political culture of the United States and that it is dangerous for democracy.

Key Concept: mainstreaming

*T*his essay explores the implications of television for a democratic system based on some theories and empirical findings from a long-term, ongoing research project called Cultural Indicators. Cultural Indicators is a three-pronged research strategy designed to investigate (1) the institutional processes underlying the production of television content, (2) the most common and stable "facts of life" in the world of television content (called *message system analysis*), and (3) relationships between exposure to television's messages and audience beliefs and behavior (called *cultivation analysis*). In particular, this essay will draw upon findings from the cultivation analysis aspects of the project.

The basic hypothesis guiding cultivation analysis is that the more time one spends watching television (that is, the more television dominates one's sources of information and consciousness), the more likely one is to hold conceptions of reality that can be traced to television's most stable and recurrent portrayals of life and society. For more than 15 years, cultivation analyses have produced consistent evidence that television viewing makes an independent contribution to people's images and assumptions about violence, sex roles, aging, occupations, education, science, health, religion, and other issues.

This essay highlights some findings from this research that relate to television's impact on political orientations, beliefs, and behavior. To most people in the United States, "politics" is a very narrow term relating to elections, campaigns, and running for office; but "politics" here is also used in the broader sense to encompass the allocation and distribution of social resources and the structures of social power. The data from these studies suggest that television does cultivate underlying values and ideologies about social power in the United States. These outcomes sometimes support but often pose a challenge to democratic principles and practices.

There are several reasons why television in America does not fit well the traditional concept of the role mass communication should play in a democratic society. The press in a democracy is supposed to be a selectively used medium, with readers searching out material which confirms and expands their point of view. Television, however, provides a relatively restricted set of choices for an almost unlimited variety of interests. Unlike print media, television is viewed relatively *non*-selectively; most people watch by the clock, not the program. Television does not require either literacy or mobility, and it provides a steady stream of politically relevant messages to nearly everyone, whether they actively seek them or not.

As with all cultural artifacts and products, television programs reflect and are shaped by cultural assumptions which are often invisible simply because they are so taken for granted. Patterns of casting and demography, conventions of portraying "human nature," and incidental, backdrop images of "reality" carry political and cultural significance.

The stories of a culture reflect and cultivate its most basic and fundamental assumptions, ideologies, and values. From myths and legends to fairy tales and nursery rhymes, from religious parables to fast-food commercials, the function of stories is to enculturate children and provide continual socialization for adults, to remind them what exists and what doesn't, what is important, good and bad, right and wrong.

Television is most of all a centralized system of storytelling. It brings a stable and coherent world of common images and messages into virtually every home in the United States. Television has become the primary, *common* source of everyday culture, politics, and values of an otherwise heterogeneous population. Tens of millions of people who had been scattered, isolated, provincial, and culturally and politically distant, are now brought into the mainstream by television.

In the average U.S. home, the television is on for more than seven hours a day. As we often hear, by the time children finish high school, they will have spent more time watching television than in school; they will have seen about 18,000 violent deaths and will have spent thousands of *hours* of their lives watching commercials. Adults spend more time watching television than doing anything else except sleeping and working. Storytelling traditionally relies upon repetition; the extent to which we are exposed to repetitive lessons through television is historically unprecedented.

The television system in the United States attracts its massive audiences by offering to all, no matter how young or old, rich or poor, the most broadly acceptable world of stories and action. Each night, 90 million people sit down and spend several hours watching mostly the same programs. Television provides, perhaps for the first time since pre-industrial religion, a strong cultural and political link between the elites and all other publics, in a shared daily ritual. As George Gerbner has put it, television is like religion, except most people watch TV more religiously. . . .

I have looked at the relationship between amount of television viewing and voting behavior over the last four U.S. presidential elections, by reanalyzing data from large national surveys. Each year, the National Opinion Research Center asks a sample of about 1500 people whether they voted in recent presidential elections, who they voted for, and, for non-voters, who they *would* have voted for if they had voted. The responses can then be compared across light, medium, and heavy television viewers.

The patterns are strong, consistent, and clear: those who watch more television are less likely to say they voted, by an average margin of about 10 percent. The relationship holds up despite statistical controls for age, income, education, sex, race, political orientation, party identification, and other powerful factors.

Over the last 12 years, heavy viewers were also more likely than light viewers to say that they either *did* or *would have* voted for the *loser*. The longer the time from the election, the wider the gap; that is, for each year that passes following an election, the more heavy viewers turn against the incumbent—including Ronald Reagan. Despite the fact that the vast bulk of political campaign money is spent on television, those who watch more television are less likely to vote, and less likely to say they voted for the winner.

This is not to imply that television alone is responsible for the steady declines in voter turnout since the 1940s. But television has turned political campaigns into a kind of spectator sport, where the only thing the viewer has to do is to tune in to see who won—even if the media have already announced it *before* the election. . . .

But the implications of television in a democratic political system go deeper than voting, candidates, and elections. Over the last 35 years television has transformed political reality in the United States, but the actual nature of that transformation has gone almost unnoticed. In part, this is because we've been asking the wrong questions.

Much research and debate on the impact of mass communication has tended to focus on individual messages, programs, series, or genres, usually in terms of their ability to produce immediate changes in audience attitudes and behavior. Also, it has been assumed that news and information programs are the major sources of people's political orientations, attitudes, and opinions.

In contrast, cultivation analysis is concerned with more general and pervasive consequences of overall immersion in a cumulative exposure to television. It sees television's impact not so much in change among individuals as in *resistance* to change, or in slow but steady shifts across generations. What cuts across most programs, what is largely inescapable regardless of whatever content "types" are "selected," is what counts. Focusing on plots and surface features may distract from what we really absorb.

The underlying political messages of regular entertainment may be among the least visible aspects of television, but they may also be among the most significant. The amount of attention given to such controversial fare as "Rambo," "White Knights," and "Amerika" may deflect attention away from the day-to-day political messages which permeate prime-time drama. From the cultivation perspective, regular, everyday entertainment may be a tremendously powerful means for expressing and sustaining cultural beliefs and values. Most people, most of the time, watch dramatic, fictional entertainment, which teaches them many basic lessons, facts, and values about social and political reality.

Television tells us, over and over, what different social types can and should do, and what fate has in store for them. Its dramatic portrayals of crime, adventure, sex roles, minorities, courtrooms and the conflicts of urban life provide vivid and consistent lessons for viewers. Those basic lessons contribute to broadly shared, common assumptions about risks and opportunities, vulnerabilities and power—the building blocks of political orientations. . . .

Institutional and economic pressures mean that these basic underlying features of the television world are remarkably stable and consistent over time, despite surface-level novelties and fads that come and go. In the United States, about $55 million of revenue rides on every rating point. So, program producers *have* to create programs with the broadest possible appeal. That means avoiding political (and most other) "extremes," or making them as bland and non-threatening as possible, glorifying conventional consumer values, and striving for a safe, respectable, "middle-of-the-road" balance in most things.

Avoiding perceived extremes has always been television's strategy, as networks and advertisers expect attacks from special interest groups on the right *and* the left. What the television industry fears most is that people might get upset with what they watch and turn off the TV; so industry takes the obvious way out—navigating between (relative) extremes, safely in the comfortable mainstream that alienates no one and attracts the largest possible audience. "Deviant" or "extreme" groups are rarely shown, or are harshly criticized. All presentations *must* appear "objective," "moderate," "non-ideological," and otherwise suitable for mass marketing.

Some people are to the left of the television mainstream, and others are to the right; in order to maximize its audience, television attempts to steer a middle course—and in the process absorbs and homogenizes people with otherwise divergent orientations. This process of convergence is called "mainstreaming." One result is that those who watch more television are more likely to call themselves moderate (and less likely to say they are liberal or conservative) than light viewers. That is, the more time people spend watching television, the less they claim to be either liberal *or* conservative, and the more they say they are "moderate, middle-of-the-road."

The images of political reality television presents to people in the United States are highly constricted. We are given a basic continuum running from a "liberal left" to a "conservative right." It's a simple continuum, not multidimensional, and has a fairly narrow range. Positions and perspectives *outside* that narrow range of political discourse essentially do not exist.

Every issue is presented as having a "liberal" and a "conservative" side— e.g., abortion, homosexuality, school prayer, gun control, racial equality, women's rights, etc.—and the most consistent message is that the "truth" always lies somewhere in between—in the middle, in the mainstream. And the more that people watch television, the more they place themselves in that moderate, middle position.

The mainstreaming effects of television are extremely interesting within groups defined by party affiliation. . . .

The more that members of all three parties watch television, the more they choose the moderate label. . . . Heavy viewing Democrats and Independents are less likely to choose either the liberal *or* conservative label. Among Republicans, heavy viewers are less likely to call themselves conservatives, and more likely to say they are either moderate or liberal. Television blurs and distorts the impact of party on where people place themselves on the political spectrum—all groups say they are "moderate" if they watch more TV.

This finding that heavy viewers see themselves as "moderate" holds up in survey after survey, in subgroup after subgroup. And, it's specific to television, not a correlate of general media use; the same results do *not* apply to radio listening or newspaper reading. It is television, and television alone, which cultivates "moderate" self-perceptions in its audiences, in line with the mainstream political lessons of television.

This may be part of a more general phenomenon: the cultivation of homogeneous, "average" self-perceptions. In addition to political moderation, the television world is dominated by characters who fit squarely in the "middle-middle" of a five-point social class category scale; middle-class characters vastly outnumber all others.

Cultivation research has found that when people whose objective social class is low watch more television, they are more likely to call themselves "middle class" as opposed to "working class." Middle-class viewers show the least sense of class distinction at different viewing levels; they are already "in" the mainstream. The upper classes, however, like the lower, show a pattern that is strongly associated with amount of television viewing; the more they watch, the *lower* their self-designated class. Heavy viewers are also more likely to say they have "average" incomes, particularly as real income increases.

Thus, the television experience seems to swamp other circumstances in thinking of one's class. Television viewing tends to blur class distinctions as it does political labels, and to make more affluent heavy viewers think of themselves as just working people of average income. Long-term, cumulative exposure to the consumer-oriented demography and middle-class supremacy of television tends to confound real class distinctions and to cultivate "average" or "middle class" self-perceptions as the norm of the television mainstream.

On the surface, mainstreaming looks like a "centering" or "middling" of political tendencies. But if we look at the actual positions heavy viewers take on specific political issues, we see that the mainstream does not run down the "middle-of-the-road."

Television viewing makes an independent contribution to what people in the United States think about the hard political issues of our times such as women and minorities, fairness and individual rights, defense spending and welfare, taxes and other issues. Its contribution reflects the most common, stable, and repetitive messages of the fictional world of dramatic television. . . .

But the patterns are for different groups; cultivation depends upon where one is in relation to the mainstream. . . . On . . . issues [such as busing, open housing, laws against intermarriage, homosexuality, abortion, and the legalization of marijuana], the traditional polarization of liberals and conservatives turns into a homogenization of views, in the direction of the television mainstream. These otherwise disparate groups find common ground in, converge, and blend into, the television mainstream.

For example, in terms of attitudes towards racial segregation, [there is a] relationship between amount of viewing and respondents' opposition to busing. Heavy viewing conservatives are more "liberal" and heavy viewing liberals more "conservative" than their respective light viewing counterparts. . . . [H]eavy viewers of all three groups are more likely to oppose laws about open housing, but . . . the relationship is strongest among those who call themselves liberal. . . . [Regarding] laws against marriages between blacks and whites, television viewing cultivates a more restrictive attitude among all three political subgroups, but this is significantly more pronounced for liberals, whose heavy viewers join in the anti-integration mainstream. Again and again, light viewers are more diverse and heavy viewers more concentrated, and the three groups converge upon the conservative position.

. . . The sample patterns show up in terms of many other issues—sexual tolerance, freedom of speech, approval of legalizing marijuana, and many, many others.

Among heavy viewers, the difference between liberals, moderates, and conservatives are greatly reduced. But the most notable trend is the erosion of the traditionally "liberal" view among heavy viewers. In general, those who call themselves conservatives are "already" in the television mainstream. But liberals express traditionally "liberal" views *only* if they are light viewers. Mainstreaming means not only a narrowing of political differences but also a significant tilt in a conservative direction. Most consistently it reveals a significant loss of support for personal and political freedoms among liberals.

Something entirely different occurs when we look at responses to questions about *economic* issues of government spending and taxes. Instead of heavy viewing liberals taking positions closer to conservatives, the opposite happens: heavy viewing conservatives, as well as moderates, converge toward the traditionally *liberal* position of wanting the government to spend *more* on social programs, such as health, the environment, welfare, the cities, etc. The more people watch, the less they say we spend "too much"; heavy viewers endorse greater government spending, rather than cuts. (Needless to say, heavy viewers are also more likely to think we should be spending more on arms and defense, although here we see the familiar pattern of liberals converging with conservatives.)

At the same time, heavy viewers are more likely to feel their taxes are too high. Those who watch more television are more likely to hold these contradictory positions simultaneously—within every demographic subgroup, heavy viewers are more likely to want more social spending *and* lower taxes.

All this relates to and clarifies television's contribution to many other conceptions of social reality. The more people watch television, the more they are fearful and afraid. They are more willing to accept repressive measures in the name of security, and to approve of more extreme ways to punish those who break the rules of the system. They are alienated, depolicitized, and afraid both of crime in the streets and of world war. They want more protection, more money for fighting crime and drug abuse, more money for defense, but—of course—no more taxes. Heavy viewers of all political persuasions hold these conflicting beliefs more than do light viewers in the same groups.

Television thus contributes to the current political scene in the United States in three ways. First, it blurs the impact of traditional party, class, regional, and other social differences. Among light viewers, factors such as whether you call yourself a liberal, moderate, or conservative, or your social class, or what region of the country you live in, are all powerful determinants of political beliefs. But if you're a heavy viewer, these factors play a much smaller role. Living in the cultural and political mainstream of television thus appears to be diminishing the influence of social forces that traditionally governed political behavior.

Second, television blends otherwise divergent perspectives and ways of labeling one's self into its own mainstream. That is, heavy viewers of all groups are more likely to call themselves moderate, average, middle class.

And third, television bends that mainstream to the purposes of the medium's own marketing and other commercial interests. The result is that heavy viewers are conservative on social issues but liberal on economic issues.

Television cultivates a set of paradoxical currents. In a nutshell, heavy viewers think like conservatives, want like liberals, and yet call themselves moderates. They are less likely to vote but quicker to turn against an incumbent. They think elected officials don't care about what happens to them but are more interested in their personal lives than in their policies. They want to cut taxes but improve education, medical care, social security. They distrust big government but want it to fix things for them, to protect them at home and from foreign threats. They praise freedom but want to restrict anyone who uses it in an unconventional way. They are losing confidence in people who run virtually all institutions, including religion, but they express trust in God, America—and television.

Taken together, these findings suggest that democracy itself may be compromised by these unintended and incidental effects of television. Some may believe that democracy works best when the people don't care much about politics but are deeply concerned about hair spray and deodorants. But the important question, and the critical challenge to democracy, is whether or not citizens are helpless in the tidal wave of the television mainstream.

The answer will depend on the ability of people whose interests are not well served by the television mainstream to mobilize and activate voters to influence both television and public policy. It will depend on our ability to equalize the flow of influence between television and the citizenry, to make television more responsive to rewards besides commercial profit. And it will depend on the extent to which this centralized system of storytelling continues to dominate the symbolic environment and our political consciousness—because these patterns are not *necessary* effects of television *per se*, but the consequences of particular institutional and commercial arrangements which have made television the mainstream of American culture.

The concept of democracy implies that citizens can participate in their political governance on a basis of equality. Numerous studies suggest that even the youngest North Americans value highly the principles of popular government, voting, equality, pluralism. But television—again, not by design, not by conspiracy, but by commercial imperative—tends to work against these principles in practice, while probably strengthening support of the principles.

Any democratic system requires communication for stability, growth, and survival. Democracy in a large and complex society depends upon mass communication to tell us things we "need" to know in a relatively "objective" and comprehensive fashion, since in a large and complex society it is virtually impossible to find out such things for ourselves *without* mass media.

Television is by no means the most powerful influence on people, but it is the most *common;* what it teaches most people, most of the time, is of the highest political, cultural, and moral importance. As mass media become more centralized and homogeneous, the cultural currents become narrower, more standardized, and more sharply defined, and mass communication becomes a more effective mechanism of social control.

In a commercial mass communication system, corporate interests rarely give way to the *public* interest. Concentration of ownership in fewer and fewer hands, and the need to attract larger and larger heterogeneous audiences, together create blander and less diverse content; when nothing but ratings and commercial profit drive the media, the result can be apathetic and alienated citizens, who nonetheless remain obedient to the authority of the marketplace.

Mass communication is the mass production of the symbolic environment, of the cultural contexts within which we live and define ourselves and others. Earlier media did give us a broader range of sometimes antagonistic perspectives and ideologies. But television has meant that more and more people are exposed to messages created and controlled by fewer and fewer, and in far greater doses, than ever before.

The television mainstream is turning out to be the true twentieth-century melting pot of the United States. Increasingly, it may be having similar consequences around the globe, as dozens and dozens of countries have found that importing U.S. programs is easier and cheaper than producing their own. International and cross-cultural extensions of the research summarized here is now being conducted or planned in numerous other countries, including Argentina, China, India, and others. The results in the United States and elsewhere will be of central significance for the theory as well as for the practice of popular democratic self-government in the television age.

REFERENCES

The theories and research findings discussed in this paper are derived from the work of the Cultural Indicators Project, directed by George Gerbner and Larry

Gross (The Annenberg School of Communications, University of Pennsylvania), Michael Morgan (Department of Communication, University of Massachusetts), and Nancy Signorielli (Department of Communication, University of Delaware). See George Gerbner, Larry Gross, Michael Morgan, and Nancy Signorielli, "The Dynamics of the Cultivation Process," in J. Bryant and D. Zillman, eds., *Perspective on Media Effects* (Hillsdale, NJ: Erlbaum, 1986), pp. 17–40; "Political Correlates of Television Viewing," *Public Opinion Quarterly,* 48 (Spring 1984), 283–300; "Charting the Mainstream: Television's Contributions to Political Orientations," *Journal of Communication,* 32:2 (Spring 1982), 100–127; "The 'Mainstreaming' of America: Violence Profile No. 11," *Journal of Communication,* 30:3 (Summer 1980), 10–29; "Television Violence, Victimization, and Power," *American Behavioral Scientists,* 23:5 (1980), 705–716; Larry Gross, "The Cultivation of Intolerance: Television, Blacks, and Gays," in G. Melischek, K. E. Rosengren, and J. Stappers, eds., *Cultural Indicators: An International Symposium* (Vienna: Austrian Academy of Sciences, 1984), pp. 345–364; Larry Gross and Michael Morgan, "Television and Enculturation," in J. Dominick and J. Fletcher, eds., *Broadcasting Research Methods* (Boston: Allyn and Bacon, 1985), pp. 221–234; Michael Morgan, "Television and the Erosion of Regional Diversity," *Journal of Broadcasting and Electronic Media,* 30:2 (Spring 1986), 123–139; and Michael Morgan, "Symbolic Victimization and Real-World Fear," *Human Communication Research,* 9:2 (1983), 146–157.

PART TWO

Media of Communication

CHAPTER 6 Media Bias and Sense Extension

6.1 MARSHALL McLUHAN

Understanding Media: The Extensions of Man

The media theories of Canadian literary critic Marshall McLuhan (1911–1980) have been hailed by some as the work of a "visionary" and by others as the work of a "crackpot." His work was influenced by the turbulent 1960s, when many new electronic forms of communication—including VCRs, satellites, portable audio technologies, and microcomputers—were becoming more widespread. McLuhan broke away from issues of media content and focused on technological form. His famous statement "The medium is the message" is an indication of the way McLuhan looked for the unique characteristics of a medium to understand how it communicates messages and influences users' perspectives. With his novel viewpoint, McLuhan influenced a host of scholars who were attracted to the idea that the medium itself has the ability to influence users' senses of space and time.

In the following selection from the introduction and a chapter of his well-known book *Understanding Media: The Extensions of Man*, 2d ed. (New American Library, 1964), McLuhan discusses some of his most controversial ideas. Taking the perspective that media creates and influences new environments, he asserts that the individual is "hypnotized" by the media experience and is unaware of the ways technology influences the environment and the content of media.

Key Concept: media form and sensory extension

Any technology gradually creates a totally new human environment. Environments are not passive wrappings but active processes. In his splendid work *Preface to Plato* (Harvard University Press, 1963), Eric Havelock contrasts the oral and written cultures of the Greeks. By Plato's time the written word had created a new environment that had begun to detribalize man. Previously the Greeks had grown up by benefit of the process of the *tribal encyclopedia.* They had memorized the poets. The poets provided specific operational wisdom for all the contingencies of life—Ann Landers in verse. With the advent of individual detribalized man, a new education was needed. Plato devised such a new program for literate men. It was based on the Ideas. With the phonetic alphabet, classified wisdom took over from the operational wisdom of Homer and Hesiod and the tribal encyclopedia. Education by classified data has been the Western program ever since.

Now, however, in the electronic age, data classification yields to pattern recognition, the key phrase at IBM. When data move instantly, classification is too fragmentary. In order to cope with data at electric speed in typical situations of "information overload," men resort to the study of configurations, like the sailor in Edgar Allan Poe's *Maelstrom.* The drop-out situation in our schools at present has only begun to develop. The young student today grows up in an electrically configured world. It is a world not of wheels but of circuits, not of fragments but of integral patterns. The student today *lives* mythically and in depth. At school, however, he encounters a situation organized by means of classified information. The subjects are unrelated. They are visually conceived in terms of a blueprint. The student can find no possible means of involvement for himself, nor can he discover how the educational scene relates to the "mythic" world of electronically processed data and experience that he takes for granted. As one IBM executive puts it, "My children had lived several lifetimes compared to their grandparents when they began grade one."

"The medium is the message" means, in terms of the electronic age, that a totally new environment has been created. The "content" of this new environment is the old mechanized environment of the industrial age. The new environment reprocesses the old one as radically as TV is reprocessing the film. For the "content" of TV is the movie. TV is environmental and imperceptible, like all environments. We are aware only of the "content" or the old environment. When machine production was new, it gradually created an environment whose content was the old environment of agrarian life and the arts and crafts. This older environment was elevated to an art form by the new mechanical environment. The machine turned Nature into an art form. For the first time men began to regard Nature as a source of aesthetic and spiritual values. They began to marvel that earlier ages had been so unaware of the world of Nature as Art. Each new technology creates an environment that is itself regarded as corrupt and degrading. Yet the new one turns its predecessor into an art form. When writing was new, Plato transformed the old oral dialogue into an art form. When printing was new the Middle Ages became an art form. "The Elizabethan world view" was a view of the Middle Ages. And the industrial age turned the Renaissance into an art form as seen in the work of Jacob Burckhardt. Siegfried Giedion, in turn, has in the electric age taught us how to see the entire process of mechanization as an art process. (*Mechanization Takes Command*). . . .

INTRODUCTION

James Reston wrote in *The New York Times* (July 7, 1957):

> A health director . . . reported this week that a small mouse, which presumably had been watching television, attacked a little girl and her full-grown cat. . . . Both mouse and cat survived, and the incident is recorded here as a reminder that things seem to be changing.

After three thousand years of explosion, by means of fragmentary and mechanical technologies, the Western world is imploding. During the mechanical ages we had extended our bodies in space. Today, after more than a century of electric technology, we have extended our central nervous system itself in a global embrace, abolishing both space and time as far as our planet is concerned. Rapidly, we approach the final phase of the extensions of man—the technological simulation of consciousness, when the creative process of knowing will be collectively and corporately extended to the whole of human society, much as we have already extended our senses and our nerves by the various media. Whether the extension of consciousness, so long sought by advertisers for specific products, will be "a good thing" is a question that admits of a wide solution. There is little possibility of answering such questions about the extensions of man without considering all of them together. Any extension, whether of skin, hand, or foot, affects the whole psychic and social complex.

Some of the principal extensions, together with some of their psychic and social consequences, are studied [here]. Just how little consideration has been given to such matters in the past can be gathered from the consternation of one of the editors of this [selection]. He noted in dismay that "seventy-five per cent of your material is new. A successful book cannot venture to be more than ten per cent new." Such a risk seems quite worth taking at the present time when the stakes are very high, and the need to understand the effects of the extensions of man becomes more urgent by the hour.

In the mechanical age now receding, many actions could be taken without too much concern. Slow movement insured that the reactions were delayed for considerable periods of time. Today the action and the reaction occur almost at the same time. We actually live mythically and integrally, as it were, but we continue to think in the old, fragmented space and time patterns of the pre-electric age.

Western man acquired from the technology of literacy the power to act without reacting. The advantages of fragmenting himself in this way are seen in the case of the surgeon who would be quite helpless if he were to become humanly involved in his operation. We acquired the art of carrying out the most dangerous social operations with complete detachment. But our detachment was a posture of noninvolvement. In the electric age, when our central nervous system is technologically extended to involve us in the whole of mankind and to incorporate the whole of mankind in us, we necessarily participate, in depth, in the consequences of our every action. It is no longer possible to adopt the aloof and dissociated role of the literate Westerner. . . .

THE MEDIUM IS THE MESSAGE

In a culture like ours, long accustomed to splitting and dividing all things as a means of control, it is sometimes a bit of a shock to be reminded that, in operational and practical fact, the medium is the message. This is merely to say that the personal and social consequences of any medium—that is, of any extension of ourselves—result from the new scale that is introduced into our affairs by each extension of ourselves, or by any new technology. Thus, with automation, for example the new patterns of human association tend to eliminate jobs, it is true. That is the negative result. Positively, automation creates roles for people, which is to say depth of involvement in their work and human association that our preceding mechanical technology had destroyed. Many people would be disposed to say that it was not the machine, but what one did with the machine, that was its meaning or message. In terms of the ways in which the machine altered our relations to one another and to ourselves, it mattered not in the least whether it turned out cornflakes or Cadillacs. The restructuring of human work and association was shaped by the technique of fragmentation that is the essence of machine technology. The essence of automation technology is the opposite. It is integral and decentralist in depth, just as the machine was fragmentary, centralist, and superficial in its patterning of human relationships.

The instance of the electric light may prove illuminating in this connection. The electric light is pure information. It is a medium without a message, as it were, unless it is used to spell out some verbal ad or name. This fact, characteristic of all media, means that the "content" of any medium is always another medium. The content of writing is speech, just as the written word is the content of print, and print is the content of the telegraph. If it is asked, "What is the content of speech?," it is necessary to say, "It is an actual process of thought, which is in itself nonverbal." An abstract painting represents direct manifestation of creative thought processes as they might appear in computer designs. What we are considering here, however, are the psychic and social consequences of the designs or patterns as they amplify or accelerate existing processes. For the "message" of any medium or technology is the change of sale or pace or pattern that it introduces into human affairs. The railway did not introduce movement or transportation or wheel or road into human society, but it accelerated and enlarged the scale of previous human functions, creating totally new kinds of cities and new kinds of work and leisure. This happened whether the railway functioned in a tropical or a northern environment, and is quite independent of the freight or content of the railway medium. The airplane, on the other hand, by accelerating the rate of transportation, tends to dissolve the railway form of city, politics, and association, quite independently of what the airplane is used for.

Let us return to the electric light. Whether the light is being used for brain surgery or night baseball is a matter of indifference. It could be argued that these activities are in some way the "content" of the electric light, since they could not exist without the electric light. This fact merely underlines the point that "the medium is the message" because it is the medium that shapes and controls the scale and form of human association and action. The content or uses of such media are as diverse as they are ineffectual in shaping the form of human association. Indeed, it is only too typical that the "content" of any medium blinds us to the character of the medium. It is only today that industries have become aware of the various kinds of business in which they are engaged. When IBM discovered that it was not in the business of making office equipment or business machines, but that it was in the business of processing information, then it began to navigate with clear vision. The General Electric Company makes a considerable portion of its profits from electric light bulbs and lighting systems. It has not yet discovered that, quite as much as A.T.&T., it is in the business of moving information. . . .

In accepting an honorary degree from the University of Notre Dame . . . , General David Sarnoff made this statement: "We are too prone to make technological instruments the scapegoats for the sins of those who wield them. The products of modern science are not in themselves good or bad; it is the way they are used that determines their value." That is the voice of the current somnambulism. Suppose we were to say, "Apple pie is in itself neither good nor bad; it is the way it is used that determines its value." Or, "The smallpox virus is in itself neither good nor bad; it is the way it is used the determines its value." Again, "Firearms are in themselves neither good nor bad; it is the way they are used that determines their value." That is, if the slugs reach the right people firearms are good. If the TV tube fires the right ammunition at the right people it is good. I am not being perverse. There is simply nothing in the Sarnoff statement that will bear scrutiny, for it ignores the nature of the medium, of any and all media, in the true Narcissus style of one hypnotized by the amputation and extension of its own being in a new technical form. General Sarnoff went on to explain his attitude to the technology of print, saying that it was true that print caused much trash to circulate, but it had also disseminated the bible and the thoughts of seers and philosophers. It has never occurred to General Sarnoff that any technology could do anything but *add* itself on to what we already are. . . .

Just before an airplane breaks the sound barrier, sound waves become visible on the wings of the plane. The sudden visibility of sound just as sound ends is an apt instance of that great pattern of being that reveals new and opposite forms just as the earlier forms reach their peak performance. Mechanization was never so vividly fragmented or sequential as in the birth of the movies, the moment that translated us beyond mechanism into the world of growth and organic interrelation. The movie, by sheer speeding up the mechanical, carried us from the world of sequence and connections into the world of creative configuration and structure. The message of the movie medium is that of transition from lineal connections to configurations. It is the transition that produced the now quite correct observation: "If it works, it's obsolete." When electric speed further takes over from mechanical movie sequences, then the lines of force in structures and in media become loud and clear. We return to the inclusive from of the icon.

To a highly literate and mechanized culture the movie appeared as a world of triumphant illusions and dreams that money could buy. It was at this moment of the movie that cubism occurred, and it has been described by E. H. Gombrich (*Art and Illusion*) as "the most radical attempt to stamp out ambiguity and to enforce one reading of the picture—that of a man-made construction, a colored canvas." For cubism substitutes all facets of an object simultaneously for the "point of view" or facet of perspective illusion. Instead of the specialized illusion of the third dimension on canvas, cubism sets up an interplay of planes and contradiction or dramatic conflict of patterns, lights, textures that "drives home the message" by involvement. This is held by many to be an exercise in painting, not in illusion.

In other words, cubism, by giving the inside and outside, the top, bottom, back, and front and the rest, in two dimensions, drops the illusion of perspective in favor of instant sensory awareness of the whole. Cubism, by seizing on instant total awareness, suddenly announced that *the medium is the message.* Is it not evident that the moment that sequence yields to the simultaneous, one is in the world of the structure and of configuration? Is that not what has happened in physics as in painting, poetry, and in communication? Specialized segments of attention have shifted to total field, and we can now say, "The medium is the message" quite naturally. Before the electric speed and total field, it was not obvious that the medium is the message. The message, it seemed, was the "content," as people used to ask what a painting was *about.* Yet they never thought to ask what a melody was about, nor what a house or a dress was about. In such matters, people retained some sense of the whole pattern, of form and function as a unity. But in the electric age this integral idea of structure and configuration has become so prevalent that educational theory has taken up the matter. Instead of working with specialized "problems" in arithmetic, the structural approach now follows the linea of force in the field of number and has small children meditating about number theory and "sets."

Cardinal Newman said of Napoleon, "He understood the grammar of gunpowder." Napoleon had paid some attention to other media as well, especially the semaphore telegraph that gave him a great advantage over his enemies. He is on record for saying that "Three hostile newspapers are more to be feared than a thousand bayonets."

. . . [Alexis] de Tocqueville, in earlier work on the French Revolution, had explained how it was the printed word that, achieving cultural saturation in the eighteenth century, had homogenized the French nation. Frenchmen were the same kind of people from north to south. The typographic principles of uniformity, continuity, and lineality had overlaid the complexities of ancient feudal and oral society. The Revolution was carried out by the new literati and lawyers.

In England, however, such was the power of the ancient oral traditions of common law, backed by the medieval institution of Parliament, that no uniformity or continuity of the new visual print culture could take complete hold. The result was that the most important event in English history has never taken place; namely, the English Revolution on the lines of the French Revolution. The American Revolution had no medieval legal institutions to discard or to root out, apart from monarchy. And many have held that the American Presidency has become very much more personal and monarchical than any European monarch ever could be.

De Tocqueville's contrast between England and America is clearly based on the fact of typography and of print culture creating uniformity and continuity. England, he says, has rejected this principle and clung to the dynamic or oral common-law tradition. Hence the discontinuity and unpredictable quality of English culture. The grammar of print cannot help to construe the message of oral and nonwritten culture and institutions. The English aristocracy was properly classified as barbarian by Matthew Arnold because its power and status had nothing to do with literacy or with the cultural forms of typography. Said the Duke of Gloucester to Edward Gibbon upon the publication of his *Decline and Fall:* "Another damned fat book, eh, Mr. Gibbon? Scribble, scribble, scribble, eh, Mr. Gibbon?" De Tocqueville was a highly literate aristocrat who was quite able to be detached from the values and assumptions of typography. That is why he alone understood the grammar of typography. And it is only on those terms, standing aside from any structure or medium, that its principles and lines of force can be discerned. For any medium has the power of imposing its own assumption on the unwary. Prediction and control consist in avoiding this subliminal state of Narcissus trance. But the greatest aid to this end is simply in knowing that the spell can occur immediately upon contact, as in the first bars of a melody.

. . . Our conventional response to all media, namely that it is how they are used that counts, is the numb stance of the technological idiot. For the "content" of a medium is like the juicy piece of meat carried by the burglar to distract the watchdog of the mind. The effect of the medium is made strong and intense just because it is given another medium as "content." The content of a movie is a novel or a play or an opera. The effect of the movie form is not related to its program content. The "content" of writing or print is speech, but the reader is almost entirely unaware either of print or of speech.

The Age of Show Business

New York University professor Neil Postman has written extensively on the way media environments influence and change social practices. Some of his books include *The Disappearance of Childhood* (Vintage Books, 1982), *Conscientious Objections* (Vintage Books, 1988), and *Technopoly* (Alfred A. Knopf, 1992).

The following selection is taken from one of his most influential books, *Amusing Ourselves to Death: Public Discourse in the Age of Show Business* (Penguin, 1985). In it, Postman shows how practices of public discourse are repackaged in media environments to be presented as forms of entertainment. He claims that when media present serious issues, television audiences in particular are left with an impression formed by television's bias for entertainment programming.

Postman focuses on the unique characteristics of media form and its ability to influence both the message and the audience's perception of the message. He points out that various cultures use television for different purposes; thus, the medium helps shape, and is also shaped by, the North American cultural experience. Finally, Postman calls for more criticism of the way media packages and presents content.

Key Concept: entertainment and media bias

A dedicated graduate student I know returned to his small apartment the night before a major examination only to discover that his solitary lamp was broken beyond repair. After a whiff of panic, he was able to restore both his equanimity and his chances for a satisfactory grade by turning on the television set, turning off the sound, and with his back to the set, using its light to read important passages on which he was to be tested. This is one use of television—as a source of illuminating the printed page.

But the television screen is more than a light source. It is also a smooth, nearly flat surface on which the printed word may be displayed. We have all stayed at hotels in which the TV set has had a special channel for describing the day's events in letters rolled endlessly across the screen. This is another use of television—as an electronic bulletin board.

Many television sets are also large and sturdy enough to bear the weight of a small library. The top of an old-fashioned RCA console can handle as many as thirty books, and I know one woman who has securely placed her entire collection of Dickens, Flaubert, and Turgenev on the top of a 21-inch Westinghouse. Here is still another use of television—as bookcase.

I bring forward these quixotic uses of television to ridicule the hope harbored by some that television can be used to support the literate tradition. Such a hope represents exactly what Marshall McLuhan used to call "rear-view mirror" thinking: the assumption that a new medium is merely an extension or amplification of an older one; that an automobile, for example, is only a fast horse, or an electric light a powerful candle. To make such a mistake in the matter at hand is to misconstrue entirely how television redefines the meaning of public discourse. Television does not extend or amplify literate culture. It attacks it. If television is a continuation of anything, it is of a tradition begun by the telegraph and photograph in the mid-nineteenth century, not by the printing press in the fifteenth.

What is television? What kinds of conversations does it permit? What are the intellectual tendencies it encourages? What sort of culture does it produce?

. . . We might say that a technology is to a medium as the brain is to the mind. Like the brain, a technology is a physical apparatus. Like the mind, a medium is a use to which a physical apparatus is put. A technology becomes a medium as it employs a particular symbolic code, as it finds its place in a particular social setting, as it insinuates itself into economic and political contexts. A technology, in other words, is merely a machine. A medium is the social and intellectual environment a machine creates.

Of course, like the brain itself, every technology has an inherent bias. It has within its physical form a predisposition toward being used in certain ways and not others. Only those who know nothing of the history of technology believe that a technology is entirely neutral. There is an old joke that mocks that naive belief. Thomas Edison, it goes, would have revealed his discovery of the electric light much sooner than he did except for the fact that every time he turned it on, he held it to his mouth and said, "Hello? Hello?"

Not very likely. Each technology has an agenda of its own. It is, as I have suggested, a metaphor waiting to unfold. The printing press, for example, had a clear bias toward being used as a linguistic medium. It is *conceivable* to use it exclusively for the reproduction of pictures. And, one imagines, the Roman Catholic Church would not have objected to its being so used in the sixteenth century. Had that been the case, the Protestant Reformation might not have occurred, for as Luther contended, with the word of God on every family's kitchen table, Christians do not require the Papacy to interpret it for them. But in fact there never was much chance that the press would be used solely, or even very much, for the duplication of icons. From its beginning in the fifteenth century, the press was perceived as an extraordinary opportunity for the display and mass distribution of written language. Everything about its technical possibilities led in that direction. One might even say it was invented for that purpose.

The technology of television has a bias, as well. It is conceivable to use television as a lamp, a surface for texts, a bookcase, even as radio. But it has not been so used and will not be so used, at least in America. Thus, in answering the question, What is television?, we must understand as a first point that we are not talking about television as a technology but television as a medium. There are many places in the world where television, though the same technology as it is in America, is an entirely different medium from that which we know. I refer to places where the majority of people do not have television sets, and those who do have only one; where only one station is available; where television does not operate around the clock; where most programs have as their purpose the direct furtherance of government ideology and policy; where commercials are unknown, and "talking heads" are the principal image; where television is mostly used as if it were radio. For these reasons and more television will not have the same meaning or power as it does in America, which is to say, it is possible for a technology to be so used that its potentialities are prevented from developing and its social consequences kept to a minimum.

But in America, this has not been the case. Television has found in liberal democracy and a relatively free market economy a nurturing climate in which its full potentialities as a technology of images could be exploited. One result of this has been that American television programs are in demand all over the world. The total estimate of U.S. television program exports is approximately 100,000 to 200,000 hours, equally divided among Latin America, Asia and Europe. Over the years, programs like "Gunsmoke," "Bonanza," "Mission: Impossible," "Star Trek," "Kojak," and more recently, "Dallas" and "Dynasty" have been as popular in England, Japan, Israel and Norway as in Omaha, Nebraska. I have heard (but not verified) that some years ago the Lapps postponed for several days their annual and, one supposes, essential migratory journey so that they could find out who shot J.R.* All of this has occurred simultaneously with the decline of America's moral and political prestige, worldwide. American television programs are in demand not because America is loved but because American television is loved.

We need not be detained too long in figuring out why. In watching American television, one is reminded of George Bernard Shaw's remark on his first seeing the glittering neon signs of Broadway and 42nd Street at night. It must be beautiful, he said, if you cannot read. American television is, indeed, a beautiful spectacle, a visual delight, pouring forth thousands of images on any given day. The average length of a shot on network television is only 3.5 seconds, so that the eye never rests, always has something new to see. Moreover, television offers viewers a variety of subject matter, requires minimal skills to comprehend it, and is largely aimed at emotional gratification. Even commercials, which some regard as an annoyance, are exquisitely crafted, always pleasing to the eye and accompanied by exciting music. There is no question but that the best photography in the world is presently seen on television commercials. American television, in other words, is devoted entirely to supplying its audience with entertainment.

---

*[J. R. Ewing, a character on the prime-time soap opera "Dallas," was shot during the final episode of the 1979–1980 season. The November 21, 1980, episode, in which the identity of the shooter was revealed, became the highest-rated entertainment program in television history.—Eds.]

Of course, to say that television is entertaining is merely banal. Such a fact is hardly threatening to a culture, not even worth writing a book about. It may even be a reason for rejoicing. Life, as we like to say, is not a highway strewn with flowers. The sight of a few blossoms here and there may make our journey a trifle more endurable. The Lapps undoubtedly thought so. We may surmise that the ninety million Americans who watch television every night also think so. But what I am claiming here is not that television is entertaining but that it has made entertainment itself the natural format for the representation of all experience. Our television set keeps us in constant communion with the world, but it does so with a face whose smiling countenance is unalterable. The problem is not that television presents us with entertaining subject matter but that all subject matter is presented as entertaining, which is another issue altogether.

To say it still another way: Entertainment is the supraideology of all discourse on television. No matter what is depicted or from what point of view, the overarching presumption is that it is there for our amusement and pleasure. That is why even on news shows which provide us daily with fragments of tragedy and barbarism, we are urged by the newscasters to "join them tomorrow." What for? One would think that several minutes of murder and mayhem would suffice as material for a month of sleepless nights. We accept the newscasters' invitation because we know that the "news" is not to be taken seriously, that it is all in fun, so to say. Everything about a news show tells us this—the good looks and amiability of the cast, their pleasant banter, the exciting music that opens and closes the show, the vivid film footage, the attractive commercials—all these and more suggest that what we have just seen is no cause for weeping. A news show, to put it plainly, is a format for entertainment, not for education, reflection or catharsis. And we must not judge too harshly those who have framed it in this way. They are not assembling the news to be read, or broadcasting it to be heard. They are televising the news to be seen. They must follow where their medium leads. There is no conspiracy here, no lack of intelligence, only a straightforward recognition that "good television" has little to do with what is "good" about exposition or other forms of verbal communication but everything to do with what the pictorial images look like.

I should like to illustrate this point by offering the case of the eighty-minute discussion provided by the ABC network on November 20, 1983, following its controversial movie *The Day After*. Though the memory of this telecast has receded for most, I choose this case because, clearly, here was television taking its most "serious" and "responsible" stance. Everything that made up this broadcast recommended it as a critical test of television's capacity to depart from an entertainment mode and rise to the level of public instruction. In the first place, the subject was the possibility of a nuclear holocaust. Second, the film itself had been attacked by several influential bodies politic, including the Reverend Jerry Falwell's Moral Majority. Thus, it was important that the network display television's value and serious intentions as a medium of information and coherent discourse. Third, on the program itself no musical theme was used as background—a significant point since almost all television programs are embedded in music, which helps to tell the audience what emotions are to be called forth. This is a standard theatrical device, and its absence on television is always ominous. Fourth, there were no commercials during the discussion, thus elevating the tone of the event to the state of reverence usually reserved for the funerals of assassinated Presidents. And finally, the participants included Henry Kissinger, Robert McNamara, and Elie Wiesel, each of whom is a symbol of sorts of serious discourse. Although Kissinger, somewhat later, made an appearance on the hit show "Dynasty," he was then and still is a paradigm of intellectual sobriety; and Wiesel, practically a walking metaphor of social conscience. Indeed, the other members of the cast—Carl Sagan, William Buckley and General Brent Scowcroft—are, each in his way, men of intellectual bearing who are not expected to participate in trivial public matters.

The program began with Ted Koppel, master of ceremonies, so to speak, indicating that what followed was not intended to be a debate but a *discussion*. And so those who are interested in philosophies of discourse had an excellent opportunity to observe what serious television means by the word "discussion." Here is what it means: Each of six men was given approximately five minutes to say something about the subject. There was, however, no agreement on exactly what the subject was, and no one felt obliged to respond to anything anyone else said. In fact, it would have been difficult to do so, since the participants were called upon seriatim, as if they were finalists in a beauty contest, each being given his share of minutes in front of the camera. Thus, if Mr. Wiesel, who was called upon last, had a response to Mr. Buckley, who was called upon first, there would have been four commentaries in between, occupying about twenty minutes, so that the audience (if not Mr. Wiesel himself) would have had difficulty remembering the argument which prompted his response. In fact, the participants—most of whom were no strangers to television—largely avoided addressing each other's points. They used their initial minutes and then their subsequent ones to intimate their position or give an impression. Dr. Kissinger, for example, seemed intent on making viewers feel sorry that he was no longer their Secretary of State by reminding everyone of books he had once written, proposals he had once made, and negotiations he had once conducted. Mr. McNamara informed the audience that he had eaten lunch in Germany that very afternoon, and went on to say that he had at least fifteen proposals to reduce nuclear arms. One would have thought that the discussion would turn on this issue, but the others seemed about as interested in it as they were in what he had for lunch in Germany. (Later, he took the initiative to mention three of his proposals but they were not discussed.) Elie Wiesel, in a series of quasi-parables and paradoxes, stressed the tragic nature of the human condition, but because he did not have the time to provide a context for his remarks, he seemed quixotic and confused, conveying an impression of an itinerant rabbi who has wandered into a coven of Gentiles.

In other words, this was no discussion as we normally use the word. Even when the "discussion" period began, there were no arguments or counterarguments, no scrutiny of assumptions, no explanations, no elaborations, no definitions. Carl Sagan made, in my opinion, the most coherent statement—a four-minute rationale for a nuclear freeze—but it contained at least two questionable assumptions and was not carefully examined. Apparently, no one wanted to take time from his own few minutes to call attention to someone else's. Mr. Koppel, for his part, felt obliged to keep the "show" moving, and though he occasionally pursued what he discerned as a line of thought, he was more concerned to give each man his fair allotment of time.

But it is not time constraints alone that produce such fragmented and discontinuous language. When a television show is in process, it is very nearly impermissible to say, "Let me think about that" or "I don't know" or "What do you mean when you say . . . ?" or "From what sources does your information come?" This type of discourse not only slows down the tempo of the show but creates the impression of uncertainty or lack of finish. It tends to reveal people in the *act of thinking,* which is as disconcerting and boring on television as it is on a Las Vegas stage. Thinking does not play well on television, a fact that television directors discovered long ago. There is not much to *see* in it. It is, in a phrase, not a performing art. But television demands a performing art, and so what the ABC network gave us was a picture of men of sophisticated verbal skills and political understanding being brought to heel by a medium that requires them to fashion performances rather than ideas. Which accounts for why the eighty minutes were very entertaining, in the way of a Samuel Beckett play: The intimations of gravity hung heavy, the meaning passeth all understanding. The performances, of course, were highly professional. Sagan abjured the turtle-neck sweater in which he starred when he did "Cosmos." He even had his hair cut for the event. His part was that of the logical scientist speaking in behalf of the planet. It is to be doubted that Paul Newman could have done better in the role, although Leonard Nimoy might have. Scowcroft was suitably military in his bearing—terse and distant, the unbreakable defender of national security. Kissinger, as always, was superb in the part of the knowing world statesman, weary of the sheer responsibility of keeping disaster at bay. Koppel played to perfection the part of a moderator, pretending, as it were, that he was sorting out ideas while, in fact, he was merely directing the performances. At the end, one could only applaud those performances, which is what a good television program always aims to achieve; that is to say, applause, not reflection.

I do not say categorically that it is impossible to use television as a carrier of coherent language or thought in process. William Buckley's own program, "Firing Line," occasionally shows people in the act of thinking but who also happen to have television cameras pointed at them. There are other programs, such as "Meet the Press" or "The Open Mind," which clearly strive to maintain a sense of intellectual decorum and typographic tradition, but they are scheduled so that they do not compete with programs of great visual interest, since otherwise, they will not be watched. After all, it is not unheard of that a format will occasionally go against the bias of its medium. For example, the most popular radio program of the early 1940's featured a ventriloquist, and in those days, I heard more than once the feet of a tap dancer on the "Major Bowes' Amateur Hour." (Indeed, if I am not mistaken, he even once featured a pantomimist.) But ventriloquism, dancing and mime do not play well on radio, just as sustained, complex talk does not play well on television. It can be made to play tolerably well if only one camera is used and the visual image is kept constant— as when the President gives a speech. But this is not television at its best, and it is not television that most people will choose to watch. The single most important fact about television is that people *watch* it, which is why it is called *"television."* And what they watch, and like to watch, are moving pic-tures—millions of them, of short duration and dynamic variety. It is in the nature of the medium that it must suppress the content of ideas in order to accommodate the requirements of visual interest; that is to say, to accommo-date the values of show business.

Film, records and radio (now that it is an adjunct of the music industry) are, of course, equally devoted to entertaining the culture, and their effects in altering the style of American discourse are not insignificant. But television is different because it encompasses all forms of discourse. No one goes to a movie to find out about government policy or the latest scientific advances. No one buys a record to find out the baseball scores or the weather or the latest mur-der. No one turns on radio anymore for soap operas or a presidential address (if a television set is at hand). But everyone goes to television for all these things and more, which is why television resonates so powerfully throughout the culture. Television is our culture's principal mode of knowing about itself. Therefore—and this is the critical point—how television stages the world be-comes the model for how the world is properly to be staged. It is not merely that on the television screen entertainment is the metaphor for all discourse. It is that off the screen the same metaphor prevails. As typography once dictated the style of conducting politics, religion, business, education, law and other important social matters, television now takes command. In courtrooms, class-rooms, operating rooms, board rooms, churches and even airplanes, Americans no longer talk to each other, they entertain each other. They do not exchange ideas; they exchange images. They do not argue with propositions; they argue with good looks, celebrities and commercials. For the message of television as metaphor is not only that all the world is a stage but that the stage is located in Las Vegas, Nevada.

In Chicago, for example, the Reverend Greg Sakowicz, a Roman Catholic priest, mixes his religious teaching with rock 'n' roll music. According to the Associated Press, the Reverend Sakowicz is both an associate pastor at the Church of the Holy Spirit in Schaumberg (a suburb of Chicago) and a disc jockey at WKQX. On his show, "The Journey Inward," Father Sakowicz chats in soft tones about such topics as family relationships or commitment, and interposes his sermons with "the sound of *Billboard's* Top 10." He says that his preaching is not done "in a churchy way," and adds, "You don't have to be boring in order to be holy."

Meanwhile in New York City at St. Patrick's Cathedral, Father John J. O'Connor put on a New York Yankee baseball cap as he mugged his way through his installation as Archbishop of the New York Archdiocese. He got off some excellent gags, at least one of which was specifically directed at Mayor Edward Koch, who was a member of his audience; that is to say, he was a congregant. At his next public performance, the new archbishop donned a New York Mets baseball cap. These events were, of course, televised, and were vastly entertaining, largely because Archbishop (now Cardinal) O'Connor has gone Father Sakowicz one better: Whereas the latter believes that you don't have to be boring to be holy, the former apparently believes you don't have to be holy at all.

In Phoenix, Arizona, Dr. Edward Dietrich performed triple bypass surgery on Bernard Schuler. The operation was successful, which was nice for Mr. Schuler. It was also on television, which was nice for America. The operation was carried by at least fifty television stations in the United States, and also by the British Broadcasting Corporation. A two-man panel of narrators (a play-by-play and color man, so to speak) kept viewers informed about what they were seeing. It was not clear as to why this event was televised, but it resulted in transforming both Dr. Dietrich and Mr. Schuler's chest into celebrities. Perhaps because he has seen too many doctor shows on television, Mr. Schuler was uncommonly confident about the outcome of his surgery. "There is no way in hell they are going to lose me on live TV," he said.

As reported with great enthusiasm by both WCBS-TV and WNBC-TV in 1984, the Philadelphia public schools have embarked on an experiment in which children will have their curriculum sung to them. Wearing Walkman equipment, students were shown listening to rock music whose lyrics were about the eight parts of speech. Mr. Jocko Henderson, who thought of this idea, is planning to delight students further by subjecting mathematics and history, as well as English, to the rigors of a rock music format. In fact, this is not Mr. Henderson's idea at all. It was pioneered by the Children's Television Workshop, whose television show "Sesame Street" is an expensive illustration of the idea that education is indistinguishable from entertainment. Nonetheless, Mr. Henderson has a point in his favor. Whereas "Sesame Street" merely attempts to make learning to read a form of light entertainment, the Philadelphia experiment aims to make the classroom itself into a rock concert.

In New Bedford, Massachusetts, a rape trial was televised, to the delight of audiences who could barely tell the difference between the trial and their favorite mid-day soap opera. In Florida, trials of varying degrees of seriousness, including murder, are regularly televised and are considered to be more entertaining than most fictional courtroom dramas. All of this is done in the interests of "public education." For the same high purpose, plans are afoot, it is rumored, to televise confessionals. To be called "Secrets of the Confessional Box," the program will, of course, carry the warning that some of its material may be offensive to children and therefore parental guidance is suggested.

On a United Airlines flight from Chicago to Vancouver, a stewardess announces that its passengers will play a game. The passenger with the most credit cards will win a bottle of champagne. A man from Boston with twelve credit cards wins. A second game requires the passengers to guess the collective age of the cabin crew. A man from Chicago guesses 128, and wins another bottle of wine. During the second game, the air turns choppy and the Fasten Seat Belt sign goes on. Very few people notice, least of all the cabin crew, who keep up a steady flow of gags on the intercom. When the plane reaches its destination, everyone seems to agree that it's fun to fly from Chicago to Vancouver.

On February 7, 1985, *The New York Times* reported that Professor Charles Pine of Rutgers University (Newark campus) was named Professor of the Year by the Council for the Support and Advancement of Education. In explaining why he has such a great impact on his students, Professor Pine said: "I have some gimmicks I use all the time. If you reach the end of the blackboard, I keep writing on the wall. It always gets a laugh. The way I show what a glass molecule does is to run over to one wall and bounce off it, and run over to the other wall." His students are, perhaps, too young to recall that James Cagney used this "molecule move" to great effect in *Yankee Doodle Dandy*. If I am not mistaken, Donald O'Connor duplicated it in *Singin' in the Rain*. So far as I know, it has been used only once before in a classroom: Hegel tried it several times in demonstrating how the dialectical method works.

The Pennsylvania Amish try to live in isolation from mainstream American culture. Among other things, their religion opposes the veneration of graven images, which means that the Amish are forbidden to see movies or to be photographed. But apparently their religion has not got around to disallowing seeing movies *when* they are being photographed. In the summer of 1984, for example, a Paramount Pictures crew descended upon Lancaster County to film the movie *Witness,* which is about a detective, played by Harrison Ford, who falls in love with an Amish woman. Although the Amish were warned by their church not to interfere with the film makers, it turned out that some Amish welders ran to see the action as soon as their work was done. Other devouts lay in the grass some distance away, and looked down on the set with binoculars. "We read about the movie in the paper," said an Amish woman. "The kids even cut out Harrison Ford's picture." She added: "But it doesn't really matter that much to them. Somebody told us he was in *Star Wars* but that doesn't mean anything to us." The last time a similar conclusion was drawn was when the executive director of the American Association of Blacksmiths remarked that he had read about the automobile but that he was convinced it would have no consequences for the future of his organization. . . .

Prior to the 1984 presidential elections, the two candidates confronted each other on television in what were called "debates." These events were not in the least like the Lincoln-Douglas debates or anything else that goes by the name. Each candidate was given five minutes to address such questions as, What is (or would be) your policy in Central America? His opposite number was then given one minute for a rebuttal. In such circumstances, complexity, documentation and logic can play no role, and, indeed, on several occasions syntax itself was abandoned entirely. It is no matter. The men were less concerned with giving arguments than with "giving off" impressions, which is what television does best. Post-debate commentary largely avoided any evaluation of the candidates' ideas, since there were none to evaluate. Instead, the debates were conceived as boxing matches, the relevant question being, Who KO'd whom? The answer was determined by the "style" of the men—how they looked, fixed their gaze, smiled, and delivered one-liners. In the second debate, President Reagan got off a swell one-liner when asked a question about his age. The following day, several newspapers indicated that Ron had KO'd Fritz with his joke. Thus, the leader of the free world is chosen by the people in the Age of Television.

What all of this means is that our culture has moved toward a new way of conducting its business, especially its important business. The nature of its discourse is changing as the demarcation line between what is show business and what is not becomes harder to see with each passing day. Our priests and presidents, our surgeons and lawyers, our educators and newscasters need worry less about satisfying the demands of their discipline than the demands of good showmanship. Had Irving Berlin changed one word in the title of his celebrated song, he would have been as prophetic, albeit more terse, as Aldous Huxley. He need only have written, There's No Business But Show Business.

Neil Postman

New Group Identities

Joshua Meyrowitz, who received his Ph.D. from New York University, is a professor at the University of New Hampshire. In the following selection from Meyrowitz's award-winning book *No Sense of Place: The Impact of Electronic Media on Social Behavior* (Oxford University Press, 1985), the author stresses how the characteristics of electronic media ultimately influence the ways individuals perceive themselves in relation to others through group identity, tolerance for diversity, and a sense of shared culture.

Meyrowitz's thesis is that electronic media influence the way people relate to physical location and access to information, and he explains how familiarity with media form influences interpersonal social dynamics. In some ways, his work reflects the concept of media having the ability to influence spatial and temporal reality. Meyrowitz addresses the long-term effects of living with electronic media by looking at the ways individuals have internalized mediated messages, but he also points to the positive and negative results of media's time- and space-binding qualities. His work further elaborates on the concepts of media form and sense extension.

Meyrowitz's work, as well as the work of recent political communication researchers, looks at the long-term effects of living with media—how people have internalized certain behaviors and standards that media have conditioned us to accept.

Key Concept: group affiliation and media bias

Group identity is based on "shared but special" information-systems. The greater the number of distinct social information-systems, the greater the number of distinct "groups"; the smaller the number of distinct information-systems, the smaller the number of distinct group identities. The merging of many formerly distinct situations through electronic media, therefore, should have an homogenizing effect on group identities.

As a result of the widespread use of television, for example, the social information available to the ghetto family now more closely resembles the information available to the middle class family. Information available to women now more closely resembles information available to men. Formerly distinct groups not only share very similar information about society in general, they also share more information about each other—information that once distinguished "insiders" from "outsiders." As a consequence, traditional distinctions among groups become partially blurred.

The change in the information characteristic of traditional groups leads to two complementary phenomena: the decreasing importance of traditional group ties and the increasing importance of other types of association.

The homogenized information networks fostered by electronic media offer individuals a comparatively holistic view of society and a wider field within which to measure their relative lot. To use George Herbert Mead's term, electronic media alter one's "generalized other"—the general sense of how other people think and evaluate one's actions. The "mediated generalized other" includes standards, values, and beliefs from outside traditional group spheres, and it thereby presents people with a new perspective from which to view their actions and identities. The new mediated generalized other bypasses face-to-face encounters in family and community and is shared by millions of others.

One result of this shared perspective and more common set of situations is that members of formerly isolated and distinct groups begin to demand "equal" rights and treatment. This analysis, therefore, offers one possible explanation for the recent, sudden rise of "minorities" as potent social and political forces. Blacks, women, hispanics, Native Americans, gays, children, prisoners, and the disabled are all groups composed of people who now feel or are seen as isolated in a corner of the larger environment, restricted and disenfranchised.

The rise of minority consciousness, according to this analysis, actually indicates the demise of one aspect of minority status in the traditional sense. Minority affiliations were once based on *isolated* information-systems and very *distinct* group experiences. The demand for full equality in roles and rights dramatizes the development, in a way, of a mass "majority," a single large "group" whose members will not tolerate any great distinctions in roles and privileges.

Today's minority consciousness is something of a paradox. Many people take renewed pride in their special identity, yet the heightened consciousness of the special group is the result of being able to view one's group from the outside; that is, it is the result of no longer being fully *in* the group. Members of today's minority groups are united in their feelings of *restriction* from certain rights and experiences. People sense they are in a minority group because they feel excluded from the larger reference group. The diminutive connotation of the term "minority" does not refer to the small number of people in the group, but rather to the limited degree of access the members feel they have to the larger society. The term "minority" as it is sometimes applied to women[1]—the majority of the population—is meaningless in any other sense. . . .

Many minorities consciously proclaim their special identity in the unconscious hope of losing at least part of it. When gays, for example, publicly protest for equal treatment under the law, including the right to teach and the recognition of homosexual marriages, they are not only saying, "I'm different and I'm proud of it," they are also saying, "I should be treated as if I'm the same as everyone else." So there is a paradoxical call for both consciousness of differences and blindness to them.

Ironically, the sense of restriction felt by many minority group members may be the result of the sudden *increase* in access to a larger, more inclusive information environment. For to know about and be constantly exposed to places you cannot go and things you are not allowed to do makes you feel more isolated than you were before. My uncle has told me many times that when he was young, he did not realize how poor his family was because everyone he knew was poor. Through television, today's ghetto children have more points of reference and higher standards for comparison. They see what they are being deprived of in every program and commercial. . . .

THE UNDERMINING OF GROUP LOCATIONS

Electronic media have had a tremendous impact on group identity by undermining the relationship between physical location and information access. Many categories of people—women, ghetto dwellers, prisoners, children—were once "naturally" restricted from much social information by being isolated in particular places. The identity and cohesion of many groupings and associations were fostered by the fact that members were "isolated together" in the same or similar locations: homes or offices, ghettos or suburbs, prisons or stores, playgrounds or bars. Such physical segregation worked to create social segregation for as long as place and situation were still closely linked. Now, however, electronic messages on television, telephone, and radio democratize and homogenize places by allowing people to experience and interact with others in spite of physical isolation. As a result, physical location now creates only one type of information-system, only one type of shared but special group experience. Electronic media begin to override group identities based on "co-presence," and they create many new forms of access and "association" that have little to do with physical location.

Electronic media have an impact on group identity by distancing people from traditional group perspectives. The use of the word "perspective" to mean both what one sees from a given location as well as one's social attitudes suggests the strong traditional relationship between physical place and social belief. Shared physical location fosters a shared perspective which, in turn, reinforces group solidarity. A shift in physical position generally leads to a shift in attitude. A common example is the change in our perception of a street or intersection as we switch from pedestrian to driver. The same principle, however, provides the basis for one of the subtlest techniques of cinematic persuasion and propaganda: the shifting of perspective and position rather than the altering of content. In the celebrated film *The Godfather,* for example, we are not asked to believe that the mafia family members are good people; we are simply "put" in their home and given their view of the world. As a result, we find ourselves in the unusual position of rooting for the criminals and cheering when government agents are killed. Similar techniques are used in war movies and westerns where, regardless of "plot," viewers tend to take the side of those whose perspective they are shown.[2]

Through visual portrayal of real and fictional events, television presents most members of our society with a crazy-quilt pattern of perspectives. Regardless of physical location and traditional group ties, people experience how the world looks and feels from other places and other role perspectives. Television's views are, to be sure, distorted and incomplete, and often they are purposefully biased for political or economic reasons. Nevertheless, television "removes" viewers from their physical locales and offers them alternative views of other people and the physical environment. The "view from no place" that television permits may have been a stimulus for the growth of such groups as Amnesty International, for the increasing awareness of ecological issues, and for the growing demand for nuclear disarmament. Such issues require an "overview," an overriding of traditional group concerns and a bypassing of needs as seen from one's particular place. (Ironically, the "liberalizing" effect of the multiple perspective view may still give a political advantage to conservatives, reactionaries, and special interest groups. After all, multiple perspectives often lead many people to an overabundance of empathy and, therefore, to political ambivalence and inaction.

The impact of electronic media on group identity may be most apparent in large cities where traditional community ties are often already weak, where people do not know all their neighbors, nor speak to everyone they see. But small towns too are experiencing a change in perspective. Media ties compete with family, church, school, and community. Media create new "communities," and a large portion of their content is shared by most people in the country. Many jokes, phrases, expression, and events heard and seen on television provide a common set of "experience" for people across the land. It is not surprising, therefore, that what sociologists refer to as the "urbanization" of America includes not only population shifts to large cities but also a general urbanization of attitudes and behaviors throughout the country.[3] Electronic media move people informationally to the same "place."

The homogenization of regional spheres is, of course, only a matter of degree. Different places are still different, but they are not as different as they once were. The psychological distinctions between states and regions were once very great. As late as the 1940s, one coast of America was something of a mystery to the other. A cross-country trip was a true adventure into the unknown.[4] But television has removed much of this sense of mystery.

The telegraph began the breakdown of communication barriers between different places. But is presented terse coded messages that had to follow the telegraph lines. Radio enhanced the process, first by sending Morse Code through the air rather than through wires and later by adding the human voice. But radio merely *reported* verbally on events in other parts of the world or country. The information was still descriptive and "second-hand," a linguistic abstraction. Radio provided "word-pictures," but the pictures had to be redrawn in each listeners's imagination. It is difficult to imagine something new and mysterious without picturing it as some variation of what one has already seen. Further, with radio each listener creates his or her own unique and subjective picture. Television, in contrast, seemingly allows the viewer to experience distant events and places directly and "objectively." It is significant that when Edward R. Murrow's radio program "Hear It Now" became television's

"See It Now," the premiere show featured a live hookup between California and New York; viewers saw the Golden Gate Bridge and the Brooklyn Bridge simultaneously on a split screen.[5] With television, the final demystification of other parts of the country began.

Electronic media, of course, are not the only causes of merging situations. High speed travel and mass production of identical clothes, appliances, and other products also have had their impact. As Daniel Boorstin's history of America suggests, the development and use of electronic media may be part of a larger trend of the homogenizing of here and there.[6] But electronic media have an effect that goes beyond other variables. Travel allows people to get from *place to place.* Identical products give *different places* the same surface look. These changes are physical not informational. Electronic media, in contrast, eat away at the very meaning of distinct places: shared by special *experience.* To be "with" other people is very different from using the same products or eating similar foods. . . .

Television's "national embrace" has an effect on local media content and local behavior. National weather reports, for example, are now included even in local news programs. And a disaster in another state—such as California mud slides or sink-holes in Florida—often receives more attention in local news and conversation than a house fire in one's home town. One result of this national and sometimes international view is that the total strangeness of "strangers" as well as the special meaning of "neighbor"—both important elements in the "them vs. us" feelings of group identity—have been muted.

It is difficult to isolate oneself from the metaphysical arena created by television. In the early days of television, the low quality of programming made it embarrassing for professors and other "highbrows" to admit that they even owned a television set, let alone that they spent any valuable time watching it. Today, however, the massive saturation of television into virtually every American home imbues the activity of watching television with multiple levels of social significance (and therefore offers convenient justifications as well). To watch television is now to hook into part of the "American experience." One can watch popular programs, not merely to see the program, but to see what others are watching. One can watch, not necessarily to stare into the eyes of America, but at least to look over the shoulders of Americans and see what they see. Television watching may not allow you to keep your finger directly on the pulse of the nation, but it does allow you to keep your finger on the pulse the nation is keeping its finger on.

Television today has a social function similar to the weather. No one takes responsibility for it, often it is bad, but nearly everyone pays attention to it and sees it as a basis of common experience and a source of topics of conversation.

The ease and speed with which one can tune into the national television forum or be in touch with other people through the telephone make it more difficult for people to isolate themselves in specific places. With electronic media, one is always "in range," others are always "within reach." To be "out of touch" today is to be abnormal. Many people now carry portable radios, or even television sets while on vacations or "retreats," and many isolated camping sites advertise that they have a TV room and a telephone. Similarly, for a person to live or vacation in a place that has no telephone is often thought to be an implicit insult to friends, relatives, and co-workers. Taking one's phone off the hook may be seen as a mark of a misanthrope. In some occupations, people are expected to wear "beepers" that make them accessible at any time wherever they are and whatever they are doing. Thus, many of the traditional behavioral characteristics of "place"—those dependent on isolation—are overridden. Indeed, electronic media have given insularity of thought and place a bad name. It now seems unnatural to be completely unaware or inaccessible. This may partially explain why the television set and the telephone recently have become fixtures even in the recreation rooms of convents and in the formerly silent halls of the Trappist monks.[7]

Electronic media create ties and associations that compete with those formed through live interaction in specific locations. Live encounters are certainly more "special" and provide stronger and deeper relationships, but their relative number is decreasing. Many business, social, and even intimate family encounters now take place through electronic media ("Long distance is the next best thing to being there.") Although close physical ties in the home are important enough to compete successfully with a small number of electronic links, the many contacts through radio, television, and telephone begin to outweigh personal interactions through sheer number. Indeed, many "family encounters" now take place in from of the television set. Whether media have actually affected the *amount* of family interaction may be less of an issue than the fact that they have changed the *uniqueness* of what goes on in the home. Because many electronic messages within a given home are also experienced simultaneously by many other families, the shared but secret behavior of the family unit is further diluted. A person's psychological affiliation with his or her nuclear family is weakened when the families of friends, co-workers, and relatives share much of the same information at the same time. The common backdrop of social experience provided by electronic media creates broader (and therefore shallower) ties and associations.

Electronic media's impact on the uniqueness of family interactions suggests a common element underlying both the 1960s fad of communal living and the stronger current trend toward single-member households.[8] Both communal living and living alone represent a breakdown of traditional family ties; both represent treating large numbers of others with equal intimacy. The commune movement involved treating strangers like family; living alone involves treating even family members like partial strangers. In an electronic society, it makes sense that the single-member household arrangement has become the stronger of the two trends. Living alone more closely reflects, in physical terms, the patterns of association fostered by electronically created information-systems. Communes, like extended families before them, involve deep, long-term, place-bound commitments with a stable group of others. In both electronic communication and single-living, however, the options of association are large and shared, but the choice is individual and idiosyncratic. Just as electronic interactions do not saturate a time/space frame, so now do many live relationships take on an ephemeral and sporadic quality.

The integration of social spheres does not simply give people new places to play their old roles; it changes the roles that are played. As place and information access become disconnected, place-specific behaviors and activities begin to fade. The psychological and social distance among physical places is muted. As a result, dress codes in schools and restaurants have come to seem antiquated or phony. And when people do "dress up" today, it is more likely than in the past to be viewed as a "costume" rather than as a clear sign of personal identity. Further, people are less likely to wear the once "appropriate" dress for their role in a given place because places and roles no longer seem that distinct. Presidents wear jeans in public and nuns shed their habits.

As different places become informationally similar, the social definitions of different locations begin to merge. Factories and lavishly decorated residential lofts can coexist in the same buildings because location now has much less to do with group identity and interaction. The workplace begins to move back into the home because business interactions and information flow are now less dependent on the physical presence of co-workers and clients. As previously distinct situations are combined, formerly distinct behavior patterns merge. One of the contingencies of establishing an office at home, for example, is the need to develop a new social role that is neither "executive-in-office" nor "spouse/parent-at-home."

Traditional groups were formed on the basis of long-term shared locations and live experience. Workers in a factory, women at home, children in school, and shoppers in a store often defined themselves in terms of the physical defined "group": the factory, the family, the school, the neighborhood. Problems with a supervisor, a husband, a teacher, or a shopkeeper were once likely to be considered personal problems between individuals. Today, however, the mediated "view from above" redefines many problems into "social issues" and into battles between "social categories." When a promotion is denied, it is now likely to be liked to sex discrimination or racism; a problem with a spouse is likely to be defined in terms of spouse abuse or sexism. A child's problem in school may end up as a court battle over educational malpractice, and an interaction with a shopkeeper may be seen as a "consumer" issue. I am not suggesting that these perceptions are necessarily "false," only that they certainly are *different.* While interactions continue to occur in specific places, they are now conceived of as taking place in a much larger social arena.

Many of today's groupings are based on single, superficial attributes shared in common rather than on an intimate web of complicated interactions and long-term shared experience. The current battles over the rights of "smokers" versus "nonsmokers," for example, suggest how removed many current groupings are from traditional place-bound group ties.

Audiences for particular group behaviors are no longer determined by physical presence, and the performance of roles on all social levels shifts as a result. Police who negotiate with the city "through the media," for example, can no longer clearly distinguish their front region image of dedicated and selfless protectors of the people from their back region haggling for more sick days, vacation time, and higher salaries. Similarly, when the U.S. Senate's debate on the Panama Canal Treaty was broadcast live in Panama, there was a merging of the back region of American-American dealings into the front region of American-Panamanian interaction. The United States could no longer conduct its internal arguments with all due intensity and bitterness without insulting Panamanians, nor could it present a unified and diplomatic front to

Panama without diminishing internal debate and discussion. Thus, the undermining of group locations leads to the dilution of traditional group behaviors and the development of "middle region" compromise behavior patterns.

NOTES

1. For an early article on "Women as a Minority Group," see Hacker, 1951.
2. Meyrowitz, 1979, pp. 71–72. A more recent example of a "disturbing identification" for many Americans is the movie "Das Boot" in which the adventures of a World War II German U-Boat crew are chronicled. In direct contrast to virtually all *our* World War II movies, the Germans become "us" and the British and Americans become "them."
3. See, for example, Popenoe, 1980, pp. 513–514.
4. One indication of this was the role that cross-country travel could still play in radio dramas. The classic 1942 radio thriller with Orson Wells, "The Hitchhiker," for example, begins with the main character assuring his mother that her fears about his planned drive from New York to California are unfounded; the drama ends with his trip transformed into a journey from sanity to near-insanity, from normal life to a sort of purgatory. And, interestingly, his one hope for remaining sane is the telephone that will link him to the known world—his mother's house.
5. Barnouw, 1970, p. 45.
6. Boorstin, 1973, pp. 307–410.
7. Since the "renewal movement" spurred by Vatican Council II in the 1960s, there has been a dramatic increase in access to electronic media among nuns and monastery brothers. Although media use varies from place to place, most nuns now have relatively free access to radio, telephone, and television (Father Francis L. Demers, Vicar for Religious, Diocese of Manchester, personal communication, May 1984). Communication among the Trappist monks was once highly restricted; brothers could not even speak to each other except in emergencies or with special permission from the Abbot. This changed in the late 1960s, however, and along with the increase in face-to-face communication has come an increase in access to electronic media. At the Abbey of the Genesee in Piffard, New York, for example, brothers now have access to a telephone (once the prerogative of the Abbot alone). The monks also use a computer for word processing and for running their bakery business, a video taping system is used to give "tours" of the facilities, and one brother is in charge of taping appropriate television programs off the air for later viewing by the monks. The Abbey also subscribes to weekly newspapers and new magazines. To maintain their goal of "solitude," however, the monks avoid watching regular broadcast television or reading daily newspapers (Brother Anthony, Guestmaster, Abbey of the Genesee, personal communication, May 1984).
8. Between 1960 and 1981 the number of people living alone in the United States nearly tripled. In 1982, the U.S. Bureau of the Census reported that nearly one out of every four households in the United States consisted of a person living alone. U.S. Bureau of the Census, 1982, p. 44. In a recent study on single-member households, Hughes and Gove, 1981, are surprised to discover that, contrary to earlier findings, people who live alone are no longer associated with many pathological behaviors, including higher rates of suicide. They suggest that their findings undermine previous thinking concerning the importance of "social integration" and the detrimental effects of "social isolation." What they overlook, however, is the opportunity that electronic media have provided for "selective integration." In an electronic age, people who live alone *physically* are no longer necessarily isolated *informationally*.

REFERENCES

Barnouw, Erik. *The Image Empire: A History of Broadcasting in the United States, Vol. 3—From 1953.* New York: Oxford Univ. Press, 1970.

Boorstin, Daniel J. *The Americans: The Democratic Experience.* New York: Random House, 1973.

Hacker, Helen M. "Women as a Minority Group." *Social Forces,* 30 (1951), 60–69.

Meyrowitz, Joshua. "Television and Interpersonal Behavior: Codes of Perception and Response." In *Inter/Media: Interpersonal Communication in a Media World.* Ed. Gary Gumpert and Robert Cathcart. New York: Oxford Univ. Press, 1979, pp. 56–76.

A.C. Nielsen, *Nielsen Report on Television.* Northbrook, IL: A.C. Nielsen Co. (An edition of this booklet is published every year.)

Popenoe, David. *Sociology.* 4rth ed. Englewood Cliffs, NJ: Prentice-Hall, 1980.

U.S. Bureau of the Census. *Statistical Abstract of the United States: 1982–83.* 103rd Ed. Washington, D.C.: U.S. Government Printing Office, 1982.

CHAPTER 7 Technology, Systems, and Human Interaction

7.1 NORBERT WIENER

The Human *Use of Human Beings: Cybernetics and Society*

Norbert Wiener (1894–1964) was a professor of mathematics at the Massachusetts Institute of Technology, where he made a significant contribution to the study of communication and media with his theory of *cybernetics.* The work he did on trying to improve the accuracy of antiaircraft gunfire during World War II resulted in the concept of cybernetics. This concept explains how self-regulating systems contribute to an understanding of the systems themselves. In other words, the way a technological system works determines how it will be controlled by and how it will exert some control over the human user. Integral to this theory is the concept of *feedback*, which has been fundamental to the development of information theory.

Wiener's concepts not only influenced other technological determinists, but they also gain greater importance as interactive technologies increas-

154

*Chapter 7
Technology,
Systems, and
Human
Interaction*

ingly become a subject of study. Cybernetic principles, for example, under-gird theories of artificial intelligence (computerized simulated thought proc-esses) and virtual reality (technologically controlled sensory manipulation). In the following selection from *The* Human *Use of Human Beings: Cyber-netics and Society* (Houghton Mifflin, 1950), Wiener looks at the way humans and machines "interact," or exert a level of control over the mes-sages transmitted. Important are Wiener's descriptions of *entropy* and *progress.*

Key Concept: human/machine interaction and cybernetics

WHAT IS CYBERNETICS?

I have been occupied for many years with problems of communication engi-neering. These have led to the design and investigation of various sorts of communication machines, some of which have shown an uncanny ability to simulate human behavior, and thereby to throw light on the possible nature of human behavior. They have even shown the existence of a tremendous possi-bility of replacing human behavior, in many cases in which the human being is relatively slow and ineffective. We are thus in an immediate need of discussing the powers of these machines as they impinge on the human being, and the consequences of this new and fundamental revolution in technique. . . .

One of the most interesting aspects of the world is that it can be consid-ered to be made up of *patterns*. A pattern is essentially an arrangement. It is characterized by the order of the elements of which it is made, rather than by the intrinsic nature of these elements. Two patterns are identical if their rela-tional structure can be put into a one-to-one correspondence, so that to each term of the one there corresponds a term of the other; and that to each relation of order between several terms of one, there corresponds a similar relation of order between the corresponding terms of the other. The simplest case of one-to-one correspondence is given by the ordinary process of counting. If I have five pennies in my pocket, and five apples in a basket, I can put my apples in a row, and lay one penny beside each. Each penny will correspond to one apple and one apple only, and each apple will correspond to one penny and one penny only. . . .

A pattern which is conceived to convey information, or something trans-missible from individual to individual, is not taken as an isolated phenome-non. To telegraph is to convey a message by the proper use of dots and dashes; and here it is necessary that these dots and dashes be a selection from among a set which contains other possibilities as well. If I am sending the letter *e,* it gains its meaning in part because I have not sent the letter *o.* If my only choice is to send the letter *e,* then the message is merely something that is either there or not there; and it conveys much less information.

In the early days of telephone engineering, the mere sending of a message was so much of a miracle that nobody asked how it should be sent. The lines were able to take care of all the information forced on them, and the real difficulties were in the design of the terminal apparatus at the sending and receiving ends. Under these conditions, the problems concerning the maximum carrying capacity of telephone lines were not yet of any importance. However, as the art developed, and ways were found to compress several messages into a single line by the use of carriers and other similar means, economy in sending speech over the telephone lines began to develop an economic importance. Let me explain what we mean by "carriers" and by "carrier-telephony."

A mathematical theorem due to Fourier states that every motion within very broad limits can be represented as a sum of the very simplest sort of vibrations which give rise to pure musical notes. A way has been found to take an oscillation on an electric line, and to shift each one of the notes that make it up, by a certain constant pitch. In this manner, we may take a pattern in which several subsidiary patterns would otherwise be placed on top of each other, and separate them so that they are placed side by side in positions, and do not produce a mere confusion. Thus we may run three lines together in the typewriter in such a way that they are superimposed and blurred, or we may write them in their proper sequence, and keep them separate. This process of moving different messages into separate positions of pitch is known as *modulation.*

After modulation, the message may be sent over a line which is already carrying a message, if the displacement in pitch is sufficient. Under proper conditions, the message already transmitted and the new message will not affect one another; and it is possible to recover from the line both the original undisplaced message and the modulated message, in such a way that they go to separate terminal equipment. The modulated message may then be subjected to a process which, is the inverse of modulation, and may be reduced to the form which it originally had before it was entrusted to the apparatus. Thus two messages may be sent along the same telephone line. By an extension of this process, many more than two messages may be sent over the same line. This process is known as carrier-telephony, and has vastly extended the usefulness of our telephone lines without any correspondingly great increase in investment.

Since the introduction of carrier methods, telephone lines have been used at a high efficiency of message transmission. Thus the question of how much information can be sent over a line has become significant, and with this, the measurement of information in general. This has been made more acute by the discovery that the very existence of electric currents in a line is the cause of what is called *line noise,* which blurs the messages, and offers an upper limit to their ability to carry information.

The earlier work on the theory of information was vitiated by the fact that it ignored noise-levels and other quantities of a somewhat random nature. It was only when the idea of randomness was fully understood, together with the applications of the related notions of probability, that the question of the carrying capacity of a telegraph or telephone line could even be asked intelligently. When this question was asked, it became clear that the problem of measuring the amount of information was of a piece with the related problem of the measurement of the regularity and irregularity of a pattern. It is quite clear that a haphazard sequence of symbols or a pattern which is purely haphazard can convey no information. Information thus must be in some way the measure of the regularity of a pattern, and in particular of the sort of pattern

156

*Chapter 7
Technology,
Systems, and
Human
Interaction*

known as *time series*. By time series, I mean a pattern in which the parts are spread in time. This regularity is to a certain extent an abnormal thing. The irregular is always commoner than the regular. Therefore, whatever definition of information and its measure we shall introduce must be something which grows when the *a priori* probability of a pattern or a time series diminishes. We shall later find the proper numerical measure for the amount of information. This range of ideas was already familiar in the branch of physics known as statistical mechanics, and was associated with the famous second law of thermodynamics, which asserts that a system may lose order and regularity spontaneously, but that it practically never gains it.

A little later . . . I shall give this law its proper statement in terms of the scientific notion of *entropy* which I shall then define. For the present this qualitative formulation of the law will suffice. The notion of information has proved to be subject to a similar law—that is, a message can lose order spontaneously in the act of transmission, but cannot gain it. For example, if one talks into a telephone with a great deal of line noise, and a great deal of loss of energy of the main message, the person at the other end may miss words that have been spoken, and may have to reconstruct them on the basis of the significant information of the context. Again, if a book is translated from one language into another, there does not exist that precise equivalence between the two languages which will permit the translation to have exactly the same meaning as the original. Under these conditions, the translator has only two alternatives: namely, to use phrases which are a little broader and vaguer than those of the original, and which certainly fail to contain its entire emotional context, or to falsify the original by introducing a message which is not precisely there, and which conveys his own meaning rather than that of the author. In either case, some of the author's meaning is lost. . . .

We ordinarily think of a message as sent from human being to human being. This need not be the case at all. If, being lazy, instead of getting out of bed in the morning, I press a button which turns on the heat, closes the window, and starts an electric heating unit under the coffeepot, I am sending messages to all these pieces of apparatus. If on the other hand, the electric egg boiler starts a whistle going after a certain number of minutes, it is sending me a message. If the thermostat records that the room is too warm, and turns off the oil burner, the message may be said to be a method of control of the oil burner. Control, in other words, is nothing but the sending of messages which effectively change the behavior of the recipient.

It is this study of messages, and in particular of the effective messages of control, which constitutes the science of Cybernetics,[1] which I christened in an earlier book. Its name signifies the art of pilot or steersman. Let it be noted that the word "governor" in a machine is simply the latinized Greek word for steersman.

. . . [S]ociety can only be understood through a study of the messages and the communication facilities which belong to it; and . . . in the future development of these messages and communication facilities, messages between man and machines, between machine and man, and between machine and machine, are destined to play an ever-increasing part. . . .

It is my thesis that the operation of the living individual and the operation of some of the newer communication machines are precisely parallel. Both of them have sensory receptors as one stage in their cycle of operation: that is, in both of them there exists a special apparatus for collecting information from the outer world at low energy levels, and for making it available in the operation of the individual or of the machine. In both cases these external messages are not taken *neat,* but through the internal transforming powers of the apparatus, whether it be alive or dead. The information is then turned into a new form available for the further stages of performance. In both the animal and the machine this performance is made to be effective on the outer world. In both of them, their *performed* action on the outer world, and not merely their *intended* action, is reported back to the central regulatory apparatus. This complex of behavior is ignored by the average man, and in particular does not play the rôle that it should in our habitual analysis of society.

. . . [W]e are studying either those respects in which the machine duplicates man, or those aspects of man which appear clearer in view of our study of the machine, or both. We begin with the two notions of *entropy* and of *progress:* notions which are completely necessary for the understanding of the orientation of man in the world, and notions which have been sadly misunderstood. . . .

A measure of information is a measure of order. Its negative will be a measure of disorder, and will be a negative number. It can be made artificially positive by adding a constant quantity, or starting from some value other than zero. This measure of disorder is known to the statistical mechanicist as *entropy,* and almost never spontaneously decreases in an isolated system. This again is the second law of thermodynamics.

NOTE

1. *Cybernetics, or Control and Communication in the Animal and the Machine;* 1949, The Technology Press of M.I.T., Cambridge; John Wiley & Sons, New York; and Hermann et Cie, Paris.

The Mathematical Theory of Communication

Mathematicians and electrical engineers have contributed heavily to the study of communication and information. Two notable examples are Claude E. Shannon (b. 1916) and Warren Weaver (1894–1978), who have contributed to the field through their work in message exchange and technological system design.

The Mathematical Theory of Communication (University of Illinois Press, 1964), from which the following selection is taken, originated as two journal articles authored by Shannon in his capacity as a Bell Labs engineer working on cryptography and published in the *Bell System Technical Journal*. Shannon's efforts toward improving coding and code-breaking during World War II were also applied to an emerging field in the design of the "thinking machine"—the computer.

Weaver had been trained as an engineer and mathematician, and he was working at the Rockefeller Foundation at the time Shannon's papers were receiving some attention. Weaver translated Shannon's highly technical writing into language that was more easily understandable by those untrained in mathematics.

Shannon specifically defined *information* as a quantitative measurement, rather than as a message that involves *meaning*. This way of thinking makes the pursuit of answers to some questions easier, but it restricts the use of the theory to addressing questions that can only be determined in quantified form.

Key Concept: information theory

INTRODUCTORY NOTE ON THE GENERAL SETTING OF THE ANALYTICAL COMMUNICATION STUDIES

Communication

The word *communication* will be used here in a very broad sense to include all of the procedures by which one mind may affect another. This, of course, involves not only written and oral speech, but also music, the pictorial arts, the theatre, the ballet, and in fact all human behavior. In some connections it may be desirable to use a still broader definition of communication, namely, one which would include the procedures by means of which one mechanism (say automatic equipment to track an airplane and to compute its probable future positions) affects another mechanism (say a guided missile chasing this airplane).

The language of this memorandum will often appear to refer to the special, but still very broad and important, field of the communication of speech; but practically everything said applies equally well to music of any sort, and to still or moving pictures, as in television.

Three Levels of Communications Problems

Relative to the broad subject of communication, there seem to be problems at three levels. Thus it seems reasonable to ask, serially:

LEVEL A. How accurately can the symbols of communication be transmitted? (The technical problem.)

LEVEL B. How precisely do the transmitted symbols convey the desired meaning? (The semantic problem.)

LEVEL C. How effectively does the received meaning affect conduct in the desired way? (The effectiveness problem.)

The *technical problems* are concerned with the accuracy of transference from sender to receiver of sets of symbols (written speech), or of a continuously varying signal (telephonic or radio transmission of voice or music), or of a continuously varying two-dimensional pattern (television), etc. Mathematically, the first involves transmission of a finite set of discrete symbols, the second the transmission of one continuous function of time, and the third the transmission of many continuous functions of time or of one continuous function of time and of two space coordinates.

The *semantic problems* are concerned with the identity, or satisfactorily close approximation, in the interpretation of meaning by the receiver, as compared with the intended meaning of the sender. This is a very deep and involved situation, even when one deals only with the relatively simpler problems of communicating through speech. . . .

The *effectiveness problems* are concerned with the success with which the meaning conveyed to the receiver leads to the desired conduct on his part. It may seem at first glance undesirably narrow to imply that the purpose of all communication is to influence the conduct of the receiver. But with any reasonably broad definition of conduct, it is clear that communication either affects conduct or is without any discernible and probable effect at all.

The problem of effectiveness involves aesthetic considerations in the case of the fine arts. In the case of speech, written or oral, it involves considerations which range all the way from the mere mechanics of style, through all the

160

*Chapter 7
Technology,
Systems, and
Human
Interaction*

psychological and emotional aspects of propaganda theory, to those value judgments which are necessary to give useful meaning to the words "success" and "desired" in the opening sentence of this section on effectiveness.

The effectiveness problem is closely interrelated with the semantic problem, and overlaps it in a rather vague way; and there is in fact overlap between all of the suggested categories of problems. . . .

COMMUNICATION PROBLEMS AT LEVEL A

A Communication System and Its Problems

. . . The *information source* selects a desired *message* out of a set of possible messages. . . . The selected message may consist of written or spoken words, or of pictures, music, etc.

The *transmitter* changes this *message* into the *signal* which is actually sent over the *communication channel* from the transmitter to the *receiver.* In the case of telephony, the channel is a wire, the signal a varying electrical current on this wire; the transmitter is the set of devices (telephone transmitter, etc.) which change the sound pressure of the voice into the varying electrical current. In telegraphy, the transmitter codes written words into sequences of interrupted currents of varying lengths (dots, dashes, spaces). In oral speech, the information source is the brain, the transmitter is the voice mechanism producing the varying sound pressure (the signal) which is transmitted through the air (the channel). In radio, the channel is simply space (or the aether, if any one still prefers that antiquated and misleading word), and the signal is the electromagnetic wave which is transmitted.

The *receiver* is a sort of inverse transmitter, changing the transmitted signal back into a message, and handing this message on to the destination. When I talk to you, my brain is the information source, yours the destination; my vocal system is the transmitter, and your ear and the associated eighth nerve is the receiver.

In the process of being transmitted, it is unfortunately characteristic that certain things are added to the signal which were not intended by the information source. These unwanted additions may be distortions of sound (in telephony, for example) or static (in radio), or distortions in shape or shading of picture (television), or errors in transmission (telegraphy or facsimile), etc. All of these changes in the transmitted signal are called *noise.*

The kind of questions which one seeks to ask concerning such a communication system are:

a. How does one measure *amount of information?*
b. How does one measure the *capacity* of a communication channel?
c. The action of the transmitter in changing the message into the signal often involves a *coding process.* What are the characteristics of an efficient coding process? And when the coding is as efficient as possible, at what rate can the channel convey information?

d. What are the general characteristics of *noise?* How does noise affect the accuracy of the message finally received at the destination? How can one minimize the undesirable effects of noise, and to what extent can they be eliminated?

e. If the signal being transmitted is *continuous* (as in oral speech or music) rather than being formed of *discrete* symbols (as in written speech, telegraphy, etc.), how does this fact affect the problem?

We will now state, without any proofs and with a minimum of mathematical terminology, the main results which Shannon has obtained.

Information

The word *information,* in this theory, is used in a special sense that must not be confused with its ordinary usage. In particular, *information* must not be confused with meaning.

In fact, two messages, one of which is heavily loaded with meaning and the other of which is pure nonsense, can be exactly equivalent, from the present viewpoint, as regards information. It is this, undoubtedly, that Shannon means when he says that "the semantic aspects of communication are irrelevant to the engineering aspects." But this does not mean that the engineering aspects are necessarily irrelevant to the semantic aspects.

To be sure, this word information in communication theory relates not so much to what you *do* say, as to what you *could* say. That is, information is a measure of one's freedom of choice when one selects a message. If one is confronted with a very elementary situation where he has to choose one of two alternative messages, then it is arbitrarily said that the information, associated with this situation, is unity. Note that it is misleading (although often convenient) to say that one or the other message conveys unit information. The concept of information applies not to the individual messages (as the concept of meaning would), but rather to the situation as a whole, the unit information indicating that in this situation one has an amount of freedom of choice, in selecting a message, which it is convenient to regard as a standard or unit amount. . . .

Coding

At the outset it was pointed out that the *transmitter* accepts the *message* and turns it into something called the *signal,* the latter being what actually passes over the channel to the *receiver.*

The transmitter, in such a case as telephony, merely changes the audible voice signal over into something (the varying electrical current on the telephone wire) which is at once clearly different but clearly equivalent. But the transmitter may carry out a much more complex operation on the message to produce the signal. It could, for example, take a written message and use some

162

Chapter 7
Technology,
Systems, and
Human
Interaction

code to encipher this message into, say a sequence of numbers; these numbers then being sent over the channel as the signal.

Thus one says, in general, that the function of the transmitter is to *encode*, and that of the receiver to *decode*, the message. The theory provides for very sophisticated transmitters and receivers—such, for example, as possess "memories," so that the way they encode a certain symbol of the message depends not only upon this one symbol, but also upon previous symbols of the message and the way they have been encoded. . . .

Remember that the entropy (or information) associated with the process which generates messages or signals is determined by the statistical character of the process—by the various probabilities for arriving at message situations and for choosing, when in those situations the next symbols. The statistical nature of *messages* is entirely determined by the character of the source. But the statistical character of the *signal* as actually transmitted by a channel, and hence the entropy in the channel, is determined both by what one attempts to feed into the channel and by the capabilities of the channel to handle different signal situations. For example, in telegraphy, there have to be spaces between dots and dots, between dots and dashes, and between dashes and dashes, or the dots and dashes would not be recognizable.

Now it turns out that when a channel does have certain constraints of this sort, which limit complete signal freedom, there are certain statistical signal characteristics which lead to a signal entropy which is larger than it would be for any other statistical signal structure, and in this important case, the signal entropy is exactly equal to the channel capacity.

In terms of these ideas, it is now possible precisely to characterize the most efficient kind of coding, The best transmitter, in fact, is that which codes the message in such a way that the signal has just those optimum statistical characteristics which are best suited to the channel to be used—which in fact maximize the signal (or one may say, the channel) entropy and make it equal to the capacity C of the channel. . . .

Noise

How does noise affect information? Information is, we must steadily remember, a measure of one's freedom of choice in selecting a message. The greater this freedom of choice, and hence the greater the information, the greater is the uncertainty that the message actually selected is some particular one. Thus greater freedom of choice, greater uncertainty, greater information go hand in hand.

If noise is introduced, then the received message contains certain distortions, certain errors, certain extraneous material, that would certainly lead one to say that the received message exhibits, because of the effects of the noise, an increased uncertainty. But if the uncertainty is increased, the information is increased, and this sounds as though the noise were beneficial!

It is generally true that when there is noise, the received signal exhibits greater information—or better, the received signal is selected out of a more varied set than is the transmitted signal. This is a situation which beautifully illustrates the semantic trap into which one can fall if he does not remember that "information" is used here with a special meaning that measures freedom of choice and hence uncertainty as to what choice has been made. It is therefore possible for the word information to have either good or bad connotations. Uncertainty which arises by virtue of freedom of choice on the part of the sender is desirable uncertainty. Uncertainty which arises because of errors or because of the influence of noise is undesirable uncertainty.

It is thus clear where the joker is in saying that the received signal has more information. Some of this information is spurious and undesirable and has been introduced via the noise. To get the useful information in the received signal we must subtract out this spurious portion.

Before we can clear up this point we have to stop for a little detour. Suppose one has two sets of symbols, such as the message symbols generated by the information source, and the signal symbols which are actually received. The probabilities of these two sets of symbols are interrelated, for clearly the probability of receiving a certain symbol depends upon what symbol was sent. With no errors from noise or from other causes, the received signals would correspond precisely to the message symbols sent; and in the presence of possible error, the probabilities for received symbols would obviously be loaded heavily on those which correspond, or closely correspond, to the message symbols sent.

Now in such a situation one can calculate what is called the entropy of one set of symbols relative to the other. Let us, for example, consider the entropy of the message relative to the signal. It is unfortunate that we cannot understand the issues involved here without going into some detail. Suppose for the moment that one knows that a certain signal symbol has actually been received. Then each *message* symbol takes on a certain probability—relatively large for the symbol identical with or the symbols similar to the one received, and relatively small for all others. Using this set of probabilities, one calculates a tentative entropy value. This is the message entropy on the assumption of a definite known received or signal symbol. Under any good conditions its value is low, since the probabilities involved are not spread around rather evenly on the various cases, but are heavily loaded on one or a few cases. Its value would be zero in any ease where noise was completely absent, for then, the signal symbol being known, all message probabilities would be zero except for one symbol (namely the one received), which would have a probability of unity.

For each assumption as to the signal symbol received, one can calculate one of these tentative message entropies. Calculate all of them, and then average them, weighting each one in accordance with the probability of the signal symbol assumed in calculating it. Entropies calculated in this way, when there are two sets of symbols to consider, are called *relative entropies*. The particular one just described is the entropy of the message relative to the signal, and Shannon has named this also the *equivocation*.

From the way this equivocation is calculated, we can see what its significance is. It measures the *average uncertainty in the message when the signal is known*. If there were no noise, then there would be no uncertainty concerning the message if the signal is known. If the information source has any residual uncertainty after the signal is known, then this must be undesirable uncertainty due to noise.

Logic and Intuition

Researchers in the area of information theory have become increasingly interested in how technologies exert control over their users and their messages. As newer media forms and new programs are developed, the relationship between the human user and the technological system becomes more acute.

Michael Heim is the author of *Electric Language: A Philosophical Study of Word Processing* (Yale University Press, 1987) and *The Metaphysics of Virtual Reality* (Oxford University Press, 1993). In the following selection from *Metaphysics,* Heim discusses ways in which people's thought processes are different when working with a computer. He defines and discusses Boolean logic to show how people "use" the internal logic of the system to process information.

Heim adds a dimension to the study of media and society that goes beyond thinking of the communication process as involving components of persons, media, and society, toward considering the human user and technological system as a combined unit. His approach also goes beyond the idea of the human/medium relationship as an organism; instead, he incorporates principles of philosophy, linguistics, and cognitive science to analyze the complexities of human thought processes as individuals work closely with technological systems.

Heim's work is important for advanced studies in communication, and the principles he proposes may be applied in the future to other fields, including electronics, mathematics, computer science, and linguistics.

Key Concept: Boolean logic

How does thinking at the computer differ from thinking with paper and pencil or thinking at the typewriter? The computer doesn't merely place another tool at your fingertips. It builds a whole new environment, an information environment in which the mind breathes a different atmosphere. The computing atmosphere belongs to an information-rich world—which soon becomes an information-polluted world.

First, the files you create grow rapidly, forming an electronic library of letters, papers, and other documents. Through on-line connections, you save pieces from the work of colleagues and friends, notes about future projects, and leftovers from database searches. Add some serendipitous items to disk storage—maybe the Gettysburg Address, the Constitution, or the King James Bible—and you find yourself soon outgrowing your disk-storage capacity. CD-Roms then spin out encyclopedias, the *Oxford English Dictionary,* or the entire corpus of ancient Greek literature. As the load of information stresses your mental capacity, you sense that you've come down with infomania.

Because the computer helped generate all this information, you naturally hope that the computer will in turn help mop up the mess. The computer can indeed hack a neat pathway through the dense information jungle. Computer data searches find references, phrases, or ideas in an instant, in the nanoseconds it takes the microprocessor to go through huge amounts of data. A word processor or database takes a key phrase and in a flash snaps a piece of information into view. So there you are, lifted by the computer out of the morass generated by computers. You can search through thousands of periodicals in minutes, without ever having to know anything about silicon microchips, high-level code, or sorting algorithms. All you need is some elementary search logic that you can learn in about an hour. Today most computer searches use elementary Boolean logic.

What is Boolean logic? Alfred Glossbrenner in *How to Look It Up Online* describes Boolean logic in terms simple enough for most computer users: "AND means a record must have both terms in it. OR means it can have either term. NOT means it cannot have the specified term." Glossbrenner chides those who belabor the complexities of Boolean logic and bewilder the user: "You sometimes get the impression that the authors would be drummed out of the manual-writers union if they didn't include complicated discussion of search logic laced with plenty of Venn diagrams—those intersecting, variously shaded circles you learned about in sophomore geometry. Forget it!" . . .

Today we interrogate the world through the computer interface, where many of our questions begin with Boolean terms. The Boolean search then guides the subconscious processes by which we characteristically model the world. Once we notice how computers structure our mental environment, we can reflect on the subconscious agencies that affect our mental life, and we are then in a position to grasp both the potential and the peril. So let's return again to those simple Venn diagrams from sophomore geometry and to the Boolean logic on which they are based.

George Boole (1815–1864) discovered the branch of mathematics known as *symbolic logic.* Boole's "algebra of logic" uses formulas to symbolize logical relations. The formulas in algebraic symbols can describe the general relationships among groups of things that have certain properties. Given a question about how one group relates to another, Boole could manipulate the equations and quickly produce an answer. First, his algebra classifies things, and then the algebraic symbols express any relationship among the things that have been classified—as if we were shuffling things in the nested drawers of a Chinese puzzle box. . . .

Historically, Boole's logic was the first system for calculating class membership, for rapidly determining whether or not something falls into one or another category or class of things. Before Boole, logic was a study of state-

166

*Chapter 7
Technology,
Systems, and
Human
Interaction*

ments about things referred to directly and intuitively at hand. After Boole, logic became a system of pure symbols. Pre-Boolean logic focused on the way that direct statements or assertions connect and hold together. A set of statements that hangs together can be a valid deductive pattern. Validity is the way that conclusions connect with their supporting reasons or premises. The traditional study of logic harked back to Aristotle, who first noticed patterns in the way we assemble statements into arguments. Aristotle called the assemblage of statements *syllogisms,* from the Greek for a pattern of reasoning. Aristotle himself used symbols sparingly in his logic, and when he did use symbols, they served merely to point out language patterns. Aristotle's symbols organized what was already given in direct statements. With Boolean logic, on the contrary, direct statements have value only as instances of the relationships among abstract symbols. Direct language becomes only one possible instance of algebraic mathematics, one possible application of mathematical logic.

Boole inverted the traditional relationship between direct and symbolic languages. He conceived of language as a system of symbols and believed that his symbols could absorb all logically correct language. By inverting statement and symbol, Boole's mathematical logic could swallow traditional logic and capture direct statements in a web of symbolic patterns. Logical argument became a branch of calculation.

The term *symbolic logic* first appeared in 1881 in a book by that title. The book's author, John Venn, introduced the first graphic display of Boole's formulas. Venn continued Boole's plan to absorb the direct statements of language into a general system of abstract algebra. With mathematics as a basis, Venn could solve certain logical difficulties that had perplexed traditional Aristotelian logicians. With mathematical precision, modern logic could present linguistic arguments and logical relationships within a total system, a formal organization having its own axioms and theorems. Systemic consistency became more important than the direct reference to things addressed in our experience.

Note already one telltale sign of infomania: the priority of system. When system precedes relevance, the way becomes clear for the primacy of information. For it to become manipulable and transmissible as information, knowledge must first be reduced to homogenized units. With the influx of homogenized bits of information, the sense of overall significance dwindles. This subtle emptying of meaning appears in the Venn diagrams that graphically display Boolean logic.

. . . From the outset, then Boolean logic assumes that as a rule, we stand at a remove from direct statements about particular things in which we existing beings are actually, personally involved.

This shift in the meaning of logical terms has drastic consequences for logic itself and for logic as a formal study. Traditional Aristotelian logic presupposed an actual subject, ideal or real, to which logical terms or words refer. Traditional logic also presupposed that logical thinking is, like spontaneous thought and speech, intimately involved with a real subject matter. Mathematical logic gained the upper hand by severing its significance from the conditions under which we make direct statements. Today, logicians like Willard Van Orman Quine can argue that a concrete and unique individual thing (to which we refer as such) has no more reality than "to be the value of a variable," at least when we consider things "from a logical point of view." The modern logical point of view begins with the system, not with concrete content. It operates in a domain of pure formality and abstract detachment. The modern logical point of view proceeds from an intricate net of abstract relations having no inherent connection to the things we directly perceive and experience.

We can contrast this aloof abstraction with the traditional logic that still swam in the element of direct experience. Traditional logic began with direct statements, insofar as its logical language presupposed as necessary the existential interpretation of statements. When we state something in everyday language, we attribute something to something; we attribute the color mauve to the wall, the quality of mercy to a creditor. We speak of what is before us, and we speak in the context of other people who may also have access to what we are talking about. We commonly assume the existence or at least the existential relevance of what we are talking about. Modern symbolic logic, on the contrary, mimics modern mathematics, which has no interest in the actually existing world, not even the world of direct statements. In this sense, modern logic operates at a remove from our everyday involvement with things.

But why pick on modern Boolean logic? Don't all logics bring abstraction and alienation? Even the words we use to pose any question testify to a gap between us and the wordless subject we are thinking or talking about. Any logic can distance us. We sometimes run across a person arguing with impeccable logic for a conclusion contrary to our own gut feelings, and we often feel overwhelmed, and forcibly so, by the sheer power of the argument itself. Logic can move like a juggernaut adrift from any personal engagement with its subject matter. Someone with a great deal less experience, for example, can make us feel compelled to accept a conclusion we know instinctively to be wrong. We feel the logical coercion even though we may have much more familiarity with the matter under discussion. Arguing with someone like Socrates or William F. Buckley can be disconcerting. We sense a line of thought pushing inexorably through the topic, perhaps even in spite of the topic. Logic, like mathematics, operates outside the intuitive wisdom of experience and common sense. Hence the mathematical idiot savant. Like math, logic can hover above particular facts and circumstances, linking chains of statements trailing from some phantom first premise. We can be perfectly logical yet float completely adrift from reality. By its very nature, logic operates with abstractions. But modern logic operates with a greater degree of abstraction than does Aristotelian logic, placing us at a further remove from experience and from felt insight. . . .

As a medium, the computer relieves us of the exertion needed to pour our thoughts into an algebraic mold. The shift from intuitive content to bit-size information proceeds invisibly and smoothly. On the machine level, the computer's microswitches in the central processing unit organize everything through a circuit based on symbolic logic, and Boolean searches simply apply that same logic to text processing. Hardly noticing this spiderlike, nondirect logic, we stand at a new remove from concretely embedded language. The computer absorbs our language so we can squirt symbols at lightning speeds or scan the whole range of human thought with Boolean searches. Because the

168

*Chapter 7
Technology,
Systems, and
Human
Interaction*

computer, not the student, does the translating, the shift takes place subtly. The computer system slides us from a direct awareness of things to the detached world of logical distance. By encoding language as data, the computer already modifies the language we use into mathematized ASCII (American Standard Code for Information Interchange). We can then operate with the certitude of Boolean formulas. The logical distance we gain offers all the allure of control and power without the pain of having to translate back and forth from our everyday approach to the things we experience.

But so what if computer power removes us from direct intuitive language? So what if Boolean logic injects greater existential distance from practical contexts than any previous logic? Don't our other text tools also operate at a remove from direct context-embedded language? Isn't any medium, by definition, a mediation? If the Boolean search operates at a great remove from direct oral discourse, don't also pen and paper, not to mention rubber erasers and Linotype typesetting machines?

Nonlinguistic tools, like erasers, do indeed insert a distance between ourselves and our context-embedded mother tongue. And, yes, using a rubber eraser does affect us in subtle, psychological ways. Teachers understand that getting a student to use an eraser marks a significant step on the road to good writing. A self-critical attitude distinguishes good from bad writing, and picking up an eraser means that we are beginning to evaluate our own words and thoughts.

But using Boolean search logic on a computer marks a giant step in the human species's relationship to thought and language. Just as the invention of the wax tablet made a giant stride in writing habits, forever marginalizing chiseled stones, so too Boolean search logic marks the new psychic framework of electronic text woven around us by computers. With electronic text we speed along a superhighway in the world of information, and Boolean search logic shifts our mental life into a high gear.

The Boolean search shows the characteristic way that we put questions to the world of information. When we pose a question to the Boolean world, we use keywords, buzzwords, and thought bits to scan the vast store of knowledge. Keeping an abstract, cybernetic distance from the sources of knowledge, we set up tiny funnels to capture the onrush of data. The funnels sift out the "hits" triggered by our keywords. Through minute logical apertures, we observe the world much like a robot rapidly surveying the surface of things. We cover an enormous amount of material in an incredibly short time, but what we see comes through narrow thought channels.

PART THREE

Critical Theory of Mass Media

CHAPTER 8 Mass Media, Power, and Ideology

8.1 HERBERT I. SCHILLER

The Mind Managers

Herbert I. Schiller has had a long and distinguished career as a critical scholar of modern mass media. His work has influenced the field of media studies worldwide. In his many books, including *Mass Communication and American Empire* (A.M. Kelley, 1969) and *Culture, Inc.* (Oxford University Press, 1989), Schiller has systematically investigated the relationship between corporate-owned and controlled mass media and the global expansion of capitalism. Within this larger project, Schiller points to what he sees as a problematic complicity between the mainstream of communication research and the agenda of private corporate and government power. Using a distinction originally made by European social critics, he differentiates between *administrative* researchers (i.e., scholars whose work obscures the connections between mass media and political-economic power) and *critical* researchers.

Schiller argues that critical scholars take the position that mass media institutions are key elements of the modern capitalist world order. He believes that mass media produce both economic profits and the ideology necessary to sustain a world system of exploitative capitalist social relationships. Schiller maintains that it is the job of the critical researcher to untangle the relationships between media and power and to expose the ideology inherent in media content.

In the following selection from his early work *The Mind Managers* (Beacon Press, 1973), Schiller employs the critical perspective to expose the operation of key ideological myths disseminated in the mass media, which act to confuse individuals and to gain their consent to the existing state of power relationships.

Key Concept: manipulation of consciousness

INTRODUCTION

America's media managers create, process, refine, and preside over the circulation of images and information which determine our beliefs and attitudes and, ultimately, our behavior. When they deliberately produce messages that do not correspond to the realities of social existence, the media managers become mind managers. Messages that intentionally create a false sense of reality and produce a consciousness that cannot comprehend or wilfully rejects the actual conditions of life, personal or social, are manipulative messages.

Manipulation of human minds, according to Paulo Freire, "is an instrument of conquest." It is one of the means by which "the dominant elites try to conform the masses to their objectives.[1] By using myths which explain, justify, and sometimes even glamorize the prevailing conditions of existence, manipulators secure popular support for a social order that is not in the majority's long-term real interest. When manipulation is successful, alternative social arrangements remain unconsidered. . . .

The permanent division of the society into two broad categories of "winners" and "losers" arises and persists as a result of the maintenance, recognition, and, indeed, sanctification of the system of private ownership of productive property and the extension of the ownership principle to all other aspects of human existence. The general acceptance of this arrangement for carrying on social activity makes it inevitable that some prosper, consolidate their success, and join the dominant shapers and molders of the community. The others, the majority, work on as mere conformists, the disadvantaged, and the manipulated; they are manipulated especially to continue to participate, if not wholeheartedly, at least positively, in the established routines. The system gives them a return adequate to achieve some marks of economic status, and manipulation leads them to hope that they might turn these routines to greater personal advantage for themselves or their children.

It is not surprising that manipulation, as an instrument of control, should reach its highest development in the United States. In America, more than anywhere else, the favorable conditions we have briefly noted permit a large fraction of the population to escape total suppression and thereby become potential actors in the historical process. Manipulation allows the appearance of active engagement while denying many of the material and *all* of the psychic benefits of genuine involvement. . . .

The means of manipulation are many, but, clearly, control of the informational and ideational apparatus at all levels is essential. This is secured by the operation of a simple rule of the market economy. Ownership and control of the mass media, like all other forms of property, is available to those with capital. Inevitably, radio- and television-station ownership, newspaper and magazine proprietorship, movie-making, and book publishing are largely in the hands of corporate chains and media conglomerates. The apparatus is thus ready to assume an active and dominant role in the manipulative process.

My intention is to identify some of these conditioning forces and to reveal the means by which they conceal their presence, deny their influence, or exercise directional control under auspices that superficially appear benign and/or natural. The search for these "hidden processes," along with their subtle mechanics, should not be mistaken for a more common kind of investigation—the exposé of clandestine activities. Conspiracy is neither invoked nor considered in these pages. Though the idea of mind management lends itself easily to such an approach, the comprehensive conditioning carried on throughout American society today does not require, and actually cannot be understood in, such terms. . . .

MANIPULATION AND THE PACKAGED CONSCIOUSNESS

Five Myths That Structure Content

1. The Myth of Individualism and Personal Choice   Manipulation's greatest triumph, most observable in the United States, is to have taken advantage of the special historical circumstances of Western development to perpetrate as truth a definition of freedom cast in individualistic terms. This enables the concept to serve a double function. It protects the ownership of productive private property while simultaneously offering itself as the guardian of the individual's well-being, suggesting, if not insisting, that the latter is unattainable without the existence of the former. Upon this central construct an entire scaffolding of manipulation is erected. What accounts for the strength of this powerful notion?

. . . The identification of personal choice with human freedom can be seen arising side-by-side with seventeenth-century individualism, both products of the emerging market economy.[2]

For several hundred years individual proprietorship, allied with technological improvement, increased output and thereby bestowed great importance on personal independence in the industrial and political processes. The view that freedom is a personal matter, and that the individual's rights supersede the group's and provide the basis for social organization, gained credibility with the rise of material rewards and leisure time. Note, however, that these conditions were not distributed evenly among all classes of Western society and that they did not begin to exist in the rest of the world. . . .

In the newly settled United States, few restraints impeded the imposition of an individualistic private entrepreneurial system and its accompanying myths of personal choice and individual freedom. Both enterprise and myth found a hospitable setting. The growth of the former and consolidation of the latter were inevitable. How far the process has been carried is evident today in the easy public acceptance of the giant multinational private corporation as an example of individual endeavor. . . .

Privatism in every sphere of life is considered normal. The American life style, from its most minor detail to its most deeply felt beliefs and practices, reflects an exclusively self-centered outlook, which is in turn an accurate image of the structure of the economy itself. The American dream includes a personal means of transportation, a single-family home, the proprietor-operated business. Such other institutions as a competitive health system are obvious, if not natural, features of the privately organized economy. . . .

Though individual freedom and personal choice are its most powerful mythic defenses, the system of private ownership and production requires and creates additional constructs, along with the techniques to transmit them. These notions either rationalize its existence and promise a great future, or divert attention from its searing inadequacies and conceal the possibilities of new departures for human development. Some of these constructs and techniques are not exclusive to the privatistic industrial order, and can be applied in any social system intent on maintaining its dominion. Other myths, and the means of circulating them, are closely associated with the specific characteristics of this social system.

2. The Myth of Neutrality For manipulation to be most effective, evidence of its presence should be nonexistent. When the manipulated believe things are the way they are naturally and inevitably, manipulation is successful. In short, manipulation requires a false reality that is a continuous denial of its existence.

It is essential, therefore, that people who are manipulated believe in the neutrality of their key social institutions. They must believe that government, the media, education, and science are beyond the clash of conflicting social interests. Government, and the national government in particular, remains the centerpiece of the neutrality myth. This myth presupposes belief in the basic integrity and nonpartisanship of government in general and of its constituent parts—Congress, the judiciary, and the Presidency. Corruption, deceit, and knavery, when they occur from time to time, are seen to be the result of human weakness. The institutions themselves are beyond reproach. The fundamental soundness of the overall system is assured by the well-designed instrumentalities that comprise the whole.

The Presidency, for instance, is beyond the reach of special interests, according to this mythology. The first and most extreme manipulative use of the Presidency, therefore, is to claim the nonpartisanship of the office, and to seem to withdraw it from clamorous conflict. . . .

The chief executive, though the most important, is but one of many governmental departments that seek to present themselves as neutral agents, embracing no objectives but the general welfare, and serving everyone impartially and disinterestedly. For half a century all the media joined in propagating the myth of the FBI as a nonpolitical and highly effective agency of law enforcement. In fact, the Bureau has been used continuously to intimidate and coerce social critics.

The mass media, too, are supposed to be neutral. Departures from even-handedness in news reportage are admitted but, the press assure us, result from human error and cannot be interpreted as flaws in the basically sound institutions of information dissemination. That the media (press, periodicals, radio, and television) are almost without exception business enterprises, receiving their revenues from commercial sales of time or space, seems to create no problems for those who defend the objectivity and integrity of the informational services.[3] . . .

Science, which more than any other intellectual activity has been integrated into the corporate economy, continues also to insist on its value-free neutrality. Unwilling to consider the implications of the sources of its funding, the directions of its research, the applications of its theories, and the character of the paradigms it creates, science promotes the notion of its insulation from the social forces that affect all other ongoing activities in the nation.

The system of schooling, from the elementary through the university level, is also, according to the manipulators, devoid of deliberate ideological purpose. Still, the product must reflect the teaching: it is astonishing how large a proportion of the graduates at each stage continue, despite all the ballyhoo about the counterculture, to believe in and observe the competitive ethic of business enterprise.

Wherever one looks in the social sphere, neutrality and objectivity are invoked to describe the functioning of value-laden and purposeful activities which lend support to the prevailing institutional system. Essential to the everyday maintenance of the control system is the carefully nurtured myth that no special groups or views have a preponderant influence on the country's important decision-making processes. . . .

3. The Myth of Unchanging Human Nature   Human expectations can be the lubricant of social change. When human expectations are low, passivity prevails. There can, of course, be various kinds of images in anyone's mind concerning political, social, economic, and personal realities. The common denominator of all such imagery, however, is the view people have of human nature. What human nature is seen to be ultimately affects the way human beings behave, not because they must act as they do but because they believe they are expected to act that way. . . .

It is predictable that in the United States a theory that emphasizes the aggressive side of human behavior and the unchangeability of human nature would find approval, permeate most work and thought, and be circulated widely by the mass media. Certainly, an economy that is built on and rewards private ownership and individual acquisition, and is subject to the personal and social conflicts these arrangement impose, can be expected to be gratified with an explanation that legitimizes its operative principles. How reassuring to consider these conflictful relationships inherent in the human condition rather than imposed by social circumstance! This outlook fits nicely too with the antiideological stance the system projects. It induces a "scientific" and "objective" approach to the human condition rigorously measuring human microbehavior in all its depravities, and for the most part ignoring the broader and less measurable social parameters.

Daily TV programming, for example, with its quota of half a dozen murders per hour, is rationalized easily by media controllers as an effort to give the people what they want. Too bad, they shrug, if human nature demands eighteen hours daily of mayhem and slaughter. . . .

Fortune finds it cheering, for example, that some American social scientists are again emphasizing "the intractability of human nature" in their explanations of social phenomena. "The orthodox view of environment as the all-important influence on people's behavior," it reports, "is yielding to a new awareness of the role of hereditary factors: enthusiasm for schemes to reform society by remolding men is giving way to a healthy appreciation of the basic intractability of human nature."[4]

The net social effects of the thesis that human nature is at fault are further disorientation, total inability to recognize the causes of malaise—much less to take any steps to overcome it—and, of most consequence, continued adherence to the *status quo*. . . .

It is to prevent social action (and it is immaterial whether the intent is articulated or not) that so much publicity and attention are devoted to every pessimistic appraisal of human potential. If we are doomed forever by our inheritance, there is not much to be done about it. But there is a good reason and a good market for undervaluing human capability. An entrenched social system depends on keeping the popular and, especially, the "enlightened" mind unsure and doubtful about its human prospects. . . .

This does not necessitate ignoring history. On the contrary, endless recitation of what happened in the past accompanies assertions about how much change is occurring under our very noses. But these are invariably *physical* changes—new means of transportation, air conditioning, space rockets, packaged foods. Mind managers dwell on these matters but carefully refrain from considering changes in social relationships or in the institutional structures that undergird the economy.

Every conceivable kind of futuristic device is canvassed and blueprinted. Yet those who will use these wonder items will apparently continue to be married, raise children in suburban homes, work for private companies, vote for a President in a two-party system, and pay a large portion of their incomes for defense, law and order, and superhighways. The world, except for some glamorous surface redecorations, will remain as it is; basic relationships will not change, because they, like human nature, are allegedly unchangeable. As for those parts of the world that have undergone far-reaching social rearrangements, reports of these transformations, if there are any, emphasize the defects, problems, and crises, which are seized upon with relish by domestic consciousness manipulators. . . .

4. The Myth of the Absence of Social Conflict . . . Consciousness controllers, in their presentation of the domestic scene, deny absolutely the presence of social conflict. On the face of it, this seems an impossible task. After all, violence is "as American as apple pie." Not only in fact but in fantasy: in films, on TV, and over the radio, the daily quota of violent scenarios offered the public is staggering. How is this carnival of conflict reconcilable with the media managers' intent to present an image of social harmony? The contradiction is easily resolved.

As presented by the national message-making apparatus, conflict is almost always an *individual* matter, in its manifestations and in its origin. The social roots of conflict just do not exist for the cultural-informational managers. True, there are "good guys" and "bad guys," but, except for such ritualized situations as westerns, which are recognized as scenarios of the past, role identification is divorced from significant social categories.

Black, brown, yellow, red, and other ethnic Americans have always fared poorly in the manufactured cultural imagery. Still, these are minorities which all segments of the white population have exploited in varying degrees. As for the great social division in the nation, between worker and owner, with rare exceptions it has been left unexamined. Attention is diverted elsewhere—generally toward the problems of the upward-striving middle segment of the population, that category with which everyone is supposed to identify. . . .

Elite control requires omission or distortion of social reality. Honest examination and discussion of social conflict can only deepen and intensify resistance to social inequity. Economically powerful groups and companies quickly get edgy when attention is called to exploitative practices in which they are engaged. *Variety*'s television editor, Les Brown, described such an incident. Coca-Cola Food Company and the Florida Fruit and Vegetable Association reacted sharply to a TV documentary, "Migrant," which centered on migrant fruit pickers in Florida. Brown wrote that "the miracle of *Migrant* was that it was televised at all." Warnings were sent to NBC not to show the program because it was "biased." Cuts in the film were demanded, and at least one was made. Finally, after the showing, "Coca-Cola shifted all its network billings to CBS and ABC."[5]

On a strictly commercial level, the presentation of social issues creates uneasiness in mass audiences, or so the audience researchers believe. To be safe, to hold onto as large a public as possible, sponsors are always eager to eliminate potentially "controversial" program material.

The entertainments and cultural products that have been most successful in the United States, those that have received the warmest support and publicity from the communications system, are invariably movies, TV programs, books, and mass entertainments (i.e., Disneyland) which may offer more than a fair quota of violence but never take up *social* conflict. . . .

5. The Myth of Media Pluralism   Personal choice exercised in an environment of cultural-information diversity is the image, circulated worldwide, of the condition of life in America. This view is also internalized in the belief structure of a large majority of Americans, which makes them particularly susceptible to thoroughgoing manipulation. It is, therefore, one of the central myths upon which mind management flourishes. Choice and diversity, though separate concepts, are in fact inseparable; choice is unattainable in any real sense without diversity. If real options are nonexistent, choosing is either meaningless or manipulative. It is manipulative when accompanied by the illusion that the choice is meaningful.

Though it cannot be verified, the odds are that the illusion of informational choice is more pervasive in the United States than anywhere else in the world. The illusion is sustained by a willingness, deliberately maintained by information controllers, to mistake *abundance of media* for *diversity of content.* . . .

The fact of the matter is that, except for a rather small and highly selective segment of the population who know what they are looking for and can therefore take advantage of the massive communications flow, most Americans are basically, though unconsciously, trapped in what amounts to a no-choice informational bind. Variety of opinion on foreign and domestic news or, for that matter, local community business, hardly exists in the media. This results essentially from the inherent identity of interests, material and ideological, of property-holders (in this case, the private owners of the communications media), and from the monopolistic character of the communications industry in general.

The limiting effects of monopoly are in need of no explanation, and communications monopolies restrict informational choice wherever they operate. They offer one version of reality—their own. In this category fall most of the nation's newspapers, magazines, and films, which are produced by national or regional communications conglomerates. The number of American cities in which competing newspapers circulate has shrunk to a handful.

While there is a competition of sorts for audiences among the three major TV networks, two conditions determine the limits of the variety presented. Though each network struggles gamely to attract as large an audience as possible, it imitates its two rivals in program format and content. If ABC is successful with a western serial, CBS and NBC will in all likelihood "compete" with "shoot-'em-ups" in the same time slot. Besides, each of the three national networks is part of, or is itself, an enormous communications business, with the drives and motivations of any other profit-seeking enterprise. This means that diversity in the informational-entertainment sector exists only in the sense that there are a number of superficially different versions of the main categories of program. For example, there are several talk shows on late-night TV; there may be half a dozen private-eye, western, or law-and-order TV serials to "choose from" in prime time; there are three network news commentators with different personalities who offer essentially identical information. One can switch the radio dial and get round-the-clock news from one or, at most, two news services; or one can hear Top 40 popular songs played by "competing" disc jockeys.

Though no single program, performer, commentator, or informational bit is necessarily identical to its competitors, *there is no significant qualitative difference.* Just as a supermarket offers six identical soaps in different colors and a drugstore sells a variety of brands of aspirin at different prices, disc jockeys play the same records between personalized advertisements for different commodities. . . .

Yet it is this condition of communicational pluralism, empty as it is of real diversity, which affords great strength to the prevailing system of consciousness-packaging. The multichannel communications flow creates confidence in, and lends credibility to, the notion of free informational choice. Meanwhile, its main effect is to provide continuous reinforcement of the *status quo.* Similar stimuli, emanating from apparently diverse sources, envelop the listener/ viewer/reader in a message/image environment that ordinarily seems uncontrolled, relatively free, and quite natural. How could it be otherwise with such an abundance of programs and transmitters? Corporate profit-seeking, the main objective of conglomeratized communications, however real and ultimately determining, is an invisible abstraction to the consumers of the cultural images. And one thing is certain: the media do not call their audiences' attention to its existence or its mode of operation. . . .

The fundamental similarity of the informational material and cultural messages that each of the mass media *independently* transmits makes it necessary to view the communications system as a totality. The media are mutually and continuously reinforcing. Since they operate according to commercial rules, rely on advertising, and are tied tightly to the corporate economy, both in their own structure and in their relationships with sponsors, the media constitute an industry, not an aggregation of independent, freewheeling informational entrepreneurs, each offering a highly individualistic product. By need and by design, the images and messages they purvey are, with few exceptions, constructed to achieve similar objectives, which are, simply put, profitability and the affirmation and maintenance of the private-ownership consumer society.

Consequently, research directed at discovering the impact of a single TV program or movie, or even an entire category of stimuli, such as "violence on TV," can often be fruitless. Who can justifiably claim that TV violence is inducing delinquent juvenile behavior when violence is endemic to all mass communications channels? Who can suggest that any single category of programming is producing male chauvinist or racist behavior when stimuli and imagery carrying such sentiments flow unceasingly through all the channels of transmission?

It is generally agreed that television is the most powerful medium; certainly its influence as a purveyor of the system's values cannot be overstated. All the same, television, no matter how powerful, itself depends on the absence of dissonant stimuli in the other media. Each of the informational channels makes its unique contribution, but the result is the same—the consolidation of the *status quo.*

NOTES

1. Paulo Freire, *Pedagogy of the Oppressed* (New York: Herder and Herder, 1971), p. 144.
2. C. B. MacPherson, *The Political Theory of Possessive Individualism* (Oxford: Clarendon Press, 1962).
3. Henry Luce, the founder of *Time, Life, Fortune, Sports Illustrated,* and other mass circulation magazines, knew otherwise. He told his staff at *Time:* "The alleged journalistic objectivity, a claim that a writer presents facts without applying any value judgment to them [is] modern usage—and that is strictly a phony. It is that that I had to renounce and denounce. So when we say the hell with objectivity, that is what we are talking about." W. A. Swanberg, *Luce and His Empire* (New York: Charles Scribner's Sons, 1972), p. 331.
4. "The Social Engineers Retreat Under Fire," *Fortune,* October 1972, p. 3.
5. Les Brown, *Television: The Business Behind The Box* (New York: Harcourt, Brace Jovanovich, 1971), pp. 196–203.

8.2 EDWARD S. HERMAN AND NOAM CHOMSKY

A Propaganda Model

Noam Chomsky is a linguistics scholar who has analyzed the integral relationship between mass media institutions, the state, and corporate power around the globe. He has also relentlessly scrutinized the connections between economic, political, and cultural institutions, and he has published the results of his studies in many books, including *The Culture of Terrorism* (South End Press, 1988) and *Necessary Illusions: Thought Control in Democratic Societies* (South End Press, 1989). Edward S. Herman is a critical researcher whose work has focused on the power of private corporations in the modern world. His publications include *Corporate Control, Corporate Power: A Twentieth Century Fund Study* (Cambridge University Press, 1981) and *Beyond Hypocrisy: Decoding the News in an Age of Propaganda* (South End Press, 1992).

In the following excerpt from their book *Manufacturing Consent: The Political Economy of the Mass Media* (Pantheon Books, 1988), Herman and Chomsky begin by defining the social function of mass media. Simply put, mass media socialize individuals into the dominant norms of society. The authors note that in any society that is characterized by systematic disparities of wealth and power, this socializing role takes the form of propaganda (i.e., pervasive misrepresentation of unequal and exploitative social relationships).

Herman and Chomsky condemn the *illegitimate* exercise of power in any society—capitalist, communist, authoritarian, etc. However, they suggest that the propaganda function of mass media is more insidious and much harder to see in societies like the United States where mass media systems are not run by the state; where they are run as private businesses; and where the press often stands in an adversarial relationship with the state and, less frequently, with corporate power. Propaganda is nonetheless the social function of such "free" media systems. Herman and Chomsky argue that only through systematic and rigorous analysis of the institutional relationships between mass media, the government, and the corporate sphere can the operation of propaganda be uncovered. To this end, Herman and Chomsky offer a propaganda, or *filtering,* model—a model that can be used by *anyone,* not just scholarly researchers.

Key Concept: media filtering

The he mass media serve as a system for communicating messages and symbols to the general populace. It is their function to amuse, entertain, and inform, and to inculcate individuals with the values, beliefs, and codes of behavior that will integrate them into the institutional structures of the larger society. In a world of concentrated wealth and major conflicts of class interest, to fulfil this role requires systematic propaganda.

Edward S. Herman and Noam Chomsky

In countries where the levers of power are in the hands of a state bureaucracy, the monopolistic control over the media, often supplemented by official censorship, makes it clear that the media serve the ends of a dominant elite. It is much more difficult to see a propaganda system at work where the media are private and formal censorship is absent. This is especially true where the media actively compete, periodically attack and expose corporate and governmental malfeasance, and aggressively portray themselves as spokesmen for free speech and the general community interest. What is not evident (and remains undiscussed in the media) is the limited nature of such critiques, as well as the huge inequality in command of resources, and its effect both on access to a private media system and on its behavior and performance.

A propaganda model focuses on this inequality of wealth and power and its multilevel effects on mass-media interests and choices. It traces the routes by which money and power are able to filter out the news fit to print, marginalize dissent, and allow the government and dominant private interests to get their messages across to the public. The essential ingredients of our propaganda model, or set of news "filters," fall under the following headings: (1) the size, concentrated ownership, owner wealth, and profit orientation of the dominant mass-media firms; (2) advertising as the primary income source of the mass media; (3) the reliance of the media on information provided by government, business, and "experts" funded and approved by these primary sources and agents of power; (4) "flak" as a means of disciplining the media; and (5) "anticommunism" as a national religion and control mechanism. These elements interact with and reinforce one another. The raw material of news must pass through successive filters, leaving only the cleansed residue fit to print. They fix the premises of discourse and interpretation, and the definition of what is newsworthy in the first place, and they explain the basis and operations of what amount to propaganda campaigns. . . .

SIZE, OWNERSHIP, AND PROFIT ORIENTATION OF THE MASS MEDIA: THE FIRST FILTER

. . . Ben Bagdikian stresses the fact that despite the large media numbers, the twenty-nine largest media systems account for over half of the output of newspapers, and most of the sales and audiences in magazines, broadcasting, books, and movies. He contends that these "constitute a new Private Ministry of Information and Culture" that can set the national agenda.[1] . . .

Many of the large media companies are fully integrated into the market, and for the others, too, the pressures of stockholders, directors, and bankers to focus on the bottom line are powerful. These pressures have intensified in recent years as media stocks have become market favorites, and actual or prospective owners of newspapers and television properties have found it possible to capitalize increased audience size and advertising revenues into multiplied values of the media franchises—and great wealth.[2] This has encouraged the entry of speculators and increased the pressure and temptation to focus more intensively on profitability. . . .

This trend toward greater integration of the media into the market system has been accelerated by the loosening of rules limiting media concentration, cross-ownership, and control by non-media companies.[3] There has also been an abandonment of restrictions—previously quite feeble anyway—on radio-TV commercials, entertainment-mayhem programming, and "fairness doctrine" threats, opening the door to the unrestrained commercial use of the airwaves.[4]

The greater profitability of the media in a deregulated environment has also led to an increase in takeovers and takeover threats, with even giants like CBS and Time, Inc., directly attacked or threatened. This has forced the managements of the media giants to incur greater debt and to focus ever more aggressively and unequivocally on profitability, in order to placate owners and reduce the attractiveness of their properties to outsiders.[5] They have lost some of their limited autonomy to bankers, institutional investors, and large individual investors whom they have had to solicit as potential "white knights."[6] . . .

The control groups of the media giants are also brought into close relationships with the mainstream of the corporate community through boards of directors and social links. In the cases of NBC and the Group W television and cable systems, their respective parents, GE and Westinghouse, are themselves mainstream corporate giants, with boards of directors that are dominated by corporate and banking executives. Many of the other large media firms have boards made up predominantly of insiders, a general characteristic of relatively small and owner-dominated companies. The larger the firm and the more widely distributed the stock, the larger the number and proportion of outside directors. The composition of the outside directors of the media giants is very similar to that of large non-media corporations. . . .

In addition to these board linkages, the large media companies all do business with commercial and investment bankers, obtaining lines of credit and loans, and receiving advice and service in selling stock and bond issues and in dealing with acquisition opportunities and takeover threats. Banks and other institutional investors are also large owners of media stock. In the early 1980s, such institutions held 44 percent of the stock of publicly owned newspapers and 35 percent of the stock of publicly owned broadcasting companies.[7] These investors are also frequently among the largest stockholders of individual companies. For example, in 1980–81, the Capital Group, an investment company system, held 7.1 percent of the stock of ABC, 6.6 percent of Knight-Ridder, 6 percent of Time, Inc., and 2.8 percent of Westinghouse.[8] These holdings, individually and collectively, do not convey control, but these large investors can make themselves heard, and their actions can affect the welfare of the companies and their managers.[9] If the managers fail to pursue actions that favor shareholder returns, institutional investors will be inclined to sell the stock (depressing its price), or to listen sympathetically to outsiders contemplating takeovers. These investors are a force helping press media companies toward strictly market (profitability) objectives. . . .

The large media companies have also diversified beyond the media field, and non-media companies have established a strong presence in the mass media. The most important cases of the latter are GE, owning RCA, which owns the NBC network, and Westinghouse, which owns major television-broadcasting stations, a cable network, and a radio-station network. GE and Westinghouse are both huge, diversified multinational companies heavily involved in the controversial areas of weapons production and nuclear power. . . . GE has contributed to the funding of the American Enterprise Institute, a right-wing think tank that supports intellectuals who will get the business message across. With the acquisition of ABC, GE should be in a far better position to assure that sound views are given proper attention.[10] The lack of outcry over its takeover of RCA and NBC resulted in part from the fact that RCA control over NBC had already breached the gate of separateness, but it also reflected the more pro-business and *laissez-faire* environment of the Reagan era. . . .

Another structural relationship of importance is the media companies' dependence on and ties with government. The radio-TV companies and networks all require government licenses and franchises and are thus potentially subject to government control or harassment. This technical legal dependency has been used as a club to discipline the media, and media policies that stray too often from an establishment orientation could activate this threat.[11] The media protect themselves from this contingency by lobbying and other political expenditures, the cultivation of political relationships, and care in policy. The political ties of the media have been impressive. . . . In television, the revolving-door flow of personnel between regulators and the regulated firms was massive during the years when the oligopolistic structure of the media and networks was being established.[12]

The great media also depend on the government for more general policy support. All business firms are interested in business taxes, interest rates, labor policies, and enforcement and nonenforcement of the antitrust laws. GE and Westinghouse depend on the government to subsidize their nuclear power and military research and development, and to create a favorable climate for their overseas sales. The *Reader's Digest, Time, Newsweek,* and movie- and television-syndication sellers also depend on diplomatic support for their rights to penetrate foreign cultures with U.S. commercial and value messages and interpretations of current affairs. The media giants, advertising agencies, and great multinational corporations have a joint and close interest in a favorable climate of investment in the Third World, and their interconnections and relationships with the government in these policies are symbiotic.[13]

In sum, the dominant media firms are quite large businesses; they are controlled by very wealthy people or by managers who are subject to sharp constraints by owners and other market-profit–oriented forces;[14] and they are closely interlocked, and have important common interests, with other major corporations, banks, and government. This is the first powerful filter that will affect news choices.

THE ADVERTISING LICENSE TO DO BUSINESS: THE SECOND FILTER

. . . With advertising, the free market does not yield a neutral system in which final buyer choice decides. The *advertisers'* choices influence media prosperity and survival.[15] The ad-based media receive an advertising subsidy that gives them a price-marketing-quality edge, which allows them to encroach on and further weaken their ad-free (or ad-disadvantaged) rivals.[16] Even if ad-based media cater to an affluent ("upscale") audience, they easily pick up a large part of the "down-scale" audience, and their rivals lose market share and are eventually driven out or marginalized. . . .

From the time of the introduction of press advertising, therefore, working-class and radical papers have been at a serious disadvantage. Their readers have tended to be of modest means, a factor that has always affected advertiser interest. One advertising executive stated in 1856 that some journals are poor vehicles because "their readers are not purchasers, and any money thrown upon them is so much thrown away."[17] . . .

The power of advertisers over television programming stems from the simple fact that they buy and pay for the programs—they are the "patrons" who provide the media subsidy. As such, the media compete for their patronage, developing specialized staff to solicit advertisers and necessarily having to explain how their programs serve advertisers' needs. The choices of these patrons greatly affect the welfare of the media, and the patrons become what William Evan calls "normative reference organizations,"[18] whose requirements and demands the media must accommodate if they are to succeed.[19]

For a television network, an audience gain or loss of one percentage point in the Nielsen ratings translates into a change in advertising revenue of from $80 to $100 million a year, with some variation depending on measures of audience "quality." The stakes in audience size and affluence are thus extremely large, and in a market system there is a strong tendency for such considerations to affect policy profoundly. This is partly a matter of institutional pressures to focus on the bottom line, partly a matter of the continuous interaction of the media organization with patrons who supply the revenue dollars. As Grant Tinker, then head of NBC-TV, observed, television "is an advertising-supported medium, and to the extent that support falls out, programming will change."[20]

Working-class and radical media also suffer from the political discrimination of advertisers. Political discrimination is structured into advertising allocations by the stress on people with money to buy. But many firms will always refuse to patronize ideological enemies and those whom they perceive as damaging their interests, and cases of overt discrimination add to the force of the voting system weighted by income. . . .

Advertisers will want, more generally, to avoid programs with serious complexities and disturbing controversies that interfere with the "buying mood." They seek programs that will lightly entertain and thus fit in with the spirit of the primary purpose of program purchases—the dissemination of a selling message. Thus over time, instead of programs like "The Selling of the Pentagon," it is a natural evolution of a market seeking sponsor dollars to offer programs such as "A Bird's-Eye View of Scotland," "Barry Goldwater's Arizona," "An Essay on Hotels," and "Mr. Rooney Goes to Dinner"—A CBS program on "how Americans eat when they dine out, where they go and why."[21] ...

Edward S. Herman and Noam Chomsky

Television stations and networks are also concerned to maintain audience "flow" levels, i.e., to keep people watching from program to program, in order to sustain advertising ratings and revenue. Airing program interludes of documentary-cultural matter that cause station switching is costly, and over time a "free" (i.e., ad-based) commercial system will tend to excise it. Such documentary-cultural-critical materials will be driven out of secondary media vehicles as well, as these companies strive to qualify for advertiser interest, although there will always be some cultural-political programming trying to come into being or surviving on the periphery of the mainstream media.

SOURCING MASS-MEDIA NEWS: THE THIRD FILTER

The mass media are drawn into a symbiotic relationship with powerful sources of information by economic necessity and reciprocity of interest. The media need a steady, reliable flow of the raw material of news. They have daily news demands and imperative news schedules that they must meet. They cannot afford to have reporters and cameras at all places where important stories may break. Economics dictates that they concentrate their resources where significant news often occurs, where important rumors and leaks abound, and where regular press conferences are held. The White House, the Pentagon, and the State Department, in Washington, D.C., are central nodes of such news activity. On a local basis, city hall and the police department are the subject of regular news "beats" for reporters. Business corporations and trade groups are also regular and credible purveyors of stories deemed newsworthy. These bureaucracies turn out a large volume of material that meets the demands of news organizations for reliable, scheduled flows. Mark Fishman calls this "the principle of bureaucratic affinity: only other bureaucracies can satisfy the input needs of a news bureaucracy."[22]

Government and corporate sources also have the great merit of being recognizable and credible by their status and prestige. This is important to the mass media. . . . Another reason for the heavy weight given to official sources is that the mass media claim to be "objective" dispensers of the news. Partly to maintain the image of objectivity, but also to protect themselves from criticisms of bias and the threat of libel suits, they need material that can be portrayed as presumptively accurate.[23] This is also partly a matter of cost: taking information from sources that may be presumed credible reduces investigative expense, whereas material from sources that are not prima facie credible, or that will elicit criticism and threats, requires careful checking and costly research.

The magnitude of the public-information operations of large government and corporate bureaucracies that constitute the primary news sources is vast and ensures special access to the media. The Pentagon, for example, has a public-information service that involves many thousands of employees, spending hundreds of millions of dollars every year and dwarfing not only the public-information resources of any dissenting individual or group but the *aggregate* of such groups. . . .

Only the corporate sector has the resources to produce public information and propaganda on the scale of the Pentagon and other government bodies. The AFSC and NCC cannot duplicate the Mobil Oil company's multimillion-dollar purchase of newspaper space and other corporate investments to get its viewpoint across.[24] The number of individual corporations with budgets for public information and lobbying in excess of those of the AFSC and NCC runs into the hundreds, perhaps even the thousands. A corporate *collective* like the U.S. Chamber of Commerce had a 1983 budget for research, communications, and political activities of $65 million.[25] By 1980, the chamber was publishing a business magazine (*Nation's Business*) with a circulation of 1.3 million and a weekly newspaper with 740,000 subscribers, and it was producing a weekly panel show distributed to 400 radio stations, as well as its own weekly panel-discussion programs carried by 128 commercial television stations.[26] . . .

To consolidate their preeminent position as sources, government and business-news promoters go to great pains to make things easy for news organizations. They provide the media organizations with facilities in which to gather; they give journalists advance copies of speeches and forthcoming reports; they schedule press conferences at hours well-geared to news deadlines;[27] they write press releases in usable language; and they carefully organize their press conferences and "photo opportunity" sessions.[28] It is the job of news officers "to meet the journalist's scheduled needs with material that their beat agency has generated at its own pace."[29]

In effect, the large bureaucracies of the powerful *subsidize* the mass media, and gain special access by their contribution to reducing the media's costs of acquiring the raw materials of, and producing, news. The large entities that provide this subsidy become "routine" news sources and have privileged access to the gates. Non-routine sources must struggle for access, and may be ignored by the arbitrary decision of the gatekeepers. It should also be noted that in the case of the largesse of the Pentagon and the State Department's Office of Public Diplomacy, the subsidy is at the taxpayers' expense, so that, in effect, the citizenry pays to be propagandized in the interest of powerful groups such as military contractors and other sponsors of state terrorism.

Because of their services, continuous contact on the beat, and mutual dependency, the powerful can use personal relationships, threats, and rewards to further influence and coerce the media. The media may feel obligated to carry extremely dubious stories and mute criticism in order not to offend their sources and disturb a close relationship.[30] It is very difficult to call authorities on whom one depends for daily news liars, even if they tell whoppers. Critical sources may be avoided not only because of their lesser availability and higher cost of establishing credibitlity, but also because the primary sources may be offended and may even threaten the media using them. . . .

The relation between power and sourcing extends beyond official and corporate provision of day-to-day news to shaping the supply of "experts." The dominance of official sources is weakened by the existence of highly respectable unofficial sources that give dissident views with great authority. This problem is alleviated by "co-opting the experts"[31]—i.e., putting them on the payroll as consultants, funding their research, and organizing think tanks that will hire them directly and help disseminate their messages. In this way bias may be structured, and the supply of experts may be skewed in the direction desired by the government and "the market."[32] As Henry Kissinger has pointed out, in this "age of the expert," the "constituency" of the expert is "those who have a vested interest in commonly held opinions; elaborating and defining its consensus at a high level has, after all, made him an expert."[33] It is therefore appropriate that this restructuring has taken place to allow the commonly held opinions (meaning those that are functional for elite interests) to continue to prevail. . . .

FLAK AND THE ENFORCERS: THE FOURTH FILTER

"Flak" refers to negative responses to a media statement or program. It may take the form of letters, telegrams, phone calls, petitions, lawsuits, speeches and bills before Congress, and other modes of complaint, threat, and punitive action. It may be organized centrally or locally, or it may consist of the entirely independent actions of individuals.

If flak is produced on a large scale, or by individuals or groups with substantial resources, it can be both uncomfortable and costly to the media. Positions have to be defended within the organization and without, sometimes before legislatures and possibly even in courts. Advertisers may withdraw patronage. Television advertising is mainly of consumer goods that are readily subject to organized boycott. During the McCarthy years, many advertisers and radio and television stations were effectively coerced into quiescence and blacklisting of employees by the threats of determined Red hunters to boycott products. Advertisers are still concerned to avoid offending constituencies that might produce flak, and their demand for suitable programming is a continuing feature of the media environment. If certain kinds of fact, position, or program are thought likely to elicit flak, this prospect can be a deterrent.

The ability to produce flak, and especially flak that is costly and threatening, is related to power. Serious flak has increased in close parallel with business's growing resentment of media criticism and the corporate offensive of the 1970s and 1980s. Flak from the powerful can be either direct or indirect. The direct would include letters or phone calls from the White House to Dan Rather or William Paley, or from the FCC to the television networks asking for documents used in putting together a program, or from irate officials of ad agencies or corporate sponsors to media officials asking for reply time or threatening retaliation.[34] The powerful can also work on the media indirectly by complaining to their own constituencies (stockholders, employees) about the media, by generating institutional advertising that does the same, and by funding right-wing monitoring or think-tank operations designed to attack the media. They may also fund political campaigns and help put into power conservative politicians who will more directly serve the interests of private power in curbing any deviationism in the media.

Along with its other political investments of the 1970s and 1980s, the corporate community sponsored the growth of institutions such as the American Legal Foundation, the Capital Legal Foundation, the Media Institute, the Center for Media and Public Affairs, and Accuracy in Media (AIM). These may be regarded as institutions organized for the specific purpose of producing flak. . . .

AIM was formed in 1969, and it grew spectacularly in the 1970s. Its annual income rose from $5,000 in 1971 to $1.5 million in the early 1980s, with funding mainly from large corporations and the wealthy heirs and foundations of the corporate system. At least eight separate oil companies were contributors to AIM in the early 1980s, but the wide representation in sponsors from the corporate community is impressive.[35] The function of AIM is to harass the media and put pressure on them to follow the corporate agenda and a hard-line, right-wing foreign policy. It presses the media to join more enthusiastically in Red-scare bandwagons, and attacks them for alleged deficiencies whenever they fail to toe the line on foreign policy. It conditions the media to expect trouble (and cost increases) for violating right-wing standards of bias.[36] . . .

Although the flak machines steadily attack the mass media, the media treat them well. They receive respectful attention, and their propagandistic role and links to a larger corporate program are rarely mentioned or analyzed. AIM head Reed Irvine's diatribes are frequently published, and right-wing network flacks who regularly assail the "liberal media," such as Michael Ledeen,[37] are given Op-Ed column space, sympathetic reviewers, and a regular place on talk shows as experts. This reflects the power of the sponsors, including the well-entrenched position of the right wing in the mass media themselves.[38]

The producers of flak add to one another's strength and reinforce the command of political authority in its news-management activities. The government is a major producer of flak, regularly assailing, threatening, and "correcting" the media, trying to contain any deviations from the established line. News management itself is designed to produce flak. In the Reagan years, Mr. Reagan was put on television to exude charm to millions, many of whom berated the media when they dared to criticize the "Great Communicator."[39]

ANTICOMMUNISM AS A CONTROL MECHANISM

A final filter is the ideology of anticommunism. Communism as the ultimate evil has always been the specter haunting property owners, as it threatens the very root of their class position and superior status. The Soviet, Chinese, and Cuban revolutions were traumas to Western elites, and the ongoing conflicts and the well-publicized abuses of Communist states have contributed to elevating opposition to communism to a first principle of Western ideology and politics. This ideology helps mobilize the populace against an enemy, and because the concept is fuzzy it can be used against anybody advocating policies that threaten property interests or support accommodation with Communist states and radicalism. It therefore helps fragment the left and labor movements and serves as a political-control mechanism. If the triumph of communism is the worst imaginable result, the support of fascism abroad is justified as a lesser evil. Opposition to social democrats who are too soft on Communists and "play into their hands" is rationalized in similar terms.

Liberals at home, often accused of being pro-Communist or insufficiently anti-Communist, are kept continuously on the defensive in a cultural milieu in which anticommunism is the dominant religion. If they allow communism, or something that can be labeled communism, to triumph in the provinces while they are in office, the political costs are heavy. Most of them have fully internalized the religion anyway, but they are all under great pressure to demonstrate their anti-Communist credentials. This causes them to behave very much like reactionaries. Their occasional support of social democrats often breaks down where the latter are insufficiently harsh on their own indigenous radicals or on popular groups that are organizing among generally marginalized sectors. . . .

The anti-Communist control mechanism reaches through the system to exercise a profound influence on the mass media. In normal times as well as in periods of Red scares, issues tend to be framed in terms of a dichotomized world of Communist and anti-Communist powers, with gains and losses allocated to contesting sides, and rooting for "our side" considered an entirely legitimate news practice. It is the mass media that identify, create, and push into the limelight a Joe McCarthy. . . . The ideology and religion of anticommunism is a potent filter.

DICHOTOMIZATION AND PROPAGANDA CAMPAIGNS

The five filters narrow the range of news that passes through the gates, and even more sharply limit what can become "big news," subject to sustained news campaigns. By definition, news from primary establishment sources meets one major filter requirement and is readily accommodated by the mass media. Messages from and about dissidents and weak, unorganized individuals and groups, domestic and foreign, are at an initial disadvantage in sourcing costs and credibility, and they often do not comport with the ideology or interests of the gatekeepers and other powerful parties that influence the filtering process.[40] . . .

In sum, a propaganda approach to media coverage suggests a systematic and highly political dichotomization in news coverage based on serviceability to important domestic power interests. This should be observable in dichotomized choices of story and in the volume and quality of coverage.

NOTES

1. Ben Bagdikian, *The Media Monopoly*, 2nd ed. (Boston: Beacon Press, 1987), p. xvi.
2. John Kluge, having taken the Metromedia system private in a leveraged buyout in 1984 worth $1.1 billion, sold off various parts of this system in 1985–86 for $5.5 billion, at a personal profit of some $3 billion (Gary Hector, "Are Shareholders Cheated by LBOs?" *Fortune*, Jan. 17, 1987, p. 100). Station KDLA-TV, in Los Angeles, which had been bought by a management-outsider group in a leveraged buyout in

1983 for $245 million, was sold to the Tribune Company for $510 million two years later (Richard Stevenson, "Tribune in TV Deal for $510 Million," *New York Times*, May 7, 1985). See also "The Media Magnates: Why Huge Fortunes Roll Off the Presses," *Fortune*, October 12, 1987.

3. The Reagan administration strengthened the control of existing holders of television-station licenses by increasing their term from three to five years, and its FCC made renewals essentially automatic. The FCC also greatly facilitated speculation and trading in television properties by a rule change reducing the required holding period before sale of a newly acquired property from three years to one year.

    The Reagan era FCC and Department of Justice also refused to challenge mergers and takeover bids that would significantly increase the concentration of power (GE–RCA) or media concentration (Capital Cities–ABC). Furthermore, beginning April 2, 1985, media owners could own as many as twelve television stations, as long as their total audience didn't exceed 25 percent of the nation's television households; and they could also hold twelve AM and twelve FM stations, as the 1953 "7-7-7 rule" was replaced with a "12-12-12 rule." See Herbert H. Howard, "Group and Cross-Media Ownership of Television Stations: 1985" (Washington: National Association of Broadcasters, 1985).

4. This was justified by Reagan-era FCC chairman Mark Fowler on the grounds that market options are opening up and that the public should be free to choose. Criticized by Fred Friendly for doing away with the law's public-interest standard, Fowler replied that Friendly "distrusts the ability of the viewing public to make decisions on its own through the marketplace mechanism. I do not" (Jeanne Saddler, "Clear Channel: Broadcast Takeovers Meet Less FCC Static, and Critics Are Upset," *Wall Street Journal*, June 11, 1985). Among other problems, Fowler ignores the fact that true freedom of choice involves the ability to select options that may not be offered by an oligopoly selling audiences to advertisers.

5. CBS increased its debt by about $1 billion in 1985 to finance the purchase of 21 percent of its own stock, in order to fend off a takeover attempt by Ted Turner. The *Wall Street Journal* noted that "With debt now standing at 60% of capital, it needs to keep advertising revenue up to repay borrowings and interest" (Peter Barnes, "CBS Profit Hinges on Better TV Ratings," June 6, 1986). With the slowed-up growth of advertising revenues, CBS embarked on an employment cutback of as many as six hundred broadcast division employees, the most extensive for CBS since the loss of cigarette advertising in 1971 (Peter Barnes, "CBS Will Cut up to 600 Posts in Broadcasting," *Wall Street Journal*, July 1, 1986). In June 1986, Time, Inc., embarked on a program to buy back as much as 10 million shares, or 16 percent of its common stock, at an expected cost of some $900 million, again to reduce the threat of a hostile takeover (Laura Landro, "Time Will Buy as Much as 16% of Its Common," *Wall Street Journal*, June 20, 1986).

6. In response to the Jesse Helms and Turner threats to CBS, Laurence Tisch, of Loews Corporation, was encouraged to increase his holdings in CBS stock, already at 11.7 percent. In August 1986, the Loews interest was raised to 24.9 percent, and Tisch obtained a position of virtual control. In combination with William Paley, who owned 8.1 percent of the shares, the chief executive officer of CBS was removed and Tisch took over that role himself, on a temporary basis (Peter Barnes, "Loews Increases Its Stake in CBS to Almost 25%," *Wall Street Journal*, Aug. 12, 1986).

7. Benjamin Compaine et al., *Anatomy of the Communications Industry: Who Owns the Media?* (White Plains, N.Y.: Knowledge Industry Publications, 1982), p. 463.

8. Ibid., pp. 458–60.

9. See Edward S. Herman, *Corporate Control, Corporate Power* (New York: Cambridge University Press, 1981), pp. 26–54.

10. The widely quoted joke by A. J. Liebling—that if you don't like what your newspaper says you are perfectly free to start or buy one of your own—stressed the impotence of the individual. In a favorable political climate such as that provided by the Reagan administration, however, a giant corporation not liking media performance *can* buy its own, as exemplified by GE.

11. On the Nixon-Agnew campaign to bully the media by publicity attacks and threats, see Marilyn Lashner, *The Chilling Effect in TV News* (New York: Praeger, 1984). Lashner concluded that the Nixon White House's attempt to quiet the media "succeeded handily, at least as far as television is concerned ..." (p. 167). See also Fred Powledge, *The Engineering of Restraint: The Nixon Administration and the Press* (Washington: Public Affairs Press, 1971), and William E. Porter, *Assault on the Media: The Nixon Years* (Ann Arbor: University of Michigan Press, 1976).

12. One study showed that of sixty-five FCC commissioners and high-level staff personnel who left the FCC between 1945 and 1970, twelve had come out of the private-communications sector before their FCC service, and thirty-four went into private-firm service after leaving the commission (Roger Noll et al., *Economic Aspects of Television Regulation* [Washington: Brookings, 1973], p. 123).

13. "The symbiotic growth of American television and global enterprise has made them so interrelated that they cannot be thought of as separate. They are essentially the same phenomenon. Preceded far and wide by military advisers, lobbyists, equipment salesmen, advertising specialists, merchandising experts, and telefilm salesmen as advance agents, the enterprise penetrates much of the non-socialist world. Television is simply its most visible portion" (Erik Barnouw, *The Sponsor* [New York: Oxford University Press, 1978], p. 158). For a broader picture, see Herbert I. Schiller, *Communication and Cultural Domination* (White Plains, N.Y.: International Arts and Sciences Press, 1976), especially chapters 3–4.

14. Is it not possible that if the populace "demands" program content greatly disliked by the owners, competition and the quest for profits will cause them to offer such programming? There is some truth in this, and it, along with the limited autonomy of media personnel, may help explain the "surprises" that crop up occasionally in the mass media. One limit to the force of public demand, however, is that the millions of customers have no means of registering their demand for products that are not offered to them. A further problem is that the owners' class interests are reinforced by a variety of other filters that we discuss below.

15. " ... producers presenting patrons [advertisers] with the greatest opportunities to make a profit through their publics will receive support while those that cannot compete on this score will not survive" (Joseph Turow, *Media Industries: The Production of News and Entertainment* [New York: Longman, 1984], p. 52).

16. Noncommercial television is also at a huge disadvantage for the same reason, and will require a public subsidy to be able to compete. Because public television does not have the built-in constraints of ownership by the wealthy, and the need to appease advertisers, it poses a threat to a narrow elite control of mass communications. This is why conservatives struggle to keep public television on a short leash, with annual funding decisions, and funding at a low level (see Barnouw, *The Sponsor*, pp. 179–82). Another option pursued in the Carter-Reagan era has been to force it into the commercial nexus by sharp defunding.

17. Quoted in Curran and Seaton, *Power Without Responsibility*, p. 43.

18. William Evan, *Organization Theory* (New York: Wiley, 1976), p. 123.

19. Turow asserts that "The continual interaction of producers and primary patrons plays a dominant part in setting the general boundary conditions for day-to-day production activity" (*Media Industries*, p. 51).

20. Quoted in Todd Gitlin, *Inside Prime Time* (New York: Pantheon, 1983), p. 253.

21. Barnouw, *The Sponsor*, p. 134.

22. Mark Fishman, *Manufacturing the News* (Austin: University of Texas Press, 1980), p. 143.

23. Gaye Tuchman, "Objectivity as Strategic Ritual: An Examination of Newsmen's Notions of Objectivity," *American Journal of Sociology* 77, no. 2 (1972), pp. 662–64.

24. In 1980, Mobil Oil had a public-relations budget of $21 million and a public-relations staff of seventy-three. Between 1976 and 1981 it produced at least a dozen televised special reports on such issues as gasoline prices, with a hired television journalist interviewing Mobil executives and other experts, that are shown frequently on television, often without indication of Mobil sponsorship. See A. Kent MacDougall, *Ninety Seconds To Tell It All* (Homewood, Ill.: Dow Jones-Irwin, 1981), pp. 117–20.

25. John S. Saloma III, *Ominous Politics: The New Conservative Labyrinth* (New York: Hill & Wang, 1984), p. 79.

26. MacDougall, *Ninety Seconds*, pp.116–17.

27. The April 14, 1986, U.S. bombing of Libya was the first military action timed to preempt attention on 7 P.M. prime-time television news. See Chomsky, *Pirates & Emperors*, p. 147.

28. For the masterful way the Reagan administration used these to manipulate the press, see "Standups," *The New Yorker*, December 2, 1985, pp. 81ff.

29. Fishman, *Manufacturing the News*, p. 153.

30. On January 16, 1986, the American Friends Service Committee issued a news release, based on extended Freedom of Information Act inquiries, which showed that there had been 381 navy nuclear-weapons accidents and "incidents" in the period 1965–77, a figure far higher than that previously claimed. The mass media did not cover this hot story directly but through the filter of the navy's reply, which downplayed the significance of the new findings and eliminated or relegated to the background the AFSC's full range of facts and interpretation of the meaning of what they had uncovered. A typical heading: "Navy Lists Nuclear Mishaps: None of 630 Imperiled Public, Service Says," *Washington Post*, January 16, 1986.

31. Bruce Owen and Ronald Braeutigam, *The Regulation Game: Strategic Use of the Administrative Process* (Cambridge, Mass.: Ballinger, 1978), p. 7.

32. See Edward S. Herman, "The Institutionalization of Bias in Economics," *Media, Culture and Society* (July 1982), pp. 275–91.

33. Henry Kissinger, *American Foreign Policy* (New York: Norton, 1969), p. 28.

34. See "The Business Campaign Against 'Trial by TV,' " *Business Week*, June 22, 1980, pp. 77–79; William H. Miller, "Fighting TV Hatchet Jobs," *Industry Week*, January 12, 1981, pp. 61–64.

35. Louis Wolf, "Accuracy in Media Rewrites News and History," *Covert Action Information Bulletin* (Spring 1984), pp. 26–29.

36. AIM's impact is hard to gauge, but it must be recognized as only a part of a larger corporate–right-wing campaign of attack. It has common funding sources with such components of the conservative labyrinth as AEI, Hoover, the Institute for Contemporary Studies, and others (see Saloma, *Ominous Politics*, esp. chapters 2, 3, and 6), and has its own special role to play. AIM's head, Reed Irvine, is a frequent participant in television talk shows, and his letters to the editor and commentary are regularly published in the mass media. The media feel obligated to provide careful responses to his detailed attacks on their news and documentaries, and the Corporation for Public Broadcasting even helped fund his group's reply to the PBS series on Vietnam. His ability to get the publisher of the *New York Times* to meet with him personally once a year—a first objective of any lobbyist—is impressive testimony to influence. On his contribution to the departure of Raymond Bonner from the *Times*, see Wolf, "Accuracy in Media Rewrites News and History," pp. 32–33.

37. For a discussion of Ledeen's views on the media, see Herman and Brodhead, *Bulgarian Connection*, pp. 166–70.

38. Among the contributors to AIM have been the Reader's Digest Association and the DeWitt Wallace Fund, Walter Annenberg, Sir James Goldsmith (owner of the French *L'Express*), and E. W. Scripps II, board chairman of a newspaper-television-radio system.

39. George Skelton, White House correspondent for the *Los Angeles Times*, noted that in reference to Reagan's errors of fact, "You write the stories once, twice, and you get a lot of mail saying, 'You're picking on the guy, you guys in the press make mistakes too.' And editors respond to that, so after a while the stories don't run anymore. We're intimidated" (quoted in Hertsgaard, "How Reagan Seduced Us").

40. Where dissidents are prepared to denounce official enemies, of course, they can pass through the mass-media filtering system, in the manner of the ex-Communist experts described in "Anticommunism as a Control Mechanism" (p. 29).

8.3 MARTIN A. LEE AND NORMAN SOLOMON

The Media Cartel: Corporate Control of the News

In the following selection from *Unreliable Sources: A Guide to Detecting Bias in News Media* (Carol Publishing Group, 1990), Martin A. Lee and Norman Solomon examine the consequences of corporate ownership of mass media. Their research is part of a larger media "watchdog" project called Fairness and Accuracy in Reporting, or FAIR, of which Lee and Solomon are a part. For FAIR the key issue is that mass media systems are not only run as profit-making ventures but they are also now owned and operated by powerful multinational corporations that have close ties to national governments. Given the propaganda function of the media, the authors believe that corporate media will systematically represent their own interests—i.e., those of their owning corporations—which include ties between the corporate sphere and the state. Lee and Solomon further contend that corporate-state power represents its own interests *not* by informing the public as to the operation of its political-economic power but by disseminating myths that operate to conceal the real function of this power and, thus, to gain public consent to the existing situation.

Lee and Solomon argue that the public must become critical consumers of media messages and learn how to detect systematic bias in favor of corporate-state interests in the mass media. In the following selection, the authors analyze the implications of corporate control of news production in the cases of the merger of Time, Inc. and Warner, Inc., and the General Electric Corporation's acquisition of the NBC television network.

Key Concept: military-industrial-media complex

*D*o the business priorities of their corporate bosses affect the way journalists cover the news? Consider network news coverage of the 1988 Winter Olympics in Calgary, Canada. All three network news divisions had to decide how much attention the Olympics warranted. NBC devoted a total of 33 minutes of national news coverage to the games, while CBS News provided 17 minutes of coverage. Compare these figures to ABC, which found the Winter Olympics worthy of 47 minutes on its nightly newscasts. Is it merely coincidental that ABC also televised the Winter Olympics and a heavy news focus helped build ratings and profits? Are we to believe that such concerns had no bearing on the "independent news judgment" of ABC producers?

ABC News found the 1988 Summer Olympic Games in Seoul, South Korea, less newsworthy than the winter games. That's because ABC didn't televise the Summer Olympics—NBC did. As it turned out, NBC News considered the summer games and their Korean hosts far more newsworthy than the other networks. NBC's inflated news coverage was geared toward attracting a larger audience—which translated into greater earnings for the network. So much for the hallowed precept that news choices are based solely on the intrinsic importance of a story and are immune to financial considerations.

The truth of the matter is that financial interests play a major role in determining what we see—and don't see—on television. Most of the top network sponsors are powerful multinational corporations. These global mammoths dominate our broadcast and print media far more extensively than most people realize. They exert tremendous leverage over the media industry because they are its principal source of revenue: TV and radio get nearly 100 percent of their income from advertisers, newspapers 75 percent, and magazines about 50 percent. . . .

TIME WARNER TANGO

"It looks like the Rolling Stones are coming here next week," remarked a security guard as he eyed a mob of would-be spectators waiting outside a packed Delaware courthouse. They were there to witness in person the Delaware Supreme Court's historic decision on the fate of Time Inc., target of one of the year's fiercest takeover battles. But only those with special passes were permitted inside on July 24, 1989; the rest had to settle for watching the courtroom drama unfold on Cable News Network. It was the first time ever in Delaware corporate law that TV cameras were allowed in a courtroom.

Even in an era of deregulated merger mania, this corporate tryst was remarkable for the attention it generated. It began in March 1989, when Time and Warner, two communications giants, announced a major stock swap as part of a friendly deal which would have effectively combined the companies, forming the largest—and arguably the most influential—media conglomerate in the world. The business profile of Time Inc., America's biggest magazine ad revenue earner and publisher (*Time, Life, Fortune, People, Sports Illustrated*, etc.), meshed particularly well with Warner, the number-one record and TV production company in the United States. With combined assets somewhere between $25 and $30 billion, they also controlled a major chunk of the cable, motion picture and book markets, including Home Box Office (the nation's largest pay TV channel), Lorimar Studios and the Book-of-the-Month Club.

Such an amalgam of lucrative components gave Time Warner distinct advantages for promoting their products in a multiplicity of media. A magazine article with the company copyright, for example, could be expanded into a Time Warner book. It could serve as the basis for a film made at an in-house studio, which would then be distributed through a movie theater chain owned by the same company. The movie doubtless will be reviewed in widely-read magazines also published by Time Warner, and the soundtrack would be issued on a company record label. To catch a re-run, turn to one of Time Warner's cable channels. "More and more, we will be dealing with closed loops," predicts Ben Bagdikian, as a handful of mega-conglomerates squeeze out others in the field.

The prospect of Time Warner commanding such a dominant position in the news and entertainment universe made executives at Paramount, another media titan, hyperactive with envy. It soon became a three-ring circus, as Paramount leaped into the fray, waving top dollar for Time Inc. stock, which shot up 45 points in a single day. Time was suddenly "in play," as market euphoria carried clusters of media stock skyward, followed by a period of wild fluctuation as rumors swept through Wall Street that other corporate heavyweights, including General Electric, might join the battle for Time.

The well-planned Time Warner merger quickly degenerated into a full-fledged corporate scramble involving investment bankers, blue chip law firms, PR strategists and a fleet of private detectives hired to dig up dirt on the other parties. Time execs rejected Paramount's hostile takeover bid and announced their intention to buy Warner outright. Paramount countered by upping its offer. There was even talk of a reverse takeover—the so-called Pac Man defense—in which Time would turn around and swallow up Paramount. Sensing opportunity amidst all the turmoil, Australian media magnate Rupert Murdoch hovered in the wings, ready to grab any loose assets shed during the scuffle. At stake were commercial empires so vast it staggered the imagination.

While Wall Street movers and shakers were having a field day, those who punched the clock day-in and day-out at Time Inc. grew increasingly nervous. Someone would have to pay for the huge debt amassed by the company, as it sought to stave off Paramount's maneuvers. Given that well-heeled executives and publishers aren't in the habit of volunteering cuts in their seven-figure salaries, it seemed likely that Time's rank-and-file would bear the brunt of the inevitable belt-tightening, layoffs and restructuring that a debt-laden company must undertake.

When the dust finally settled, the Delaware Supreme Court upheld Time's proposed $14 billion buyout of Warner, leaving Paramount to search elsewhere for media industry prey. Most of the press covered the entire ordeal simply as a business story without dwelling on the social and political consequences of such a merger. The main criticisms were voiced by big media execs concerned about facing an even bigger bully on the block. A *New York Times* article, headlined "Time Deal Worrying Competitors," featured comments to that effect by Robert Wright, president of NBC, owned by little ol' GE. Journalists covering the Time Warner merger rarely featured statements by public interest critics warning that mass media concentration in fewer and fewer corporate hands poses a serious threat to pluralism, democratic discourse and the First Amendment. . . .

MILITARY-INDUSTRIAL-MEDIA COMPLEX:
THE CASE OF GENERAL ELECTRIC AND NBC

In January 1961, shortly before he handed over the formal reins of power, President Dwight Eisenhower issued a blunt warning to the American people about the "immense military establishment" whose "total influence—economic, political, even spiritual—is felt in every city, every state house, every office of the federal government." The departing chief added: "We must guard against the acquisition of unwarranted influence . . . by the military-industrial complex. The potential for disastrous rise of misplaced power exists and will persist."

General Electric, a financial and industrial behemoth with annual sales topping $50 billion, has long been a key player in the military-industrial complex. Ranked second among U.S. military contractors, GE makes the detonators for every nuclear bomb in America's arsenal. There are few modern weapons systems that GE has not been instrumental in developing. In addition to nuclear and conventional arms, GE manufactures refrigerators, electric motors, medical equipment, plastics, light bulbs and communications satellites. It also owns the Wall Street firm Kidder-Peabody. When it acquired RCA, the parent company of NBC, for $6.28 billion in 1986—at that point the largest non-oil corporate merger in U.S. history—GE added a formidable media component to its worldwide business empire.

The saga of GE—marked by fraud, scandals, labor strife and contempt for the natural environment—illustrates the dangers of misplaced power that Eisenhower spoke about, but which the U.S. media rarely probe at length. Here are a few examples: In 1932, GE initiated a policy of planned obsolescence and cut the life of light bulbs in order to boost sales during the Depression. During World War II, GE was convicted of illegally collaborating with Germany's Krupp company, a linchpin of the Nazi war machine. And in 1961, GE was convicted of price-fixing, bid-rigging and antitrust violations, for which it had to pay a large fine in addition to a $57 million settlement with the U.S. government and other customers. Three GE officials served brief jail terms. But GE's attorney Clark Clifford (chair of the CIA's Foreign Intelligence Advisory Board and a future Defense Secretary) convinced the IRS that the damages GE had to pay for its criminal activities could be written off as a tax-deductible business expense!

With the IRS doling out favors to big business, the pattern of corruption continued. In 1981, GE was found guilty of bribing a Puerto Rican official to obtain a $92 million contract to build a power plant on the island. GE paid no income tax that year, even though its pre-tax earnings were a nifty $2.66 billion; what's more, GE somehow qualified for a $90 million rebate from the IRS. (Is that what they mean by "free enterprise"?) In 1985, GE became the first weapons contractor to be found guilty of defrauding the U.S. government by overcharging on military contracts.

Ronald Reagan: GE Front-Man

GE's well-documented record of deceit should have been grounds for the Justice Department to disqualify the company from acquiring NBC. But GE had friends in high places and the deal went through without a hitch. The fact that Ronald Reagan had previously spent eight years on GE's payroll as the company's chief PR spokesman undoubtedly helped matters. Publicist Edward Langley, who has written on Reagan's GE years, described GE as "a company so obsessed with conservatism that it was not unlike the John Birch Society."

Reagan signed on with GE in 1954, when his acting career was floundering. He hosted and occasionally starred in the long-running *General Electric Theater* series that aired on CBS. Soon Reagan began touring the country at GE's behest, making speeches against communism, labor unions, social security, public housing and, of course, corporate taxes. These GE-sponsored lectures laid the groundwork for Reagan's political career, and the rest, as they say, is history.

A number of Reagan cabinet officials had close relations with GE. William French Smith, Reagan's personal attorney, joined GE's board of directors shortly after leaving the administration. It was during Smith's tenure as U.S. Attorney General in the mid-1980s that the Justice Department modified anti-trust regulations, thereby enabling GE to buy NBC.

It wasn't always so easy to pull off this kind of merger. ITT's attempt to acquire ABC in 1966–67 provoked a public outcry; the plan was nixed after the Justice Department found that ITT control "could compromise the independence of ABC's news coverage of political events in countries where ITT has interests." The same logic could have been applied to GE, which operates in 50 foreign countries, but its purchase of NBC in 1986 was hardly debated in Washington or the U.S. media.

NBC is one of GE's most profitable assets, largely due to austerity measures such as reducing the news division staff from 1,400 to 1,000. This was par for the course at a GE-owned company. In less than a decade since John Welsh became GE's CEO in 1981, over a hundred thousand employees were laid off—25 percent of GE's total work force. These cutbacks occurred at a time when the company was earning record profits. Welsh has been nicknamed "Neutron Jack" because, like the neutron bomb, he makes people disappear but leaves the buildings standing.

The Nuts and Bolts of Censorship

How has ownership by GE influenced what we see—or don't see—on NBC News programs? NBC has repeatedly insisted that its relationship to GE does not affect its news coverage. But certain incidents suggest otherwise.

For example, a reference to the General Electric Company was surgically removed from a report on substandard products before it aired on NBC's *Today* show on November 30, 1989. The report focused on a federal investigation of inferior bolts used by GE and other firms in building airplanes, bridges, nuclear missile silos and equipment for the NASA space program. It said that 60 percent of the 200 billion bolts used annually in the U.S. may be faulty. The censored portion of the *Today* show included this passage: "Recently, General Electric engineers discovered they had a big problem. One out of three bolts from one of their major suppliers was bad. Even more alarming, GE accepted the bad bolts without any certification of compliance for eight years."

Peter Karl, the journalist who produced the segment, called NBC's decision to eliminate references to GE "insidious." He cited the "chilling effect" on a network that is "overprotective of a corporate owner."

In March 1987, NBC news broadcast a special documentary, "Nuclear Power: In France It works," which could have passed for an hour-long nuclear power commercial. In an upbeat introduction, NBC anchor Tom Brokaw neglected to state that his corporate patron is America's second-largest nuclear energy vendor, with 39 nuclear power reactors in the U.S., and the third-leading nuclear weapons producer—facts which gave rise to the moniker "Nuclear Broadcasting Company" among disgruntled NBC staff.

Herein lay a fundamental conflict of interest, which Brokaw didn't own up to. Citizens' fear of nuclear technology could cut into GE's profits—and these fears were a key target of this so-called "News Special." An NBC crew toured France as if on a pilgrimage to the atomic land of Oz, off to see the wizardry of safe nuclear power plants. "Looking at a foreign country where nuclear power is a fact of life may restore some reason to the discussion at home," said correspondent Steven Delaney. "In most countries, especially the U.S., emotions drive the nuclear debate and that makes rational dialogue very difficult."

Having sung the praises of the French nuclear industry, NBC News bluffed when discussing what to do with radioactive waste, some of which remains lethal for dozens of centuries or longer: "The French will probably succeed in their disposal plan for the same reasons the rest of their nuclear program works . . . The French have more faith than we do in the government's competence to manage the nuclear program, and the French government has less tolerance for endless dissent."

Unfortunately, faith and lack of tolerance for dissent will not solve critical nuclear problems, even in France. One month after NBC aired its pro-nuclear broadcast, there were accidents at two French nuclear power installations, injuring seven workers. The *Christian Science Monitor* wrote of a "potentially explosive debate" in France, with polls showing a third of the French public opposing nuclear power. While the accidents were widely discussed in the French media and some U.S. newspapers, NBC TV did not report the story.

A telling sidelight to this incident occurred the following year when NBC's pro-nuke documentary won first prize for science journalism in a competition sponsored by the Westinghouse Foundation, an affiliate of Westinghouse Electric Company. Like GE, Westinghouse is a military-industrial powerhouse with large investments in nuclear power and weapons, as well as in broadcast media. Westinghouse owns Group W Cable and is the second largest radio station operator in the United States.

Westinghouse gave NBC its journalism trophy not long after GE was publicly implicated in yet another major scandal. A member of the Nuclear Regulatory Commission (NRC) resigned, charging that GE had "struck a deal" with the NRC to keep secret the contents of a 1975 GE internal report critical of its faulty nuclear reactor design. The report—which documented problems such as earthquake hazards and radiation dangers for plant workers—

prompted suits by three Midwest utility companies which claimed that GE knowingly installed unsafe systems. Ironically, Jim Lawless, the *Cleveland Plain Dealer* reporter who first exposed the GE nuclear cover-up, was yanked from the utilities beat after the parent company of Cleveland's powerful electric utility complained to the *Plain Dealer*'s management about alleged "bias" in coverage by Lawless.

In 1986, New York State officials banned recreational and commercial bass fishing after GE had polluted the Hudson River with 400,000 ponds of carcinogenic PCBs. Moreover, according to EPA's 1989 Superfund list, GE was responsible for 47 toxic waste sites around the country—the most of any firm cited.

Not surprisingly, NBC News staffers haven't shown much zeal for investigating environmental abuse by the company that pays their salaries. Nor have they done much digging into Kidder-Peabody, GE's brokerage subsidiary, which has been implicated in insider trading scandals on Wall Street. And the worldwide consumer boycott of GE products launched by INFACT, a group opposed to nuclear profiteering, hasn't been a hot topic on NBC News either. INFACT's TV commercials, urging consumers not to buy GE products, were banned by NBC and other television broadcasters.

Conflicts of Interest

GE and other military contractors made out like bandits during the Reagan administration, which presided over the largest peacetime military build-up in U.S. history. And bandits is exactly what they are, as the Pentagon procurement scandal, involving dozens of military contractors, amply demonstrates. GE was pegged with a 321-count indictment in November 1988 for trying to defraud the Department of Defense.

Despite such shenanigans, GE continued to receive hefty Defense Department contracts. Star Wars research was a veritable cash cow for GE and other high-tech weapons manufacturers. An article in the *New York Times* business section pointed out that the Star Wars program (and, by implication, GE contracts) could be scuttled if a major arms control agreement were reached or if a Democrat got elected to the White House. Star Wars subsequently became an issue during the 1988 presidential campaign; Bush was for it and Dukakis was against it. Thus NBC's owner had a material interest in the outcome of the election. NBC President Robert Wright donated money to the Bush campaign, as did GE chief "Neutron Jack" Welsh. NBC News employees didn't have to be told that a Dukakis victory—or tough, critical reporting on Star Wars—could cost GE millions of dollars.

Given GE's far-flung, diversified interests, there aren't many subjects that NBC News could cover that would not have a direct or indirect bearing on its corporate parent. Conflicts of interest are unavoidable as long as GE owns NBC. "As a newswriter I'm constantly aware who my boss is," a disaffected NBC News staffer told the media watch group FAIR shortly before he was laid off by the network.

Of course, NBC News doesn't completely ignore embarrassing stories about its owner. That would be too blatant, particularly when other news outlets refer in passing to GE corruption. When GE was indicted for its role in the 1988 Pentagon procurement scandal, *NBC Nightly News* gave a straightforward report—that lasted about ten seconds. There was little follow-up on this scandal by any of the major networks. The corporate zeitgeist doesn't encourage a sustained in-depth investigation of such matters.

It would be an overstatement to say that the topic of GE's ownership is banned entirely from NBC broadcasts. Occasionally, David Letterman will make a few joking references to GE on his late-night show. In that ha-ha context, a bit of lampooning about corporate daddy is permissible. At first glance a concession to openness and self-criticism, such quips may be just the reverse— a kind of inoculation, making light of potential conflicts of interests and ethical quagmires. Like the Fool in a Shakespeare play, Letterman is allowed to utter some jestful references to what's really going on beneath the pretenses. But as for serious examination by NBC News, forget it . . .

Nor are the other major networks in much of a position to cast the first stone. CapCities/ABC and CBS are interlinked with other huge conglomerates that are part of the military-industrial complex. The boards of directors of the Big Three are composed of executives, lawyers, financiers and former government officials who represent the biggest banks and corporations in the U.S., including military and nuclear contractors, oil companies, agribusiness, insurance and utility firms.

So too with leading newspapers and other major media. The *New York Times*, for example, is not only the newspaper of record for the Fortune 500; it is also a member in good standing of that elite club. There are numerous interlocks between the board of directors of the *New York Times* and the nuclear industry, which partially explains why it has been a fanatical supporter of nuclear weapon and atomic power plants.

Among the 14-member *New York Times* corporate board is George B. Munroe, retired chair and CEO of Phelps Dodge, a notorious anti-union company involved in uranium mining. Munroe and other *Times* board member, George Shinn, are also directors of Manufacturers Hanover, a bank that lent money to bail out LILCO, a New York utility, as plans for the Shoreham nuclear power plant fell to widespread citizen opposition. (The *Times* steadfastly backed the Shoreham project in dozens of strident editorials, without letting its readers know of these corporate links.) In addition, *Times* board member William R. Cross is vice chairman of the credit policy committee of Morgan bank, another LILCO creditor. And Marian S. Heiskell, sister of *Times* publisher and CEO Arthur Ochs Sulzberger, sits on the board of Con Edison, another nuclear utility.

Time Warner, the world's biggest media corporation, has so many interlocks with Fortune 500 companies that its board reads like a Who's Who of U.S. business and finance. Directors include representatives from military contractors such as General Dynamics, IBM and AT&T, as well as movers and shakers from Mobile Oil, Atlantic Richfield, Xerox and a number of major international banks. But Time Warner and other mass media won't discuss conflicts of interest inherent in interlocking directorates and how these may affect the selection and presentation of news stories. That subject is strictly taboo.

*Martin A. Lee
and Norman
Soloman*

Blueblood media and their corporate cousins have a vast stake in decisions made by the U.S. government. Through elite policy-shaping groups like
the Council on Foreign Relations and the Business Roundtable, they steer the
ship of state in what they deem to be a financially advantageous direction. (GE,
CapCities, CBS, the *New York Times* and the *Washington Post* all have board
members who sit on the Council on Foreign Relations.) They have much to
gain from a favorable investment climate in Third World countries and bloated
military budgets at home.

This was made explicit by former GE President Charles Wilson, a long-
time advocate of a permanent war economy, who worked with the Pentagon's
Office of Defense Mobilization during the 1950s. In a speech before the American newspaper Publishers Association, he urged the media to rally behind the
government's Cold War crusade. "The free world is in mortal danger. If the
people were not convinced of that, it would be impossible for Congress to vote
vast sums now being spent to avert that danger," said Wilson. "With the support of public opinion, as marshalled by the press, we are off to a good start . . .
It is our job—yours and mine—to keep our people convinced that the only way
to keep disaster away from our shores is to build America's might."

Nowadays, General Electric doesn't need to marshall the press to persuade the masses; it owns the press—or at least a sizable chunk of it. Moreover
GE's board of directors interlocks with various media, including the Washington Post Company, Harper & Row (book publishers), and the Gannett Foundation. GE also owns a cable channel (CNBC) and sponsors news programs on
other networks, such as ABC's *This Week With David Brinkley*, CNN's *Crossfire*,
and the *McLaughlin Group* on PBS. As a communications manager at GE explained, "We insist on a program environment that reinforces our corporate
messages."

In what has become standard operating procedure for mega-corporations,
GE spends millions of dollars each year sprucing up its image. But behind the
catchy PR slogan, "We bring good things to life," lurks a legacy of faulty
nuclear reactors, toxic waste dumps, bribery, cheating and cover-up. The
chasm between this reality and GE's heroic self-image underscores an essential
point: advertising is institutionalized lying, and such lies are tolerated, even
encouraged, because they serve the needs of the corporate establishment. Network news is brought to us by sponsors that lie routinely, matter-of-factly, as it
were. Under such circumstances how truthful can we expect the news to be?

The Think Tank Scam

In an effort to get the corporate message across and maximize sympathetic public opinion, GE and like-minded business firms fill the coffers of
influential conservative think tanks. Representatives from these well-heeled
organizations are quoted regularly in the press and they often pose as unbiased
"experts" on television news and public affairs shows. In this capacity they
directly serve the interests of the corporations which hold their purse strings.

The American Enterprise Institute (AEI) runs a highly effective PR operation AEI resident scholars, such as would-be Supreme Court justice Robert Bork and former U.N. ambassador Jeane Kirkpatrick, generate a steady flow of opinion columns on political, social and economic issues that are syndicated in hundreds of news dailies; other AEI associates serve as paid consultants for the three main TV networks. AEI "quotemaster" Norman J. Ornstein claimed to have logged 1,294 calls from 183 news organizations in 1988.

AEI receives financial support from various news media, including the *New York Times,* the Philip L. Graham Fund (*Washington Post*) and Times-Mirror (parent company of the *Los Angeles Times*). Among AEI's favorite whipping boys is Jesse Jackson, whose populist, anti-corporate presidential campaigning undoubtedly annoyed the high-brow business executives from Mobile Oil, Proctor & Gamble, Chase Manhattan, Citibank, Rockwell International and GE who sit on AEI's board of trustees.

GE also supports the Center for Strategic and International Studies (CSIS), an AEI spinoff based in Washington. CSIS functions as a way station for U.S. intelligence operatives as they shuttle back and forth through the revolving door that links the public (or at least as public as spooks can be) and private sectors. Representatives from CSIS and the Rand Corporation, another CIA-linked think tank, frequently appear on TV to comment on terrorism and other "national security" issues. Directors of GE and CBS sit on the Rand Corporation board. During one six-week period, CSIS fellows tallied 650 media "contacts"—TV appearances, opinion columns and quotations in news stories.

The Heritage Foundation, which functioned virtually as a shadow government during much of the Reagan administration, is another media favorite, according to a survey of news sources conducted by the University of Windsor. Burton Yale Pines, formerly a *Time* magazine associate editor and AEI "resident journalist," went on to become vice president of Heritage. GE director Henry H. Henley Jr. is a Heritage board member. Funders include Henley's company—Cluett, Peabody—along with Joseph Coors, the Reader's Digest Foundation (which also finances AEI), Mobil Oil and other major corporations. According to *The Nation* magazine, Heritage also received money on the sly from South Korean intelligence to support its Asian Studies Center.

It's another closed loop: Analysts from think tanks funded by GE and the Fortune 500 elite appear as "independent experts" on TV networks owned and sponsored by the same corporations. When the networks want someone to ratify corporate news and opinion, they turn to a stable of approved think tank specialists. Not surprisingly these well-paid sluggers go to bat for big business and the national security state, confirming biases already deeply-ingrained in U.S. media. Thus we see a lot of "hot spot" coverage on TV that gives the impression that the world is not a safe place for Americans; this unsettling picture is invariably confirmed by the same coterie of pundits who exude a false aura of objectivity as they define security in terms of brute military force rather than a healthy environment workplace safety and a strong, equitable economy. The prevalence of conservative think-tank mavens on TV and in the press is yet another symptom of corporate domination of the mass media.

CHAPTER 9 Advertising, Media, and Society

9.1 STUART EWEN

Captains of Consciousness: Advertising and the Social Roots of the Consumer Culture

Stuart Ewen, whose work represents a critical perspective in media studies, does not regard advertising as a form of market information designed to help consumers make choices in the marketplace. Nor does Ewen regard advertising simply as another cultural industry alongside television, movies, or radio, transmitting its own brand of consumer propaganda. Rather, he believes that advertising is the economic, social, and ideological keystone of modern capitalist societies. In the following selection from his historical analysis of advertising *Captains of Consciousness: Advertising and the Social Roots of the Consumer Culture* (McGraw-Hill, 1976), Ewen shows that advertising rose to solve, at one stroke, a profound double crisis in the United States at the turn of the twentieth century. By socializing the emerging working class to identify themselves primarily as consumers, advertising helped create a demand for goods, which prevented economic stagnation and gave workers imaginary power and freedom associated with products in ads, thereby staving off the threat of working-class conflict. Ewen reveals *how* advertising acted to form this new consciousness; it did not simply deceive the working class as to the nature and benefits of new products but it *mobilized the instincts* and *civilized the self*, both in terms of consuming industrially produced commodities.

Ewen is a professor of history at Hunter College in New York City. He has expanded his critique of the social and historical role of advertising to include the broader issues of commercial imagery and the associated phenomenon of style in contemporary culture in *All Consuming Images: The Politics of Style in Contemporary Culture* (Basic Books, 1988) and *Channels of Desire: Mass Images and the Shaping of American Consciousness*, 2d ed. (University of Minnesota Press, 1992), coauthored with Elizabeth Ewen.

Key Concept: the social production of consumers

"SHORTER HOURS, HIGHER WAGES . . ."

In 1910, Henry Ford instituted the "line production system" for "maximum production economy" in his Highland Park, Michigan, plant.[1] The innovation, though in many ways unsophisticated, and hardly educated as to its own implications, was the beginning of a momentous transformation in America's capacity to produce. In quantitative terms, the change was staggering. On the 1910 line, the time required to assemble a chassis was twelve hours and twenty-eight minutes. "By spring of 1914, the Highland Park plant was turning out over 1,000 vehicles a day, and the average labor time for assembling a chassis had dropped to one hour and thirty-three minutes."[2]

Mass production was a way of making production more economical. Through his use of the assembly line, Ford was able to utilize "expensive, single-purpose" machinery along with "quickly trained, single-purpose" workmen to make a single-model, inexpensive automobile at a rate which, with increasing sophistication, continued to dwarf not only the production levels of premassified industry, but the output of less refined mass production systems.[3]

By the 1920s, interest in and employment of the industrial potential of mass production extended far beyond the automobile industry. In recognition of such industrial developments, the United States Special Census of 1921 and 1923 offered a study of productive capacity[4] which was one of the first general discussions of its kind.[5] Consumer goods manufacturers were coming to recognize that mass production and mass distribution were "necessary" steps toward survival in a competitive market. Edward Filene, of the Boston department store family, a businessman founder of the consumer union movement, articulated the competitive compulsion of mass production. Competition, said Filene, "will compel us to Fordize American business and industry."[6]

And yet, what Filene and others meant by "Fordizing" American industry transcended the myopic vision of Henry Ford. While Ford stubbornly held to the notion that "the work and the work *alone* controls us,"[7] others in the automobile industry[8] and, (for our purposes) more importantly, ideologues of mass industry outside of the auto industry viewed the strategy of production in far broader social terms. Before mass production, industry had produced for a limited, largely middle- and upper-class market. With a burgeoning productive capacity, industry now required an equivalent increase in potential consumers of its goods. "Scientific production promised to make the conventional notion of the self-reliant producer/consumer anachronistic."[9]

The mechanism of mass production could not function unless markets became more dynamic, growing horizontally (nationally), vertically (into social classes not previously among the consumers) and ideologically. Now men and women had to be habituated to respond to the demands of the productive machinery. The corollary to a freely growing system of goods production was a "systematic, nationwide plan . . . to endow the masses with more buying power," a freely growing system of consumer production.[10] . . .

As capitalism became characterized by mass production and the subsequent need for mass distribution, traditional expedients for the real or attempted manipulation of labor were transformed. While the nineteenth-century industrialist coerced labor (both on and off the job) to serve as the "wheelhorse" of industry, modernizing capitalism sought to change "wheelhorse" to "worker" and "worker" to "consumer."[11]

For the workers, the movement toward mass production had severely changed the character of labor. The worker had become a decreasingly "significant" unit of production within the modern manufacturing process. "The man who had been the more or less creative maker of the whole of an article became the tender of a machine that made only one small part of the article."[12] The time required to teach the worker the "adept performance" of his "operation on assembly work" was a matter of a few hours.[13] This development had significant repercussions both in terms of the way in which a laborer viewed his proletarian status and in terms of the manufacturer's need to mass distribute the mountainous fruits of mass production. The two phenomena merged in the redefinition of the proletarian status. While mass production defined labor's work in terms of monotony and rationalized its product to a fragment, some businessmen spoke of "economic freedom" or "industrial democracy"[14] as the blessing promised the worker by modern production methods. Yet the "freedom" and "democracy" offered by mass industry stopped short of a freedom to define the uses or to rearrange the relationships of production. . . .

Not only was this alleged democracy designed to define the modern worker as a smoothly running unit of industrial production, it also tended to define protest and proletarian unrest in terms of the desire to consume, making these profitable as well. By the demand of workers for the right to be better consumers, the aspirations of labor would be profitably coordinated with the aspirations of capital. Such convictions implicitly attempted to divest protest of its anticapitalist content. Modern labor protest should have no basis in class antagonism.[15]

By the twenties, the ideological vanguard of the business community saw the need to endow the masses with what the economic historian Norman Ware has called the money, commodity, and psychic wages (satisfactions) correlative and responsive to the route of industrial capitalism.[16] There was a dramatic movement toward objective conditions which would make mass consumption feasible: higher wages and shorter hours. . . .

The question of shorter hours was also tantamount to offering labor the "chance" to expand the consumer market. And yet, this notion of "chance," like the notions of "industrial democracy" and "economic freedom," were subterfuges in so much as these alleged freedoms and choices meant merely a transformed version of capitalism's incessant need to mold a work force in its own image. "As modern industry . . . [was] geared to mass production, time out for mass consumption becomes as much a necessity as time in for production."[17] The shortening of hours was seen as a qualitative as well as quantitative change in the worker's life, without significantly altering his relation to power over the uses and means of production. . . . Shorter hours and higher wages were seen as a first step in a broader offensive against notions of thrift and an attempt to habituate a national population to the exigencies of mass production. . . . Now priorities demanded that the worker spend his wages and leisure time on the consumer market. . . .

Within the vision of consumption as a "school of freedom," the entry onto the consumer market was described as a "civilizing" experience. "Civilization" was the expanded cultural world which flowed from capitalism's broad capacity to commodify material resources. The experience of civilization was the cultural world this capacity produced.

And yet the "school of freedom" posed various problems. The democratic terminology within which the profitable vision of consumption was posed did not reveal the social and economic realities that threatened that vision. In terms of economic development, the financial growth of industrial corporations averaged 286 percent between 1922 and 1929. Despite wage hikes and relatively shorter hours in some industries,[18] the average manufacturing wage-earner showed a wage increase of only 14 percent during this same period.[19] The discrepancy between purchasing power and the rate of industrial growth was dealt with in part by the significant development of installment selling[20] which grew as an attempt to bolster "inadequate" markets in the economically depressed years of the early twenties.

Despite the initiation of a corporate credit system which offered consumers supplementary money, the growth of the productive system forced many industrial ideologues to realize the continuous need to habituate people psychically to consumption beyond mere changes in the productive order which they inhabited.

MOBILIZING THE INSTINCTS

. . . Modern advertising must be seen as a direct response to the needs of mass industrial capitalism. Second in procession after the manager of the production line, noted Whiting Williams [personnel director for a steel company and an ideologue of "scientific" management], "came the leader who possessed the ability to develop and direct men's desires and demands in a way to furnish the organized mass sales required for the mass production made possible by the massed dollars."[21] Advertising, as a part of mass distribution within modernizing industries, became a major sector for business investment. Within the automobile industry, initiated by the broad and highly diversified G.M. oligopoly, distribution came to account for about one half of that investment. Among producers of smaller consumer goods, the percentage of capital devoted to product proliferation was often greater.[22] ...

Advertising offered itself as a means of efficiently creating consumers and as a way of homogeneously "controlling the consumption of a product."[23] Although many corporations boasted of having attained national markets without the aid of advertising, the trade journal *Printers' Ink* argued that these "phantom national markets" were actually inefficient, unpredictable and scattered agglomerations of heterogeneous local markets.[24] The significance of the notion of efficiency in the creation of consumers lies in the fact that the modern advertising industry, like the modern manufacturing plant, was an agent of consolidated and multi-leveled commerce. As Ford's assembly line utilized "expensive single-purpose machinery" to produce automobiles inexpensively and at a rate that dwarfed traditional methods, the costly machinery of advertising that Coolidge had described set out to produce consumers, likewise inexpensively and at a rate that dwarfed traditional methods. To create consumers efficiently the advertising industry had to develop universal notions of what makes people respond, going beyond the "horse sense" psychology that had characterized the earlier industry.[25] Such general conceptions of human instinct promised to provide ways of reaching a mass audience via a universal appeal. Considering the task of having to build a mass ad industry to attend to the needs of mass production, the ad men welcomed the work of psychologists in the articulation of these general conceptions.[26] ...

While agreeing that "human nature is more difficult to control than material nature,"[27] ad men spoke in specific terms of "human instincts" which if properly understood could induce people "to buy a given product if it was scientifically presented. If advertising copy appealed to the right instincts, the urge to buy would surely be excited."[28] The utilitarian value of a product or the traditional notion of mechanical quality were no longer sufficient inducements to move merchandise at the necessary rate and volume required by mass production.

Such traditional appeals would not change the disposition of potential markets toward consumption of given products. Instead each product would be offered in isolation, not in terms of the nature of the consumer, but through an argument based on the intrinsic qualities of the item itself.

The advertisers were concerned with effecting a self-conscious change in the psychic economy, which could not come about if they spent all their time talking about a product and none talking about the "reader." Advertising literature, following the advent of mass production methods, increasingly spoke in terms of appeals to instinct. Anticipating later implementation, by 1911, Walter Dill Scott, psychologist/author of *Influencing Men in Business*, noted that "goods offered as means of gaining social prestige make their appeals to one of the most profound of the human instincts."[29] Yet the instinct for "social prestige," as well as others of a broad "constellation"[30] of instincts, was channeled into the terms of the productive system. The use value of "prestige," of "beauty," of "acquisition," of "self-adornment," and of "play" were all placed in the service of advertising's basic purpose—to provide effective mass distribution of products. . . .

Advertising demanded but a momentary participation in the logic of consumption. Yet hopefully that moment would be expanded into a life style by its educational value. A given ad asked not only that an individual buy its product, but that he experience a self-conscious perspective that he had previously been socially and psychically denied. By that perspective, he could ameliorate social and personal frustrations through access to the marketplace.

In light of such notions as [Floyd Henry] Allport's "social self" and other self-objectifying visions of popularity and success,[34] a new cultural logic was projected by advertising beyond the strictly pecuniary one of creating the desire to consume. The social perception was one in which people ameliorated the negative condition of social objectification through consumption—material objectification. The negative condition was portrayed as social failure derived from continual public scrutiny. The positive goal emanated from one's *modern* decision to armor himself against such scrutiny with the accumulated "benefits" of industrial production. Social responsibility and social self-preservation were being correlated to an allegedly existential decision that one made to present a mass-produced public face. Man, traditionally seen as exemplary of God's perfect product, was not hardly viable in comparison with the man-made products of industrial expertise. . . . Such social production of consumers represented a shift in social and political priorities which has since characterized much of the "life" of American industrial capitalism. The functional goal of national advertising was the creation of desires and habits. In tune with the need for mass distribution that accompanied the development of mass production capabilities, advertising was trying to produce in readers personal needs which would dependently fluctuate with the expanding marketplace. . . .

ADVERTISING: CIVILIZING THE *SELF*

In his sympathetic book on the *History and Development of Advertising*, Frank Presbrey articulated the conception of a predictable, buying, national population in proud and patriotic terms. "To national Advertising," noted Presbrey, "has recently been attributed most of the growth of a national homogeneity in our people, a uniformity of ideas which, despite the mixture of races, is found to be greater here than in European countries whose population is made up almost wholly of people of one race and would seem easier to nationalize in all respects.[32] Presbrey's conception of "national homogeneity" was a translucent reference to what Calvin Coolidge saw as "the enormous capacity for consumption of all kinds of commodities which characterizes our country."[33]

The idea that advertising was producing a homogeneous national character was likened within the trade as a "civilizing influence comparable in its cultural effects to those of other epoch-making developments in history."[34] Yet not all of the conceptions of advertising were expressed in such epic and transhistorical terminology. Sensitive to the political and economic context of such notions as "civilizing," "national homogeneity" and "capacity for consumption," William Allen White bridged the gap between "civilization" and civil society, noting that modern advertising was particularly a formation of advanced capitalist production. Aiming his critique at internal and external "revolutionist" threats to capitalism, White turned contemporary conceptions of revolution to their head. Reasserting the efficacy of the American Revolutionary tradition, he argued that advertising men were the true "revolutionists." Juxtaposing the consumer market to revolution of a socialistic variety, White presented a satirical political strategy to halt the "golden quest" for consumer goods. "I would cut out the advertising and fill the editorial and news pages with material supplied by communists and reds. That would stop buying—distribution of things. It would bring an impasse in civilization, which would immediately begin to decay."[35] Identifying ad men with the integrity and survival of the American heritage, White numbered advertising among our sacred cultural institutions.

Through advertising, then, consumption took on a clearly cultural tone. Within governmental and business rhetoric, consumption assumed an ideological veil of nationalism and democratic lingo. The mass "American type," which defined unity on the bases of common ethnicity, language, class or literature, was ostensibly born out of common desires—mass responses to the demands of capitalist production. Mass industry, requiring a corresponding mass individual, cryptically named him "Civilized American" and implicated his national heritage in the marketplace. By defining himself and his desires in terms of the good of capitalist production, the worker would implicitly accept the foundations of modern industrial life. By transforming the notion of "class" into "mass," business hoped to create an "individual" who could locate his needs and frustrations in terms of the consumption of goods rather than the quality and content of his life (work). . . .

In an attempt to massify men's consumption in step with the requirements of the productive machinery, advertising increasingly offered mass-produced solutions to "instinctive" strivings as well as to the ills of mass society itself. If it was industrial capitalism around which crowded cities were being built and which had spawned much of the danger to health, the frustration, the loneliness and the insecurity of modern industrial life, the advertising of the period denied complicity. Rather, the logic of contemporaneous advertising read, one can free oneself from the ills of modern life by embroiling oneself in the maintenance of that life. A 1924 ad for Pompeian facial products argued that

> unless you are one woman in a thousand, you must use powder and rouge. Modern living has robbed women of much of their natural color . . . taken away the conditions that once gave natural roses in the cheeks.[36]

Within such literature, the term "modern living" was an ahistorical epithet, devoid of the notion "Modern Industrial Society," and teeming with visions of the benefits of civilization which had emerged, one would think, quite apart from the social conditions and relations to which these "benefits" therapeutically addressed themselves. On the printed page, modern living was defined as heated houses, easy transportation, and the conveniences of the household. To the reader it may have meant something considerably different: light-starved housing, industrial pollution, poor nutrition, boredom. In either sense, modern life offered the same sallow skin and called for a solution through consumption. Within such advertisements, business called for a transformation of the critique of bourgeois society to an implicit commitment to that society.

The advertising which attempted to create the dependable mass of consumers required by modern industry often did so by playing upon the fears and frustrations evoked by mass society—offering mass produced visions of individualism by which people could extricate themselves from the mass. The rationale was simple. If a person was unhappy within mass industrial society, advertising was attempting to put that unhappiness to work in the name of that society.

In an attempt to boost mass sales of soap, the Cleanliness Institute, a cryptic front group for the soap and glycerine producers' association, pushed soap as a "Kit for Climbers" (social, no doubt). The illustration was a multitudinous mountain of men, each climbing over one another to reach the summit. At the top of this indistinguishable mass stood one figure, his arms outstretched toward the sun, whose rays spelled out the words "Heart's Desire." The ad cautioned that "in any path of life, that long way to the top is hard enough—so make the going easier with soap and water." In an attempt to build a responsive mass market, the Cleanliness Institute appealed to what they must have known was a major dissatisfaction with the reality of mass life. Their solution was a sort of mass pseudodemassification. . . .

Listerine, whose ads had taken the word *halitosis* out of the inner reaches of the dictionary and placed it on "stage, screen and in the home," offered this anecdote:

> He was conscious that something stood between him and greater business success—between him and greater popularity. Some subtle something he couldn't lay his hands on . . . Finally, one day, it dawned on him . . . the truth that his friends had been too delicate to mention.[37]

When a critical understanding of modern production might have helped many to understand what actually stood "between them and greater business success," this ad attempted to focus man's critique against himself—his body had kept him from happiness. Within the world view of a society which was more and more divorcing men from any notion of craft or from any definable sort of product, it was also logical that "you couldn't blame a man for firing an employee with halitosis to hire one without it." The contingency of a man's job was offered a nonviolent, apolitical solution. If man was the victim of himself, the fruits of mass production were his savior. Ads constantly hammered away at everything that was his own—his bodily functions, his self-esteem—and offered something of theirs as a socially more effective substitute.

. . . Correlative to Allport's vision of "social self," advertising offered the next best thing—*a commodity self*—to people who were unhappy or could be convinced that they were unhappy about their lives. Each portion of the body was to be viewed critically, as a *potential* bauble in a successful assemblage. Woodbury's soap was offered as a perfect treatment for the "newly important face of Smart Today;" another product promised to keep teeth white: "A flashing smile is worth more than a good sized bank account. It wins friends." After she has used Caro Cocoanut Oil Shampoo, a dashing gentleman informs the lady, "I'm crazy about your hair. *It's* the most beautiful of any here tonight." Within the vision offered by such ads, not only were social grace and success attainable: they were also defined through the use of specific products. You don't make friends, your smile "wins" them; your embellished hair, and not you, is beautiful. . . .

During the twenties, civil society was increasingly characterized by mass industrial production. In an attempt to implicate men and women within the efficient process of production, advertising built a vision of culture which bound old notions of Civilization to the new realities of civil society. In what was viewed as their instinctual search for traditional ideals, people were offered a vision of civilized man which was transvaluated in terms of the pecuniary exigencies of society. Within a society that defined real life in terms of the monotonous insecurities of mass production, advertising attempted to create an alternative organization of life which would serve to channel man's desires for self, for social success, for leisure away from himself and his works, and toward a commoditized acceptance of "Civilization."

NOTES

1. Alfred Dupont Chandler, *Giant Enterprise, Ford, General Motors and the Automobile Industry* (1964), p. 29. Chandler is citing the *Federal Trade Commission Report on the Motor Vehicle Industry.*
2. *Ibid.,* p. 26.
3. " . . . during a period of eighteen years commencing in 1908, Ford Motor Company manufactured and offered for sale only one basic model of passenger automobile. . . . This was the [black] Model T." See Chandler, pp. 27, 37.
4. Harold Loeb, *National Survey of Potential Product Capacity* (1935), p. 3.
5. This may be seen as a response to a combination of things. Aside from the fact of proliferating mass production methods, the 1921 depression/buyers' strike served as an impetus to this study.
6. Edward A. Filene, *The Way Out: A Forecast of Coming Changes in American Business and Industry* (1924), p. 93.
7. Chandler, p. 143.
8. Notably Alfred P. Sloan of General Motors. Sloan saw productive strategy in broad social terms. His biography, *My Life With General Motors* (1960), gives an account of these early developments.
9. Loeb, p. xv, in regard to "the capacity of the nation to produce goods and services. If full advantage were taken of existing resources, man power, and knowledge . . . every new invention, every improved method, every advance in management technique will increase the final quantitative estimate." Such a question would be answered by "a running inventory of our approach to perfection rather than a research into existing capacity as determined by production." The survey considered such a potential too open-ended to effect meaningful speculation.
10. Edward A. Filene, *The Consumer's Dollar* (1934), p. 13.

11. Whiting Williams, *What's on the Worker's Mind* (1920), p. 317.
12. Filene, *The Way Out*, pp. 62–63.
13. Williams, *Mainsprings*, p. 51.
14. Filene, *The Way Out*, p. 127.
15. By the 1920s widespread elements of the union movement had accepted such an ideology. Among others, William English Walling of the Labor Progressives dissolved the class struggle in one fell swoop. Virtually paraphrasing the ideologues of scientifically planned capitalism, he felt that "to bring labor to the maximum productivity, the American labor movement believes, requires new organization and policies in the administration of industry." See William Walling, *American Labor and American Democracy* (1926), p. 233.

    Walling Spoke of *labor* and *consumer* as interrelated aspects of the total life of the American worker. His concern for consumer rights reflected the ideology of progressive capital no less than did the writings of Edward Filene, who, although he had one foot in the "consumer category," placed his other on the side of financial power rather than in the monotony of factory life.
16. Norman Ware, *Labor in Modern Industrial Society* (1935), p. 88.
17. Ware, *Labor in Modern Industrial Society*, p. 101.
18. Ware, *Labor in Modern Industrial Society*, p. 95. According to Ware's studies, union manufacturing labor averaged 40–48 hours per week. Nonunion labor in similar industries averaged 50 hours per week, while labor in more traditional areas, mills and shops, worked 48–60 hours per week.
19. *Ibid.* p. 16–17.
20. Robert S. Lynd, "The People as Consumers," *Recent Social Trends in the United States: Report of the President's Research Committee on Social Trends*, Vol. II (1933), p. 862. Such credit buying was initiated primarily in the automobile industry with the General Motors Acceptance Corporation (GMAC).
21. Williams, *What's on the Worker's Mind*, p. 317.
22. "In some lines, such as whiskey and milk, distribution cost is from four to ten times the cost of production." Chandler, p. 157.
23. Editorial, "Senator Borah on Marketing," *P.I.*, CXXIV, No. 5 (August 2, 1923), p. 152
24. Editorial, "The Phantom of National Distribution," *P.I.*, CXXIV, No. 12 (September 20, 1923), p. 180.
25. Baritz, p. 27.
26. *Ibid.*, p. 26.
27. Walter Dill Scott, *Influencing Men in Business* (originally published 1911; 1928 revised edition enlarged by Delton T. Howard), p. 3.
28. Loren Baritz,, *The Servants of Power* (1960), p. 26.
29. Scott, p. 132.
30. Baritz, p. 26.
31. "Physical or sex attraction . . . other things being equal, qualities which make one pleasing to look at or to caress render their possessor popular to many and loved by not a few." Floyd Henry Allport, *Social Psychology* (1924), p. 365.
32. Frank Spencer Presbrey, *The History and Development of Advertising* (1929), p. 613.
33. *Ibid.*, p. 622.
34. *Ibid.*, p. 608.
35. *Ibid.*, p. 610
36. *Ladies' Home Journal* (May 1924), p. 161.
37. *Ibid.*, p. 133.

9.2 DALLAS W. SMYTHE

The Role of the Mass Media and Popular Culture in Defining Development

Dallas W. Smythe (1907–1992) was a critical scholar of mass communication. Concerned about the domination of Canadian culture by the United States, Smythe worked for a time at the Federal Communications Commission (FCC), which oversees the operation of the predominantly commercial mass media in the United States. Over the years, Smythe was commissioned by the Canadian government to study the situation of broadcasting in Canada, which is dominated by the Canadian Broadcasting Corporation (CBC).

The accumulated results of Smythe's work were synthesized in a study of the impact of U.S. commercial media on Canada entitled *Dependency Road: Communications, Capitalism, Consciousness, and Canada* (Ablex, 1981). In the following selection from that book, Smythe focuses on the integral relationship between advertising, media, and audiences. Smythe argues that advertising-supported media systems produce audiences as the commodity through which they make economic profit. TV networks, for example, attract people to watch by offering a regular schedule of programs during prime-time viewing hours. The resulting audiences are sold by the networks to advertisers. Thus, Smythe believes, advertising-supported media are a peculiar form of market; they do not sell cultural goods to people, they sell people to advertisers. Once sold to advertisers, media audiences perform key services for the capitalist economy at large. In fact, Smythe says, audiences are put to work for the capitalist economy in specific ways that are crucial to the reproduction of capitalist social relations.

Key Concept: audience work

*T*he mass media of communications (television, radio, press, magazines, cinema, and books), the related arts (e.g., popular music, comic books), and consumer goods and services (clothing, cosmetics, fast food, etc.) set the daily agenda for the populations of advanced capitalist countries and increasingly for Third World nations. It follows, therefore, that the policy which governs what appears on the daily agenda produced by these institutions has a special role in defining the process of "development" for those populations.

What do I mean by *agenda*? As Ortega y Gasset remarked, "Living is nothing more or less than doing one thing instead of another." Individuals daily live by giving *priorities* to their problems. Whether implicitly or explicitly, they use their time and resources to attend to their problems according to some ordering of these priorities. It is when they act as part of *institutions* that the agenda-setting function becomes a collective rather than an individual process.

Human beings are human because and by means of the relationships or process that links them together. Institutions are social habits—systematic and perpetuated relationships between people. Institutions have specialized agendas for their own actions. Thus, the family is primarily concerned with the nurture of children. Work organizations (factories or farms) are primarily concerned with "production" activities. Military and other security institutions specialize on the use of force to perpetuate a particular class structure's control of people and other resources. The formal educational system is primarily concerned with instructing the next generation in the techniques and values of the dominant social system. Medical institutions are principally concerned with the treatment of illness and accidents. Religious institutions have a special concern with theological and ethical aspects of birth, life, and death.

Each of these institutions also embodies in its actions and propagates the agenda which follows from the ideological theory and practice of the whole social system of which it is a part. Therefore each of these institutions incidentally to its prime purpose states and reinforces priorities in the systemic agendas to which the population gives attention. For example, the military discipline instructs young people in the values of private property and individual subordination to a hierarchy of authority. All these institutions are very old, dating from prehistoric times. As compared with them, the mass media of communications are very young institutions (printing since the late nineteenth century, electronic media since the early twentieth century). What has been distinctive about the capitalist mass media is their *specialized function* of legitimizing and directing the development of the social system. . . .

The real world context for the present dominant institutional structures developed over the past four centuries is that of capitalism. It is a system based on private property in the means of production and consumption and on the appropriation of the surplus product of labor by the owners of capital. It is a worldwide system of interrelated markets for commodities. These markets, through more or less monopolistic prices, determine *what* is to be produced, *how much* is to be produced, *for whom* it is to be produced, and *how* it is to be produced. The answers given through these markets to the *how* question determine the kind, amount, and location of specialization of work and production, as well as the kind, timing, extent, and location of invention and innovation of new products and techniques of productive activity. . . .

Today, the mass media (press, television, radio, magazines, books, cinema) are the central means of forming attitudes, values, and buying behavior—consciousness in action, to put it succinctly. They are the "shock troops" of Consciousness Industry. It is obvious to all—and is the main concern of liberal and radical critics—that the way the mass media select and present news, portray ethnic groups in the "entertainment," and handle public controversial issues powerfully affects people's behavior. . . . Here we are concerned to show that the mass media have a more basic influence on our lives and our ideology because they, together with advertisers, take a central part in the process by which the monopoly-capitalist system grows or declines in strength. In the core area, the mass media *produce* audiences and *sell* them to advertisers of consumer goods and services, political candidates, and groups interested in controversial public issues. These audiences *work* to market these things to themselves. *At the same time,* these audiences have their basic human concerns, and part of the *work* they must do is to reproduce their labor power. This work embodies their resistance to the power of Consciousness Industry. That power appears to them through the total mass media *message* (consisting of advertising, entertainment, information, news), through the physical consumer goods, political candidates, and through tangible evidences of social relations problems. . . .

Although the mass media began the *mass* production of information, they are linked through interlocking business organization and a complex of largely managed, i.e., oligopolistic, markets with a much broader base of information production and exchange. The whole complex is Consciousness Industry. Advertising, market research, photography, the commercial application of art to product and container design, the fine arts, teaching machines and related software and educational testing, as well as the formal educational system, are all part of it. The mass media are also linked through corporate ties and intersecting markets with professional and amateur sports, the performing arts, comic books, toys, games, the production and sale of recorded music, hotel, airlines, and a wide variety of consumer goods industries (automobiles, clothing, jewelry, cosmetics, etc.) through "tie-in" contracts and their advertising service to these industries. They are also mutually interdependent with telecommunications operations (point-to-point electronic communications), the computerized storage, transmission, retrieval, and processing of digital information and the industries which produce the equipment for telecommunications and computer operations and which conduce research and development in electronics, physics, and chemistry. The information sector of the United States government and military is at least as large as the civilian telecommunications sector, and both are linked with the mass media by giant corporations. The telecommunications and computer industries dwarf the mass media in terms of revenues and assets and simultaneously generate technical innovations (e.g., television, tele-processing of data) and enlarge their economic and political power by doing so. . . .

The secret of the growth of Consciousness Industry in the past century will be found in (1) the relation of advertising to the news, entertainment, and information material in the mass media: (2) the relations of both the material and advertising to real consumer goods and services, political candidates, and public issues; (3) the relations of advertising and consumer goods and services to the people who consume them; (4) the effective control of people's lives which the monopoly capitalist corporations dominating the foregoing three sets of relationships try to establish and maintain. The capitalist system cultivates the illusion that the three streams of information and things are independent, the advertising merely "supports" or "makes possible" the news, information, and entertainment, which in turn are *separate* from the consumer goods and services we buy. This is untrue. The commercial mass media *are* advertising in their entirety. Advertising messages provide news (that a particular product or sponsor has something "new" to deserve the attention of the audience), entertainment (many television commercials are more entertaining than the programs in which they are imbedded), and information about prices and alleged qualities of the advertised product of the "sponsoring" organization. And both advertising and the "program material" reflect, mystify, and are essential to the sale of goods and services. The program material is produced and distributed in order to attract and hold the attention of the audience so that its members may be counted (by audience survey organizations which then certify the size and character of the audience produced) and sold to the advertiser.

... [R]eaders and audience members of advertising-supported mass media are a commodity produced and sold to advertisers *because they perform a valuable service for the advertisers.* This is why the advertisers buy them. What is the valuable service audiences perform? It is three kinds of work:

1. They market consumer goods and services to themselves.
2. They learn to vote for one candidate (or issue) or another in the political arena.
3. They learn and reaffirm belief in the rightness of their politico-economic system. . . .

Audience power work for Consciousness Industry produces a particular kind of human nature or consciousness, focusing its energies on the consumption of commodities, which [psychoanalyst] Erich Fromm called *homo consumens*—people who live and work to perpetuate the capitalist system built on the commoditization of life. This is not to say that individuals, the family, and other institutions, such as labor unions and the church, are powerless. They resist the pressures of the capitalist system. . . . But for about a century the kind of human nature produced in the core area has, to a large degree, been the product of Consciousness Industry. People with this nature exist primarily to serve the system; the system is *not* under the control, serving them. . . .

The necessity for consumers to buy new products is guaranteed by (1) style changes; (2) quality control in manufacture, not to maximize product life but to produce lives which will end shortly after warranty periods expire so that there is predictable "junking" of products because it would cost more to repair than replace them. And the stylistic features of all consumer goods and services are based on calculated manipulation of public taste so that increasingly consumers pay for images rather than use-values. Having analyzed the

American development of science, capital equipment, and production, Professor David Noble of MIT begins his *America by Design*:

> Modern Americans confront a world in which everything changes, yet nothing moves. The perpetual rush to novelty that characterizes the modern marketplace, with its escalating promise of technological transcendence, is matched by the persistence of pre-formed patterns of life which promise merely more of the same. Each major scientific advance, while appearing to presage an entirely new society, attests rather to the vigor and resilience of the old order that produced it. Every new, seemingly bold departure ends by following an already familiar path (Noble, 1977, p. xvii).

There are two broad classes of markets in which giant corporations make the "sales effort" which stimulates the realization of surplus that powers the monopoly-capitalist system. First, and most easily recognizable, is the Civilian Sales sector where ordinary civilians buy their consumer goods and services. But it left to depend on this sector alone for its growth, the monopoly-capitalist system would be plunged into ruinous depression. The Military Sales and Welfare sector must be maintained as a giant and increasingly generous "pump primer" in order to compensate for the "leakiness" of the system—the tendency for surplus to be accumulated (or hoarded) by corporations and their direct beneficiaries rather than distributed to workers so that they in turn could buy the consumer goods and services produced. Of course the Military Sales effort also serves to ensure the security of the capitalist system against dissidents and criminals at home and liberation movements in the economic colonies around the world.

 . . . The prime item on the agenda of Consciousness Industry is producing *people* motivated to buy the "new models" of consumer goods and services and motivated to pay the taxes which support the swelling budgets for the Military Sales effort. . . .

In economic terms there are three types of commodities (e.g., wheat), intermediate products (e.g., flour), and end products (e.g., bread). In economic terms, the audiences of the mass media are intermediate products. Like other factors of production, they are consumed in producing, i.e., selling, the end product; their production and use by the advertiser is a marketing cost. The end product of the giant corporations in the consumer goods and services sector is those consumer goods and services. The audiences produced by the mass media are only part of the means to the sale of that end product. But at the larger, systemic level, people, working via audiences to market goods and services to themselves, and their consciousness ultimately are the *systemic* end product: *they* are produced by the system ready to buy consumer goods and to pay taxes and to work in their alienating jobs in order to continue buying tomorrow. The message of the system is a slogan in fine print on a full-page advertisement in the *New York Times*: "Buy something." That way you help keep up the GNP and perhaps keep your job and paycheck so that next time around you will still be able to "buy something."

The media function of producing audiences is not limited to audiences designed to market consumer goods and services. It also includes the production of audiences designed to produce the end product: votes for candidates for political office, and public opinion on "political" matters. . . .

The practice of news management is universal on the part of party candidates, heads of states, government agencies, business corporations, and their organized pressure groups often working through trade associations for the various industries and government intelligence agencies (CIA, etc.). Political parties and candidates advertise heavily in the mass media, and their relation to audiences is the same as that of consumer goods manufacturers. The content of news space in the print media, television, and radio is mostly the result of press releases and publicity-getting events which are staged in order to *make* news. Advertising agency executives have estimated that as much as 85 percent of news is "planted" through the staging of pseudo events (press conferences, publicity stunts, etc.) rather than the result of the initiative of editors and reporters. The objective of political advertising and news management is the same as that of advertisers of consumer goods. It is to produce people who are ready to support a particular policy, rather than some other policy, be it buying brand X rather than brand Y of automobile, or "supporting" one or another political candidate, or supporting employment preference for ethnic minorities or WASPS, or supporting Israel or the Arabs in their long struggle in the Middle East. The mass media thus daily set the agenda of issues and images to which everyone pays some attention. . . .

To be effective, advertising, like the avowedly news, entertainment and information interlarded between the advertisements, must have the same qualities as the ostensibly nonadvertising content: it must catch and hold audience attention and present its message in an entertaining way; that is, it must tell an effective story of some kind. Advertising is storytelling. So also is the news. No matter the claims that news is "objective"; obviously it is not. It has a subjective perspective—determined by stylized customs. Even weather reports on television tell a story about what tomorrow's weather will be. And of course, the so-called entertainment programs on television are stories told in stylized, commoditized ways. TV advertisements cost more than the surrounding program material by a factor of from eight to ten to one per minute of air time. They therefore contain the *concentrated* entertaining and informative qualities which are spread out more thinly in the nonadvertising program content.

A second reason for treating advertising and the surrounding program content as inextricably intermixed is, as alluded to, that the advertisers require that the program content be suited to the advertisements. For example, advertisements for foreign travel in newspapers *must* appear adjacent to the "news stories" of the tourist attractions of visiting Hawaii, or Europe, or if you are in the United State, visiting Canada. And there are very many examples of television programs which reached the air only to be canceled (or never passed the "pilot" stage) not because they were not entertaining, but because they did not produce the particular audience demographics which advertisers demanded. A third reason, which applies particularly to news, is that the great bulk of the news is itself produced by business enterprises, government agencies, and occasionally other institutions (churches, labor unions, and special interest groups, e.g., environmental protection associations)—and hence has the same manipulative intentions as does explicit advertising.

A fourth reason for treating the advertising and nonadvertising content of the mass media as essentially connected with each other is that the business organizations which operate them so consider them. In the early years of the mass media . . . the press in fact generally allowed advertisers to supply directly the news which the latter wished to see published. Only by a long struggle to eliminate the cruder manifestations of such direct dictation have the mass media achieved limited "believability" for the autonomy of the editorial side of the media. (In newspapers the travel and real estate sections still commonly allow advertisers to determine the editorial content.) Edward L. Bernays declared:

> At its 1888 convention, the American Newspaper Publishers Association openly worried about the effects of press agentry. . . . But there was no real effort to eliminate free publicity until about twenty years later (Bernays, 1952, p. 61).

How different from the nonadvertising content of the mass media which are openly dominated by advertising is the content of other branches of popular cultural industry, such as motion pictures, popular music, paperback books, and comic books? After all, the customers pay for them at the box office or cash register and not indirectly by working for advertisers. From a broad systemic point of view, however, the content of these popular cultural industrial products is *not* different from that in the advertiser-dominated mass media. It is axiomatic in the trade that if a story has what it takes to sell, it matters not whether it first appears in a book, a popular song or musical genre (like rock music), in a movie, or in television-radio. Cross-marketing of nonadvertising material is essential to capitalist popular culture. The Beatles' records dominated radio station programming for a time. "Hit songs" in the juke boxes are takeouts from Hollywood film sound tracks. *Roots*, beginning as a book, was a successful television series. *Peyton Place* was profitable in television, cinema houses, and as a paperback. As the connections noted here are not confined within the media, no matter how broadly defined, but extend to tangible commodity markets. . . . The point is not merely that these specific cultural commodities were cross-marketed, but that the qualities of form and content which made them successful in one or another branch of cultural industry, whether explicitly advertiser-dominated or not, are deliberately cultivated by *all* branches of cultural industry.

. . . The mass media screen in the values of the capitalist system and screen out other values—a function which [has been termed] the "hegemonic filter." The agenda set by the mass media is explicitly or implicitly (in much so-called entertainment, e.g., professional sports)—although traditional contradictory elements are included in it—ideologically loaded to support the system. A condensed summary of such values illustrates.

Human nature is portrayed as fixed ("you cannot change human nature"). It is typically and incurably selfish. Therefore, "look out for number one." Let the other fellow take care of himself. In every area, what is private is better than what is public. Private business is clean and efficient. But some people are dishonest and mean and they will be punished by a heroic individual or the efficient military or police forces. Public government is inherently dirty and inefficient, and of course, politics is a dirty business. It follows that prices charged by private business are good because private businessmen "have to meet a payroll" and are efficient. But taxes (which in economic terms are indistinguishable from prices) are bad; and because public officers need not "show a profit," they are inefficient. Private property is virtually sacred. And public planning which would tell private owners what to do with their property is inherently bad. But sometimes bad, miserly landlords should be punished by the community. In fact, that government is best which governs least, leaving everything possible to be provided by the "market." We should be "objective" and respect each other's opinions, unless the others are Communists. In that case they are part of a bad international conspiracy. They are not good Canadians or Americans and ought to be sent back where they came from....

Although its core values are static and rigid, the capitalists system has the necessary flexibility to cope with internal structural conflicts which would otherwise be disruptive. This is a particular virtue of the policy of the mass media which air and coopt such drives. Thus the mass media facilitated the move to the Right which the capitalist system initiated with the Cold War anti-Communist inquisition inaugurated by Richard Nixon and associates in the United States in 1946. And the Black civil rights movement, the anti–Vietnam war movement of the late 1960s and the exposure of the corruption of President Nixon in the Watergate matter were also facilitated by the mass media. Symptomatic of this cooptative capacity of the system was the full-page advertisement in the *New York Times* for a bank. It features a blown-up photograph of Che Guevara and the copy ran about as follows: "We would hire this man if we could. For we are making a revolution in banking." Through this cooptative flexibility, individual and ethnic alienation is kept within tolerable limits for the system. Consciousness Industry *leads* in the cooptation. The distinctive clothing, jewelry, hairstyling, and music of the counterculture of the 1960s was quickly adopted and profitably mass produced and mass marketed. This effectively liquidated its cultural characteristics of "protest" and completed the erosion of potential for structural change or revolution which the young radicals of the 1960s hoped to develop.

The enormous mass of advertisements and other mass media content which bombards the individual in the advanced capitalist state from *all* the mass media has the systemic effect of a barrage of noise which effectively exhausts the time and energies of the population. This is a powerful deterrent to consideration of the possibilities of alternative systems of social relationships. As Robert Merton and Paul Lazarsfeld wrote in 1948, in a scene which did not yet include mass television, the net effect is to "dysfunctionally narcotize" the population:

For these media not only continue to affirm the *status quo*, but, in the same measure they fail to raise essential questions about the structure of society (Lazarsfeld and Merton, 1949, p. 459).

By attending to the agenda set for them by the mass media, the actions of audiences working for advertisers, narcotizes the population. People are diverted from giving high and continuous priority to the political, economic, and social crises which are marginally on or off the agenda and not dealt with, such as the ecological disasters which the rape of natural resources, environmental pollution, and the threat of extinction of life by nuclear weapons make very real possibilities. . . .

If the role of the mass media and popular culture today is to define development, what do we mean by *development?* Countless United Nations, UNESCO documents and commissions, as well as individual scholars have defined it in terms such as these: Development is the process of creating the conditions for every individual to live in such relations with other human beings and his/her fellow animals and the remainder of the physical environment as will realize the potential of all. It is also the only tenable definition of *peace.* Because we have not yet in the multimillion year evolution of life on this planet approached an awareness of the qualities inherent in that potential, it is impossible now to describe the objective of development more exactly.

Life proceeds through a process of contradictions and the struggles which embody them. The common denominator which runs through these struggles through recorded history to date appears to be the efforts of some social formations to oppress and exploit other social formations (men vs. women, boss vs. workers, rich vs. poor, white vs. nonwhite, for example). The terms *developed* nations, *developing* nations, *underdeveloped* nations have entered our vocabulary within the past 35 years as a result of the struggles focused in international forums such as the United Nations. The concept of development in these terms has been shaped by experience to date. And that experience has been mostly that of the capitalist world order (for the past 400 years at least). It therefore is not surprising that for the greater part of the world's population today, *development* is defined by the capitalist system through the agenda set by its Consciousness Industry, with the communications media as the leading edge of the process. . . .

Regardless of the immediate achievements of capitalist or socialist systems, the rivalry between them reveals for all to see the *processual* nature of development. Now everyone has a real basis to ask questions like these: Who will determine the kind of development which is to be pursued? How? When? Why? And most fundamentally, for whose benefit, i.e., for the benefit of which class of people? The answers given to these questions will describe the *development* any people will experience. In the total power struggle between class interests which *is* the process of development, the peculiar technical forms of power embodied in the mass media where they themselves are developed will play the agenda-setting role in all ideological systems. The mass media, as the specialized institutions created for this purpose, will guide (but not decide in any deterministic fashion) the evolving struggle between contradictory power concentrations within the system. What is *omitted* from the agenda set daily by the mass media for people's attention will hardly shape the strategic level of policy determination for that society. What is generally unconsidered or discontinuously considered cannot enter into mass consciousness.

REFERENCES

Bernays, Edward L. "The Engineering of Consent," *Annuals of the American Academy of Political and Social Science*, Vol. 250, March 1947, pp. 113–120.

Lazarsfeld, P. F., and Merton, R. K. "Mass Communications, Popular Taste, and Organized Social Action," in Bryson, L., Ed., *The Communication of Ideas.* New York: Harper & Row, 1948. (Also published in Schramm, W., Ed., *Mass Communications.* Urbana: University of Illinois Press, 1949.)

Noble, David F. *America by Design: Science, Technology and the Rise of Corporate Capitalism,* New York: Knopf, 1977.

9.3 SUT JHALLY

Image-Based Culture: Advertising and Popular Culture

Sut Jhally is a professor of communication at the University of Massachu-setts, Amherst. A scholar in the critical study of mass media, he also directs the Media Education Foundation, located in Northampton, Massachusetts, which produces an ongoing series of videotapes that critique key public issues in mass media and popular culture. Perhaps the most widely viewed of these programs is Jhally's *Dreamworlds* (Media Education Foundation, 1990; recently revised and updated as *Dreamworlds II,* 1995), which util-izes the imagery of rock video to criticize the ways in which women are represented and to show the links between these images and real-life vio-lence against women.

Jhally holds that we cannot understand anything coherent about contem-porary mass media and popular culture unless we understand their integral relationship with advertising. His work started with critical analyses of advertising, exemplified by *Social Communication in Advertising,* 2d ed. (Routledge, 1990), coauthored with Canadian communication scholars Wil-liam Leiss and Stephen Kline, and *Codes of Advertising* (St. Martin's Press, 1987). Jhally has ranged out from this direct critique of advertising to consider questions of race, class, and the media in *Enlightened Racism* (Westview, 1992), coauthored with Justin Lewis, and of the social issues treated in his series of videotapes.

In the following selection from "Image-Based Culture: Advertising and Popular Culture," *The World and I* (July 1990), Jhally shows how the com-mercial imagery of advertising has spread to other areas of popular culture, and he discusses the impact of this on the formation of individual and social identities. Due to the central economic and cultural role of advertising, commercial images permeate everyday life. As a result, it is difficult for people to distance themselves enough so that they can critically reflect on the effect of these images on their lives. Furthermore, Jhally argues, since

223

powerful and pleasurable images form the mainstream of popular culture, it
is difficult to reject them, even if they are harmful. Jhally concludes that
citizens must engage in a *cultural politics of images* to combat the negative
effects of advertising.

Key Concept: discourse through and about objects

*B*ecause we live inside the consumer culture, and most of us have done
so for most of our lives, it is sometimes difficult to locate the origins of our
most cherished values and assumptions. They simply appear to be part of our
natural world. It is a useful exercise, therefore, to examine how our culture has
come to be defined and shaped in specific ways. . . .

In this context, it is instructive to focus upon that period in our history
that marks the transition point in the development of an image-saturated society—the 1920s. In that decade the advertising industry was faced with a curious problem—the need to sell increasing quantities of "nonessential" goods in
a competitive marketplace using the potentialities offered by printing and color
photography. Whereas the initial period of national advertising (from approximately the 1880s to the 1920s) had focused largely in a celebratory manner on
the products themselves and had used text for "reason why" advertising (even
if making the most outrageous claims), the 1920s saw the progressive integration of people (via visual representation) into the messages. Interestingly, in
this stage we do not see representations of "real" people in advertisements, but
rather we see representations of people who "stand for" reigning social values
such as family structure, status differentiation, and hierarchical authority.

While this period is instructive from the viewpoint of content, it is
equally fascinating from the viewpoint of *form;* for while the possibilities of
using visual imagery existed with the development of new technologies, there
was no guarantee that the audience was sufficiently literate in visual imagery
to properly decode the ever-more complex messages. Thus, the advertising
industry had to educate as well as sell, and many of the ads of this period were
a fascinating combination where the written (textual) material explained the
visual material. The consumer society was literally being taught how to read
the commercial messages. By the postwar period the education was complete
and the function of written text moved away from explaining the visual and
toward a more cryptic form where it appears as a "key" to the visual "puzzle."
In the contemporary world, messages about goods are all pervasive—advertising has increasingly filled up the spaces of our daily existence. Our media are
dominated by advertising images, public space has been taken over by "information" about products, and most of our sporting and cultural events are
accompanied by the name of a corporate sponsor. There is even an attempt to
get television commercials into the nations' high schools under the pretense of
"free" news programming. As we head toward the twenty-first century, advertising is ubiquitous—it is the air that we breathe as we live our daily lives.

ADVERTISING AND THE GOOD LIFE: IMAGE AND 'REALITY'

[Advertising is] part of "a discourse through and about objects" because it does not merely tell us about things but of how things are connected to important domains of our lives. Fundamentally, advertising talks to us as individuals and addresses us about how we can become *happy*. The answers it provides are all oriented to the marketplace, through the purchase of goods or services. To understand the system of images that constitutes advertising we need to inquire into the definition of happiness and satisfaction in contemporary social life.

Quality of life surveys that ask people what they are seeking in life—what it is that makes them happy—report quite consistent results. The conditions that people are searching for—what they perceive will make them happy—are things such as having personal autonomy and control of one's life, self-esteem, a happy family life, loving relations, a relaxed, tension-free leisure time, and good friendships. The unifying theme of this list is that these things are not fundamentally connected to goods. It is primarily "social" life and not "material" life that seems to be the locus of perceived happiness. Commodities are only *weakly related* to these sources of satisfaction[1]

A market society, however, is guided by the principle that satisfaction should be achieved via the marketplace, and through its institutions and structures it orients behavior in that direction. The data from the quality of life studies are not lost on advertisers. If goods themselves are not the locus of perceived happiness, then they need to be connected in some way with those things that are. Thus advertising promotes images of what the audience conceives of as "the good life": Beer can be connected with anything from eroticism to male fraternity to the purity of the old West; food can be tied up with family relations or health; investment advice offers early retirements in tropical settings. The marketplace cannot directly offer the real thing, but it can offer visions of it connected with the purchase of products.

Advertising thus does not work by creating values and attitudes out of nothing but by drawing upon and rechanneling concerns that the target audience (and the culture) already shares. . . .

What are the consequences of such a system of images and goods? Given that the "real" sources of satisfaction cannot be provided by the purchase of commodities (merely the "image" of that source), it should not be surprising that happiness and contentment a pear illusory in contemporary society. . . .

It is not simply a matter of being "tricked" by the false blandishments of advertising. The problem is with the institutional structure of a market society that propels definition of satisfaction *through* the commodity/image system. The modern context, then, provides a curious satisfaction experience—one that William Leiss describes as an ensemble of satisfactions and dissatisfactions" in which the consumption of commodities mediated by the image-system of advertising leads to consumer uncertainty and confusion.[2] The image-system of the marketplace reflects our desires and dreams, yet we have only the pleasure of the images to sustain us in our actual experience with goods.

The commodity image-system thus provides a particular vision of the world—a particular mode of self-validation that is integrally connected with what one *has* rather than what one *is*—a distinction often referred to as one between "having" and "being," with the latter now being defined through the former. As such, it constitutes a way of life that is defined and structured in quite specific political ways. Some commentators have even described advertising as part of a new *religious* system in which people construct their identities through the commodity form, and in which commodities are part of a supernatural magical world where anything is possible with the purchase of a product The commodity as displayed in advertising plays a mixture of psychological, social, and physical roles in its relations with people. The object world interacts with the human world at the most basic and fundamental of levels, performing seemingly magical feats of enchantment and transformation, bringing instant happiness and gratification, capturing the forces of nature, and acting as a passport to hitherto untraveled domains and group relationships.[3]

In short, the advertising image-system constantly propels us toward things as means to satisfaction. In the sense that every ad says it is better to buy than not to buy, we can best regard advertising as a *propaganda* system for commodities. In the image-system as a whole, happiness lies at the end of a purchase. Moreover, this is not a minor propaganda system—it is all pervasive. It should not surprise us then to discover that the problem that it poses—how to get more things for everyone (as that is the root to happiness)—guides our political debates. The goal of *economic growth* (on which the commodity vision is based) is an unquestioned and sacred proposition of the political culture. As the environmental costs of the strategy of unbridled economic growth be come more obvious, it is clear we must, as a society, engage in debate concerning the nature of future economic growth. However, as long as the commodity image system maintains its ubiquitous presence and influence, the possibilities of opening such a debate are remote. At the very moment we most desperately need to pose new questions within the political culture, the commodity image-system propels us with even greater certainty and persuasion along a path that, unless checked, is destined to end in disaster. . . .

THE SPREAD OF IMAGE-BASED INFLUENCE

While the commodity image-system is primarily about satisfaction, its influence and effect are not limited to that alone. I want to briefly consider four other areas in the contemporary world where the commodity system has its greatest impact The first is in the area of gender identity. Many commercial messages use images and representations of men and women as central components of their strategy to both get attention and persuade. Of course, they do not use any gender images but images drawn from a narrow and quite concentrated pool. As Erving Goffman has shown, ads draw heavily upon the domain of gender display—not the way that men and women actually behave but the ways in which we think men and women behave.[4] It is because these conventions of gender display are so easily recognized by the audience that they figure so prominently in the image-system. Also, images having to do with gender strike at the core of individual identity; our understanding of ourselves as either male or female (socially defined within this society at this time) is central to our understanding of who we are. What better place to choose than an area of social life that can be communicated at a glance and that reaches into the core of individual identity.

However, we should not confuse these portrayals as true reflections of gender. In advertising, gender (especially for women) is defined almost exclusively along the lines of sexuality. The image-system thus distorts our perceptions and offers little that balances out the stress on sexuality.

If only one or two advertisers used this strategy, then the image-system would not have the present distorted feature. The problem is that the vast majority do so. The iconography of the culture, perhaps more than any previous society, seems to be obsessed with sexuality. The end result is that the commodity is part of an increasingly eroticized world—that we live in a culture that is more and more defined erotically through commodities.

Second, the image-system has spread its influence to the realm of electoral politics. Much has been written (mostly negatively) about the role that television advertising now plays within national electoral politics. The presidency seems most susceptible to "image-politics," as it is the office most reliant on television advertising. The social commentary on politics from this perspective has mostly concerned the manner in which the focus has shifted from discussion of real "issues" to a focus on symbolism and emotionally based imagery.

. . . The fact that large numbers of people are changing their minds on who to vote for after seeing a thirty-second television commercial says a great deal about the nature of the political culture. It means that politics (for a significant portion of the electorate) is largely conducted on a symbolic realm, and that a notion of politics that is based upon people having a coherent and deep vision of their relationship to the social world is no longer relevant. Politics is not about issues; it is about "feeling good" or "feeling bad" about a candidate—and all it takes to change this is a thirty-second commercial.

The grammar of these images, then, clearly is different to the grammar of verbal or written language. The intrusion of the image-system into the world of electoral politics has meant that the majority of committed voters are held ransom by those who are uncommitted (the undecided or swing votes), and that these groups are influenced differently—and have a different relationship to politics—than those who have an old style view of politics. These huge swings of opinion, based upon information provided by the image-system, suggest that the political culture is incredibly superficial and does not correspond to what we normally think of as "politics."

Third, the commodity image-system is now implicated, due to changes in the way that toys are marketed, in the very structure and experience of children's play. With both children's television programming and commercials oriented around the sale of toys, writers such as Stephen Kline argue that the context within which kids play is now structured around marketing considerations. In consequence, "Children's imaginative play has become the target of marketing strategy, allowing marketers to define the limits of children's imaginations. . . . Play in fact has become highly ritualized—less an exploration and solidification of personal experiences and developing conceptual schema than a rearticulation of the fantasy world provided by market designers. Imaginative play has shifted one degree closer to mere imitation and assimilation." Further, the segmentation of the child audience in terms of both age and gender has led to a situation where parents find it difficult to play with their children because they do not share the marketing fantasy world that toy advertisers have created and where there is a growing divide between boys and girls at play. . . .

Fourth, the visual image-system has colonized areas of life that were previously largely defined (although not solely) by auditory perception and experience. The 1980s has seen a change in the way that popular music commodities (records, tapes, compact discs) are marketed, with a music video becoming an indispensable component of an overall strategy. These videos are produced as commercials for musical commodities by the advertising industry, using techniques learned from the marketing of products. Viewing these videos, there often seems to be little link between the song and the visual. In the sense that they are commercials for records, there of course does not have to be. Video makers are in the same position as ad makers in terms of trying to get attention for their message and making it visually pleasurable. It is little wonder then that representations involving sexuality figure so prominently (as in the case of regular product advertising). The visuals are chosen for their ability to sell. . . .

SPEED AND FRAGMENTATION: TOWARD A TWENTY-FIRST-CENTURY CONSCIOUSNESS

In addition to issues connected with the colonization of the commodity image-system of other areas of social life (gender socialization, politics, children's play, popular cultural forms) there are also important broader issues connected with its relation to modes of perception and forms of consciousness within contemporary society.

The visual images that dominate public space and public discourse are, in the video age, not static They do not stand still for us to examine and linger over. They are here for a couple of seconds and then they are gone. Television advertising is the epitome of this speed-up. There is nothing mysterious in terms of how it arose. As commercial time slots declined from sixty seconds to thirty seconds (and recently to fifteen seconds and even shorter), advertisers responded by creating a new type of advertising—what is called the "vignette approach"—in which narrative and "reason-why" advertising are subsumed under a rapid succession of life-style images, meticulously timed with music, that directly sell feeling and emotion rather than products. . . .

The speed-up is also a response by advertisers to two other factors: the increasing "clutter" of the commercial environment and the coming of age, in terms of disposable income, of a generation that grew up on television and commercials. The need for a commercial to stand out to a visually sophisticated audience drove the image-system to a greater frenzy of concentrated shorts. Again, sexuality became a key feature of the image-system within this.

The speed-up has two consequences. First, it has the effect of drawing the viewer into the message. One cannot watch these messages casually; they require undivided attention. Intensely pleasurable images, often sexual, are integrated into a flow of images. Watching has to be even more attentive to catch the brief shots of visual pleasure. The space "in between" the good parts can then be filled with other information, so that the commodity being advertised becomes a rich and complex sign.

Second, the speed-up has replaced narrative and rational response with images and emotional response. Speed and fragmentation are not particularly conducive to *thinking*. They induce *feeling*. The speed and fragmentation that characterize the commodity image-system may have a similar effect on the construction of consciousness. In one series of ads for MTV, a teenage boy or girl engages in a continuous monologue of events, characters, feelings, and emotions without any apparent connecting theme. As the video images mirror the fragmentation of thoughts, the ad ends with the plug: "Finally, a channel for the way you *think*." The generalization of this speed/fragmentation strategy to the entire domain of image culture may in fact mean that this is the form that thought increasingly is taking at the end of the twentieth century.

POLITICAL IMPLICATIONS: EDUCATION IN AN IMAGE-SATURATED SOCIETY

The real question concerning . . . [the commodity image-system] has to do with the political implications that one may draw from this kind of approach. Put simply: Is there a problem with this situation, and if so what precisely is it? Further, what solutions may be offered?

. . . In the history of twentieth-century capitalism the world of substance has been hidden and given a false veil by the world of appearances. People have given up control of the real world and immersed themselves in the ultimately illusory world of appearances. Surface has triumphed over substance.

The question is, how is substance (reality) revealed? Given that our understanding of reality is always socially constructed (that "ideology" is present in any system or situation), visual images are the central mode through which the modern world understands itself. Images are the dominant language of the modern world. We are stuck with them. Further, we have to acknowledge the pleasure that such images provide. This is not simply trickery or manipulation—the pleasure is substantive.

I would focus a cultural politics on two related strategies. First, the struggle to reconstruct the existence and meaning of the world of substance has to take place on the terrain of the image-system. . . .

The second aspect of the strategy centers less on revealing matters of substance (the underlying reality) than on opening up further the analysis of the contemporary image-system, in particular, *democratizing* the image-system.

At present the "discourse through and about objects" is profoundly authoritarian—it reflects only a few narrow (mostly corporate) interests. The institutions of the world of substance be engaged to open up the public discourse to new and varied (and dissenting) voices.

The other set of concerns are connected to issues of *literacy* in an image-saturated society. . . . While we can read the images quite adequately (for the purposes of their creators) we do not know how to *produce* them. Such skills, or knowledge of the process, must be a prerequisite for functional literacy in the contemporary world. . . .

Finally, information about the institutional context of the production and consumption of the image-system should be a prerequisite for literacy in the modern world. . . .

As Noam Chomsky puts it (taking about the media in general) in his book *Necessary Illusions:* "Citizens of the democratic societies should undertake a course of intellectual self-defense to protect themselves from manipulation and control, and to lay the basis for meaningful democracy."[5] Such a course of action will not be easy, for the institutional structure of the image-system will work against it. However, the invigoration of democracy depends upon the struggle being engaged.

NOTES

1. See. Fred Hirsch, *Social Limits to Growth* (Cambridge: Harvard University Press, 1976).
2. William Leiss, *The Limits to Satisfaction* (Toronto: Toronto University Press, 1976).
3. See Sut Jhally, *The Codes of Advertising* (New York: St. Martin's Press, 1987) and John Kavanaugh. *Following Christ in a Consumer Society* (New York: Orbis, 1981).
4. Erving Goffman, *Gender Advertisements* (New York: Harper & Row, 1979).
5. Noam Chomsky, *Necessary Illusions: Thought Control in Democratic Societies* (Boston: South End Press), viii.

PART FOUR

Media, Culture, and Society

CHAPTER 10 Mass Communication as Cultural Process

10.1 JAMES W. CAREY

A Cultural Approach to Communication

The following selection is from James W. Carey's *Communication as Culture: Essays on Media and Society* (Unwin Hyman, 1989), which is a part of an expanding interdisciplinary field that has come to be called "cultural studies" and whose roots are found within both the United States and Great Britain. Carey, an American communication scholar, argues that any form of communication is not simply about the transmission of information from a "source" (TV network, news journalist, and the like, who produce and transmit messages according to a specific purpose) to a "receiver" (an individual consumer of media messages who is affected one way or another by the message). Rather, he believes that mass communication is a *ritual* process, involving the *shared construction* of the patterns of social behavior, social interaction, and social significance. From this perspective the content of a TV program or a Hollywood film should be regarded as fundamentally similar to that of social rituals, such as the marriage ceremony or the telling of mythical stories.

234

*Chapter 10
Mass
Communication
as Cultural
Process*

Carey emphasizes the shared construction of social meaning. The British strand in cultural studies focuses on questions concerning power and conflict in society. Around the turn of the twentieth century, when the United States was embroiled in the transition from a rural society to an urban, industrial society, many feared that the intimate, interpersonal bonds of small-town society would be overwhelmed by the anonymous forces of the city. There was concern that the new mass media of newspapers, magazines, and radio might exacerbate this tendency by transmitting messages designed to manipulate people's opinions and behaviors from anonymous and powerful sources such as the government or product advertisers. However, there also existed the potential for mass media to draw together otherwise dispersed and isolated urban populations in new forms of community and ritual processes.

In the following selection, Carey argues that the dominance of a transmission view of the mass communication process follows precisely from such concerns about the "massification" of society. He argues that we must recover a working sense of communication as the shared construction of social relationships, not simply as the exercise of power "from above."

Key Concept: ritual view of communication

*T*wo alternative conceptions of communication have been alive in American culture since this term entered common discourse in the nineteenth century. Both definitions derive, as with much in secular culture, from religious origins, though they refer to somewhat different regions of religious experience. We might label these descriptions, if only to provide handy pegs upon which to hang our thought, a transmission view of communication and a ritual view of communication.

The transmission view of communication is the commonest in our cultures—perhaps in all industrial culture—and dominates contemporary dictionary entries under the term. It is defined by terms such as "imparting," "sending," "transmitting," or "giving information to others." It is formed from a metaphor of geography or transportation. In the nineteenth century but to a lesser extent today, the movement of goods or people and the movement of information were seen as essentially identical processes and both were described by the common noun "communication." The center of this idea of communication is the transmission of signals or messages over distance for the purpose of control. It is a view of communication that derives from one of the most ancient of human dreams: the desire to increase the speed and effect of messages as they travel in space. From the time upper and lower Egypt were unified under the First Dynasty down through the invention of the telegraph, transportation and communication were inseparably linked. Although messages might be centrally produced and controlled, through monopolization of writing or the rapid production of print, these messages, carried in the hands of a messenger or between the bindings of a book, still had to be distributed, if they were to have their desired effect, by rapid transportation. The telegraph ended the identity but did not destroy the metaphor. Our basic orientation to communication remains grounded, at, the deepest roots of our thinking, in the idea of transmission: communication is a process whereby messages are transmitted and distributed in space for the control of distance and people.

I said this view originated in religion, though the foregoing sentences seem more indebted to politics, economics, and technology. Nonetheless, the roots of the transmission view of communication, in our culture at least, lie in essentially religious attitudes. I can illustrate this by a devious though, in detail, inadequate path.

In its modem dress the transmission view of communication arises, as the *Oxford English Dictionary* will attest, at the onset of the age of exploration and discovery. We have been reminded rather too often that the motives behind this vast movement in space were political and mercantilistic. Certainly those motives were present, but their importance should not obscure the equally compelling fact that a major motive behind this movement in space, particularly as evidenced by the Dutch Reformed Church in South Africa or the Puritans in New England, was religious. The desire to escape the boundaries of Europe, to create a new life, to found new communities, to carve a New Jerusalem out of the woods of Massachusetts, were primary motives behind the unprecedented movement of whIte European civilization over virtually the entire globe. The vast and, for the first time, democratic migration in space was above all an attempt to trade an old world for a new and represented the profound belief that movement in space could be in itself a redemptive act. It is a belief Americans have never quite escaped.

Transportation, particularly when it brought the Christian community of Europe into contact with the heathen community of the Americas, was seen as a form of communication with profoundly religious implications. This movement in space was an attempt to establish and extend the kingdom of God, to create the conditions under which godly understanding might be realized, to produce a heavenly though still terrestrial city.

The moral meaning of transportation, then, was the establishment and extension of God's kingdom on earth. The moral meaning of communication was the same. By the middle of the nineteenth century the telegraph broke the identity of communication and transportation but also led a preacher of the era, Gardner Spring, to exclaim that we were on the "border of a spiritual harvest because thought now travels by steam and magnetic wires" (Miller, 1965: 48). Similarly, in 1848 "James L. Batchelder could declare that the Almighty himself had constructed the railroad for missionary purposes and, as Samuel Morse prophesied with the first telegraphic message, the purpose of the invention was not to spread the price of pork but to ask the question 'What Hath God Wrought?' " (Miller, 1965: 52). This new technology entered American discussions not as a mundane fact but as divinely inspired for the purposes of spreading the Christian message farther and faster, eclipsing time and transcending space, saving the heathen, bringing closer and making more probable the day of salvation.

Soon, as the forces of science and secularization gained ground, the obvious religious metaphors fell away and the technology of communication itself moved to the center of thought. Moreover, the superiority of communication

236

*Chapter 10
Mass
Communication
as Cultural
Process*

over transportation was assured by the observation of one nineteenth century commentator that the telegraph was important because it involved not the mere "modification of matter but the transmission of thought." Communication was viewed as a process and a technology that would, sometimes for religious purposes, spread, transmit, and disseminate knowledge, ideas, and information farther and faster with the goal of controlling space and people.

There were dissenters, of course, and I have already quoted Thoreau's disenchanted remark on the telegraph. More pessimistically, John C. Calhoun saw the "subjugation of electricity to the mechanical necessities of man . . . (as) the last era in human civilization" (quoted in Miller, 1965: 307). But the dissenters were few, and the transmission view of communication, albeit in increasingly secularized and scientific form, has dominated our thought and culture since that time. Moreover, as can be seen in contemporary popular commentary and even in technical discussions of new communications technology, the historic religious undercurrent has never been eliminated from our thought. From the telegraph to the computer the same sense of profound possibility for moral improvement is present whenever these machines are invoked. And we need not be reminded of the regularity with which improved communication is invoked by an army of teachers, preachers, and columnists as the talisman of all our troubles. More controversially, the same root attitudes, as I can only assert here rather than demonstrate, are at work in most of our scientifically sophisticated views of communication.

The ritual view of communication, though a minor thread in our national thought, is by far the older of those views—old enough in fact for dictionaries to list it under "Archaic." In a ritual definition, communication is linked to terms such as "sharing," "participation," "association," "fellowship," and "the possession of a common faith." This definition exploits the ancient identity and common roots of the terms "commonness," "communion," "community," and "communication." A ritual view of communication is directed not toward the extension of messages in space but toward the maintenance of society in time; not the act of imparting information but the representation of shared beliefs.

If the archetypal case of communication under a transmission view is the extension of messages across geography for the purpose of control, the archetypal case under a ritual view is the sacred ceremony that draws persons together in fellowship and commonality.

The indebtedness of the ritual view of communication to religion is apparent in the name chosen to label it. Moreover, it derives from a view of religion that downplays the role of the sermon, the instruction and admonition, in order to highlight the role of the prayer, the chant, and the ceremony. It sees the original or highest manifestation of communication not in the transmission of intelligent information but in the construction and maintenance of an ordered, meaningful cultural world that can serve as a control and container for human action.

This view has also been shorn of its explicitly religious origins, but it has never completely escaped its metaphoric root. Writers in this tradition often trace their heritage, in part, to Durkheim's *Elementary Forms of Religious Life* and to the argument stated elsewhere that "society substitutes for the world revealed to our senses a different world that is a projection of the ideals created by the community" (1953: 95). This projection of community ideals and their embodiment in material form—dance, plays, architecture, news stories, strings of speech—creates an artificial though nonetheless real symbolic order that operates to provide not information but confirmation, not to alter attitudes or change minds but to represent an underlying order of things, not to perform functions but to manifest an ongoing and fragile social process.

The ritual view of communication has not been a dominant motif in American scholarship. Our thought and work have been glued to a transmission view of communication because this view is congenial with the underlying well-springs of American culture, sources that feed into our scientific life as well as our common, public understandings. There is an irony in this. We have not explored the ritual view of communication because the concept of culture is such a weak and evanescent notion in American social thought. We understand that other people have culture in the anthropological sense and we regularly record it—often mischievously and patronizing. But when we turn critical attention to American culture the concept dissolves into a residual category useful only when psychological and sociological data are exhausted. We realize that the underprivileged live in a culture of poverty, use the notion of middle-class culture as an epithet, and occasionally applaud our high and generally scientific culture. But the notion of culture is not a hard-edged term of intellectual discourse for domestic purposes. This intellectual aversion to the idea of culture derives in part from our obsessive individualism, which makes psychological life the paramount reality; from our Puritanism, which leads to disdain for the significance of human activity that is not practical and work oriented; and from our isolation of science from culture: science provides culture-free truth whereas culture provides ethnocentric error.

. . . Perhaps, then, some of the difference between a transmission and a ritual view of communication can be grasped by briefly looking at alternative conceptions of the role of the newspaper in social life.

If one examines a newspaper under a transmission view of communication, one sees the medium as an instrument for disseminating news and knowledge, sometimes *divertissement,* in larger and larger packages over greater distances. Questions arise as to the effects of this on audiences: news as enlightening or obscuring reality, as changing or hardening attitudes, as breeding credibility or doubt. Questions also are raised concerning the functions of news and the newspaper: Does it maintain the integration of society or its maladaption? Does it function or misfunction to maintain stability or promote the instability of personalities? Some such mechanical analysis normally accompanies a "transmission" argument.

A ritual view of communication will focus on a different range of problems in examining a newspaper. It will, for example, view reading a newspaper less as sending or gaining information and more as attending a mass, a situation in which nothing new is learned but in which a particular view of the world is portrayed and confirmed. News reading, and writing, is a ritual act and moreover a dramatic one. What is arrayed before the reader is not pure information but a portrayal of the contending forces in the world. Moreover, as readers make their way through the paper, they engage in a continual shift of roles or of dramatic focus. A story on the monetary crisis salutes them as

238

*Chapter 10
Mass
Communication
as Cultural
Process*

American patriots fighting those ancient enemies Germany and Japan; a story on the meeting of the women's political caucus casts them into the liberation movement as supporter or opponent; a tale of violence on the campus evokes their class antagonisms and resentments. The model here is not that of information acquisition, though such acquisition occurs, but of dramatic action in which the reader joins a world of contending forces as an observer at a play. We do not encounter questions about the effect or functions of messages as such, but the role of presentation and involvement in the structuring of the reader's life and time. We recognize, as with religious rituals, that news changes little and yet is intrinsically satisfying; it performs few functions yet is habitually consumed. Newspapers do not operate as a source of effects or functions but as dramatically satisfying, which is not to say pleasing, presentations of what the world at root is. And it is in this role—that of a text—that a newspaper is seen; like a Balinese cockfight, a Dickens novel, an Elizabethan drama, a student rally, it is a presentation of reality that gives life an overall form, order, and tone.

Moreover, news is a historic reality. It is a form of culture invented by a particular class at a particular point of history—in this case by the middle class largely in the eighteenth century. Like any invented cultural form, news both forms and reflects a particular "hunger for experience," a desire to do away with the epic, heroic, and traditional in favor of the unique, original, novel, new—news. This "hunger" itself has a history grounded in the changing style and fortunes of the middle class and as such does not represent a universal taste or necessarily legitimate form of knowledge (Park, 1955: 71–88) but an invention in historical time, that like most other human inventions, will dissolve when the class that sponsors it and its possibility of having significance for us evaporates.

Under a ritual view, then, news is not information but drama. It does not describe the world but portrays an arena of dramatic forces and action; it exists solely in historical time; and it invites our participation on the basis of our assuming, often vicariously, social roles within it.

Neither of these counterposed views of communication necessarily denies what the other affirms. A ritual view does not exclude the processes of information transmission or attitude change. It merely contends that one cannot understand these processes aright except insofar as they are cast within an essentially ritualistic view of communication and social order. Similarly, even writers indissolubly wedded to the transmission view of communication must include some notion . . . to attest however tardily to the place of ritual action in social life. Nonetheless, in intellectual matters origins determine endings, and the exact point at which one attempts to unhinge the problem of communication largely determines the path the analysis can follow. . . .

The transmission view of communication has dominated American thought since the 1920s. When I first came into this field I felt that this view of communication, expressed in behavioral and functional terms, was exhausted.

But where does one turn, even provisionally, for the resources with which to get a fresh perspective on communication? For me at least the resources were found by going back to the work of Weber, Durkheim, de Tocqueville, and

Huizinga, as well as by utilizing contemporaries such as Kenneth Burke, Hugh Duncan, Adolph Portman, Thomas Kuhn, Peter Berger, and Clifford Geertz. Basically, however, the most viable though still inadequate tradition of social thought on communication comes from those colleagues and descendants of Dewey in the Chicago School: from Mead and Cooley through Robert Park and on to Erving Goffman.

From such sources one can draw a definition of communication of disarming simplicity yet, I think, of some intellectual power and scope: communication is a symbolic process whereby reality is produced, maintained, repaired, and transformed.

Let me attempt to unpack that long first clause emphasizing the symbolic production of reality.

. . . Both our common sense and scientific realism attest to the fact that there is, first, a real world of objects, events, and processes that we observe. Second, there is language or symbols that name these events in the real world and create more or less adequate descriptions of them. There is reality and then, after the fact, our accounts of it. We insist there is a distinction between reality and fantasy; we insist that our terms stand in relation to this world as shadow and substance. While language often distorts, obfuscates, and confuses our perception of this external world, we rarely dispute this matter-of-fact realism. We peel away semantic layers of terms and meanings to uncover this more substantial domain of existence. Language stands to reality as secondary stands to primary in the old Galilean paradigm from which this view derives.

By the first clause I mean to invert this relationship, not to make any large metaphysical claims but rather, by reordering the relation of communication to reality, to render communication a far more problematic activity than it ordinarily seems.

. . . Reality is not given, not humanly existent, independent of language and toward which language stands as a pale refraction. Rather, reality is brought into existence, is produced, by communication—by, in short, the construction, apprehension, and utilization of symbolic forms. Reality, while not a mere function of symbolic forms, is produced by terministic systems—or by humans who produce such system—that focus its existence in specific terms.

Under the sway of realism we ordinarily assume there is an order to existence that the human mind through some faculty may discover and describe. I am suggesting that reality is not there to discover in any significant detail. The world is entropic—that is, not strictly ordered—though its variety is constrained enough that the mind can grasp its outline and implant an order over and within the broad and elastic constraints of nature. To put it colloquially, there are no lines of latitude and longitude in nature, but by overlaying the globe with this particular, though not exclusively correct, symbolic organization, order is imposed on spatial organization and certain, limited human purposes served.

Let us suppose one had to teach a child of six or seven how to get from home to school. The child has driven by the school, which is some six or seven blocks away, so he recognizes it, but he has no idea of the relation between his house and school. The space between these points might as well be, as the saying goes, a trackless desert. What does one do in such a situation?

240

*Chapter 10
Mass
Communication
as Cultural
Process*

There are a number of options. One might let the child discover the route by trial and error, correcting him as he goes, in faithful imitation of a conditioning experiment. One might have the child follow an adult, as I'm told the Apaches do, "imprinting" the route on the child. However, the ordinary method is simply to draw the child a map. By arranging lines, angles, names, squares denoting streets and buildings in a pattern on paper, one transforms vacant space into a featured environment. Although some environments are easier to feature than others—hence trackless desert-space is understood and manageable when it is represented in symbolic form.

The map stands as a representation of an environment capable of clarifying a problematic situation. It is capable of guiding behavior and simultaneously transforming undifferentiated space into configured—that is, known, apprehended, understood—space.

Note also that an environment, any given space, can be mapped in a number of different modes. For example, we might map a particularly important space by producing a poetic or musical description. As in the song that goes, in part; "first you turn it to the left, then you turn it to the right," a space can be mapped by a stream of poetic speech that expresses a spatial essence and that also ensures, by exploiting the mnemonic devices of song and poetry, that the "map" can be retained in memory. By recalling the poem at appropriate moments, space can be effectively configured.

A third means of mapping space is danced ritual. The movements of the dance can parallel appropriate movements through space. By learning the dance the child acquires a representation of the space that on another occasion can guide behavior.

Space can be mapped, then, in different modes—utilizing lines on a page, sounds in air, movements in a dance. All three are symbolic forms, though the symbols differ; visual, oral, and kinesthetic. Moreover, each of the symbolic forms possesses two distinguishing characteristics: displacement and productivity. Like ordinary language, each mode allows one to speak about or represent some thing when the thing in question is not present. This capacity of displacement, of producing a complicated act when the "real" stimulus is not physically present, is another often noted though not fully explored capacity. Second, each of these symbolic forms is productive, for a person in command of the symbols is capable of producing an infinite number of representations on the basis of a finite number of symbolic elements. As with language, so with other symbolic forms: a finite set of words or a finite set of phonemes can produce, through grammatical combination, an infinite set of sentences.

We often argue that a map represents a simplification of or an abstraction from an environment. Not all the features of an environment are modeled, for the purpose of the representation is to express not the possible complexity of things but their simplicity. Space is made manageable by the reduction of information. By doing this, however, different maps bring the same environment alive in different ways; they produce quite different realities. Therefore, to live within the purview of different maps is to live within different realities. Consequently, maps not only constitute the activity known as mapmaking; they constitute nature itself. . . .

This particular miracle we perform daily and hourly—the miracle of producing reality and then living within and under the fact of our own production—rests upon a particular quality of symbols: their ability to be both representations "of" and "for" reality. . . .

It is no different with a religious ritual. In one mode it represents the nature of human life, its condition and meaning, and in another mode—its "for" mode—it induces the dispositions it pretends merely to portray.

All human activity is such an exercise (can one resist the word "ritual"?) in squaring the circle. We first produce the world by symbolic work and then take up residence in the world we have produced. Alas, there is magic in our self deceptions.

We not only produce reality but we must likewise maintain what we have produced, for there are always new generations coming along for whom our productions are incipiently problematic and for whom reality must be regenerated and made authoritative. Reality must be repaired for it consistently breaks down: people get lost physically and spiritually, experiments fail, evidence counter to the representation is produced, mental derangement sets in—all threats to our models of and for reality that lead to intense repair work. Finally, we must, often with fear and regret, toss away our authoritative representations of reality and begin to build the world anew. . . .

To study communication is to examine the actual social process wherein significant symbolic forms are created, apprehended, and used. . . .

Our attempts to construct, maintain, repair, and transform reality are publicly observable activities that occur in historical time. We create, express, and convey our knowledge of and attitudes toward reality through the construction of a variety of symbol systems: art, science, journalism, religion, common sense, mythology. How do we do this? What are the differences between these forms? What are the historical and comparative variations in them? How do changes in communication technology influence what we can concretely create and apprehend? How do groups in society struggle over the definition of what is real? These are some of the questions, rather too simply put, that communication studies must answer.

Finally, let me emphasize an ironic aspect to the study of communication, a way in which our subject matter doubles back on itself and presents us with a host of ethical problems. One of the activities in which we characteristically engage, as in this essay, is communication about communication itself. However, communication is not some pure phenomenon we can discover; there is no such thing as communication to be revealed in nature through some objective method free from the corruption of culture. We understand communication insofar as we are able to build models or representations of this process. But our models of communication, like all models, have this dual aspect—an "of" aspect and a "for" aspect. In one mode communication models tell us what the process is; in their second mode they produce the behavior they have described. Communication can be modeled in several empirically adequate ways, but these several models have different ethical implications for they produce different forms of social relations. . . .

Models of communication are, then, not merely representations of communication but representations *for* communication: templates that guide, un-

242

*Chapter 10
Mass
Communication
as Cultural
Process*

availing or not, concrete processes of human interaction, mass and interpersonal. Therefore, to study communication involves examining the construction, apprehension, and use of models of communication themselves—their construction in common sense, art, and science, their historically specific creation and use: in encounters between parent and child, advertisers and consumer, welfare worker and supplicant, teacher and student. Behind and within these encounters lie models of human contact and interaction.

Our models of communication, consequently, create what we disingenuously pretend they merely describe. As a result our science is, to use a term of Alvin Gouldner's, a reflexive one. We not only describe behavior; we create a particular corner of culture—culture that determines, in part, the kind of communicative world we inhabit.

. . . If one tries to examine society as a form of communication, one sees it as a process whereby reality is created, shared, modified, and preserved. When this process becomes opaque, when we lack models of and for reality that make the world apprehensible, when we are unable to describe and share it; when because of a failure in our models of communication we are unable to connect with others, we encounter problems of communication in their most potent form.

10.2 DICK HEBDIGE

From Culture to Hegemony

Dick Hebdige studied at the Center for Contemporary Cultural Studies (CCCS) at the University of Birmingham, England, at a time when professors and graduate students at the center were collaborating on studies of the relationship between media, culture, and society. An important empirical focus of the CCCS at that time was so-called spectacular youth subcultures, which were prominent in Great Britain in the aftermath of World War II.

These subcultures—including the "teddy boys," "mods," and "rockers" of the 1950s and 1960s—distinguished themselves through modes of dress, speaking, and behavior that seemed designed to outrage mainstream, adult British society. The initial response of many sociologists and criminologists was to label these subcultures as "deviant" and "delinquent." However, members of the CCCS argued that subcultures were not deviant; rather they represented a set of deliberate and coherent symbolic strategies for coping with historical changes in working-class life in Great Britain. Hebdige's contribution to the CCCS collaborative study *Resistance Through Rituals* (Hutchinson, 1976) was interpreting the "meaning of mod" style as a response to the gap between the post–World War II promise of consumer affluence disseminated through the mass media and by the British government and the reality that working-class kids had a very limited ability, over the long term, to participate in this affluence.

In the study from which the following selection has been taken, *Subculture: The Meaning of Style* (Routledge, 1979), Hebdige shows that if mod was a subcultural response to the problems of "growing up working class" in the 1960s, then the nihilism of the punk subculture of the 1970s was the symbolic response of a later working-class generation, one largely doomed to the hopelessness of permanent unemployment. According to Hebdige, it is not simply the content of mass media and popular culture but their social uses that is important.

In the following selection, Hebdige lays out the conceptual tools he used to pry apart the meaning of punk subcultural practices, from an essentially ritual definition of culture through the important concept of *hegemony*, which has come to play a central theoretical role in the study of contemporary mass media and popular culture. Hebdige has gone on to apply these concepts to the study of reggae music and West Indian culture in *Cut 'n' Mix: Culture, Identity and Caribbean Music* (Methuen, 1987).

Key Concept: hegemony

CULTURE

Culture: cultivation, tending, in Christian authors, worship; the action or practice of cultivating the soil; tillage, husbandry; the cultivation or rearing of certain animals (e.g. fish); the artificial development of microscopic organisms, organisms so produced; the cultivating or development (of the mind, faculties, manners), improvement or refinement by education and training; the condition of being trained or refined; the intellectual side of civilization; the prosecution or special attention or study of any subject or pursuit.

—*Oxford English Dictionary*

Culture is a notoriously ambiguous concept as the above definition demonstrates. Refracted through centuries of usage, the word has acquired a number of quite different, often contradictory, meanings. Even as a scientific term, it refers both to a process (artificial development of microscopic organisms) and a product (organisms so produced). More specifically, since the end of the eighteenth century, it has been used by English intellectuals and literary figures to focus critical attention on a whole range of controversial issues. The 'quality of life', the effects in human terms of mechanization, the division of labour and the creation of a mass society have all been discussed within the larger confines of what Raymond Williams has called the 'Culture and Society' debate (Williams, 1961). It was through this tradition of dissent and criticism that the dream of the 'organic society'—of society as an integrated, meaningful whole—was largely kept alive. The dream had two basic trajectories. One led back to the past and to the feudal ideal of a hierarchically ordered community. Here, culture assumed an almost sacred function. Its 'harmonious perfection' (Arnold, 1868) was posited against the Waste-land of contemporary life.

The other trajectory, less heavily supported, led towards the future, to a socialist Utopia where the distinction between labour and leisure was to be annulled. Two basic definitions of culture emerged from this tradition, though these were by no means necessarily congruent with the two trajectories outlined above. The first—the one which is probably most familiar to the reader—was essentially classical and conservative. It represented culture as a standard of aesthetic excellence: 'the best that has been thought and said in the world' (Arnold, 1868), and it derived from an appreciation of 'classic' aesthetic form (opera, ballet, drama, literature, art). The second, traced back by Williams to Herder and the eighteenth century (Williams, 1976), was rooted in anthropology. Here the term 'culture' referred to a

. . . particular way of life which expresses certain meanings and values not only in art and learning, but also in institutions and ordinary behaviour. The analysis of culture, from such a definition, is the clarification of the meanings and values implicit and explicit in a particular way of life, a particular culture. (Williams, 1965)

This definition obviously had a much broader range. It encompassed, in T. S. Eliot's words,

> ... all the characteristic activities and interests of a people. Derby Day, Henley Regatta, Cowes, the 12th of August, a cup final, the dog races, the pin table, the dart-board, Wensleydale cheese, boiled cabbage cut into sections, beetroot in vinegar, 19th Century Gothic churches, the music of Elgar. . . . (Eliot, 1948)

As Williams noted, such a definition could only be supported if a new theoretical initiative was taken. The theory of culture now involved the 'study of relationships between elements in a whole way of life' (Williams, 1965). The emphasis shifted from immutable to historical criteria, from fixity to transformation:

> ... an emphasis [which] from studying particular meanings and values seeks not so much to compare these, as a way of establishing a scale, but by studying their modes of change to discover certain general causes or 'trends' by which social and cultural developments as a whole can be better understood. (Williams, 1965)

Williams was, then, proposing an altogether broader formulation of the relationships between culture and society, one which through the analysis of 'particular meanings and values' sought to uncover the concealed fundamentals of history; the 'general causes' and broad social 'trends' which lie behind the manifest appearances of an 'everyday life'.

In the early years, when it was being established in the Universities, Cultural Studies sat rather uncomfortably on the fence between these two conflicting definitions—culture as a standard of excellence, culture as a 'whole way of life'—unable to determine which represented the most fruitful line of enquiry. Richard Hoggart and Raymond Williams portrayed working-class culture sympathetically in wistful accounts of pre-scholarship boyhoods (Leeds for Hoggart (1958), a Welsh mining village for Williams (1960)) but their work displayed a strong bias towards literature and literacy and an equally strong moral tone. Hoggart deplored the way in which the traditional working-class community—a community of tried and tested values despite the dour landscape in which it had been set—was being undermined and replaced by a 'Candy Floss World' of thrills and cheap fiction which was somehow bland *and* sleazy. Williams tentatively endorsed the new mass communications but was concerned to establish aesthetic and moral criteria for distinguishing the worthwhile products from the 'trash'; the jazz—'a real musical form'—and the football—'a wonderful game'—from the 'rape novel, the Sunday strip paper and the latest Tin Pan drool' (Williams, 1965). In 1966 Hoggart laid down the basic premises upon which Cultural Studies were based:

> First, without appreciating good literature, no one will really understand the nature of society, second, literary critical analysis can be applied to certain social phenomena other than 'academically respectable' literature (for example, the popular arts, mass communications) so as to illuminate their meanings for individuals and their societies. (Hoggart, 1966)

246

Chapter 10
Mass
Communication
as Cultural
Process

The implicit assumption that it still required a literary sensibility to 'read' society with the requisite subtlety, and that the two ideas of culture could be ultimately reconciled was also, paradoxically, to inform the early work of the French writer, Roland Barthes, though here it found validation in a method—semiotics—a way of reading signs (Hawkes, 1977).

BARTHES: MYTHS AND SIGNS

Using models derived from the work of the Swiss linguist Ferdinand de Saussure Barthes sought to expose the *arbitrary* nature of cultural phenomena, to uncover the latent meanings of an everyday life which, to all intents and purposes, was 'perfectly natural'. Unlike Hoggart, Barthes was not concerned with distinguishing the good from the bad in modern mass culture, but rather with showing how *all* the apparently spontaneous forms and rituals of contemporary bourgeois societies are subject to a systematic distortion, liable at any moment to be dehistoricized, 'naturalized', converted into myth:

> The whole of France is steeped in this anonymous ideology: our press, our films, our theatre, our pulp literature, our rituals, our Justice, our diplomacy, our conversations, our remarks about the weather, a murder trial, a touching wedding, the cooking we dream of, the garments we wear, everything in everyday life is dependent on the representation which the bourgeoisie *has and makes us have* of the relations between men and the world. (Barthes, 1972)

Like Eliot, Barthes' notion of culture extends beyond the library, the opera-house and the theatre to encompass the whole of everyday life. But this everyday life is for Barthes overlaid with a significance which is at once more insidious and more systematically organized. Starting from the premise that 'myth is a type of speech', Barthes set out in *Mythologies* to examine the normally hidden set of rules, codes and conventions through which meanings particular to specific social groups (i.e. those in power) are rendered universal and 'given' for the whole of society. He found in phenomena as disparate as a wrestling match, a writer on holiday, a tourist-guide book, the same artificial nature, the same ideological core. Each had been exposed to the same prevailing rhetoric (the rhetoric of common sense) and turned into myth, into a mere element in a 'second-order semiological system' (Barthes, 1972). (Barthes uses the example of a photograph in *Paris-Match* of a Negro soldier saluting the French flag, which has a first and second order connotation: (1) a gesture of loyalty, but also (2) 'France is a great empire, and all her sons, without colour discrimination, faithfully serve under her flag'.)

Barthes' application of a method rooted in linguistics to other systems of discourse outside language (fashion, film, food, etc.) opened up completely new possibilities for contemporary cultural studies. It was hoped that the invisible seam between language, experience and reality could be located and prised open through a semiotic analysis of this kind: that the gulf between the alienated intellectual and the 'real' world could be rendered meaningful and, miraculously, at the same time, be made to disappear. Moreover, under

Barthes' direction, semiotics promised nothing less than the reconciliation of the two conflicting definitions of culture upon which Cultural Studies was so ambiguously posited—a marriage of moral conviction (in this case, Barthes' Marxist beliefs) and popular themes: the study of a society's total way of life.

This is not to say that semiotics was easily assimilable within the Cultural Studies project. Though Barthes shared the literary preoccupations of Hoggart and Williams, his work introduced a new Marxist 'problematic' which was alien to the British tradition of concerned and largely untheorized 'social commentary'. As a result, the old debate seemed suddenly limited. In E. P. Thompson's words it appeared to reflect the parochial concerns of a group of 'gentlemen amateurs'. Thompson sought to replace Williams' definition of the theory of culture as 'a theory of relations between elements in a whole way of life' with his own more rigorously Marxist formulation: 'the study of relationships in a whole way of *conflict*'. A more analytical framework was required; a new vocabulary had to be learned. As part of this process of theorization, the word 'ideology' came to acquire a much wider range of meanings than had previously been the case. We have seen how Barthes found an 'anonymous ideology' penetrating every possible level of social life, inscribed in the most mundane of rituals, framing the most casual social encounters. But how can ideology be 'anonymous, and how can it assume such a broad significance? Before we attempt any reading of subcultural style, we must first define the term 'ideology' more precisely.

IDEOLOGY: A *LIVED* RELATION

In the *German Ideology,* Marx shows how the basis of the capitalist economic structure (surplus value, neatly defined by Godelier as 'Profit . . . is unpaid work' (Godelier, 1970) is hidden from the consciousness of the agents of production. The failure to see through appearances to the real relations which underlie them does not occur as the direct result of some kind of masking operation consciously carried out by individuals, social groups or institutions. On the contrary, ideology by definition thrives *beneath* consciousness. It is here, at the level of 'normal common sense', that ideological frames of reference are most firmly sedimented and most effective, because it is here that their ideological nature is most effectively concealed. As Stuart Hall puts it:

> It is precisely its 'spontaneous' quality, its transparency, its 'naturalness', its refusal to be made to examine the premises on which it is founded, its resistance to change or to correction, its effect of instant recognition, and the closed circle in which it moves which makes common sense, at one and the same time, 'spontaneous', ideological and *unconscious*. You cannot learn, through common sense, *how things are:* you can only discover *where* they fit into the existing scheme of things. In this way, its very taken-for-grantedness is what establishes it as a medium in which its own premises and presuppositions are being rendered *invisible* by its apparent transparency. (Hall, 1977)

Since ideology saturates everyday discourse in the form of common sense, it cannot be bracketed off from everyday life as a self-contained set of 'political

248

*Chapter 10
Mass
Communication
as Cultural
Process*

opinions' or 'biased views'. Neither can it be reduced to the abstract dimensions of a 'world view' or used in the crude Marxist sense to designate 'false consciousness'. Instead, as Louis Althusser has pointed out:

> . . . ideology has very little to do with 'consciousness'. . . . It is profoundly *unconscious*. . . . Ideology is indeed a system of representation, but in the majority of cases these representations have nothing to do with 'consciousness': they are usually images and occasionally concepts, but it is above all as *structures* that they impose on the vast majority of men, not via their 'consciousness'. They are perceived-accepted-suffered cultural objects and they act functionally on men via a process that escapes them. (Althusser, 1969)

Although Althusser is here referring to structures like the family, cultural and political institutions, etc., we can illustrate the point quite simply by taking as our example a physical structure. Most modern institutes of education, despite the apparent neutrality of the materials from which they are constructed (red brick, white tile, etc.) carry within themselves implicit ideological assumptions which are literally structured into the architecture itself. The categorization of knowledge into arts and sciences is reproduced in the faculty system which houses different disciplines in different buildings, and most colleges maintain the traditional divisions by devoting a separate floor to each subject. Moreover, the hierarchical relationship between teacher and taught is inscribed in the very lay-out of the lecture theatre where the seating arrangements—benches rising in tiers before a raised lectern—dictate the flow of information and serve to 'naturalize' professorial authority. Thus, a whole range of decisions about what is and what is not possible within education have been made, however unconsciously, before the content of individual courses is even decided.

These decisions help to set the limits not only on what is taught but on *how* it is taught. Here the buildings literally *reproduce* in concrete terms prevailing (ideological) notions about what education *is* and it is through this process that the educational structure, which can, of course, be altered, is placed beyond question and appears to us as a 'given' (i.e. as immutable). In this case, the frames of our thinking have been translated into actual bricks and mortar.

Social relations and processes are then appropriated by individuals only through the forms in which they are represented to those individuals. These forms are, as we have seen, by no means transparent. They are shrouded in a 'common sense' which simultaneously validates and mystifies them. It is precisely these 'perceived-accepted-suffered cultural objects' which semiotics sets out to 'interrogate' and decipher. All aspects of culture possess a semiotic value, and the most taken-for-granted phenomena can function as signs: as elements in communication systems governed by semantic rules and codes which are not themselves directly apprehended in experience. These signs are, then, as opaque as the social relations which produce them and which they represent. In other words, there is an ideological dimension to every signification:

> A sign does not simply exist as part of reality—it reflects and refracts another reality. Therefore it may distort that reality or be true to it, or may perceive it from a special point of view, and so forth. Every sign is subject to the criteria of

ideological evaluation. . . . The domain of ideology coincides with the domain of signs. They equate with one another. Whenever a sign is present, ideology is present too. Everything ideological possesses a semiotic value. (Volosinov, 1973)

To uncover the ideological dimension of signs we must first try to disentangle the codes through which meaning is organized. 'Connotative' codes are particularly important. As Stuart Hall has argued, they ' . . . cover the face of social life and render it classifiable, intelligible, meaningful' (Hall, 1977). He goes on to describe these codes as 'maps of meaning' which are of necessity the product of selection. They cut across a range of potential meanings, making certain meanings available and ruling others out of court. We tend to live inside these maps as surely as we live in the 'real' world: they 'think' us as much as we 'think' them, and this in itself is quite 'natural'. All human societies *reproduce* themselves in this way through a process of 'naturalization'. It is through this process—a kind of inevitable reflex of all social life—that *particular* sets of social relations, *particular* ways of organizing the world appear to us as if they were universal and timeless. This is what Althusser (1971) means when he says that 'ideology has no history' and that ideology in this general sense will always be an 'essential element of every social formation' (Althusser and Balibar, 1968).

However, in highly complex societies like ours, which function through a finely graded system of divided (i.e. specialized) labour, the crucial question has to do with which specific ideologies, representing the interests of which specific groups and classes will prevail at any given moment, in any given situation. To deal with this question, we must first consider how power is distributed in our society. That is, we must ask which groups and classes have how much say in defining, ordering and classifying out the social world. For instance, if we pause to reflect for a moment, it should be obvious that access to the means by which ideas are disseminated in our society (i.e. principally the mass media) is *not* the same for all classes. Some groups have more say, more opportunity to make the rules, to organize meaning, while others are less favourably placed, have less power to produce and impose their definitions of the world on the world.

Thus, when we come to look beneath the level of 'ideology-in-general' at the way in which specific ideologies work, how some gain dominance and others remain marginal, we can see that in advanced Western democracies the ideological field is by no means neutral. To return to the 'connotative' codes to which Stuart Hall refers we can see that these 'maps of meaning' are charged with a potentially explosive significance because they are traced and re-traced along the lines laid down by the *dominant* discourses about reality, the *dominant* ideologies. They thus tend to represent, in however obscure and contradictory a fashion, the interests of the *dominant* groups in society.

To understand this point we should refer to Marx:

The ideas of the ruling class are in every epoch the ruling ideas, i.e. the class which is the ruling *material* force of society is at the same time its ruling *intellectual* force. The class which has the means of material production at its disposal, has control at the same time over the means of mental production, so that generally

250

*Chapter 10
Mass
Communication
as Cultural
Process*

speaking, the ideas of those who lack the means of mental production are subject to it. The ruling ideas are nothing more than the ideal expression of the dominant material relationships grasped as ideas; hence of the relationships which make the one class the ruling class, therefore the ideas of its dominance. (Marx and Engels, 1970)

This is the basis of Antonio Gramsci's theory of *hegemony* which provides the most adequate account of how dominance is sustained in advanced capitalist societies.

HEGEMONY: THE MOVING EQUILIBRIUM

'Society cannot share a common communication system so long as it is split into warring classes.'

—Brecht, *A Short Organum for the Theatre.*

The term hegemony refers to a situation in which a provisional alliance of certain social groups can exert 'total social authority' over other subordinate groups, not simply by coercion or by the direct imposition of ruling ideas, but by 'winning and shaping consent so that the power of the dominant classes appears both legitimate and natural' (Hall, 1977). Hegemony can only be maintained so long as the dominant classes 'succeed in framing all competing definitions within their range' (Hall, 1977), so that subordinate groups are, if not controlled; then at least contained within an ideological space which does not seem at all 'ideological': which appears instead to be permanent and 'natural', to lie outside history, to be beyond particular interests (see *Social Trends*, no. 6, 1975).

This is how, according to Barthes, 'mythology' performs its vital function of naturalization and normalization and it is in his book *Mythologies* that Barthes demonstrates most forcefully the full extension of these normalized forms and meanings. However, Gramsci adds the important proviso that hegemonic power, precisely *because* it requires the consent of the dominated majority, can never be permanently exercised by the same alliance of 'class fractions'. As has been pointed out, 'Hegemony... is not universal and "given" to the continuing rule of a particular class. It has to be won, reproduced, sustained. Hegemony is, as Gramsci said, a "moving equilibrium" containing relations of forces favourable or unfavourable to this or that tendency' (Hall *et al.*, 1976a).

In the same way, forms cannot be permanently normalized. They can always be deconstructed, demystified, by a 'mythologist' like Barthes. Moreover commodities can be symbolically 'repossessed' in everyday life, and endowed with implicitly oppositional meanings, by the very groups who originally produced them. The symbiosis in which ideology and social order, production and reproduction, are linked is then neither fixed nor guaranteed. It can be prised open. The consensus can be fractured, challenged, overruled, and resistance to the groups in dominance cannot always be lightly dismissed or automatically incorporated. Although, as Lefebvre has written, we live in a society where '. . . objects in practice become signs and signs objects and a second nature takes the place of the first—the initial layer of perceptible reality' (Lefebvre, 1971), there are, as he goes on to affirm, always 'objections and contradictions which hinder the closing of the circuit' between sign and object, production and reproduction.

. . . For the sign-community, the community of myth-consumers, is not a uniform body. As Volosinov has written, it is cut through by class:

> Class does not coincide with the sign community, i.e. with the totality of users of the same set of signs of ideological communication. Thus various different classes will use one and the same language. As a result, differently oriented accents intersect in every ideological sign. Sign becomes the arena of the class struggle. (Volosinov, 1973)

The struggle between different discourses, different definitions and meanings within ideology is therefore always, at the same time, a struggle within signification: a struggle for possession of the sign which extends to even the most mundane areas of everyday life.

REFERENCES

Althusser, L. (1969), *For Marx*, Allen Lane.

____ (1971), 'Ideology and Ideological State Apparatuses', in *Lenin and Philosophy and Other Essays*, New Left Books.

Althusser, L. and Balibar, E. (1968), *Reading Capital*, New Left Books.

Arnold, M. (1868), *Culture and Anarchy*.

Barthes, R. (1972), *Mythologies*, Paladin.

Eliot, T. S. (1948), *Notes Towards a Definition of Culture*, Faber.

Godelier, M. (1970), 'Structure and Contradiction in "Capital"', in M. Lane (ed.), *Structuralism: A Reader*, Cape.

Halls, S. (1977), 'Culture the Media and the "Ideological Effect"', in J. Curran *et al.* (eds), *Mass Communication and Society*, Arnold.

Hawkes, T. (1977), *Structuralism and Semiotics*, Methuen.

Hoggart, R. (1958), *The Uses of Literacy*, Penguin.

____ (1966), 'Literature and Society', *American Scholar*, Spring.

Lefebvre, H. (1971), *Everyday Life in the Modern World*, Allen Lane.

Marx, K. and Engels, F. (1970), *The German Ideology*, Lawrence & Wishart.

Volosinov, V. N. (1973), *Marxism and the Philosophy of Language*, Seminar Press.

Williams, R. (1960), *Border Country*, Penguin.

____ (1961), *Culture and Society*, Penguin.

____ (1965), *The Long Revolution*, Penguin.

____ (1976), *Keywords*, Fontana.

CHAPTER 11 Cultural Criticism of Mass Media

Working Class Culture in the Electronic Age

Before beginning his career as a scholar and public critic, Stanley Aronowitz was an industrial worker and a union activist. Thus, he brings to his critical scholarship a mix of theory and practice. Today Aronowitz teaches at the Graduate Center of the City University of New York, and he has published numerous books. Throughout his work—both as an academic and as a union activist—Aronowitz has focused on the relationship between culture, education, and the declining fortunes of the working class in modern capitalism. In *False Promises: The Shaping of American Working Class Consciousness* (McGraw-Hill, 1973), he argues that it was not just economic decision making and political policy that caused labor to lose power in the years following World War II. Transformations in education, steady suburbanization, and the spread of mass-mediated culture, primarily through television, shifted working-class consciousness away from awareness of laborers' social and cultural distinctiveness and of their subordinate position in society. In *Education Under Siege* (Bergin & Garvey, 1985), Aronowitz focuses on the social logic of education in the United States.

In "Working Class Culture in the Electronic Age," in Ian Angus and Sut Jhally, eds., *Cultural Politics in Contemporary America* (Routledge, 1989), from which the following selection has been taken, Aronowitz reveals both the ritual nature of working-class culture and the workings of hegemony in the contemporary breakup of that culture. He does this by tracing a key set of historical displacements, which involved the simultaneous movement of workers from closely knit city neighborhoods to the dispersed living patterns of the suburbs and the substitution of mass media images for the cultural institutions of the old neighborhoods, particularly the masculine culture of the local bar.

Key Concept: displacement of working-class culture in mass media representations

*I*ndividual and collective identities are constructed on three articulated sites: the biological, the social, and the cultural. The biologically given characteristics which we bring to every social interaction are often covered over by social relations (such as the family and the school) and the technological sensorium that we call mass or popular culture. In western culture these biological givens assume meaning over which individuals have some control, but are often beyond our powers to reverse. Our race and sex confer boundaries as well as possibilities in various relations, particularly the kind of friends we can make, work we can do, mates that are available to us. Of course, the meanings of race and sex, like those of class, are socially constituted—there is no "inherent" significance to these identities as social signs. However, we are born into these identities, given the social arrangements.

The second crucial site is our interaction with family, school, the workplace, and other conventional institutions such as the Church. These relationships are often conceived as self-determining, that is, free of their biological givens. Obviously, parents and teachers treat boys and girls differently: we might say they enjoy/suffer a different moral development regardless of class membership or race. As many writers have argued, the family remains, perhaps, the crucial site for reproducing sexual differences.

While schools are crucial secondary institutions in, reproducing sexual difference, they play a major part in the reproduction of racial difference, the specific forms of which remain to be fully explored. It is enough here to point out that the school is the first place the child experiences as racially segregated, since modernism ended gender segregation. It is in school that the child experiences itself as white or black: needless to say, textbooks make clear to blacks their subordinate status, apart from any overt content. Black images, even when they appear, are tokens of the power of the civil rights movement over the past thirty years, but black history and black culture remain absent, a silence which signifies relations of domination. Of course, there are less subtle signs of difference: the failure of racial integration since the Supreme Court decision outlawing segregation thirty-five years ago is an overwhelming feature of public schooling. White kids learn that they are of a specific race simply by virtue of the absence of blacks in their classrooms. Blacks understand this by parental instruction, but realize that race means subordination by virtue of second-class education, the inferior resources made available to them, and finally come to realize that their individual and collective life chances have been decided long before they enter the workworld (a realization white working-class kids only have by secondary school).

Class representations are largely constructed by mass-mediated culture, especially since the working-class community, like the urban-based mass-production industries that created it, passed into history . . . . I especially want to trace the *displacement* of representations of the working class in this realm. I will show that there are no longer direct representations of the interactions among workers in American television, but that these have been refracted through the police shows that still (in 1988) dominate prime time.

Mass-media representations can no longer be grouped under institutional socializations which include the family, peer interactions, and schools. The media are *unique* sites precisely because of the specific place of technology in the production of culture. . . . Louis Althusser's claim that the school is the chief ideological state apparatus may hold for the production of the *symbolic* system, that constellation of signs and codes through which is construed the field of what counts as reliable knowledge.[1] But the mass media construct the *social imaginary,* the place where kids situate themselves in their emotional life, where the future appears as a narration of possibilities. . . .

The electronic media can determine, to some degree, *how* social life is represented (that is, their autonomous field of action consists in modes of representation), but not whether a social category *will* be represented. Therefore, it is literally not possible to totally exclude working-class representations, but is it equally improbable that these representations would remain direct under conditions where the cultural traditions of workers are disappearing or occupying smaller social spaces.

When I worked in the steel mills, the barroom was far more than a place to have a casual beer or to get drunk. It was scene of union politics, the site of convivial relationships that were hard to sustain on the shop floor because of the noise, frequent speedups, and the ever watchful eye of the foreman. Of course we had the john, but only for twenty minutes at a time; as the metal was heating up in furnaces, we often took a break. Sometimes the john substituted for the barroom. Animated arguments took place about baseball, women, or an incident that had just occurred, usually one in which one of our fellow workers was hurt (I remember Felix who caught a hot wire in his leg). But inevitably, the warning buzzer would interrupt our discussions—metal was nearly ready to come out and be drawn into wire.

So, the "gin mill" was the place where our collective identity as a community was forged and reproduced. Even when we had harsh disagreements about things that really mattered (whether we should stop work over a safety grievance or whether Jackie Robinson was a better second baseman that Billy

Martin, a tinderbox of an issue in 1960), we knew that the next day we would have to pull together in the hot mill, that our disputes were in the family. We also knew that we had to fight the boss together, not only for the ordinary reasons of better pay and benefits, but for our survival. The mill was a dangerous place and, for most of us, losing a limb meant losing the best paying job we were ever likely to own, for in the union shops of the 1950s and early 1960s, the job was property right. As we used to say, the only reason you could get fired was if you punched the foreman while sober.

Steelwork was definitely male culture. As in Freud's essay on femininity, women were the mysterious "other." We did not know much about them and, apart from the incessant desire that occupied our prurient conversations, they did not enter into our working lives. Women were an obscure object of our desire, but desire also reached out for a secure collective identity. . . .

I went to christenings and confirmations in the area around the place which was located in an industrial suburb. Most of the families were of eastern and southern European backgrounds, not only Italians and Poles (although they were in the majority), but also Czechs, Russians, and Greeks. People lived around the northern New Jersey plants in wood frame one-family houses or in "uppers" (the second and third floors of multiple dwellings). Those of us who were not veterans of the Second World War or the Korean War did not qualify for special mortgage deals, so we rented apartments that ate about 25% of our monthly pay. However, a growing minority of my friends were moving to the middle-class suburbs where single-family housing developments were mushrooming, or more graphically, springing up like weeds. . . .

Suburban flight was made feasible by low-interest mortgages, but also by the federal highway program initiated by President Harry Truman and fulfilled by the Eisenhower administration. In earlier years, living fifteen or twenty miles from the plant was simply not an option because the roads were invariably local. Such a round trip could take more than two hours. Now, barring traffic jams, evening- and night-shift workers could make it to work in twenty minutes, and those working days simply left home before rush hour and came back late. For many, being away from the wife and kids presented few, if any, problems; male culture excluded women and the notion that men should share child care was simply unthinkable in most families in those days. Certainly, many workers were left behind—blacks and Hispanics, young workers not yet able to raise a down payment or still unmarried and older workers who had literally failed to recover from the depression wipe-out.

White working-class flight was engendered, in part, by the influx of southern and Caribbean blacks into large northern cities, and also by the failure of federal and state lawmakers to expand the federal housing program beyond the poor. . . . Racism was not the "cause" of white flight in the sense that individuals who harbored these attitudes decided to move to get away from blacks. Racism is the result of a combination of developments. In addition to the urban housing shortage (where virtually no new one-family moderate income homes were constructed after the war), the era was marked by a precipitous decline in services—schools, hospitals, and amenities such as recreation and child care were in either serious disrepair or overcrowded.

In historical retrospect, the deterioration of the urban regions after the war was federal and corporate policy. By the mid 1960s center-city industrial plants were closing down. In Harrison, the industrial suburb of Newark, General Motors removed its roller bearing plant to the Union county suburb, Kenilworth. General Electric closed its lamp factory in the black section of Newark, and by the end of the decade, no major industrial plant remained in that city. Jersey City and Hoboken suffered similar fates; industrial expansion was still a powerful spur to economic growth, but not in the big cities. Capital and white working-class flight go together with the federal housing and highway programs, and the enthusiasm of local communities to give away the keys to the town to any corporation willing to build a plant, office building, or research facility.

The dispersion of white workers into the suburbs did not immediately destroy working-class communities, although they were considerably weakened by the late 1950s. The gin mill next to the production mill retained its pride of place. Sometimes this function was performed by a bar located in a local union hall or in a fraternal association of, say, Poles or Ukrainians. Typically, a worker would "stop" at the bar after going off shift for an hour or two before going to a home that could be as far as even forty miles away. There, he would play darts, shuffle board, or pool, or sit at the bar and just drink and talk.

Those who worked days arrived home at 7 p.m. (the shift ended at 3 p.m.). After supper, if there were no chores, the family might sit in front of the television set. The television explosion of the 1950s is generally acknowledged to have changed the leisure-time activities of Americans. The simulations that film brought to theater audiences now became daily fare.

Until the early 1960s, a small number of films and TV shows offered direct representations of white workers (usually in a comic or pathetic mode) but the mode of this presentation changed in the next decades. Workers became the object of liberal scorn, portrayed as racist and sexist, and equally important, as politically and socially conservative. Archie Bunker *(All in the Family* [1971–83]) was not only a comic character: he was a moral agent suffused with evil, a direct violation of the code according to which the working class (however scarce its media image) was invariably a hero. In contrast to Marlon Brando's 1954 portrayal *(On the Waterfront)* of a benighted but brave longshoreman who, in the last analysis, comes down for truth and justice, Bunker is a troglodyte, a "hard hat" whose wrath is aimed at the young, the poor, and the blacks.

It was hard for working-class kids to identify with Archie, but he was, as late as the mid-1970s a palpable working-class figure, recognizable by his syntax, his body language, his gruff, semi-articulate speech that parodied the results of working-class culture. As I shall demonstrate, Archie proved to be a rearguard character. After his demise (or, rather, his good fortune in having moved up the social ladder), specifically working-class representations disappear with him. Today, working-class kids may still look forward to getting working-class jobs, but forging a class identity is more difficult than ever. They confront a media complex that consistently denies their existence. However, in what amounts to a grudging acknowledgment that it is really impossible to achieve this result, working-class male identity is *displaced* to other, upwardly mobile occupations (e.g. police, football players, and other sites where conventional masculine roles are ubiquitous). . . .

Electronically mediated cultural forms play an enlarged role in the formation of cultural identities. Of course, the claim that media are so hegemonic that they exclude the influence of family, peers, and schools appears excessive. But, it would be a serious error to conclude that it is an even match. I claim that electronically mediated cultural forms have the upper hand because they carry the authority of the society that, over the last half century, has displaced patriarchial authority. For the discourse of social authority promises what family and friends cannot deliver: a qualitatively better life, consumption on an expanded scale, a chance to move beyond the limits of traditional working-class life.

No institution represents the promise of this type of transcendence more than the school, for its curriculum is widely understood as a ticket to class mobility. However, the *content* of that alternative is offered working-class kids by the situation comedies of television, the celluloid dreams of the movies, and especially the advertisements which evoke lifestyles considered worthy of emulation. I argue that the relationship between schooling and media representations of vocational and cultural aspirations has become symbiotic: to the extent that the curriculum is almost entirely geared to the presumed occupational requirements of modern corporations and the state, the dependence of what counts as education on the collective cultural ideal is almost total. For these occupational requirements, especially in large parts of the service sector, are not so much technical as they are ideological. That is, just as many advertisements sell not products but capitalism, so school learning is organized around behaviors required by types of bureaucratic work, as well as the rewards offered by consumer society for performance according to established corporate norms. The student is no longer (if *he* ever was) enthusiastic about discovering new things to know, much less Truth. Rather, he wants to find out how the real world works, especially what it takes to achieve a certain level of consumption. In this, the high school is the major site where the "real" world of work is discovered. The student remembers little or nothing of the content of knowledge (facts of history, how to perform algebraic equations, the story line of *Silas Marner*) but remembers how to succeed in receiving good grades, gaining admission to a decent college, or university, and how to curry favor with authorities—teachers, counselors, employers.

Working-class kids often fail to get the message right. As Paul Willis tells us, their rebellion against school authority, manifested as the refusal to internalize the two parts of the curriculum (its manifest "knowledge-based" content and its latent demand for discipline and respect for authority) ensures that they will get working-class jobs rather than make it up the ladder. But, while assembly-line, construction, and other heavy industrial labor was available for school leavers until the 1970s in the US and UK, these options are today foreclosed by the restructured world economy. Parents, especially fathers, can no longer serve as substitute representations of viable occupational alternatives to those imposed by school and the media. Peers may discourage an individual from integrating into the prescribed curricula, but the cultural ideal is now increasingly provided by the media. As this ideal erases working-class representations so the class sensorium disappears.

. . . Indeed, if identification is a basis for the forging of a personal identity, school and media consort to persuade, cajole, and, by the absence of representations, force working-class kids to accept middle-class identities as the only legitimate option available to them. However, it is obvious that many will choose neither to accept this course or, having bought into the aspirations, will "fail" to make the grade. The result for both groups is cultural homelessness. . . .

The stimulation of the unconscious by "imaging" (the term is Teresa di Lauretis's[2]) consists in simulating the dream work so that identities are formed through identification with the gendered characters that appear on the screen. Aural media are also powerful desiring machines, but sound is burdened with an enormous load because images must be produced by the listener. Identification can be fomented but with difficulty. The film form invokes the stark real-life character. Di Lauretis argues that women do not insert themselves into film culture, that they are absent in imagining. They cannot identify with the actual representations of women on the screen, for these women are the objects of male desire—they do not occupy subject positions from which emanates a distinctive female voice. Thus, there is no chance for identification unless women accept the object space to which they have been assigned.

Males identify with characters (protagonists, heroes) who are the subjects of narratives; women are objects of desire/exchange/conflict among males and only assume distinctive character when they occupy male-subject positions from which, in both comedies and drama they must inevitably fall (e.g. the Spencer Tracy/Katherine Hepburn comedies such as *Women of the Year* [1942] and *Desk Set* [1957], and the Joan Crawford soap operas such as *Mildred Pierce* [1945], in which women who speak as male characters find that adopting these personae invites self-destruction). Male workers do find representations in film and television in the 1950s. The characters of Ralph Cramden and Ed Norton in *The Honeymooners* (1951–56; revived 1966–70 as part of *The Jackie Gleason Show*) and Chester Riley in *The Life of Riley* (1949–58) are comically absurd, the situations often artificial and juvenile, but family relationships articulate with the prevalent war between the sexes, the distinctiveness of male culture, the absence of a corresponding women's community.

Ralph Cramden is a bus driver who, like many working-class men, dreams of escaping his routine, relatively low-paid job by entering a constant succession of bound-to-fail business schemes. His driving ambition for wealth and social position is lodged entirely in his (male) imaginary. Ralph's wife Alice can barely disguise contempt for his fantasies and foolish projects—most of which serve not to enhance the opportunity for real social mobility, but Ralph's pathetic efforts to establish his dominance in the home. On the other side is Norton, a sewer worker who harbors neither illusion nor the desire to flee his job. The sewer affords him a considerable measure of autonomy, at least in comparison to factory work or even driving a bus. He enjoys the lack of responsibility his job entails but fervently asserts its dignified character against the constant chidings of his quixotic friend.

As with most television situation comedies, the characters have a cartoon quality: there is no room for complexity in the representations. Additionally, the stripped-down sets evoke 1930s depression decorum rather than the postwar era. The honeymooners have been left behind the white urban exodus; they are transhistorical working-class types. Norton is invariably dressed in a T-shirt and wears his hat indoors. Cramden dons the uniform of a bus driver, signifying the ambiguity of his situation. Clearly he is a wage laborer, but his will is that of a petty official since genuine wealth has been foreclosed to him. Cramden displaces his frustration onto intrafamilial quarrels. His wife's housework never counts as real work—his characteristic posture is that of an inquisitor (what have you been doing all day?). Since she rarely awards him the deference he urgently needs, given his relatively degraded social position, his usual gesture is the verbal threat of violence (against women): "one of these days . . . pow, right in the kisser." Alice seems bored by his remonstrations, and we, the audience, know that Ralph is simply too henpecked . . . to follow through.

The Honeymooners retains its large audience after thirty years because it displays the range of class and gender relations. Its class ideology is represented by the absence of the labor process except discursively. The family relations displace the class relations, as Ralph seeks to dominate Alice, who as the real proletarian remains recalcitrant. Here we see the inner core of male fantasies: lacking the power individually to achieve the freedom wealth presumably affords, domination becomes she object of male desire.

Caricature notwithstanding, working-class life demanded representations in the 1950s and early 1960s. By the latter half of the decade, the dispersion of working-class culture made direct representation improbable. . . .

Working-class culture is preeminently urban; it belongs to the industrializing era which, by the late 1960s has passed. Post-industrial culture is already post-modern: it is marked by boundary crossing. As David Halle found, while working-class culture still finds renewal on the shop floor, its residential base is dispersed.[3] In the suburbs of major metropolitan centers, industrial workers mow their lawns alongside professionals, managers, and small business neighbors.

In the 1977–78 season, Archie Bunker, the Queens, New York political and social neanderthal, opened a gin mill. Having pushed himself up into the business-owning small middle class, Archie left his working-class roots behind, not only in his newly found proprietorship, but also in his contacts. In this assimilation, he continued the tendencies of the earlier incarnation of the show; recall, the Bunker family lived in that part of New York that most resembled the suburbs. The only Black family he knew owned and operated a dry cleaning business (the Jeffersons, their *own* TV series beginning in 1975). In other words, he rubbed shoulders with those who had more completely achieved one of the crucial elements of the American dream, a business of one's own. So it is entirely reasonable that Archie should aspire to gaining a toehold in the social ladder. With that, the Archie of *Archie Bunker's Place* (the series' new name, as of 1979) disappears into the middle class.

From the mid-1970s, there simply are no direct representations of working-class males (much less women) in television. Representations are dispersed to beer advertisements (thirty-second images of football players hoisting their favorite brands, jostling each other in timid evocations of the ribbing characteristic of working-class bar culture), and cop shows in which characteristic working-class culture is displaced and recontextualized in the stationhouse, on the streets, and the bars in which cops congregate. These are displacements, so we see only the reminders—conviviality and friendship that is overdetermined by the Police buddy system, the obligatory partnership. It is in these interactions, when the partners of say, *Hill Street Blues* (first aired, 1981), discuss their personal problems or their troubles with the Department, that the old class solidarity bonds are permitted to come to the surface, often against the Captain or even the lieutenants who are a step above the line and possess some authority. We know that the patrolmen (and some patrolwomen) may rise to Sergeant, but are not likely to make Lieutenant, much less Captain. These are not educated men and women. Their bravery entitles them to recognition, not rank. They have their own hangouts, their personal troubles (especially with their love lives). In contrast, officials, whatever their origins, do not congregate in barrooms; they have no sharer of their troubles because they must observe the tacit code of hierarchy.

In recent films, displacement of class to the police continues, but is joined by displacement or sex/gender relations to class as well. Hollywood movies . . . are marked by a conventional theme in contemporary narrative: the working-class man is powerfully attracted to an upper-class woman, disrupting not only the prohibition of interclass romance, but also the family romance. In these instances, to be working class is identified with masculinity, upper class with femininity. . . .

Someone to Watch Over Me finds a cop of plainly working-class parentage, married to a tough, fiesty working-class woman, who live together with their kids in a modest single-family house in Queens. Archie Bunker's kid has become a cop. The cop is assigned to protect an upper-class woman, ensconced in a Manhattan townhouse. He is assigned the midnight shift and quickly has an affair with her, an event that disrupts his tension-filled but stable home life. . . . The film reenacts a crucial male working-class fantasy: to dominate a beautiful rich woman, to make the "impossible dream" real.

. . . The cop is socialized into a conventional honorific position—the centurian—but finds it suffused with mediocrity and, most important of all, marked by repetition and continuity with the anterior generation. What is new is adventure, which can only be fulfilled by sexual indiscretion, "penetration" into the forbidden territory of the upper class. But beside the exotic, for the cop, buried in the routine tasks dictated by a bureaucracy that seems entirely beyond his power to control, sex becomes the power that can propel him out of his own real-life subordination.

It may be that today sex discourse refers to class issues; but it is also true class discourse refers to gender domination. The import of the image of the working class cum cop engaging in sexual relations with a women in an entirely improbable class position is not that American society is somehow democratic—these relationships end in disaster. They are themselves sundered, but more importantly they wreck families, personal lives, and so forth. The significance is otherwise. Class is no barrier when upper-class women are involved. In current representations, the reverse is rarely portrayed.' Femininity is not a universal signifier. That privilege is reserved for male culture. . . .

In short, in contrast to the 1950s when a viable working-class culture, connected to powerful large-scale industry, was accorded considerable status in media representations, class has been displaced in two ways: first, to other signifiers of masculinity, and second, to the code violations entailed in sexual relations between working-class or declassed men and upper-class women. In this case, sex/class relations are reversed. Men, despite lower-class roots, achieve class parity with women due to the status conferred upon masculine sexuality and its powers by society.

   . . . [T]he sex/class/power axis in television and movies constitutes a critique of the cultural ideal of consumer society that passes for the 1980s equivalent of the mobility myth. For the entrepreneurial ambition which motored two generations of immigrants in the 20th century has disappeared from view; the remainder is the civil service which has become the far horizon of well-being for a new working class that can no longer count on high-paying factory jobs. The army and the police have replaced industrial labor for working-class men, for whom professional options simply never existed.

   Male bonding persists in these contexts, but not the solidarity that is born of mutual recognition among production workers who share a common fate as well as a common existence. . . .

   The only vital life consists in dreams of power, the most vivid form of which is male sexuality. Contrasted to earlier direct representations in which sex is virtually absent from discourse, but where class persists, today's movies and television programs code sex, class, and power interchangeably. As with the earlier genre, women do not occupy subject positions: they remain the palpable objects of male desire, and by this precise relation experience class reversal.

NOTES

1. Louis Althusser, "Ideology and Ideological State Apparatuses," in *Lenin and Philosophy* (London: New Left Books, 1971).
2. Teresa Di Lauretis, *Alice Doesn't: Feminism, Semiotics, Cinema* (Bloomington: Indiana University Press, 1984) pp. 37–69.
3. David Halle, *America's Working Men: Work, Home and Politics Among the Blue-collar Property Owners* (Chicago: University of Chicago Press, 1984).

Articulating the (Im)possible: The Contradictory Fantasies of "Curing" AIDS

In the following excerpt from *Unstable Frontiers: Technomedicine and the Cultural Politics of "Curing" AIDS* (University of Minnesota Press, 1994), John Nguyet Erni puts a cultural approach to work in order to disrupt assumptions about the nature of illness. He draws on the theoretical concepts of *culture* and *hegemony,* adding to them the important notion of *discourse* developed by the French social theorist Michel Foucault. Through the intersection of a number of powerful fields of communication, particularly those of journalism and medicine, AIDS is defined as a simple, though deadly, biological fact. Yet there are many contradictions and ambiguities in the medical "facts" of AIDS as reported by the press.

Erni shows that this ambiguity is not simply the product of scientific uncertainty—as if medical research has not yet been able to pin down the real nature of the AIDS virus. The "facts" of AIDS are complex cultural constructs. Media coverage of AIDS puts conflicting metaphors to work linking the illness, the realities of human life, and the institution of medical research and treatment into an overarching "discourse of cure." This discourse, like all others, operates to institute and maintain social relationships of power through its contradictions and ambiguities. In the following selection, Erni cites the specific strategies of power involved in the contradictory discourse of "curing" AIDS.

Erni is an assistant professor of communication at the University of New Hampshire. His work is part of a broad refocusing of cultural studies—a "return to its roots" after years of important theoretical study—on analysis and criticism of key relationships in everyday life.

Key Concept: discourse

*T*he *AIDS Quarterly*, a television series created by PBS in 1989, opens with the following narration, backed by a solemn sound track reminiscent of the sound effects of a detective or horror film:

> The human immunodeficiency virus is not, in the strictest sense, a form of life. Until it is inside a host's body, it is no more alive than a rock or a stone. It is a protein-coded mass of genetic instructions 150 times smaller than the white blood cell it attacks. After penetrating, it multiplies until the cell bursts and dies. This continues for years. Cell by cell, the virus destroys its carrier's immune system. The person becomes ill from a series of infections that are progressively serious and rare and finally fatal. This is AIDS.

This narrative is accompanied by an image of the HIV, electronically colorized dark blue and green constantly shifting hues and intensities. A mediated spectacle is thus created, bound by the conventions of the representation of a mystical reality, projected as a new truth, and mobilized as a new frontier to be conquered. Since the onset of the AIDS epidemic, the HIV has become the center of an electrifying biomedical and cultural imagination, full of grave implications. Technoscience has made it possible to visualize and speak about this new truth. Yet, as the narrative indicates, it is, at best, an ambiguous truth: HIV is both lifeless and actively alive. It is a graspable, seeable, and somewhat innocent reality (as common as a rock or a stone) but simultaneously an unfamiliar object, a concept that exists only in the eyes of technology, a life-threatening entity beyond our control. Contradictory cultural constructs like this pervade the popular understanding of the discourse of AIDS treatment.

. . . [T]he contradictory images of narratives of HIV, such as the one created in *The AIDS Quarterly*, are central to the definition of the curability of AIDS, so that before one determines what to use to cure AIDS or how to cure AIDS, one must negotiate, by analysis and intuition, the contradictory meanings of HIV. . . . [T]he social constructedness of HIV . . . gives rise to perceptions of a relative potency/impotency of the virus—a matter that is a point of bitter debate among scientists today. But such perceptions would find it excruciatingly difficult to establish widespread credibility if they had not been overdetermined by the two ruling structures of fantasies of AIDS in our culture.

The fantasy structure of morbidity proliferates paranoiac identification of menace and emotional moribundity, bound by a series of morbid narratives, including most visibly the constructions of HIV as monstrosity, the intensively visual depictions of the disfigurement and wasting of the body, the horrifying statistical projections and death counting, the fantasy of "gay genocide," and of course the trauma of AZT.

The fantasy structure of containment, while consistently admitting the difficulty of finding a cure, couples curing with controlling in a regime of maximized hyperrationality. It too is enacted within a discursive boundary that activates—or habitually resuscitates—a set of narratives, including most visibly the ongoing coverage of AIDS drug and vaccine development; the mobilization of "AIDS education" campaigns, often condensed to the highly ambivalent injunction "Knowledge = Cure"; and the institutionalization of a rhetoric of reform of the technomedical paradigm of drug research and regulations. . . .

This regime of control/containment focuses on the strategic conviction that while rationality, control, the constriction of behavior, even the repression of desire will not directly constitute a cure, they can lengthen the time and reconstitute the spaces deemed respectably necessary for controlling the disease. Although I do not assume stability in any of these strands of narratives contained in the fantasies of morbidity and containment, I am convinced that they have profoundly circumscribed the entire question of "curing" AIDS—circumscribed, that is, the inauguration of the stable definitions of AIDS as both curable and incurable. . . .

"AIDS IS INCURABLE": THE STRUCTURE OF MORBIDITY

If a masterful assertion and reassertion of the invincibility of AIDS can be made (and made with the passionate conviction we have witnessed in all these years of the epidemic), it has to be in large part incurred by the immensely figurative statement that "AIDS is invariably fatal"—figurative not because it is fictional but because, in a far more productive way, it abides by a looming fantasy structure of morbidity as it actively constructs the morbid scene. The statement "Aids is invariably fatal" has been so central and so deeply permeated into every discourse, from the most austere professional scientific language to the news, that the site of its origin is no longer possible to locate.

The contention that "AIDS is invariably fatal," as opposed to "AIDS causes death" or just "AIDS is fatal," depends on the weighty inscriptions of the following truth claims, listed here in order of expanding intensity and complexity:

1. HIV *inevitably* causes AIDS.
2. Epidemiological information will *always* be unambiguously reflective of reality.
3. Although HIV is thought to be vastly mutable, its infectivity will be *permanently* immutable; infection will be carried out in a permanent and progressive irreversibility.
4. Treatment will *inevitably* fail.
5. The manifestation of illness may not always be uniform, but death will be the *universal* result.

Each of the qualifying linguistic markers—always, permanently, inevitably, universal—must appear in these truth claims with spectacular force in order to anchor and naturalize the compelling clause "invariably fatal." At the same time, these qualifiers do not necessarily connote something already accomplished. In fact, the rigid inevitability they connote suggests a sense of something constantly in progress; they help to launch the more powerful assertion "It *will* happen" rather than "It *has* happened." Morbidity is always less of an achievement that a prospect.

The interconnecting (and competing) discourses of science, including virology, epidemiology, immunology, and clinical research, are the grounds for the inevitability suggested by the combination of "invariably" and "fatal." Two things give this combination its rhetorical force. The first is the creation of a linear momentum, a medical domino theory of sorts provided by the scientific definition of AIDS as consisting of several progressive and irreversible stages of deterioration, as evidenced by the elaboration of the theory of a temporally linear HIV life cycle and the epidemiological tracking of symptom development over time. The second is the creation of a specified destiny, namely the stage of "full-blown AIDS" ("full-blown" means "mature" and "large as life"), in which time has run out and life itself is replaced by deadly symptoms. Susan Sontag has written, "construing [AIDS] as divided into distinct stages was the necessary way of implementing the metaphor of 'full-blown' disease" (1989, p. 29). The phrase "invariably fatal" therefore depends on the installation of a temporality of symptom development; it need not pronounce death itself in order to promise the prospect of death. . . .

To the degree that "AIDS is invariably fatal" means that "AIDS *will be* fatal," the tragedy becomes both more and less catastrophic, because fatality, in this statement, is being constructed to be at once a prominent and an imminent calamity. In speaking about the apocalyptic visión surrounding AIDS in general, Sontag has made a similar observation:

> With the inflation of apocalyptic rhetoric has come the increasing unreality of the apocalypse. . . . A permanent modern scenario: apocalypse looms . . . and it doesn't occur. . . . There is what is happening now. And there is what it portends: the imminent, but not yet actual, and not really graspable, disaster. Two kinds of disaster, actually. And a gap between them, in which the imagination flounders. (1989, pp. 87–90)

. . . Even though in recent years, as a result of increased understanding of the disease, the plague model of interpretation has been shifted to the chronic disease model, suggesting that an extended survival period is now possible, the discourse about the horror of AIDS remains dangerously pervasive. New understanding has not shattered the intensive social discussion of the HIV as the impossible obstacle in the scientific crusade against the disease, the culprit of horror.

A virus is a biological entity as well as socially produced text, absorbed in the gaze of medical researchers, offered up by journalists as the center of the mystery of AIDS. The visual image of HIV purports to tell the "truth" of a complex reality; seeing literally becomes knowing (Grover, 1989; McGrath, 1990).

Milan Kundera has said: "Once we can name each part of our body, that body disturbs us less." But whether the discursive constructions of HIV—the "naming" of AIDS body—disturb us less or not depends on how they are deployed and what audience they implicate. In fact, the emphasis on the widespread but "low-keyed" infectivity of HIV—the so-called silent infection—provokes fear in everyone; no one, it seems, is less disturbed. Overall, media and biomedical discourses construct HIV as the abhorrent figure, frequently invoking images of familiar characters in science fictions and detective stories:

- HIV is an insidious, indiscriminate killer.
- HIV is a time bomb, gradually wasting away its carrier's life.
- It has a brilliant genetic design that facilitates undetectable infection.
- Its genetic component replicates and mutates wildly.
- It is the invading battalion, turning the body into a war zone.
- It infects like a violent postmodern military attack.
- Its power lies in its ability to claim territories and remain there to reproduce its own kind.
- It knows how to hide itself in order to carry out its secret mission; its is the evasive Trojan horse.
- Eventually, it penetrates significant zones of the body.
- It evolves from a family of deadly viruses.
- Its origin is unmistakably foreign and alien; it either comes from subhuman species (monkeys) or from bizarre human sexual practices.

Consider also this narrative by two leading biomedical researchers of AIDS:

> This picture is a daunting one. HIV is able to slip into cells and remain there for life. Its elaborate genetic regulation enables it to lie low, hidden from immune surveillance; to replicate slowly, possibly deranging the host cell's own genetic controls as it does so, or to initiate a burst of growth that kills the infected cell. (Haseltine and Wong-Staal, 1988, p. 62)

Detective story meets science fiction. In the popular lexicons of Star Wars, serial killing, perversion, and deception, the HIV has proved an ideally comprehensible subject. As the preceding listing suggests, the virus has become a coherent character, perfectly endowed with (malignant) intentions, purposes, schedules, targets, and even preferences (Williamson, 1989).

A journalist describes the HIV as "wandering through the world of life, looking for living cells to infect" (Schmeck, 1987). Similarly a television special report called "AIDS Now" produced by Channel 4 in England features a detective taking on the case of a criminal suspect, the HIV. Coded in all the conventions of the detective story (dark, wet streets; dim lighting; mysterious music; and, of course, the detective in raincoat and hat), the investigation unfolds as the detective replays evidence on a video recording machines, looking for traces of the mysterious killer. Most of the prominent medical researchers, journalists, and social policy makers featured in the video express fear and pessimism about locating the killer or gaining information about its motives and its next attack. Sound familiar? More questions are asked than answers given, and the audience is left more disturbed than ever. The case is pending, more work is needed, and in the meantime the killer remains elusive. Throughout the program, the story of the HIV is named "The Case of a Promiscuous Parasite."

If the fantasy structure of morbidity revolves around temporalized notions of imminence, expectedness, permanent inevitability, and so on, then it also must depend on the constant marking and monitoring or charged sites or morbidity in the "AIDS body," marking, in a fairly literal sense, the body parts that are scientifically demonstrated to be the zones of infection/zones of horror and monitoring their imminent deterioration. The "AIDS body" therefore comes to stand for the literal and figurative object of the (in)curable in a journalistic and medical culture obsessed with morbidity.

. . . Cases in point are the photographs that appeared after the revelation of Rock Hudson's illness in 1985, which focused on the physical transformation of Hudson's face and body, and the brutally manipulative television use of PWA [person with AIDS] Kenny Ramsaur's face before and after his illness in 1983 and of another PWA, Fabian Bridges, in 1985.

In recent years, however, the "face of AIDS" has received a different treatment by the media. As political activism has grown and, to a smaller degree, as public outcry has expressed distaste for the dehumanizing staging of debililated AIDS patients in the media, the emaciated face has gradually lost its powerful hold on the popular morbid imagination. Yet this trend has not by any means diminished attention to the face as a crucial trope for suffering, horror, and morbidity. The different treatment is in part a result of the normalization of AIDS . . . and from the same normalization process has sprung a more subtle but no less potent imaging of the "AIDS face" in the popular media. . . .

In 1992, in a highly controversial media advertising campaign, the face of AIDS, already immortalized in the photographic representations of the crisis as a whole, reappeared in the image of an AIDS patient on his deathbed in an immodest Benetton advertisement. Given the pervasiveness of the visual horror in the photographs of AIDS, few failed to recognize this as an image of a dying AIDS patient. By 1993, an image of a dying person with AIDS had become routine; no ethical answerability of prudence was thought necessary to accompany such an image. What is also routine, in the visual form in which the image is shaped, is that the dying person, David Kirby, is surrounded by family (belonging to the photographic tradition of a family portrait), and that this gathering takes place in a hospital or a hospice (the "natural" dignified sites of death). The collective cultural fantasy of family unity typified in such a portrait, even in a tragic moment, appears to be a point of cognitive articulation with the inventive message in Benetton's benign logo: "UNITED COLORS OF BENETTON."

. . . Nothing in the Benetton photograph is more culturally naturalized as the mark of death than the AIDS patient's gaunt, barren, emotionless face, a face that relinquishes consciousness and therefore relinquishes the space of the living. The common recognition that Kirby's face resembles that of Christ (the photographer's intent?) aligns, even by coincidence, this image with the space of extreme suffering fixed in Christ's face, which is, in Christian iconography, commonly recognized as the site of excruciating morbidity: at the moment of his abandonment, Christ suffers, and suffers only, in his face. All the volatile suggestiveness of the image fortifies the morbidity so deeply articulated with AIDS.

By locking the gaze of the reader onto Kirby's face while he in turn directs his own empty gaze toward somewhere and nowhere—he is already elsewhere—the image both seduces our attention and abandons it into a non-space; it draws us toward a place where any meaning and no meaning can coexist. The image of Kirby, particularly his face, suggests that the space of the living *is being* evacuated, as opposed to *has been* evacuated, and therefore provides us with a prolonged glimpse at the abject trajectory of morbidity itself.

One may then say that the image's shock value lies in its normality, not the normality of the appearance of such an image in the pages of *Vogue, Cosmopolitan,* or *Details*, but the numbing shock of a glimpse of morbid death associated with AIDS, the banal news in an unexpected space of a popular magazine. . . .

The deep codes of fear and repugnance that saturate the cultural fantasy of the *danse macabre* surrounding AIDS show up in the continual rupture, for over twelve years now, of an arsenal of lethal representations—that AIDS is "invariably fatal," that HIV is permanently monstrous, that all people with AIDS are the clinical embodiment of grotesque disfigurement (of both body and character), that AIDS statistics authorize the de facto sign of inevitable massive deaths. This atmosphere seems vindictively eager to imagine a historical prospect of the eradication of "homosexual acts," whether carried out by homosexuals or not, and, by extension, the eradication of the figure of the homosexual. Present within the fantasy structure of morbidity is the idea of, even a yearning for, a "cure" that would restore history, itself ravaged by the AIDS crisis, through an order of eradication. . . . It is not too much to claim that the convergent injunctions of "AIDS is a gay disease" and "AIDS is invariably fatal" have been inaugurated, with spectacular sovereignty, as the amalgamized definition of AIDS in all veins of popular and official rhetorics. . . .

SCIENCE FICTIONS: THE FANTASY OF CONTROL/CONTAINMENT

Side by side with the overall construction of the impossibility of AIDS is a fantasy structure that proclaims the immense curative power of medical science to fight AIDS through a paradigm of hyperrationality. Through the years, the press has reported the steady supply of experimental drugs and new inventions provided by AIDS researchers. A cursory look at reports on the science of AIDS treatment in the news and in medical journals reveals a steady impulse of rigorous scientific innovations. Although the stories about drug and vaccine research are not always coded as "breakthrough" news, they typically appear as accumulative evidence signifying scientific progress, complete with detailed tables and graphs demonstrating how the drugs or vaccines would "really" work. . . .

Besides the attention given to the productiveness of science, there are signs of traditional and reformed coalition efforts to develop AIDS treatment. The models represented by the Community Research Initiative based in New York and Project Inform based in San Francisco are examples of such coalitions, which involve the participation of the government, the private sectors, and grass-roots activist groups. Although such efforts are a positive sign, unfortunately journalists have generally failed to acknowledge that within these organizations, AIDS community activists and workers continue to struggle to maintain a sense of autonomy in their collaboration with technomedicine and financial institutions. The activists' strategic cooperation with mainstream medicine is often viewed, naively, as their willingness to be co-opted (see, for example, Kolata, 1988b). . . .

Almost as quickly as the epidemic began to affect a large number of people, and as the media and the government continued to conduct scientific research with discriminatory presumptions, PWAs created an elaborate network of physicians and agencies who would provide alternative forms of treatment for AIDS. . . .

The alternative treatment movement is a form of political resistance that, through adopting a self-empowerment model of community organizing, challenges and hyperrationalized form of technology held sacred by many mainstream scientists. The restrictive control in orthodox science has in some ways intensified the AIDS communities' attempt to take control of their own medical matters. Although alternative treatments did not of course originate with the AIDS crisis, their use and the status of alternative treatment research have never been so organized. What unorthodox medical practices do is suggest a different conception of the relation of the body and technomedicine. Like the discourse of dominant medical science, unorthodox medicine establishes its validity through empirical experiential evidence of those who use it, but contrary to it, such treatment offers a stunning range of methods systematically excluded by technomedicine. More important, it stresses the relative autonomy of PWAs vis-à-vis treatment, encourages self-education, and promotes a discourse of empowerment.

Increasingly, the alternative treatment movement has met so many needs that some PWAs would choose to participate in it before they would turn to mainstream treatment protocols (Serinus, 1990/91). Far from being able to consolidate its control, the restrictive practices of technomedicine have sparked a proliferation of drug searches outside of the dominant institutional setting. Alternative treatment thus represents a partial recuperation of the patients' own control of their bodies. The mainsteam media and medical institutions are sharply critical of it, however. Federal health officials have taken action to stifle the grass-roots movement, for fear that it may promote quack medicine and profiteering (Robbins, 1988). Frank Young, the former FDA commissioner, comments about the movement that "every time there's a desperate disease, people try to get rich on the suffering" (quoted in Hammer, 1988, p. 41). The profit motive, always the underlying motive for official, "reputable" AIDS research, is suddenly deemed problematic and thus must be controlled.

Likewise, the mainstream press cannot seem to evaluate the significance of the alternative treatment movement without situating it in the ideological framework of "official medicine." The reporting of health fraud is an important task, provided that sufficiently specific information on a case-by-case basis is clearly identified, thereby avoiding commentaries that would, in one stroke, condemn all forms of alternative medical practices. However, the press reporting of the movement in the AIDS crisis has tended to devalue it simply on the grounds that it falls outside of official medicine. No attempt is made to differentiate the mostly nontoxic forms of holistic medicine from potentially harmful substances found in the underground market. As a whole, the movement is typically coded as quackery, as an anarchistic/guerrilla operation. People who use alternative medicine are frequently constructed as exiles from their own society, uneducated consumers, gullible, desperate, or ignorant (Clark et al., 1985; Geitner, 1988; Hammer, 1988; Kolata, 1988a; Robbins, 1988; Ticer, 1985). Community-based clinics that provide vital information and services of alternative treatment are termed "guerrilla clinics," operating in "the world of mischief and hucksterism," "spreading disinformation, panic, and fear" (Monmaney et al., 1987). The buyers' clubs' purchase and importation of drugs from foreign countries is often dramatized along the lines of an international criminal plot.

> In a brightly lit alley in Tokyo's Roppongi district, a veteran smuggler heads toward his first deal of the evening. Clutching a paper bag stuffed with crisp 10,000-yen notes, he enters a small pharmacy and within minutes carries out twelve boxes filled with $40,000 worth of round white tablets, soon to be shipped to AIDS patients across America. The dealer is a registered nurse from Los Angeles, known as "Dextran Man" to most of his desperate customers . . . It remains illegal to manufacture or sell [Dextran Sulphate] in the United States, and that has created a flourishing gray market that's fueled by altruism and greed. (Hammer, 1988, p. 41)

What was once viewed as a medical issue is now signified as a social and criminal concern, complete with the identification of the suspect and his background, the location of the crime, the illegal substance, the destination, and even the motive. . . .

The disqualification of alternative forms of treatment, which is congruent with the fantasy of control/containment, constitutes one of the gravest obstacles in the overall effort to develop treatment for HIV/AIDS. To many living in communities affected by HIV/AIDS, the pointed refusal to recognize the potential usefulness of alternative treatment methods has compounded their feeling of rejection by society: their effort to diversify the possibilities for healing, even as these methods carry a certain level of risk, is viewed by society as one more feature of their supposed deviancy. But it has also galvanized more systematic and more accurate delivery and monitoring of treatment information in those communities, leading to the professional crosschecking of medical opinions, the results of which are made available to PWAs in community newsletters, pamphlets, fact sheets, and regular information update meetings. Knowledge, it has been recognized, is no longer the monopoly of mainstream science. This community belief in the usefulness and power of knowledge/information, however, duplicates a broader, more endemic discourse that has been a highly visible feature of the popular lexicon of AIDS for many years, a discourse articulated in a peculiar injunction: "Knowledge = Cure." . . .

A hidden rhetorical and ethical structure underlies this injunction in health education that directs different strategic cognitive associations regarding the matters of knowledge and curing at what are perceived as "high-risk" or "low-risk" groups. The ubiquitous label of a "general public" commonly denotes low-risk, uninfected, nongay, non-drug users (e.g., heterosexuals). Compacted within this label is an eager belief in its mythic wholeness; that is, a belief that the so-called high-risk groups cannot already be part of it. "Closeted" gays and bisexuals and "closeted" drug users, however, exist and give a new meaning to the label. Within the infected groups is the morally and politically motivated distinction between "innocent" and "guilty" people, whose purpose is mainly to map different fantasy structures onto these categories. In other words, there is a certain circular totality in which the contradictory fantasies of morbidity/control generate categories of victim subjects, which in turn valorize the transcendent fantasies. As Cindy Patton has made clear, one of the most virulent effects of such a distinction is the creation of the assumption that the "general public" and the "infected innocent groups" receive information because they have a *right* to know, whereas the "infected guilty groups" receive information because they have an *obligation* to know so as to protect the non-guilty groups (1990, p. 103). The acquisition of knowledge is thus studded with prejudicial assumptions.

SUMMARY

The two ruling structures of fantasies of AIDS in our culture are organic vectors of contradictions that have helped establish the stable definitions of AIDS as both curable and incurable. The whole question of "curing AIDS" is overdetermined by the two fantasies of morbidity and containment. Morbid fantasies of course titillate containment fantasies, and in this mutual seduction we revisit the lethal discourse that links the durable image of gay death with the emerging definitions of "curing AIDS." For medical science and the media, the focus of HIV as a prime image of a constitutive paradigm for virtually *all* understanding of AIDS and for struggling with treatment issues is among other things testimony to the power of, and the fascination with, the idea of death. In contemporary gay cultures, such a fascination with death is often viewed as an indelible mark in the specific redefinition of homosexuality since 1981.

The powerful resistance to the possibility that HIV is not uniformly and universally fatal, that the bodies of PWAs are not uniformly and universally objects of disintegration, that not every PWA is crazy about becoming the subject of scientific experiments, that not all forms and practices of alternative treatment methods are useless, and that "health education" is not always politically or culturally just education reveals to all of us, especially to gay people, an excruciatingly adamant imagination that is attempting to remove the people most affected by, and most visible in, the AIDS crisis from the spaces of life, living, safety, compassion, and power—and ultimately from the space of being "cured."

REFERENCES

Clark, M., et al. (1985, August 5). AIDS exiles in Paris. *Newsweek*, p. 71.

Geitner, P. (1988, June 19). Desperation drives victims to try unapproved drugs. *Champaign-Urbana News-Gazette*, p. B4.

Grover, J. Z. (1989, Summer). Visible lesions: Images of people with AIDS. *Afterimage*, 17(1), 10–16.

Hammer, J. (1988, August 15). Inside the illegal AIDS drug trade. *Newsweek*, pp. 41–42.

Haseltine, W., and F. Wong-Staal. (1988, October). The molecular biology of the AIDS virus. *Scientific American*, 259(4), 52–63.

Kolata, G. (1988a, July 10). AIDS patients and their above-ground underground. *New York Times*, p. E32.

Kolata, G. (1988b, November 26). Odd alliance would speed new drugs. *New York Times*, p. A9.

McGrath, R. (1990). Dangerous liaison: Health, disease, and representation. In T. Boffin and S. Gupta (Eds.), *Ecstatic Antibodies: Resisting the AIDS Mythology*. London: Rivers Oram. 142–155

Monmaney, T., et al. (1987, June 1). Preying on AIDS patients. *Newsweek*, pp. 52–54.

Patton, C. (1990). *Inventing AIDS*. New York: Routledge.

Robbins, W. (1988, March 16). Doctors urge campaign against AIDS quackery. *New York Times*, p. A21.

Schmeck, H. (1987, March 17). AIDS drug offers hope but cure remains distant. *New York Times*, pp. A1, 16.

Serinus, J. (1990/91, December/January). The latest non-toxic natural therapies for AIDS. *PW Alive*, 3(4), 1–13.

Sontag, S. (1989). *AIDS and Its Metaphors*. New York: Farrar, Straus, and Giroux.

Ticer, S. (1985, December 2). "Fast-buck" artists are making a killing on AIDS. *Business Week*, pp. 85–86.

Treichler, P. A. (1992). AIDS, HIV, and the cultural construction of reality. In G. Herdt and S. Linderbaum (Eds.), *The Time of AIDS: Social Analysis, Theory, and Method*. Newbury Park, Calif.: Sage. 65–98.

Williamson, J. (1989). Every virus tells a story: The meanings of HIV and AIDS. In S. Watney and E. Carter (Eds.), *Taking Liberties: AIDS and Cultural Politics*. London, Serpent's Tail. 69–80.

CHAPTER 12 Feminist Media Criticism

12.1 MOLLY HASKELL

The Big Lie

Molly Haskell is both a scholar and a critic of popular culture who has written for such periodicals as *Ms., Vogue, Film Comment, The Saturday Review,* and *Mademoiselle.* When her book-length study *From Reverence to Rape: The Treatment of Women in the Movies* (Holt, Rinehart & Winston, 1974) was first published, critics noted the way Haskell systematically developed a chronology of women's portrayals in film from the 1920s through 1973. Haskell wrote this book at a time when the attention of the feminist movement was turning toward culture and focusing on the ways in which stereotyping of women in mass media reinforced the wider subordination of women in society. *From Reverence to Rape* is considered one of the first in-depth critical works on the representation of women in film.

   In the following selection from that book, Haskell uses her knowledge of film history and her ability to critically analyze film imagery to reveal the contradictory way in which women have been represented in the movies. On the one hand, cinematic images of women consistently show them in subordinate roles. On the other hand, female characters provide a vehicle for the attainment of power and status. This provides important insight into the ways in which mass media representations can at the same time reflect and challenge wider social relations of gender.

Key Concept: contradictory representations of women in film

*T*he big lie perpetrated on Western society is the idea of women's inferiority, a lie so deeply ingrained in our social behavior that merely to recognize it is to risk unraveling the entire fabric of civilization. [Psychiatrist] Alfred Adler, unique among his professional colleagues as well as among his sex in acknowledging that occasionally women had ambitions similar to men's, called attention to this "mistake"—the notion of women's inferiority and men's superiority—fifty years ago. At about the same time, Virginia Woolf wrote, "Women have served all these centuries as looking glasses possessing the magic and delicious power of reflecting the figure of man at twice its natural size." How ironic that it was in the security of this enlarged image of himself, an image provided by wives or, more often, mothers, that man went forth to fight, conquer, legislate, create. And woman stayed home without so much as "a room of her own," her only "fulfillment" the hope of bearing a son to whom she could pass on the notion of male superiority.

The prejudice against women is no less pernicious because it is based on a fallacy. Indeed, to have sanctioned by law and custom a judgment that goes against our instincts is the cornerstone of bad faith on which monuments of misunderstanding have been erected. We can see that women live longer than men, give birth, and endure pain bravely; yet they are the "weaker sex." They can read and write as well as men—are actually *more* verbal according to aptitude tests. And they are encouraged to pursue advanced education as long as they don't forget their paramount destiny to marry and become mothers, an injunction that effectively dilutes intellectual concentration and discourages ambition. Women are not "real women" unless they marry and bear children, and even those without the inclination are often pressured into motherhood and just as often make a mess of it. The inequity is perpetuated as women transmit their sense of incompleteness to their daughters. But men, too, are victimized by the lie. Secretly they must wonder how they came to be entitled to their sense of superiority if it is to these "inferior" creatures they owe the debt of their existence. And defensively, they may feel "emasculated" by any show of strength or word of criticism from their nominal dependents.

In the movie business we have had an industry dedicated for the most part to reinforcing the lie. As the propaganda arm of the American Dream machine, Hollywood promoted a romantic fantasy of marital roles and conjugal euphoria and chronically ignored the facts and fears arising from an awareness of The End—the winding down of love, change, divorce, depression, mutation, death itself. But like the latent content of any good dream, unconscious elements, often elaborately disguised, came to trouble our sleep and stick pins in our technicolored balloons. The very unwillingness of the narrative to pursue love into marriage (except in the "woman's film," where the degree of rationalization needed to justify the disappointments of marriage made its own subversive comment) betrayed a certain skepticism. Not only did unconscious elements obtrude in the films, but they were part of the very nature of the industry itself.

The anomaly that women are the majority of the human race, half of its brains, half of its procreative power, most of its nurturing power, and yet are its servants and romantic slaves was brought home with peculiar force in the Hollywood film. Through the myths of subjection and sacrifice that were its fictional currency and the machinations of its moguls in the front offices, the film industry maneuvered to keep women in their place; and yet these very myths and this machinery catapulted women into spheres of power beyond the wildest dreams of most of their sex.

This is the contradiction that runs through the history of film, a kink in the machine of sociologists' generalizations: We see the *June Bride* played by Bette Davis surrender her independence at the altar; the actress played by Margaret Sullavan in *The Moon's Our Home* submit to the straitjacket in which Henry Fonda enfolds and symbolically subjugates her; Katharine Hepburn's *Alice Adams* achieve her highest ambitions in the arms of Fred MacMurray; Rosalind Russell as an advertising executive in *Take a Letter, Darling* find happiness in the same arms; Joan Crawford as the head of a trucking firm in *They All Kissed the Bride* go weak in the knees at the sight of the labor leader played by Melvyn Douglas. And yet we remember Bette Davis not as the blushing bride but as the aggressive reporter and sometime-bitch; Margaret Sullavan leading Fonda on a wild-goose chase through the backwoods of Vermont; Katharine Hepburn standing on the "secretarial stairway" to independence; Rosalind Russell giving MacMurray the eye as her prospective secretary; and Joan Crawford looking about as wobbly as the Statue of Liberty.

This tension—between the spirited single girl and the whimpering bride, between the "star" and the "stereotype"—existed for good reason. Audiences for the most part were not interested in seeing, and Hollywood was not interested in sponsoring, a smart, ambitious woman as a popular heroine. A woman who could compete and conceivably win in a man's world would defy emotional gravity, would go against the grain of prevailing notions about the female sex. A woman's intelligence was the equivalent of a man's penis: something to be kept out of sight. Ambition in a woman had either to be deflected into the vicarious drives of her loved ones or to be mocked and belittled. A movie heroine could act on the same power and career drives as a man only if, at the climax, they took second place to the sacred love of a man. Otherwise she forfeited her right to that love.

According to society's accepted role definitions, which films have always reflected in microcosm, the interests of men and women are not only different, but actually opposed. A man is supposedly most himself when he is driving to achieve, to create, to conquer; he is least himself when reflecting or making love. A woman is supposedly most herself in the throes of emotion (the love of man or of children), and least herself, that is, least "womanly," in the pursuit of knowledge or success. The stigma becomes a self-fulfilling prophecy. By defying cultural expectations, by insisting on professional relationships with men who want only to flatter and flirt with her, a woman becomes "unfeminine" and undesirable, she becomes, in short, a monster. This may explain why there is something monstrous in all the great women stars and why we often like the "best friends" better than the heroines, or the actresses who never quite got to the top (Ann Dvorak, Geraldine Fitzgerald, Mary Astor) better than the ones who did (Joan Crawford, Bette Davis, Elizabeth Taylor). The arrogance, the toughness were not merely make-believe. In a woman's "unnatural" climb to success, she *did* have to step on toes, jangle nerves, antagonize men, and run the risk of not being loved.

In no more than one out of a thousand movies was a woman allowed to sacrifice love for career rather than the other way around. Yet, in real life, the stars did it all the time, either by choice or by default—the result of devoting so much time and energy to a career and of achieving such fame that marriage suffered and the home fell apart. Even with allowances made for the general instability of Hollywood, the nature and number of these breakups suggest that no man could stand being overshadowed by a successful wife. The male ego was sacred; the woman's was presumed to be nonexistent. And yet, what was the "star" but a woman supremely driven to survive, a barely clothed ego on display for all the world to see.

The personality of the star, the mere fact of being a star, was as important as the roles they played, and affected the very conception of those roles. In her original literary form —the long-forgotten 1920s novel by Olive Higgins Prouty —Stella Dallas was the prototypical lower-class "woman as martyr." As played by Belle Bennett in Henry King's silent-film version, she is a tasteful and remote figure of pity. But as played front and center, tacky, tactless, and bravura by Barbara Stanwyck in King Vidor's 1937 remake, she is something else again. Stanwyck, in what may be at once the most excruciating and exhilarating performance on film, takes Stella onto a plane where, no longer just Everywoman as victim, she is an outrageous creature who breaks our hearts even as she grates on our nerves. As the boozy, overdressed, social-climbing mother, Stella/Stanwyck ignores the socially accepted "oughts" by which she could keep our—and her daughter's—sympathy; she risks losing both by exposing in egregious detail the seedy and insensitive side of her nature, the unlovable side of her love. Stanwyck brings us to admire something that is both herself and the character; she gives us a Stella that exceeds in stupidity and beauty and daring the temperate limitations of her literary model and all the generalizations about the second sex.

Again, in *Woman of the Year,* screenwriters Ring Lardner, Jr., and Michael Kanin did everything possible to sabotage the career woman played by Katharine Hepburn. In their hands she becomes a Lady Macbeth of overweening ambition with so little of the "milk of human kindness" that she is guilty of criminal negligence toward the child she and her husband Spencer Tracy have adopted. Tracy, by contrast, is a doting father—though never to the neglect of his newspaper work, which seems to say that love and ambition can coexist in a man but not in a woman. Yet, because of the strength of character and integrity Hepburn brought to the screen, and the soft and sensual radiance with which director George Stevens illuminated her (thereby contradicting the screenplay), she transcended the meannesses of the plot without in any way excusing them. . . .

Women have figured more prominently in film than in any other art, industry, or profession (and film is all three) dominated by men. Although few have made it to the seignorial ranks of director and producer, women have succeeded in every other area where size or physical strength was not a factor: as screenwriters, particularly in the twenties and thirties; as editors; as production and costume designers; as critics; and of course, and most especially, as actresses—as the stars who not only invaded our dream lives but began shaping the way we thought about ourselves before we knew enough to close the door. In the roles of love goddesses, mothers, martyrs, spinsters, broads, virgins, vamps, prudes, adventuresses, she-devils, and sex kittens, they embodied stereotypes and, occasionally, transcended them.

Some, like Mae West, Greta Garbo, Katharine Hepburn, and Joan Crawford, were institutions: stars powerful, eccentric, or intimidating enough to choose their projects and determine their own images, for at least some of their careers. Others, like Lillian Gish, Marlene Dietrich, and Monica Vitti were Galateas, molded and magnificently served by their Pygmalions; or, like Marion Davies and Jean Simmons, ruined by their patrons. Having made it as a star on her own, Norma Shearer sustained her career by marrying M-G-M's boy-genius Irving Thalberg. But not all of David Selznick's more tasteful efforts on Jennifer Jones' behalf (*Carrie,* with Laurence Olivier, William Wyler directing; *We Were Strangers,* with John Garfield, John Huston directing) could turn her into a star, probably because women didn't like her. There were actresses like Bette Davis and Ida Lupino who got off on the wrong foot through miscasting or mismanagement, but eventually found themselves. (In the You-Can't-Win department, Davis tells the story of being sent onto the set of the first film of a prop man-turned-director named William Wyler, force-dressed in a low-cut cotton dress that made her feel common, only to have Wyler turn to an assistant and say, "What do you think of these girls who show their chests and think they can get jobs?") There were others—Patricia Neal, Geraldine Fitzgerald, Mary Astor—who were also-rans, actresses of promise who never became stars, but who were as vivid in one or two roles as others were in a lifetime. . . .

And women, in the early and middle ages of film, dominated. It is only recently that men have come to monopolize the popularity polls, the credits, and the romantic spotlight by allocating to themselves not just the traditional male warrior and adventurer roles, but those of the sex object and glamour queen as well. Back in the twenties and thirties, and to a lesser extent the forties, women were at the center. This was amply reflected in the billings, which revealed the shifts in star dynamics from decade to decade. Women were often billed ahead of men, either singly, as in the silents, or as the pivotal member of a team, the dominant form of the thirties. In the forties, because of the shortage of male stars during the war, available leading men were treated as spear-carriers and made to follow women on the marquee.

Far more than men, women were the vessels of men's and women's fantasies and the barometers of changing fashion. Like two-way mirrors linking the immediate past with the immediate future, women in the movies reflected, perpetuated, and in some respects offered innovations on the roles of women in society. Shopgirls copied them, housewives escaped through them. Through the documentary authenticity (new hair styles, fashions in dress, and even fads in physical beauty) that actresses brought to their roles and the familiar, simplified tales in which they played, movie heroines were viscerally immediate and accountable to audiences in a way that the heroines of literature, highbrow or popular, were not. Movie stars, as well as the women they played—Stella Dallas, Mrs. Miniver, Mildred Pierce, Jezebel—were not like the women in print or on canvas. They belonged to us and spoke to each of us personally from what, until the sixties and seventies, was the heart and emotional center of film itself.

Yet, considering the importance of these women in our lives and their centrality to film history, it is astonishing how little attention has been paid them, how little serious analysis, or even tribute, beyond the palpitating prose of the old-time fan-magazine writers or the prying, lively, but no more serious approach of the "new interviewers." At one extreme are the coffee-table picture books, with their two-sentence captions; at the other, film histories that sweep along their predetermined courses, touching on actresses only as they substantiate whatever trends and developments are being promulgated by the author. The political, socially conscious school of criticism (for years the most influential) fathered by the Scots film historian John Grierson, established the line, perfectly consonant with Anglo-American sexual attitudes, that such matters as love, romance, and the loss of virginity were women's concerns and belonged, in a properly demeaned and trivialized fashion, to that untouchable of film categories, the "woman's film." The contempt for the "woman's film" is still a general cultural attitude, not only restricted to critics who mistake "important subjects" for great films (and what could be more important than love anyway?), but conveyed in the snickering response of the supermale, himself a more sophisticated version of the little boy who holds his nose and groans during the hugging and kissing scenes. Critic John Simon describes the dissection of the morality of love and the complex inter-play of feeling and conscience in Eric Rohmer's *Claire's Knee* as "triviality" and the "height of inconsequence." Most men, even in New York art-film audiences, would rather see *The Dirty Dozen, Deliverance, The French Connection,* and *The Godfather* several times apiece than see *Petulia, Sunday, Bloody Sunday,* or *The Touch* once. It is said that many wives got their husbands to go to *A Man and a Woman* for the automobile-racing scenes. . . .

We need more of a sense of film history, and of the context in which films were released and images were formed. Gloria Steinem can write an intelligent and sympathetic article on Marilyn Monroe, and yet miss the satirical point of Howard Hawks' *Gentlemen Prefer Blondes,* which consciously exposes Monroe's ooh-la-la image and the men who collaborate to maintain it. Betty Friedan can write a stolid appraisal of *Husbands* that, like most sociological criticism, takes no account of the film's failures and accomplishments qua film, but sees it only as a convenient substantiation of *The Feminine Mystique.* A soapbox feminist can excoriate Hitchcock in *The New York Times* for the rape in *Frenzy,* ignoring point of view, context, style, the complex interplay of misogyny and sympathy in Hitchcock, and the equally complex interplay of fear and desire by which women respond to the image of rape. Another critic can write a feminist critique of *Last Tango in Paris* as a male fantasy ignoring both the empirical fact that it is largely women, rather than men, who respond to the film, and the more subtle implication that our rearguard fantasies of rape, sadism, submission, liberation, and anonymous sex are as important a key to our emancipation, our self-understanding, as our more advanced and admirable efforts at self-definition. The same critic, offering a plot synopsis to substantiate her claim to the film's sexist point of view, reveals the irrelevancy of this technique, for *Last Tango* is about Brando, is Brando, and our reaction to the film will depend, directly and chemically, on our response to Brando. The plots in five movies may be identical, may all show women degraded and humiliated and chained to stereotype, and we will react differently to each one, depending on the woman, and the director's treatment of her.

For despite their impact on cinema, there have been few women in positions of creative authority that would have fostered the development of a woman's point of view. There have been shamefully few women directors (though no fewer, perhaps, than women orchestra conductors or prime ministers or reverends or stage directors), and fewer still in America than in Europe where the unions are less powerfully chauvinistic and the whole structure of filmmaking is looser. In an issue of *Film Comment*, historian Richard Henshaw compiled filmographies of the 150 women known to have directed films. Of the forty-five Americans, no more than five or six names are known to the general public (and of these, several—Lillian Gish, Ida Lupino, Barbara Loden—are known as actresses rather than as directors), and hardly more to film buffs.

The reason, aside from union prejudice, is obvious. Directing—giving orders, mastering not only people but machinery—is a typically masculine, even militaristic, activity. The existence of such a dominant authority figure—and in this respect, the great directors, the *auteurs*, impose their ideas more forcefully than the mere technicians—would seem to present an inherently sexist situation. Decrying such use of power, feminist film critics have hastened to disavow auteurism, but in the next breath they will raise a merely competent director like Ida Lupino to that category, by assuming she has enough artistic control of her projects and enough creative vision to invest her films with a subversive ideology. The attack on auteurism is less theoretical than emotional (and no less valid for that)—an expression of indignation that all the great directors have been men, rather a soundly argued dismissal of these directors and the historical tool (auteurism) that embraces them. For there are certainly subversive elements, obtrusions of a woman's point of view, in the work of men directors, particularly in classical filmmaking, before the twin male cults (director as superstud and superstar) converged to demote women, once again, to chicks, chattels, and pure figures of fantasy.

Lawless Seeing

For feminist media critic Annette Kuhn, the problems with media representations of women go beyond questions of their content. In the following selection from her collection of studies *The Power of the Image: Essays on Representation and Sexuality* (Routledge & Kegan Paul, 1985), Kuhn argues that the activity of looking at images constructs power relationships between women and men. Presenting oneself solely to be looked at—as women in pornographic pictures do—amounts to submitting oneself to another, to making oneself open and vulnerable. Feminist film critic Laura Mulvey noted in her study "Visual Pleasure and Narrative Cinema," *Screen* (vol. 16, no. 3, 1975) that it is precisely this power relationship that explains the pleasure that is involved in looking, whether at real people or at cinematic, pornographic, or other kinds of representations. Mulvey and others argue that in Western culture women are presented far more often than men as objects to be looked at.

They also argue that the incessant media representation of women as passive and willing objects of masculine sexual desire operates to *amplify* and *legitimate* real-life violence against women. It is important to note that in the following selection, Kuhn is *not* making a morally based critique of pornography, such as those mounted by other feminists and by elements of the so-called Christian right in the United States.

More of Kuhn's research into the relationship between film representations, gender, and sexuality can be found in *Women's Pictures: Feminism and Cinema* (Routledge, Chapman & Hall, 1982) and *Cinema, Censorship, and Sexuality, 1909–1925* (Routledge, 1988).

Key Concept: looking as a relationship of power

*R*epresentations are productive: photographs, far from merely reproducing a pre-existing world, constitute a highly coded discourse which, among other things, constructs whatever is in the image as object of consumption—consumption by looking, as well as often quite literally by purchase. It is no coincidence, therefore, that in many highly socially visible (and profitable) forms of photography women dominate the image. Where photography takes women as its subject matter, it also constructs 'woman' as a set of meanings which then enter cultural and economic circulation on their own account. Women appear in many types of photography: the glamour portraits of women movie stars and the quasi-documentary pictures of early twentieth-century prostitutes looked at in the last chapter are only two of many categories, each one constructing a different type of woman. Cultural meanings centred on the signifier 'woman' may become relatively fixed in use: but a certain range of meaning is still available.

It is true (if somewhat reductive) to say that in a patriarchal culture most representations of women are readable as connoting 'otherness' or difference—difference from the norm of patriarchy, that is. The fact that they do this in distinct and often contradictory ways in various media, genres and contexts is an important justification for the practice of analysing and deconstructing culturally dominant images. Pornography is of particular interest here because, in its frank obsession with sex, its construction of sexual difference is relatively transparent. The production of woman as 'other' demands that pornography speak both to and from a masculine subject position. This [selection] explores the question of how certain widely-used forms of pornography (the argument restricts itself mainly to pinups and softcore, venturing only briefly and tentatively into a consideration of hardcore and violent pornography) construct femininity and female sexuality as objects of obsessively repetitive investigation by spectator/consumers whose desire to fathom these mysteries is constantly being evoked. . . .

The question of what is to be done about pornography—however impertinent it may at first sight appear to be in relation to a project of deconstructing porn's strategies of address—cannot and should not be sidestepped. It may usefully be rephrased in the present context as an inquiry about the usefulness of the sort of analysis offered here. Such analysis can help clarify thinking in a notoriously difficult and emotionally-charged area, an area in which questions of policy and political strategy are always particularly prominent. Moreover, the activity of analysis may be regarded as a strategy in its own right: it seems entirely appropriate, by deconstructing its operations, to debunk and demystify pornography. There is perhaps a certain pleasure, too, in taking issue with porn's inflated self-image as sexually liberating, and so radically shifting the terms of a discourse in which pornography is constructed, by its defenders and its moralist antagonists alike, as a distinct and privileged regime of representation. . . .

What does pornography do? What does it say? Who does it speak to? Where does it speak from? On one level, the contemporary pornography industry may be seen as part of a general trend to increased investment in, and consumption of, leisure goods and services, part of that tendency to promote privatised forms of rapid gratification which characterises late capitalism. Accepting this, though, many would nevertheless argue that what is specific about porn is its preoccupation with a certain subject matter: sex. Is this perhaps what makes pornography so engaging and yet so disturbing? . . .

Whatever it does, pornography is, of course, exactly a commodity: it is produced, bought and sold. To the extent that porn participates in the disruptive potential of sexual passion, it is indeed dangerous merchandise. But in its attempt to articulate sexual fantasy through particular regimes of representation, pornography seeks at the same time to contain these very qualities of fascination and disruption—in the process becoming literal, earnest, clinical. Porn is often, in consequence, profoundly disappointing to its consumers, whose dissatisfaction may well be one of the things that keeps the trade so buoyant: there is always the hope, after all, that it can be assuaged by trying (and buying) again. Although its users often say that pornography is repetitive and boring, it is obviously dangerous as well, since it has to be kept out of sight. In order to maintain its attraction, porn demands strictures, controls, censorship. Exposed to the light of day, it risks a loss of power. Pornography invites policing.

If pornography is about sex, there is nothing at all straightforward about that, either. In the first place, it is unlikely that porn is *only* about sex. Moreover, it works in highly specific ways, deploying particular modes of representation in particular social-historical contexts. . . .

The word pornography, a nineteenth-century coinage, referred originally to writings about the lives and activities of prostitutes. In its earliest sense, therefore, pornography was rather limited in its approach to the representation of sex and sexual activity. This link with prostitution gives pornography a lowlife cast, which must have produced a titillating association with the desirably/undesirably forbidden, the illicit, the underground, certainly for consumers of a particular social class. . . .

When the term pornography first came into use, virtually the only medium in which representations could be reproduced in very large numbers was print. The printed word demands literacy, and not everyone was able to read. As a written medium, pornography was consequently limited as to the audience it could reach, and seems to have been something of a gentleman's pastime. Porn did of course exist in visual media as well: but paintings and drawings also found a numerically small and socially exclusive market. Engravings and broadsheets, which did not call for literacy, were rather more widely circulated, but were still by no means a mass medium. Developments in techniques of mechanical reproduction of photographic images and consequently in the capacity to produce large quantities cheaply opened up limitless horizons for pornographers. The apparent realism of the photographic image undoubtedly proved an added attraction for consumers, too. Mechanical reproduction of still photographic images, then, offered a breakthrough in the public availability of pornography. The advent of cheap, mass-produced visual pornography opened the market to the less well-off, foreign immigrants, the illiterate, the working classes.

Today, pornography using photographic reproduction and its variants is very much in the ascendant, while literary porn appeals only to a relatively limited market, attracting little in the way either of opprobrium or of censorship. Magazines and individual photographs deal in still images, while cinema—which entered the field of pornography early in its own history—adds movement and narrativity to the photographic image. Current growth media for pornography are television and video: porn users with the appropriate equipment can subscribe to cable-TV stations which broadcast nothing but softcore, or may rent or buy hardcore and softcore on videotape to view at home. Present-day pornography is produced across a range of media, from the printed word through to television, though the market is dominated by visual forms drawing on various conventions of photographic realism. As representation, porn also has genres and subgenres of its own, its own favourite themes and subject matters. In addition to mass-market pornography aimed at a relatively wide audience, parts of the porn trade also cater for sectional interests and minority sexual tastes. . . .

Probably the most widespread format in which pornography appears at present is still photographs, usually printed in books or magazines. Porn on videotape and, to a lesser extent, pornographic movies are also very popular, but their consumption requires hardware and/or premises which are not universally accessible. Pornographic photos, magazines and books can be easily and cheaply distributed wherever mail is delivered. They do not demand literacy in any language and are highly flexible—they can be consumed in many social circumstances and locations. At the same time, to the extent that pornographic photographs, as representation, have certain qualities in common with porn in other visual media, many of the arguments relating to this medium are applicable also to other forms of visual pornography.

One of the defining features of photography as against certain other forms of visual representation—painting and drawing, say—is its capacity to appear 'truthful'. Photography seems to record, rather than interpret, the piece of the world in front of the camera. A human artist may filter the 'real world' through her or his creative imagination, but the camera and lens are often regarded simply as pieces of machinery which allow an image, a duplicate, of the world to be transferred onto film. A photograph stands as evidence that whatever is inside the frame of the image 'really' happened, was 'really' there: it is authentic, convincing, true. But photography actually involves just as much artifice as does any other mode of visual representation. There is plenty of scope for human intervention at every stage of making photographs: photos are no more innocent of cultural formation than any other product of human society. Nevertheless, photos do offer themselves up as in some sense real, embodying a particular kind of truth: even if they do not produce their meanings in a direct, unmediated way they often seem to do so. Photographs say to the spectator: this is actual, this is how it is, you need make no effort to understand this, you have only to recognise it—isn't this just the way you see it out there in the world?

. . . The truth/authenticity potential of photography is tied in with the idea that seeing is believing. Photography draws on an ideology of the visible as evidence. The eye of the camera is neutral, it sees the world as it is: we look at a photograph and see a slice of the world. To complete the circuit of recording, visibility and truth set up by the photograph, there has to be someone looking at it. The spectator looks at the photograph, and the look of the camera is completed by the look of the spectator: the photograph says that these two looks are one and the same. Meaning is produced, finally, in the spectator's look: looking is crucial in reading photographs.

The spectator's look at a photograph is not limited in time, however: she or he may merely glance at the image, may study it at length, or come back to it again and again. This sets the still photo apart from other media—such as film and television—which draw on, but are not exhausted by, conventions of photographic representation. At the same time it is not usual, either, to look at a photographic still in isolation: it may be in a magazine, captioned or surrounded by print, or it may be one of a series of images to be read in sequence as a story in photos. The immediate context in which an image appears will set limits on the ways in which it is likely to be read.

The spectator's look, then, is key in the reading of photographs. This look distinguishes photos from non-visual forms of representation, and also from non-photographic visual representations. Moreover, it is inflected in specific ways in relation to photographic stills as against, say, movies. The spectator can choose to gaze at length, to return again and again, to a favourite photograph. Looking may turn into contemplation, even into voyeurism. The voyeur's pleasure depends on the object of this look being unable to see him: to this extent, it is a pleasure of power, and the look a controlling one. Photographs are well equipped to produce this kind of pleasure: the apparent authenticity of what is in the image combines with the fact that it is of course actually not there—and so can be looked at for as long as desired, because the circuit of pleasure will never be broken by a returned look. Authenticity, visibility, looking, voyeurism, pleasure—these are the terms through which photographs produce meanings for their spectators. But how does all this tie in with pornography's ideological project of constructing sexual difference by, in, representation? How is this project realised in pornographic photographs?

Any sustained examination of photographic pornography will show that it draws consistently on a circumscribed set of conventions of photographic representation. These conventions relate both to the formal organisation of the pictures and also to the kinds of contents and narrative themes that repeatedly come up in them. They do, however, vary somewhat between different pornographic genres: while softcore, for example, consistently uses images of women on their own, in most forms of hardcore women are not portrayed on their own and are usually less central to what is represented. In some instances—notably gay male porn—women do not appear at all. But pornography's ideological project of constructing sexual difference usually, though by no means inevitably, demands that women be represented in some way or other. . . .

[Consider a photo in which an] attractive woman takes a solitary bath and is carried away by the sensuousness of it all. The spectator sneaks a look at her enjoyment of an apparently unselfconscious moment of pleasure in herself: the Peeping Tom's favourite fantasy. Since she does not know he is there, he can take a good look at what a woman gets up to when she is on her own. He might even find out what women are really like, what their pleasure really is.

The voyeur's conviction is that the riddle of femininity will ultimately yield its solution if he looks long enough and hard enough. Since his desire is pinned to the actual process of investigation/scrutiny, though, the maintenance of desire depends upon the riddle's solution remaining just out of sight. Fortunately, the picture obliges. As a photograph, it starts out by exploiting the codes of authenticity attaching to the medium: the photo says that this woman, and so perhaps all women, do really pleasure themselves in this way. The spectator can indulge in the 'lawless seeing' permitted by the photo's reassurance that the woman is unaware of his look: her eyes are closed, her face averted. He can gaze as long as he likes at her body, with its signs of difference on display. . . .

At the same time, of course, the spectator is aware that he is looking not at life but at a photograph. At a certain point, the artifice of the representation reasserts itself. On one level, this adds to his pleasure. The disposition of the woman's face suggests that she is unaware of the spectator's presence: she does not look out at him, at the camera. This is reinforced by the spectator's knowledge that this is 'only' a photograph: she could never look back at him in any case, precisely because this is nothing but a picture. A photograph, however much it may pretend to authenticity, must always in the final instance admit that this is not real, in the sense that what is in the picture is not here, but elsewhere. This very quality of absence may augment the voyeuristic pleasure of the spectator's look. On another level, though, the artifice of the photograph will ensure that his desire remains ungratified. Since he knows it is artifice, how can he be sure after all that it really is telling him anything about femininity, about woman's pleasure? The question remains unanswered: he is condemned to endless investigation.

This kind of engagement depends upon the spectator's seeing the woman in the picture as other, as a fit object of investigation-by-scrutiny. To this extent, it is a masculine engagement—which is why I have used the pronoun 'he' when discussing the spectator. The photograph speaks to a masculine subject, constructing woman as object, femininity as otherness. This does not mean that female spectators cannot, or do not, engage in a 'masculine' way with photographs like this, nor does it mean that women cannot adopt a position of voyeurism. Masculinity is not the same as maleness, even if it may be conventional in our society to construct it so. Women can and do derive pleasure from images of women, a fact which betokens the unfixity of sexual identity and the fluidity of our engagement with certain types of image. If women enjoy this picture, it is possible that they are adopting a masculine subject position in doing so. There is another possibility, however. A spectator (male or female) has the option of identifying with, rather than objectifying, the woman in the picture. The photo might evoke memories or fantasies of similar pleasures enjoyed by the spectator. In this case the pleasure of looking is not completely voyeuristic. Indeed, an important attribute of this kind of softcore image is its openness: it may be read in a variety of ways. Its original context (a series of narratively-organised still photographs published in a men's pinup magazine) certainly proposes a masculine subject position for a male spectator. But other positions are possible, too. . . .

THE INVITATION

Pornographic images participate in photography's more general project of privileging the visible, of equating visibility with truth. But porn inflects this concern with its own ruling obsessions—sexuality and sexual difference—which are made visible, become a spectacle which reveals itself to the spectator. The spectator is invited to look—with the promise that he will derive both pleasure and knowledge from his looking. His quest is mapped out for him in pornographic photographs—which always speak to his desire for pleasurable looking.

The desire for pleasurable looking—scopophilia—manifests itself in a variety of ways, voyeurism being only one. In voyeurism, the subject of the look, the Peeping Tom, separates himself in the act of looking from the object, which cannot look back at him. But although the power inherent in the voyeur's look, the power of catching its object unawares, may be pleasurable in itself, the object's unfathomable desire remains. What if she is not interested in him after all? Pornography promises to circumvent such a threat to the voyeur's pleasure by saying he can have it both ways. While in various respects the photograph proposes that the woman in the picture is unaware of the spectator's look, the risk of her indifference is mitigated by the fact that her body may at the same time be arranged as if on display for him. This implies an unspoken exhibitionism on the part of the object of the look, thus permitting the spectator a twofold pleasure. This combination of visual pleasures is taken one step further in what is probably the most commonplace of all the conventions of pornography, of softcore in particular, the 'come-on'. . . .

The come-on is perhaps the more culturally prominent of the two staples of softcore pornography (the other being the image of the solitary woman caught up in her own pleasure). In both, though, facial expression functions crucially to produce meaning: if the one—the come-on—offers a direct sexual invitation, the other puts woman's autonomous sexual pleasure on display for the spectator. In pinup photos, the face is a key signifier, a central element in the image's production of meaning and its address to the spectator. It is never let out of the picture, for pinups cannot be as specific, nor as explicit, as hardcore in their reduction of sexual difference to bodily difference. Pinups, in consequence, are more open, capable of a wider range of readings, than hardcore. In a relatively open image, the fixation of meaning depends partly on the extent to which textual signifiers operate in accord with one another. It also depends in some degree on what the spectator brings to his reading of the image. In the instance of pinup photographs, the formal organisation of the images themselves, taken together with the contexts in which they normally appear (men's 'entertainment' magazines), would as a rule privilege a 'masculine' reading by male consumers. Their potential for instability, though, does suggest that pinup photographs may be open to a range of readings, particularly when placed in different contexts.

Facial expression, the come-on look in particular, is a key moment in the pinup's construction of a masculine subject position for the spectator. In offering itself as both spectacle and truth, the photograph suggests that the woman in the picture, rather than the image itself, is responsible for soliciting the spectator's gaze. In doing this, the photograph constructs her body as an object of scrutiny, suggesting at the same time that female sexuality is active, that women may invite sex. The pinup's singular preoccupation with the female body is tied in with the project of defining the 'true' nature of female sexuality. Femaleness and femininity are constructed as a set of bodily attributes reducible to a sexuality which puts itself on display for a masculine spectator. In these ways the pinup invites the spectator to participate in a masculine definition of femininity.

12.3 ELAYNE RAPPING

Hollywood's Mid-1980s Feminist Heroines

Elayne Rapping, a scholar and a critic, has focused much of her work on the representation of gender relations on television and in the movies. In this, she differs from earlier feminist critics who were primarily concerned with stereotypical images of women in mass media and popular culture. Rapping has written book-length scholarly studies, including *The Looking Glass World of Nonfiction TV* (South End, 1987), and she has published numerous articles in *The Nation, The Progressive, The Guardian,* and other journals.

In the following selection from the collection of her critical essays *Mediations: Forays into the Culture and Gender Wars* (South End Press, 1994), Rapping offers an analysis of TV movies that are aimed at women, partly in response to the critique offered by Susan Faludi in her best-selling book *Backlash: The Undeclared War Against American Women* (Crown Publishers, 1991). In that book, Faludi argues that by the mid- to late-1970s, mass media and popular culture in the United States had responded in positive, but very limited, ways to the issues raised by the feminist movement. For example, more independent female characters populated the movies and TV shows of the time. But through the 1980s, she contends, mass media reflected a broad and powerful backlash against the gains made by feminism. Independent career women were demonized in many Hollywood films, such as *Fatal Attraction.* Faludi argues that through the 1980s there was a return to the image of "happy homemaker" and nurturing mother as the most fulfilling roles for female characters on TV and in the movies.

Rapping responds to Faludi's critique by showing how made-for-TV movies aimed at female viewers have continue to address important women's issues raised by the feminist movement, such as abortion and violence against women. Rapping considers the representation of women on TV a hegemonic process, involving struggles over defining the social world. The producers of TV programs realize that they must attract—not alienate—their audience. However, Rapping does not say that all is well with mass media images of women. She shows how key social antagonisms and conflicts are translated into individual problems and are inevitably resolved, all according to the cultural logic of advertising-supported television, which almost never indicts the social system or leaves its viewers pondering ambiguous or "dark" issues during commercial breaks.

Key Concept: "domesticating" women's social issues

*P*owerful, autonomous women have never been strangers to the Hollywood movie screen. The weak, simpering stereotypes that feminists, since the 1960s, have brought so vividly to our attention—the sex kittens and servants, the Marilyn Monroes and June Allysons—have always had their tougher counterparts.

In fact, as Molly Haskell demonstrated in *From Reverence to Rape: The Treatment of Women in the Movies,* the heroines of the 1930s and 1940s were generally far more active, assertive, and in dependent than their 1950s and 1960s sisters. Stars like Katharine Hepburn and Rosalind Russell often played women with serious careers who went toe to toe with their male counterparts and in some case—Irene Dunne as the mayor of the town in *Together Again* or Russell as an advertising executive in *Take a Letter, Darling*—were socially and professionally above their male suitors.

Not that their positions were presented as unproblematic, of course. The conflict between work and love, "femininity" and "ambition," were central themes in all these films. As often as not these women were portrayed as deeply flawed and neurotic, or even, with the coming of *film noir,* downright evil. Joan Crawford, in *Mildred Pierce,* paid dearly for her business success, losing her husband and her children. Those women whose power—realistically enough—was portrayed as sexual rather than social or economic, were, in spite of their attractiveness, often shown as cold-blooded monsters. Joan Bennet in *Scarlet Street,* Barbara Stanwyck in *Double Indemnity,* and Bette Davis in any number of films were typical of Hollywood's underlying fear and hatred of the strong sexual woman.

The reemergence of the strong heroine in the 1970s was not, as is sometimes assumed, a great leap forward, although the "new woman" was presented differently, reflecting the influence of the newly visible women's movement, the changes in family life brought about by feminism, and changes in the economy and women's place in it. The most typical films of the 1950s and 1960s presented women in sexually and socially conservative, "Stand by Your Man" stereotypes. From *The Tender Trap* and *Pillow Talk,* to *Easy Rider* and *Alice's Restaurant,* women were seen as coy, game-playing man-traps or Earth Mothers.

No wonder, then, that the 1970s' preoccupation with "the problems of the modern woman," the breakdown of the traditional family, and the social upheaval caused by changing sex roles seemed progressive. Films such as *Alice Doesn't Live Here Anymore* and *An Unmarried Woman* seemed to—and in certain ways did—point out the very real oppression and diminishment of human capacity suffered by traditionally married women in families. In these films, the end of marriage—foisted upon the heroines by circumstance—was portrayed as liberating, offering the chance for growth, fulfillment, and independence at last. In fact, the futures of these heroines were not as realistic as they were portrayed to be. In both cases, a new, "better" man was a major part of the happy ending. In *An Unmarried Woman*—and this is typical of Hollywood's "women's lib" scenarios—class privilege allows the heroine to escape the most serious consequences of divorce, and the feminization of poverty.

In the later 1970s and early 1980s this genre switched its focus on women to the problems of men. In most "family breakdown" movies of that time, the father and husband suddenly becomes the "hero," the good guy who changes and grows into a responsible, nurturing provider/parent, while the estranged wife is the heavy. In *Kramer vs. Kramer* and *Ordinary People*, for example, it is Dad who "communicates," nurtures, and holds the family together while Mom is selfish, weak, and irresponsible in her emotional or actual abandonment of the family. Even in *Tootsie*, it is a man, impersonating a woman, who is the feminist heroine.

This brief and necessarily sketchy survey of major Hollywood trends in portraying women serves as background against which to understand the crop of mid-1980s films featuring strong independent women. For Hollywood, while responding to real changes in women's status, always has its own agenda, its own axe to grind, in its treatment of these themes. While its messages and images change, and are interestingly contradictory, it is not—with rare exceptions—wholeheartedly or sincerely on women's side. Without feminist interventions, it is Hollywood's style to "keep up with the times" while framing and limiting whatever apparently progressive messages it sends out in order to undercut the real demands and rights of women and to preserve the class- and sex-based power relations upon which our social and economic system is based.

The mid-1980s crop of movies featuring strong, independent women in responsible, successful positions provides an excellent opportunity to look closely at how this is done. The fall of 1985 gave us a remarkable number of releases featuring major stars in just such roles. Unlike any of the trends just described, these films actually took as a given that women were here to stay, in every important area of American public life, and that men, romance, and marriage were not indispensable components of a meaningful female existence. Five of these film—*Sweet Dreams, Jagged Edge, Marie, Agnes of God,* and *Plenty*—provide a nicely varied sample of the structural, stylistic, and dramatic ploys with which Hollywood manages to pay lip service to feminist themes and issues while at the same time seriously, if subtly, undermining those themes and demeaning, in many ways, the image of the "new woman" it seems to present.

That there are five—actually more—major actresses suitable to play strong female roles is itself a tribute to feminism and the women's movement. Jane Fonda, Meryl Streep, Jessica Lange, Glenn Close, and Sissy Spacek make up an impressive group, the likes of which have not been seen since the 1930s and 1940s, with the Crawfords, Davises, Stanwycks, and Bacalls. While the taint of "evil" associated with these women was gone in the 1980s, this new crop of women characters suffered from equally negative, if more subtle flaws, at least from a feminist perspective.

The five films fall into two categories. Three are standard Hollywood formula pieces, while two are more highbrow adaptations from stage dramas.

Marie is actually closer to the conventions of made-for-TV movies about women than to any theatrical film genre. *Jagged Edge* is a courtroom/mystery thriller and *Sweet Dreams* is a typical Hollywood star biography of country singer Patsy Cline, which traces her path from rags to riches to tragic death. *Agnes of God* and *Plenty*, in contrast, were originally plays.

It is interesting that the women characters themselves, and their respective fates, are in certain ways more positively presented in the less serious offerings. Jessica Lange's Patsy Cline, for example, is a tough, talented, ambitious woman who knows she's as good as any man in the field, and isn't afraid to push the point. Since the real Cline lived decades ago, some of the characterization in the film is anachronistic in its feminist spirit. "Hell, no," she hoots at the promoter who asks her if she wants to be Kitty Wells, "I wanna be Hank Williams!"

Cline is also, unlike the other heroines considered here, blatantly and aggressively sexual. Unlike the 1940s heroines whose sexuality damned them, she is not a temptress of adventures. She wants a home and kids and loves her husband, played by Ed Harris, to distraction. The film does a good job of dramatizing the tensions that arise within the marriage because of Cline's fame and wealth. In recognizably 1980s fashion, in their relationship the man is ambivalent about the woman's success and power. He falls for her because of her power and talent, but he wavers dangerously between adulation and resentment at what soon becomes his secondary role in the household.

Because *Sweet Dreams* uses the Hollywood star tragedy formula, it avoids dealing with the sexual issues it raises. In fact, while the fine performances of the principals tend to obscure this, it is the slightest and most meaningless of the films. It has no point, really, because it can't decide what the point of Cline's dilemma should be. So it lets life provide an easy out: early death for the heroine. Jessica Lange's performance is masterful and her character intriguing, but we never get below the surface of the character or the issues, and the film remains a clichéd piece of Hollywood fluff about celebrity and its tragic costs.

Marie, on the other hand, does have a point It too uses a hackneyed formula to get around the real issues of women in society today. It tells the "true story" of Marie Ragghianti, a formerly abused wife and single mother, who gets a meant-to-be token job in the Tennessee governor's office and proceeds to single-handedly and doggedly expose the corruption she discovers in the penal system.

Sissy Spacek plays Marie as a modern-day Dickens heroine. She is sweet, demure, immune to sensual urges, fanatical in her mothering and so honest and determined to "do the right thing" that she quickly becomes a tremendous bore to watch. In one scene illustrating her competence and drive, she ingeniously saves her son's life in a roadstop bathroom. In fact, her single-mindedness in questioning, facing down, and proving herself right against a doctor's erroneous diagnosis of her son's condition is exactly analogous to her behavior at work. There too she refuses to be intimidated or stopped by evil, incompetent, male authority figures. A court finds her innocent of trumped-up charges made up to fire her, and in the process exposes the state's financial hanky-panky.

Formally, this morality tale is dull as dust. In TV-movie manner it plods along from scenes of domestic violence, to the hard work of going to college while raising kids and caring for an invalid mother, to her professional triumphs and troubles. Nothing is unpredictable here. Nothing is emotionally, politically, or psychologically subtle.

The character of Marie was meant, clearly, to be inspirationally feminist. It is, in fact, reactionary, both politically and sexually. Since these movies rarely provide a social or political context for their messages, the audience is left with some implicit but dangerous ideas. For one thing, Marie is a law-and-order girl, after the heart of Ronald Reagan. She acts out all the patriotic, mindless rules about "doing right" and "obeying the law" that the Right so loves. In fact, her efforts, though this is never spelled out, strengthen the penal code and ensure longer sentences and less likelihood of parole for all prisoners.

That "feminism" was used to sell this message is significant, and it fits perfectly with Marie's sexual persona. She is a true Madonna—of the Immaculate Conception, not the Material Girl, variety—of virtue and maternal instinct. Women are working these days, the film tells us, but they aren't slighting their motherly duties or becoming sexually loose because of it. And their work is an extension of their domestic mothering role: to uphold morality and keep things organized and running according to God's will.

Jagged Edge, in which Glenn Close plays an attorney who defends an accused wife-murderer, falls in love with him, wins his case, and finds out he's guilty, is as slick and formulaic as *Marie*, but far more interesting as a film as well as a social statement. It provides a nice example of how Hollywood formulas subvert and co-opt whatever serious, socially threatening issues a film may raise. If Patsy Cline has no real character, and Marie Ragghianti is a modern Little Nell, Glenn Close, as Teddy Barnes, is a real, contradictory woman. She is tough, competent, aggressive, and independent in her work, but she is also emotionally vulnerable and needy, idealistic, and, at times, manipulable. She is a devoted single mother, but her kids are not her whole emotional focus.

She is, then, what early feminist film critics used to cry out for—a "positive role model," but with enough flaws to be credible. In subtle ways, nevertheless, her character—because of her femininity—is portrayed as less capable of succeeding in a man's world than soppy little Sissy Spacek. Most obviously, she is taken in by a cold-blooded sociopathic murderer who happens to be a hunk, with charm to spare. She believes absolutely that he is innocent while her DA opponent, a political cynic and sleaze whose methods are unethical and illegal, sees through the guy immediately.

This film presents a world in which men, and the institutions they rule, are hopelessly corrupt, immoral, and unfeeling. A good woman, no matter how principled and competent, is no match for the devious male minds she must confront. The suggestion that Teddy lets her heart rule her head is obvious. In *Marie*, the Norman Rockwell world buckled easily in the face of Marie's moral authority, while in *Jagged Edge*, a much more believable version of public life, Teddy buckles and can't really play with the big boys.

There are two aspects of the style and setting of this film that further subvert whatever progressive message it might have had. For one thing, all evil is seen to lie solely in political rather than corporate institutions, and in the hearts of individual "bad" men. Teddy, in fact, had worked for the sleazy DA, become disillusioned with criminal law, and moved over to what is presented as "cleaner" corporate work. From a Left perspective, this is definitely a frying-pan/fire decision.

The film's most clever subversion of social implications is the ending. Teddy actually faces down the killer and shoots him in cold blood, before he can kill her. This "solution" is a kind of feminist *Death Wish* ploy. The women in the audience are relieved—Teddy is dramatically returned to stature—but the problem of social evil, and of ruthlessness and violence in powerful men and their institutions, is ignored. Teddy represents many feminist virtues (if we ignore questions of class), but is socially and politically ineffectual precisely because of those virtues. She is left with no emotionally suitable male partners who are on her level intellectually or morally. The solution for Teddy is a retreat from public life, since her integrity and emotional priorities signal weakness, and, implicitly, social eccentricity, at least in the world she inhabits.

In all three films, we see the way Hollywood, at its commercial best, deals with social change and the demands of the relatively powerless. It is easier than one might think to present women as feminist role models and allow them to "be the best you can be," as a popular cosmetic commercial put it, as long as you can contain their strengths and virtues in a form which implicitly subverts their radical thrust. Popular genre forms, by definition, limit the scope and seriousness of subversive challenges to the status quo. The audience expects certain things and not others: it has been trained from childhood to understand these forms. Whether it's a star biography, an uplifting morality tale, or a courtroom thriller, most of the complexities and contradictions of American social and political life are left out.

The legal and governmental worlds of *Jagged Edge* and *Marie* are contained within the limits of the plot, the problem to be solved in a neat 90 minutes or so. No larger questions can arise about, say, the "left" or "right" of Marie's positions, or the political and economic context that produces the kind of corruption and immorality that Teddy Barnes confronts. We are primed to look for clues and happy endings, to find and expunge the bad guys. *Sweet Dreams* similarly flattens and frames the issue of success and celebrity.

Hollywood addresses some of the issues left out of classic pop genres in the stage adaptations. Not surprisingly, the images and fates of the heroines are a lot more depressing, for theses films were not necessarily made to be box office blockbusters. They were aimed, primarily, at a different audience—the relatively select group of thinkers and doers who read *The New York Times* rather than *USA Today* and watch the "MacNeil Lehrer News Hour" rather than CNN's "Headline News." Because they were meant to reach the educated "opinion makers," these films took feminism's challenge to established power far more seriously.

Their analyses of the "modern woman" were therefore more mean-spirited and philosophically devastating than the films mentioned above. In fact, both *Agnes of God* and *Plenty* represented a retreat to the Freudian, implicitly woman-hating and -fearing images of the 1940s. But the flaws upon which they focused, and the punishments meted out, were different. Because of the impact of feminism, it was no longer fashionable to portray sexually or socially power-ful women as Jezebels or unfeminine victims of penis envy. Instead, they had more demeaning, even pathetic flaws.

In both films, the heroines present real challenges to the legitimacy of powerful institutions and the assumptions and values that sustain them. In both cases, the filmmakers presented a broad, intricate picture of the workings of those institutions, and then proceeded to discredit the heroines' challenges through character assassination.

In *Agnes*, Jane Fonda plays an ultra-rational psychiatrist determined to prove that a delusionary young nun, Sister Agnes (Meg Tilly), who has borne and apparently murdered a child, was raped rather than "visited by the Holy Ghost," which is the feisty Mother Superior's position.

The ideological issues dominate the film. Anne Bancroft's Mother Supe-rior is a woman of the world—she married, had children, and finally turned to the convent as a solace (and escape) from the failures and disappointments of her earlier "normal" life. Fonda's Dr. Livingston, on the other hand, is single, childless, and has left the church because of her emotionally traumatic experi-ences with religion. The cards are clearly stacked from the start. Bancroft's reasons for turning to religion are seen as valid, since she is now content as she never was in the "world of sorrow" that society had been for her and for the young, emotionally disturbed nun. Agnes, we learn, was abused both mentally and physically as a child.

Dr. Livingston's life is less fulfilling. She is estranged from her mother, has no permanent man, no visible friends or family, and is all business, from her tailored beiges and grays, to her orderly, modern apartment. The church, on the other hand, offers a true community, tradition, culture, and the joy and passion that come with faith.

To see Bancroft and Fonda square off for the young nun's soul is to see Hollywood's dirtiest of dirty pools, where women are concerned. Bancroft, after all, is as tough and hip as Fonda, and more experienced to boot (she even smokes). But the institution she represents is anathema to feminist ideals, for reasons that surely don't need to be explained. Patriarchy, celibacy, retreat from social and political life—these are values that nuns themselves are fighting to change today.

In the end, the church wins and Fonda falters in her convictions. The film ends with a statement from the doctor to the effect that she has been moved and changed by the young nun's (deranged) faith and hopes that there just may be some truth to her religious beliefs, fantastic as they seem. Needless to say, the church in question bears no relation to the progressive church of libera-tion theology. The conclusion, therefore, must be interpreted as extremely reac-tionary, both sexually and politically. The "liberated woman" ends up looking very unattractive indeed, while mysticism and blind obedience to institutional authority win the day.

Plenty, which, like *Sweet Dreams*, was set in earlier times but informed by a 1980s sensibility, goes even further than *Agnes* in subverting feminist ideals, and making them, and those who try to live by them, seem seriously flawed and emotionally unstable. This time the setting and themes are political, not religious. Susan Traherne (Meryl Streep) had been a fighter in the French Resistance during World War II. She had loved the adventure and the sense of doing important work for deeply held political principles. Her return to civilian life is a letdown. She goes from job to job—diplomatic service, TV advertising, even office work—and finds them all deadening.

Plenty includes some truly remarkable lines and situations, given its early-1950s setting. Traherne's best friend, for example, is quite eloquent on the matter of male resentment of female friendships. At one point, Traherne enlists a young working-class man to father a child for her, which she will raise alone. At another point, we see her, the lone woman at a meeting, making a suggestion that is ignored, only to be enthusiastically endorsed when a male rephrases it. Her response is a cynical shrug of the shoulders; she is used to such treatment. Finally, in one of the film's great lines, she tells her friend that she rarely says what she really thinks publicly, in front of the men she knows, "for fear of blowing them out of the room."

This is clearly a woman modern audiences will find familiar. The film, however, sets her up from the start as neurotic. Even in her war scenes she is seen giving in to fear and clinging to a male comrade. While men—heroes at least—never behave this way in war movies, fear is not, certainly, an unusual or abnormal reaction to war.

As the movie progresses, she goes from shaky to thoroughly incompetent. She marries her diplomat husband in a moment of weakness and gratitude after having a "breakdown" when her attempts to become pregnant fail. From there, the film drags us through a series of embarrassing and increasingly hysterical scenes in which she breaks protocol, shocks guests, and at times viciously tirades against British imperialist policies.

When her husband finally castigates her for her "selfishness" and unrealistic fantasies of a better, more meaningful life and world, the audience is meant to feel, "It's about time." He is, after all, a long-suffering, loving, if dull sort, who "deserves" a wife who will help, not hurt his career. The final scenes, which find her in a cheap room, stoned, and reliving the idealism and excitement of her political days, are a damning indictment of what her husband sees as her wasted life.

The film never explains why she does not pursue what at one point seems to be an interest in painting, or why she stays in such an unsuitable marriage. But the unmentioned answer is obvious—this was the 1950s. Because the film and the heroine are so very up-to-date, however, it's hard to remember that. And that is exactly the point of the film's entirely sexist strategy. It takes a woman easily identifiable as a modern-day feminist, a woman of power, drive, and social concerns, and puts her in a setting in which these traits are only interpretable as "crazy."

The 1980s in many ways were a return to 1950s values. The people who have always hated and feared feminism were more influential than ever. It makes sense, then, that this movie, like *Agnes of God*, put forth an image of the "liberated woman" in a contradictory way. On one level, all these films support and accept everything the Women's Movement pushed for in the 1960s and 1970s. On another, more subtle level, however, they are stabs in the back: reactionary attacks on those very ideals. "You've come a long way, Baby," they all seem to say, "Now let's see how you like the bed you've made for yourself."

Hollywood's bed, plush as it looked, was not the one women ordered. Feminism assumes that society itself needs to change in important, democratizing ways. By omitting or distorting every aspect of the larger social world, and its effects on women, Hollywood gives women a message so depressing that it is almost a threat. There is very little in any of these films that would make a young woman envy these heroines. In fact, the Katharine Hepburns and Lauren Bacalls look a lot more enviable in every way. "You've come a long way," indeed.

CHAPTER 13

Media and
Race

13.1 J. FRED MacDONALD

The Perimeters of Black Expression: The Cases of Paul Robeson and Nat King Cole

African American documentarian and cultural critic Marlon Riggs, in his
film *Color Adjustment* (California Newsreel, 1991), argues that even in the
early days of "segregated" TV programs, such as the controversial *Amos 'n'
Andy*, commercial television has not simply presented racist stereotypes.
Neither has TV just progressed toward more realistic and enlightened images of African American life. Rather, Riggs says, commercial television has
undergone what he terms a constant process of "color adjustment." Forced
to fit its representation of race relations to the realities of social conflict and
change, particularly through the years of the civil rights movement, TV has
always made those adjustments according to its own peculiar cultural logic
(i.e., its relentless portrayal of the myth of the "middle-class, white, American, suburban dream"). Only if the image of African Americans could be fit

into the terms of this myth could it be represented in the living rooms of white America.

J. Fred MacDonald argues along these same lines in *Blacks and White TV: African Americans in Television Since 1948,* 2d ed. (Nelson-Hall, 1992). In this book, the author provides a comprehensive view not just of racist stereotyping on television but of struggles by African Americans to achieve fair representation within the mainstream of U.S. popular culture. This perspective on the representation of race relations in popular culture as an important part of the ongoing struggle for civil rights is shared by many African American media scholars.

In the following selection from *Blacks and White TV,* MacDonald shows how the state of wider race relations, together with the structures of commercial TV, placed powerful constraints on how African Americans could represent themselves within U.S. popular culture. He presents two examples: first, the direct, racially motivated censorship of Paul Robeson; and second, the limited success of the *Nat King Cole Show* of the 1960s.

MacDonald is a professor of history at Northeastern Illinois University in Chicago. His publications, which focus mainly on television, include *Television and the Red Menace: The Video Road to Vietnam* (Praeger, 1985) and *One Nation Under Television: The Rise and Decline of Network TV* (Pantheon, 1990).

Key Concept: racist constraints on African American self-expression

THE CASE OF PAUL ROBESON

Paul Robeson was a singular American. He was a brilliant student, graduating with honors from Rutgers University, and then earning a law degree at Columbia University. An outstanding athlete, he was named an All-American football player in 1917 and 1918. He was also a premier operatic bass, and a sensitive interpreter of folk music. He is well remembered as an impressive stage and screen actor. Yet, Robeson jeopardized his professional success by insisting that his first social priority was to speak for black Americans—that no matter what praise he received from the world of culture, he was still a part of an abused minority whose plight was dismal and whose champions were few.

Robeson used his international fame as a platform from which to denounce the hypocrisy of a society founded on personal liberty, yet tolerant of segregation, inequitable Jim Crow laws, and lynchings. In stressing his point, Robeson publicly announced his approval of the Soviet Union as the highest arrangement of social equality in the world.

Although Robeson was not a member of the Communist party, his passion for the betterment of African Americans frequently led him parallel to Communist ideology. Throughout the 1930s, he was a familiar spokesman for the Soviet formula: a blend of socialism, pacifism, and egalitarian rhetoric.

While he was tolerated in the Depression years, during World War II—a time when the United States was a military ally of the Soviet Union—Robeson became a political asset. He often appeared on radio as a spokesman for the Allied cause. On several occasions his voice was beamed around the world via shortwave. In his speeches and concerts, and by his physical presence, Robeson suggested that the lot of the black American was improving. In the fervor of the war against a racist Fascist enemy, his crusade against American bigotry seemed also to be reaching fruition.

The postwar world, however, was different for Robeson. Personally, he found in the newly established Progressive party a legitimate political organization through which to channel his reformist energies. As did millions of citizens, he rallied behind the Progressive candidate in the presidential elections of 1948, former Vice-President Henry Wallace. Robeson seemed genuinely inspired when, in a campaign speech in Washington, D.C., he told an audience, "We have taken the offensive against fascism! We will take the power from their hands and through our representatives we will direct the future destiny of our nation."[1]

The least of Robeson's postwar defeats was the dismal showing made by Wallace in the November elections. In a society now locked in a cold war with the Russian rival, Robeson's progressive politics were labeled "communistic" and "treasonable." He consistently suffered because of his outspoken political views. Speeches were abruptly canceled, concerts were called off, biographies of Robeson were banned from public libraries, and rioting often occured during his appearances.

His pro-Russian views put Robeson in an untenable position. When congress held hearings on legislation outlawing the Communist party, Robeson was asked to testify on the issue. When he proclaimed that it was "unthinkable" that American blacks would "go to war on behalf of those who have oppressed us for generations" and against the USSR, "a country which in one generation has raised our people to full human dignity of mankind," he was denounced by social leaders, black and white.

Robeson's alienation from American society reached its peak in 1950 when, in the midst of an anti-Communist hysteria aggravated by the outbreak of hostilities in Korea, the State Department revoked his passport. Until the Supreme Court ruled this action unconstitutional, Robeson was unable to perform at home or travel abroad. This "imprisonment" lasted for eight years.

It was in this atmosphere that he was invited in 1950 to appear in New York City on *Today with Mrs. Roosevelt*, a Sunday afternoon discussion program on NBC hosted by Eleanor Roosevelt. Robeson was asked to represent the Progressive party in a discussion of "The Position of the Negro in American Political Life." The public affairs show was scheduled for March 19. Joining him and Roosevelt were to be Rep. Adam Clayton Powell, a liberal Democrat, and Perry Howard, a black Republican committeeman from Mississippi. The program never took place.

Instead of discussing black politics, Robeson became the first person officially banned from American television. Less than twenty-four hours after his appearance was announced, it was canceled. The decision was made by NBC, although neither Mrs. Roosevelt nor Elliott Roosevelt and Martin Jones, coproducers of the program, seemed to resent the network directive. The NBC decision was bluntly pronounced by a vice-president.

We are all agreed that Mr. Robeson's appearance would lead only to misunderstanding and confusion, and no good purpose would be served in having him speak on the issue of the Negro in politics. The announcement that Mr. Robeson would be a participant was premature and I cannot understand why it was made.[2]

The banning of Robeson from *Today with Mrs. Roosevelt* was a reaction to an unprecedented barrage of public criticism which followed the march 12 announcement of his appearance. Most strident in its criticism of Robeson was the Hearst newspaper, the *New York Journal-American.* In the midst of the cold war, his newspaper specialized in sensationalism and innuendo. In glaring headlines and flamboyant stories, it "exposed" Communists in the government, Russian aggression around the world, and threats of an H-bomb and a biochemical World War III.

In its March 13 editions, the *Journal-American* placed on the front page the story of Robeson's scheduled appearance. Next to it was a story supportive of Senator Joseph McCarthy, who had just named two State Department aides as "pro-Communist." In the Robeson report, the black celebrity was described as "pro-Communist," "Moscow-admired," and "long a champion of things Russian." The paper quoted a black former Communist who had told congressional investigators that Robeson was secretly a member of the party with ambitions of becoming "the Black Stalin of America."

More effective in precipitating the cancellation of Robeson, however, were the hundreds of war veterans who phoned NBC about their displeasure. On September 12 and 13, the network offices in New York City received more than 300 hostile telephone calls. The protest was loosely organized by several veterans' organizations, and it was fueled by the sensational story printed in the *Journal-American.*

Following NBC's capitulation, veterans' leaders were anxious to trumpet their victory. And the *Journal-American* gave them news space in which to boast.[3] The state commander of the New York American Legion alleged that Robeson's appearance "would have incited hatred and bigotry." He contended that the presence of Robeson "on any NBC program would have been an outrage to every decent American." The New York State commander of the Catholic War Veterans agreed. He declared that his organization "believes that the time has come for broadcasting systems to become conscious of their great responsibility to American citizens."

Other officials were also happy to state their case. Another leader of the Catholic War Veterans was pleased with NBC's decisiveness. "We commend NBC's prompt action in cancelling the appearance of Robeson," he declared. He clearly hoped that this action was precedent-setting. "We want programs," the official asserted, "that will not feature any individual whose affiliations are in conflict with American ideology."

The war veterans, however, were not alone in attacking Robeson. Rabbi Benjamin Schultz of the Joint Committee Against Communism wondered why "anyone would select Robeson, an avowed champion of Russia, to speak for any section of American Negroes!" And H. V. Kaltenborn, the venerable NBC commentator who once had championed the cause of the Scottsboro boys and had spoken for the Loyalist, anti-Franco side in the Spanish Civil War, now blasted Robeson. Contending that Communists "are not intellectually honest," and that "deceit and falsehood are part of their stock in trade," Kaltenborn concluded:

> The issue of free speech for Communists would arise far less frequently and would be much easier to handle if we outlawed the Communist Party. It is an association of subversive agents of a foreign government. It is not a political party. There is no reason to grant freedom of speech to any member of a group which proposes to use it to destroy it.[4]

Robeson had few supporters. Except for the Baltimore *Afro-American* which headlined "Air Not Free at NBC,"[5] the black press remained strangely silent. A few union members, mainly the Harlem Trade Union Council, picketed the NBC offices. The American Civil Liberties Union also backed Robeson's position. It formally protested the network action as "censorship by private pressure."[6]

For her part, Eleanor Roosevelt was unrepentant. After first denying that she personally had asked Robeson to participate (the invitation was made to the Progressive party, and the party selected Robeson, its vice-president), Roosevelt told a delegation of angry Young Progressives that she would never share a program with Robeson "because it would give the impression that she endorsed his left-wing political views, with which she sharply differs."[7]

Robeson, however, was not silent. He used the occasion to attack NBC. "It is not surprising to me," he asserted, "that a huge network which practically excludes colored persons from its large army of professional personnel should balk at a discussion of the colored group in American politics which professes to present all points of view."

According to Robeson, NBC "evidently does not want colored Americans reminded too forcibly of the fact which becomes increasingly evident . . . that is, that there is no real hope for my people—American working men of the majority of the population—in the two old parties which are wedded to a program of cold war abroad and privation and suppression of popular dissent at home."[8]

The decision to ban Robeson from American television had political and racial dimensions. Politically, it was simply too controversial for a commercial network to air the views of an admitted leftist at a time when cold war tensions were nationally unsettling. Further, a young network was not going to incur the wrath of government and the public at a time when its investment in the nascent industry was substantial and TV was still not entrenched as a mass medium. When Robeson was rebuked by people as diverse as Jackie Robinson and members of Congress, questions about free speech were academic to NBC.

Without being enunciated, there was a racial component to the Robeson affair. He was an outspoken political activist. A powerful man with deep convictions, he was not content with personal success gained while other African Americans remained deprived. And Robeson was unrelenting. The day before his NBC appearance was announced, he was quoted as saying that "Russia's program of raising the little people of all races to basic equality in their nation and in the world is the opposite of what our country and England and the Fascists stand for."[9]

Because of his international and national prestige, Robeson was a political force. Because he was a black man, this force was inherently racial. Unlike other black spokesmen, Robeson was neither an academic like W. E. B. DuBois, nor narrowly focused like A. Philip Randolph—neither a reactive voice like those in the National Association for the Advancement of Colored People, nor tied to an unjust national system like those in Congress. From his cultural position, he brought humanistic criticism to bear upon the American conscience. In his rhetoric, moreover, he linked the African-American cause with decolonization in Africa and Asia and with the condition of oppressed people around the world.

Except for rare appearances by men like Ralph Bunche of the United Nations and Walter White of the NAACP, black political leaders were practically absent from early TV. It was unrealistic to expect network television to accommodate a racial threat such as Robeson. Magnified by his international reputation, whatever he had said about the condition of black Americans in 1950 would have had impact throughout the world. In censoring Robeson, network and program personnel were declaring that criticism of American racism was not permissible if that criticism was profound, uncompromising, and internationally provocative. The line of demarcation was clearly drawn: television would not tolerate militant African-American reformers.

That perimeter endured throughout the 1950s. Eight years after the incident with NBC, Robeson encountered the same situation when he was slated to appear on a local public affairs television program in Chicago. When in late March 1958, it was announced that Robeson would be a guest on *V.I.P.*—hosted on WBKB, the ABC station, by Norman Ross—popular reaction precipitated postponement and then cancellation of the appearance. Instead of a half-hour interview with Robeson, Chicago viewers saw a travelogue about India. Robeson was not only banned from *V.I.P.,* he was never permitted to appear on American television to discuss his ideas.

THE CASE OF NAT KING COLE

At first glance Nat King Cole appears to have been the diametric opposite of Paul Robeson. Nonpolitical and noncontroversial, Cole was a jazz pianist and vocalist whose mellow King Cole Trio enjoyed wide acceptance throughout the 1940s. In the following decade, when he disbanded his Trio and pursued a career as a singer of popular ballads, Cole continued to receive approval from black and white listeners.

If any black performer seemed destined for his own network TV series, it was Cole. He had already hosted an NBC radio series, *King Cole Trio Time,* which in 1946 had been sponsored nationally by Wildroot hair tonic. At a time when most African-American singers imitated the group harmonies of gospel ensembles, trios like the Ink Spots, or the rhythm and blues sound whose roots lay in less sophisticated folk music forms, Cole was a well-trained, disciplined vocal artist. Only Billy Daniels and Billy Eckstine rivaled him in vocal polish, and neither had the number of hit recordings produced by Cole.

Between 1944 and 1957, Cole had forty-five recordings which were listed in the competitive charts maintained by *Billboard* magazine. Several of these songs—"For Sentimental Reasons," "Nature Boy," "Mona Lisa," and "Too Young"—reached the number one position, and thirteen were listed in the top ten. In the period 1940–1955, Cole records were on the *Billboard* charts for a total of 274 weeks. This made him the ninth most popular recording personality in that fifteen-year period—ahead of such celebrities as Frank Sinatra, Doris Day, Tommy Dorsey, and Dinah Shore.

Cole did well in early television. He appeared on network TV as early as June 1, 1948 when he was the principal guest on the CBS human interest series, *We, the People,* when it debuted as the first regularly-scheduled program aired simultaneously on radio and television. Throughout the first half of the 1950s he performed as a visitor on most top-rated variety programs. Whenever he appeared with such personalities as Ed Sullivan, Jackie Gleason, Red Skelton, or Perry Como, Cole's style always elicited strong audience approval. In mid-1954 when he signed with CBS to make ten guest appearances, it was rumored that this was in preparation for his own forthcoming show.

Compared to Robeson and his social militancy, Cole was assimilated, unthreatening, and popularly accepted. While he was not the first black host of his own network series, as the top African American recording artist of his generation Cole had the best chance of success. The premier of the *Nat King Cole Show* on NBC on November 5, 1956 seemed to open a new era for black performers.

The program was a weekly quarter-hour feature which on Mondays led into the evening news with Chet Huntley and David Brinkley at 7:45 P.M. (EST). It was a spirited program with a pleasant mixture of upbeat tunes and slower ballads. Cole was backed by reputable orchestras—Gordon Jenkins when the show emanated from New York City, and Nelson Riddle when in Hollywood. An occasional guest, such as Count Basie, also enhanced the offering.

Cole was aware of the significance of his program. He referred to himself as "the Jackie Robinson of television." In 1956, he defined his undertaking as a struggle against racism.

> I have a fight right now in my own business in TV. I realize what TV is doing. I know they are freezing the Negro out. I know that no Negro has a TV show. I'm breaking that down. I'm fighting on the inside, without publicity.[10]

That conviction stayed with Cole throughout his television career. In September 1957, he told *TV Guide* that his program was "a step in the right direction" toward allaying network fears about black shows being televised to prejudiced viewers.[11]

Unfortunately, the seeds of destruction were within the *Nat King Cole Show* from the beginning. First, the program was never popular. Opposite on CBS was *Robin Hood,* one of the top-rated shows on TV, which attracted over half the audience at 7:30 P.M. . . . .

Coupled with poor ratings, the *Nat King Cole Show* suffered from lack of a consistent national sponsor. Occasionally the quarter-hour show was bankrolled by Arrid deodorant and/or Rise shaving cream. More often than not, the program was sustained by NBC. Cole seemed painfully aware of his tenuous predicament. The words with which he ended the program of February 11, 1957 were less than confident. With his theme song playing in the background, Cole told his viewers:

> Well, I guess folks, that's about it for tonight. We expect to be around this same time next week—same station—same show, we hope. Until then, see you later.

Despite poor ratings and a sporadic pattern of sponsorship, NBC expanded the *Nat King Cole Show* to thirty minutes, raised its operating budget, and as a summer experiment placed the program in prime time competition. The revamped show premiered on Tuesday, July 2, at 10 P.M. (EST). Opposite it was a formidable CBS rival, *The $64,000 Question*—the fourth-ranking program during the 1956–57 season.

Cole and his friends seemed determined to save the series by showing its potential to attract viewers. More important, the show became a battlefield in the civil rights movement. To rescue the most dignified black program in TV history, some of the biggest talents in show business volunteered to appear on the *Nat King Cole Show* for the union-approved minimum wage. Men and women whose energies commanded TV salaries in five figures now appeared with Cole for a few hundred dollars. Among them were Ella Fitzgerald, Tony Martin, Julius LaRosa, Peggy Lee, the King Sisters, Sammy Davis, Jr., Pearl Bailey, Robert Mitchum, Frankie Laine, and Mel Torme.

With a new time and an extended format, ratings of the *Nat King Cole Show* improved. When Harry Belafonte was a guest on the program of August 6, the show came within three Trendex rating points of its CBS rival. Cole later noted that his summer program was the top-rated show in New York City, and that it was eighth in the Los Angeles area.[12]

The insurmountable problem for Cole, however, was his failure to attract a national sponsor. Despite improved popularity, with no advertiser willing to buy the series, NBC was compelled to sell the time slot to the Singer Sewing Machine Company for *The Californians,* an adult western which premiered in the fall.

In defense of NBC, the network tried to salvage the program. It had sustained the series throughout the summer, and beginning September 17, it carried the half-hour *Nat King Cole Show* on Tuesday evenings at 7:30 P.M. (EST). Now the show was offered as a cooperatively sponsored feature. By this arrangement a local business, or a national advertiser wanting only single-market exposure, could purchase the show in a given city. Thus, Regal beer sponsored the program in New Orleans; Coca-Cola paid for it in Houston; in San Francisco its underwriter was Italian Swiss Colony wine; Rheingold beer handled it in Hartford and New York City; and in Los Angeles it had two sponsors, Gallo wine and Colgate toothpaste. Still, the program attracted only thirty sponsors nationwide.

As far as the network was concerned, the cooperative arrangement was not as profitable as having a single national sponsor. During the summer NBC had sustained the series in seventy-six cities. With a low number of co-op advertisers in the fall, the network demanded that the show be rescheduled in January to a less expensive time slot—Saturdays at 7:00 P.M. This move, however, was unacceptable to Cole. Given the day and time (6:00 P.M. in the midwest and 5 P.M. in some areas), a time when "most people are eating or shopping," Cole accepted the cancellation of his series. The last telecast of the *Nat King Cole Show* was on December 17, 1957.

The *Nat King Cole Show* was not a failure. For fifty-nine consecutive weeks it appeared on NBC. During that span, the network acted responsibly toward Cole. Unlike Robeson's assessment of the network, Cole praised NBC for maintaining "democratic and wise public relations"[13] in backing his efforts. According to Cole, his cancellation by NBC was a function of TV reality: "They wanted me on the network; they wanted to keep me. But they had to shift me around because I didn't have a network sponsor and shows with single, network sponsors get preferential treatment."[14]

Cole, however, did name a culprit in his television demise. The focus of his animosity was the advertising industry which, he claimed, never really tried to sell his program to a national account. For a man with a reputation for reserve and gentility, Cole was vitriolic when he wrote in *Ebony* that "Madison Avenue, the center of the advertising industry, and their big clients didn't want their products associated with Negroes." Cole asserted that he never found a sponsor because "Madison Avenue said I couldn't be sold, that no national advertiser would take a chance on offending Southerners."

Ironically, experience with television led him to a position remarkably similar to that of Robeson, the leftist activist who approved of the classless Soviet Union and its Marxian social and economic arrangement. "It's not the people in the South who create racial problems," Cole argued, "it's the people who govern the South." According to the singer, most southerners "are fine people. But those who govern isolate the people by advocating a rigid policy of discrimination; whether the people want it or not, they are not allowed to participate in mixed audiences because of their laws."[15]

As Cole saw it, bigotry was purposely nurtured by an influential minority, "those who govern and those who incite others through organizations such as the White Citizens Council."[16] Significantly, he dismissed most white southern bigots as small-minded people who worried about lesser matters such as "the mixing of the races."[17] But he attacked the "big men" who exploited the situation.

In Cole's quasi-Marxian analysis, "the big men" were those "who control Wall Street, the men who run Madison Avenue." And they, in Cole's view, "are worried about economics." In a statement worthy of Robeson, Cole wrote that "racial prejudice is more finance than romance."

Bitter, disappointed, and frustrated by his experience, Cole refused to blame his cancellation on southern prejudice, for as he noted, "After all, Madison Avenue is in the North." In absolving the South, he alleged that "I think sometimes the South is used as a football to take some of the stain off us in the North."[18]

In a conclusion with which Robeson would have concurred, he called upon all blacks to organize and assert their financial strength to offset "the big men." According to him, "We need to show the strength of the Negro market." He continued:

> Negroes above all, must become financially independent. All things, as intelligent Negroes know, boil down to money. We must, before it is to late, solidify our positions. We must support organizations like the Urban League and the NAACP. . . . They are all working for racial betterment. Negroes, too, must invest more, not only in entertainment enterprises, but in all businesses. We should put our money to work because money is what the people working against us respect.[19]

Emerging through the frustration in Cole's argument was an insightful description of the reluctance of the advertising industry to sell his series. Madison Avenue did not think the show would survive. Even with a new format and improved summer ratings, agency interest in selling the program to an advertiser was not kindled. At the base of this lack of enthusiasm was the sensitivity of Madison Avenue to the so-called Southern Market. Ironically, five months before the *Nat King Cole Show* premiered, *Variety* reported that pressure from advertisers with southern markets was "setting back by many years the advancement made in television toward providing equal job opportunities regardless of race, creed, or color." With the civil rights movement swelling in the South, national advertisers and their agencies feared offending white consumers who were resisting the movement toward integration. Their answer was to keep blacks off national television as much as possible. "At one major agency," *Variety* noted, "the word has gone out: 'No Negro performers allowed.' "[20]

After ten years of popularly accepted television, it was legitimate to wonder where by the late 1950s black Americans had gone. In a nation where more than 10 percent of the population was African American, TV was nowhere near 10 percent black. Several citizens openly expressed their bewilderment at this situation. Natalie Fuller Shean, a woman from New York City who described herself as "nobody, just a housewife," wondered in 1956 if there existed in television "a conscious ban against the use of Negro actors. . . . I see very few on TV, and I often see none at all being intelligently used on shows in situations where they logically belong."[21] Several months later Thurgood Marshall, then the special counsel for the NAACP, protested conditions in a letter to *Variety*. He wrote about "the spotty use of Negro actors and actresses on the legitimate stage as well as in television and films save in 'token' jobs or in stereotyped roles."[22] As late as 1959, a reader of *TV Guide* questioned in that journal: "Why can't some of the detective and comedy series work Negroes into their scripts, making them an ordinary part of television life as they are an ordinary part of everyday life?"[23]

The prejudice-free enterprise that *Ebony* magazine foresaw for TV in 1950 was nonexistent by 1957. Fewer and fewer blacks were finding significant employment in the television industry. The collapse of the *Nat King Cole Show* served only to reaffirm what many felt to be true: television was no place for African-American talents to seek success. Nonetheless, in the next stage of the history of blacks in TV substantial changes would be effected. Not because of any great liberal change of heart at the networks, but as an outgrowth of the dynamics of the civil rights movement, the posture of blacks in television would be substantially realigned and improved. In the late 1950s and throughout the next decade all social life in the United States would be touched by TV and its depiction of the black minority. In many ways, too, a growing fairness in that video image became a barometer of the nation's progress toward realizing its professed democratic ideals.

NOTES

1. Dorothy Butler Gilliam, *Paul Robeson All-American* (Washington, D.C.: New Republic Book Co., 1976), p. 54.
2. *New York Times,* March 14, 1950.
3. *New York Journal-American,* March 13, 1950.
4. Ibid.
5. *Baltimore Afro-American,* March 25, 1950.
6. *Variety,* April 5, 1950, p. 35; *New York Times,* April 3, 1950.
7. *New York Amsterdam News,* March 25, 1950.
8. *Baltimore Afro-American,* March 25, 1950.
9. Ibid., March 11, 1950.
10. *Ebony,* Oct. 1956, p. 48.
11. *TV Guide,* Sept. 7, 1957, p. 15.
12. Nat King Cole, "Why I Quit My Show," *Ebony,* Feb. 1958, p. 30.
13. *Variety,* Sept. 11, 1957, p. 22.
14. Cole, "Why I Quit My Show." p. 30.
15. *Variety,* Sept. 11, 1957, p. 22.
16. Ibid., p. 2.
17. Cole, "Why I Quit My Show," p. 31.
18. *Variety,* Sept. 11, 1957, p. 2.
19. Cole, "Why I Quit My Show," p. 32.
20. *Variety,* June 20, 1956, p. 17.
21. Ibid., Aug. 1, 1956, p. 24.
22. Ibid., Nov. 21, 1956, p. 2.
23. Jay S. Harris, ed., *TV Guide: The First 25 Years* (New York: Simon and Schuster, 1978), p. 45. This letter appeared only in the Northeastern regional issues of *TV Guide,* since letters to the editor were submitted and published on a regional basis.

13.2 MICHAEL ERIC DYSON

The Culture of Hip-Hop

Michael Eric Dyson, a professor at the University of North Carolina, Chapel Hill, is an African American cultural critic who applies many tools of cultural criticism to a wide range of issues concerning African American life, racism, mass media, and popular culture. His work is part of a wider movement of African American critical scholarship, which includes the work of bell hooks (see her *Black Looks: Race and Representation* [South End, 1992]) and Cornel West (see his *Race Matters* [Beacon Press, 1993]).

The following selection is excerpted from an article that originally appeared in *Z Magazine* and is reprinted in *Reflecting Black: African-American Cultural Criticism* (University of Minnesota Press, 1993), a collection of Dyson's critical studies focusing on such pop culture phenomena as Spike Lee's films, Michael Jackson's musical performances, Michael Jordan's status as a sports icon, *The Cosby Show,* and the culture of hip-hop and rap music. Dyson's purpose is not to evaluate these African American cultural forms as "good or bad," or "beautiful or ugly," in relation to the popular culture of white America. In each study Dyson dissects the relationship of African American cultural practices to a social order that has been constructed around changing race relations.

Dyson does not regard the representation of blacks in popular culture as a simple matter of racist stereotyping. The culture of hip-hop—the focus of the following selection—is particularly revealing in this regard because it involves a complex and contradictory response by young African Americans to the structures of racist domination. Dyson argues that most white critical response to hip-hop culture, particularly to what is termed "gansta rap" with its explicit threats of violence against white authority, errs by ignoring this point. Hip-hop offers a field for the symbolic expression of the difficulties of growing up black in the United States. Hip-hop, Dyson suggests, is a hegemonic field of struggle over defining social identities and social relationships—in this case, race relations.

Key Concept: cultural resistance

*F*rom the very beginning of its recent history, hip-hop music—or rap, as it has come to be known—has faced various obstacles. Initially, rap was deemed a passing fad, a playful and ephemeral black cultural form that steamed off the musical energies of urban black teens. As it became obvious that rap was here to stay, a permanent fixture in black ghetto youths' musical landscape, the reactions changed from dismissal to denigration, and rap music came under attack from both black and white quarters. Is rap really as dangerous as many critics argue? Or are there redeeming characteristics to rap music that warrant our critical attention? I will attempt to answer these and other questions as I explore the culture of hip-hop.

Trying to pinpoint the exact origin of rap is a tricky process that depends on when one acknowledges a particular cultural expression or product as rap. Rap can be traced back to the revolutionary verse of Gil Scott-Heron and the Last Poets, to Pigmeat Markham's "Here Come de Judge," and even to Bessie Smith's rapping to a beat in some of her blues. We can also cite ancient African oral traditions as the antecedents to various contemporary African-American cultural practices. In any case, the modern history of rap probably begins in 1979 with the rap song "Rapper's Delight," by the Sugarhill Gang. Although there were other (mostly underground) examples of rap, this record is regarded as the signal barrier breaker, birthing hip-hop and consolidating the infant art form's popularity. This first stage in rap record production was characterized by rappers placing their rhythmic, repetitive speech over well-known (mostly R & B) black music hits. "Rapper's Delight" was rapped over the music to a song made by the popular seventies R & B group Chic, titled "Good Times." Although rap would later enhance its technical virtuosity through instrumentation, drum machines, and "sampling" existing records—thus making it creatively symbiotic—the first stage was benignly parasitic upon existing black music.

As rap grew, it was still limited to mostly inner-city neighborhoods and particularly its place of origin, New York City. Rap artists like Funky 4 Plus 1, Kool Moe Dee, Busy Bee, Afrika Bambaata, Cold Rush Brothers, Kurtis Blow, DJ Kool Hurk, and Grandmaster Melle Mel were experimenting with this developing musical genre. As it evolved, rap began to describe and analyze the social, economic, and political factors that led to its emergence and development: drug addiction, police brutality, teen pregnancy, and various forms of material deprivation. This new development was both expressed and precipitated by Kurtis Blow's "Those Are the Breaks" and by the most influential and important rap song to emerge in rap's early history, "The Message," by Grandmaster Flash and The Furious Five. The picture this song painted of inner-city life for black Americans—the hues of dark social misery and stains of profound urban catastrophe—screeched against the canvas of most suburban sensibilities:

> You'll grow up in the ghetto living second rate / And your eyes will sing a song of deep hate / The places you play and where you stay, / Looks like one great big alleyway / You'll admire all the number book takers / Thugs, pimps, and pushers, and the big money makers / Drivin' big cars, spendin' twenties and tens, And you want to grow up to be just like them / . . . It's like a jungle sometimes / It makes me wonder how I keep from goin' under.

"The Message," along with Flash's "New York, New York," pioneered the social awakening of rap into a form combining social protest, musical creation, and cultural expression.

As its fortunes slowly grew, rap was still viewed by the music industry as an epiphenomenal cultural activity that would cease as black youth became bored and moved on to another diversion, as they did with break-dancing and graffiti art. But the successes of the rap group Run-D.M.C. moved rap into a different sphere of artistic expression that signaled its increasing control of its own destiny. Run-D.M.C. is widely recognized as the progenitor of modern rap's creative integration of social commentary, diverse musical elements, and uncompromising cultural identification—an integration that pushed the music into the mainstream and secured its future as an American musical genre with an identifiable tradition. Run-D.M.C.'s stunning commercial and critical success almost single-handedly landed rap in the homes of many black and non-black youths across America by producing the first rap album to be certified gold (five hundred thousand copies sold), the first rap song to be featured on the twenty-four-hour music video channel MTV, and the first rap album (1987's *Raising Hell*) to go triple platinum (3 million copies sold).

On *Raising Hell*, Run-D.M.C. showcased the sophisticated technical virtuosity of its DJ Jam Master Jay—the raw shrieks, scratches, glitches, and language of the street, plus the innovative and ingenious appropriation of hard-rock guitar riffs. In doing this, Run-D.M.C. symbolically and substantively wedded two traditions—the waning subversion of rock music and the rising, incendiary aesthetic of hip-hop music—to produce a provocative musical hybrid of fiery lyricism and potent critique. *Raising Hell* ended with the rap anthem, "Proud to Be Black," intoning its unabashed racial pride:

> Ya know I'm proud to be black ya'll, And that's a fact ya'll / . . . Now Harriet Tubman was born a slave, She was a tiny black woman when she was raised / She was livin' to be givin', There's a lot that she gave / There's not a slave in this day and age, I'm proud to be black.

At the same time, rap, propelled by Run-D.M.C.'s epochal success, found an arena in which to concentrate its subversive cultural didacticism aimed at addressing racism, classism, social neglect, and urban pain: the rap concert, where rappers are allowed to engage in ritualistic refusals of censored speech. The rap concert also creates space for cultural resistance and personal agency, loosing the strictures of the tyrannizing surveillance and demoralizing condemnation of mainstream society and encouraging relatively autonomous, often enabling, forms of self-expression and cultural creativity.

However, Run-D.M.C.'s success, which greatly increased the visibility and commercial appeal of rap music through record sales and rap concerts, brought along another charge that has had a negative impact on rap's perception by the general public: the claim that rap expresses and causes violence. Tipper Gore has repeatedly said that rap music appeals to "angry, disillusioned, unloved kids" and that it tells them it is "okay to beat people up." Violent incidents at rap concerts in Los Angeles, Pittsburgh, Cleveland, Atlanta, Cincinnati, and New York City have only reinforced the popular perception that rap is intimately linked to violent social behavior by mostly black and Latino inner-city youth. Countless black parents, too, have had negative reactions to rap, and the black radio and media establishment, although not as vocal as Gore, have voted on her side with their allocation of much less airplay and print coverage to rap than is warranted by its impressive record sales.

Such reactions betray a shallow understanding of rap, which in many cases results from people's unwillingness to listen to rap lyrics, many of which counsel antiviolent and antidrug behavior among the youths who are their avid audience. Many rappers have spoken directly against violence, such as KRS-One in his "Stop the Violence." Another rap record produced by KRS-One in 1989, the top-selling *Self Destruction*, insists that violence predates rap and speaks against escalating black-on-black crime, which erodes the social and communal fabric of already debased black inner cities across America:

> Well, today's topic is self-destruction, It really ain't the rap audience that's buggin' / It's one or two suckers, ignorant brothers, Tryin' to rob and steal from one another / ... 'Cause the way we live is positive. We don't kill our relatives / ... Back in the sixties our brothers and sisters were hanged. How could you gang-bang? / I never, ever ran from the Ku Klux Klan, and I shouldn't have to run from a black man, 'Cause that's / Self-destruction, ya headed for self-destruction.

Despite such potent messages, many mainstream blacks and whites persist in categorically negative appraisals of rap, refusing to distinguish between enabling, productive rap messages and the social violence that exists in many inner-city communities and that is often reflected in rap songs. Of course, it is difficult for a culture that is serious about the maintenance of social arrangements, economic conditions, and political choices that create and reproduce poverty, racism, sexism, classism, and violence to display a significant appreciation for musical expressions that contest the existence of such problems in black and Latino communities. Also disappointing is the continued complicity of black radio stations in denying rap its rightful place of prominence on their playlists. The conspiracy of silence and invisibility has affected the black print media, as well. Although rapper M. C. Shan believes that most antirap bias arises from outside the black community, he faults black radio for depriving rap of adequate airplay and laments the fact that "if a white rock 'n' roll magazine like *Rolling Stone* or *Spin* can put a rapper on the cover and *Ebony* and *Jet* won't, that means there's really something wrong."

In this regard, rap music is emblematic of the glacial shift in aesthetic sensibilities between blacks of different generations, and it draws attention to the severe economic barriers that increasingly divide ghetto poor blacks from middle- and upper-middle-class blacks. Rap reflects the intraracial class division that has plagued African-American communities for the last thirty years. The increasing social isolation, economic hardship, political demoralization, and cultural exploitation endured by most ghetto poor communities in the past few decades have given rise to a form of musical expression that captures the terms of ghetto poor existence. I am not suggesting that rap has been limited to the ghetto poor, but only that its major themes and styles continue to be drawn from the conflicts and contradictions of black urban life. One of the later trends in rap music is the development of "pop" rap by groups like JJ Fad, The Fat Boys, DJ Jazzy Jeff and The Fresh Prince, and Tone Loc. DJ Jazzy Jeff and The

Fresh Prince, for example, are two suburbanites from South West Philadelphia and Winfield. (For that matter, members of the most radical rap group, Public Enemy, are suburbanites from Long Island.) DJ Jazzy Jeff and The Fresh Prince's album, *He's the DJ, I'm the Rapper,* sold over 3 million copies, boosted by the enormously successful single "Parents Just Don't Understand." This record, which rapped humorously about various crises associated with being a teen, struck a chord with teenagers across the racial and class spectra, signaling the exploration of rap's populist terrain. The Fresh Prince's present success as the star of his own Quincy Jones–produced television series is further testimony to his popular appeal.

Tone Loc's success also expresses rap's division between "hardcore" (social consciousness and racial pride backed by driving rhythms) and "pop" (exploration of common territory between races and classes, usually devoid of social message). This division, while expressing the commercial expansion of rap, also means that companies and willing radio executives have increasingly chosen pop rap as more acceptable than its more realistic, politically conscious counterpart. (This bias is also evident in the selection of award recipients in the . . . rap category at the annual Grammy Awards.) Tone Loc is an L.A. rapper whose first single, "Wild Thing," sold over 2 million copies, topping *Billboard's* "Hot Singles Chart," the first rap song to achieve this height. Tone Loc's success was sparked by his video's placement in heavy rotation on MTV, which devotes an hour on Saturdays to "Yo! MTV Raps," a show that became so popular that a daily hour segment was added.

The success of such artists as Tone Loc and DJ Jazzy Jeff and The Fresh Prince inevitably raises the specter of mainstream dilution, the threat to every emergent form of cultural production in American society, particularly the fecund musical tradition that comes from black America. For many, this means the sanitizing of rap's expression of urban realities, resulting in sterile hip-hop that, devoid of its original fire, will offend no one. This scenario, of course, is a familiar denouement to the story of most formerly subversive musical genres. Also, MTV's avid acceptance of rap and the staging of rap concerts run by white promoters willing to take a chance on rap artists add further commentary to the sad state of cultural affairs in many black communities: the continued refusal to acknowledge authentic (not to mention desirable) forms of rap artistry ensures rap's existence on the margins of many black communities.

Perhaps the example of another neglected and devalued black musical tradition, the blues, can be helpful for understanding what is occurring among rap, segments of the black community, and mainstream American society. The blues now has a mostly young white audience. Blacks do not largely support the blues through concert patronage or record buying, thus neglecting a musical genre that was once closely identified with devalued and despised people: poor southern agrarian blacks and the northern urban black poor, the first stratum of the developing underclass. The blues functioned for another generation of blacks much as rap functions for young blacks today: as a source of racial identity, permitting forms of boasting and asserting machismo for devalued black men suffering from social degradation, allowing commentary on social and personal conditions in uncensored language, and fostering the ability to transform hurt and anguish into art and commerce. Even in its heyday, however, the blues existed as a secular musical genre over against the religious traditions that saw the blues as "devil's music" and the conservative black cultural perspectives of the blues as barbaric. These feelings, along with the direction of southern agrarian musical energies into a more accessible and populist soul music, ensured the contraction of the economic and cultural basis for expressing life experience in the blues idiom.

Robert Cray's . . . success in mainstreaming the blues perhaps completes the cycle of survival for devalued forms of black music: it originates in a context of anguish and pain and joy and happiness, it expresses those emotions and ideas in a musical language and idiom peculiar to its view of life, it is altered as a result of cultural sensibilities and economic factors, and it undergoes distribution, packaging and consumption for leisurely or cathartic pleasure through concert attendance or record buying. Also, in the process, artists are sometimes removed from the immediate context and original site of their artistic production. Moreover, besides the everyday ways in which the music is used for a variety of entertainment functions, it may occasionally be employed in contexts that undermine its critique of the status quo, and it may be used to legitimize a cultural or social setting that, in negative ways, has partially given rise to its expression.

Interestingly, a new wave of rap artists may be accomplishing this goal, but with foreboding consequences. For example, N.W.A. (Niggaz With Attitudes) reflects the brutal circumstances that define the boundaries within which most ghetto poor black youth in Los Angeles must live. For the most part they—unlike their socially conscientious counterparts Public Enemy, Boogie Down Productions, and Stetsasonic—have no ethical remove from the violence, gang-bangin', and drugs in L.A.'s inner city. In their song "——Tha Police," N.W.A. gives a sample of their reality:

> . . . A young nigger got it bad 'cause I'm brown / And not the other color, so police think, / They have the authority to kill a minority / . . . Searchin' my car looking for the product, / Thinkin' every nigger is sellin' narcotic / . . . But don't let it be a black and a white one, / 'Cause they'll slam ya down to the street top, / Black police showin' out for the white cop.

Such expressions of violence certainly reflect the actual life circumstances of many black and Latino youth caught in the desperate cycle of drugs and gangs involved in L.A. ghetto living. N.W.A. celebrates a lethal mix of civil terrorism and personal cynicism. Their attitude is both one answer to, and the logical outcome of, the violence, racism, and oppression in American culture. On the other hand, their vision must be criticized, for the stakes are too high for the luxury of moral neutrality. Having at least partially lived the life they rap about, N.W.A. understands the viciousness of police brutality. However, they must also be challenged to develop an ethical perspective on the drug gangs that duplicate police violence in black-on-black crime. While rappers like N.W.A. perform an invaluable service by rapping in poignant and realistic terms about urban underclass existence, they must be challenged to expand their moral vocabulary and be more sophisticated in their understanding that description alone is insufficient to address the crises of black urban life. . . .

Also problematic is the sexist sentiment that pervades so much of rap music. It is a rampant sexism that continues to mediate the relations within the younger black generation with lamentable intensity. While it is true that rap's sexism is indeed a barometer of the general tenor and mood that mediates black male-female relations, it is not the role of women alone to challenge it. Reproach must flow from women *and* men who are sensitive to the ongoing sexist attitudes and behavior that dominate black male-female relationships. . . .

Fortunately, many of the problems related to rap—particularly with black radio, media, and community acceptance—have only fostered a sense of camaraderie that transcends in crucial ways the fierce competitive streak in rap (which, at its best moments, urges rappers on to creative musical heights). While the "dis" rap . . . is alive and well, the overall feeling among rap artists that rap must flourish outside the sanctions of traditional means of garnering high visibility or securing record sales has directed a communal energy into the production of their music. The current state of affairs has also precipitated cooperative entrepreneurial activity among young black persons. The rap industry has spawned a number of independent labels, providing young blacks (mostly men) with experience as heads of their own businesses and with exposure as managers of talent, positions that might otherwise be unavailable to them. Until recently, rap flourished, for the most part, outside of the tight artistic and economic constraints imposed by major music corporations. Although many independent companies have struck distribution deals with major labels—such as Atlantic, MCA, Columbia, and Warner Brothers—it has usually been the case, until the late 1980s, that the inexperience of major labels with rap, coupled with their relatively conservative musical tastes, has enabled the independent labels to control their destinies by teaching the major music corporations invaluable lessons about street sales, the necessity of having a fast rate of delivery from the production of a record to its date of distribution, and remaining close to the sensibilities of the street, while experimenting with their marketing approach in ways that reflect the diversification of styles in rap.

Rap expresses the ongoing preoccupation with literacy and orality that has characterized African-American communities since the inception of legally coerced illiteracy during slavery. Rap artists explore grammatical creativity, verbal wizardry, and linguistic innovation in refining the art of oral communication. The rap artist, as Cornel West has indicated, is a bridge figure who combines the two potent traditions in black culture: preaching and music. The rap artist appeals to the rhetorical practices eloquently honed in African-American religious experiences and the cultural potency of black singing/musical traditions to produce an engaging hybrid. They are truly urban griots dispensing social and cultural critique, verbal shamans exorcising the demons of cultural amnesia. The culture of hip-hop has generated a lexicon of life that expresses rap's B-boy/B-girl worldview, a perspective that takes delight in undermining "correct" English usage while celebrating the culturally encoded phrases that communicate in rap's idiom.

Rap has also retrieved historic black ideas, movements, and figures in combating the racial amnesia that threatens to relegate the achievements of the black past to the ash heap of dismemory. Such actions have brought a renewed sense of historical pride to young black minds that provides a solid base for racial self-esteem. Rap music has also focused renewed attention on black nationalist and black radical thought. This revival has been best symbolized by the rap group Public Enemy. Public Enemy announced its black nationalism in embryonic form on their first album, *Yo! Bum Rush the Show,* but their vision sprang forward full-blown in their important *It Takes a Nation of Millions to Hold Us Back.* The album's explicit black nationalist language and cultural sensibilities were joined with a powerful mix of music, beats, screams, noise, and rhythms from the streets. Its message is provocative, even jarring, a précis of the contained chaos and channeled rage that informs the most politically astute rappers. On the cut "Bring the Noise," they intone:

> We got to demonstrate, come on now, they're gonna have to wait / Till we get it right / Radio stations I question their blackness / They call themselves black, but we'll see if they'll play this / Turn it up! Bring the noise!

Public Enemy also speaks of the criminality of prison conditions and how dope dealers fail the black community. Their historical revivalism is noteworthy, for instance, as they rap on "Party for Your Right to Fight":

> Power Equality / And we're out to get it / I know some of you ain't wit' it / This party started right in '66 / With a pro-Black radical mix / Then at the hour of twelve / . . . J. Edgar Hoover, and he coulda' proved to 'ya / He had King and X set up / Also the party with Newton, Cleaver, and Seale / . . . Word from the honorable Elijah Muhummad / Know who you are to be Black / . . . the original Black Asiatic man.

Public Enemy troubled even more sociocultural waters with their Nation of Islam views, saying in "Don't Believe the Hype":

> The follower of Farrakhan / Don't tell me that you understand / Until you hear the man.

Such rap displays the power and pitfalls associated with the revival of earlier forms of black radicalism, nationalism, and cultural expression. The salutary aspect of the historical revival is that it raises consciousness about important figures, movements, and ideas, prompting rappers to express their visions of life in American culture. This renewed historicism permits young blacks to discern links between the past and their own present circumstances, using the past as a fertile source of social reflection, cultural creation, and political resistance.

On the other hand, it has also led to perspectives that do not provide *critical* reflection on the past. Rather, many rappers attempt to duplicate the past without challenging or expanding it. Thus, their historical insight fails to illumine our current cultural problems as powerfully as it might, and the present generation of black youth fails to benefit as fully from the lessons that it so powerfully revives. This is an unfortunate result of the lack of understanding and communication among various segments of the black community, particularly along generational and class lines, problems symbolized in the black community's response to rap. Historical revival cries out for contexts that render the past understandable and usable. This cannot occur if large segments of the black community continue to be segregated from one of the most exciting cultural transformations occurring in contemporary American life: the artistic expression, cultural exploration, political activity, and historic revival of hip-hop artists. . . .

Rap is a form of profound musical, cultural, and social creativity. It expresses the desire of young black people to reclaim their history, reactivate forms of black radicalism, and contest the powers of despair and economic depression that presently besiege the black community. Besides being the most powerful form of black musical expression today, rap projects a style of self into the world that generates forms of cultural resistance and transforms the ugly terrain of ghetto existence into a searing portrait of life as it must be lived by millions of voiceless people. For that reason alone, rap deserves attention and should be taken seriously; and for its productive and healthy moments, it should be promoted as a worthy form of artistic expression and cultural projection and an enabling source of black juvenile and communal solidarity.

Boyz N the Hood *and* Jungle Fever

Michele Wallace, together with other African American women critics such as bell hooks, combines feminist concerns with a specific focus on African American popular culture. In her ground-breaking study *Black Macho and the Myth of the Superwoman* (Dial, 1979), she argued that the importance of the struggle for self-representation in the mass media should not hide the problem of gender domination within African American society. "Black-macho" is, in part, a response by African American men to wider racist oppression in America. The celebration of this sort of masculinity in the "blaxploitation" films of the 1970s, such as *Shaft*, hurt both black men and black women, in particular by legitimating violence toward black women. Wallace has since extended and refined this analysis, as can be seen in the collection of her studies entitled *Invisibility Blues* (Verso, 1990).

The following selection is from "*Boyz N the Hood* and *Jungle Fever*," in Gina Dent, ed., *Black Popular Culture* (Bay Press, 1992). In it, Wallace examines recent popular films made by John Singleton and Spike Lee. She recalls that when she first saw Singleton's *Boyz N the Hood,* she was overwhelmed by the dramatic power of its representation of African American life. However, after a second viewing of the film, she became troubled by its representation of women. Wallace saw young, black, male film-makers, such as Singleton and Lee, demonizing single, black mothers, in particular their sexuality. Thus, at the very moment that such movies powerfully dramatize the joys and tragedies of African American life, they obscure the plight of black women. As a result, Wallace argues, black feminist viewers can "enjoy [their] own symbolic decimation"—a socially dangerous situation.

Key Concept: the demonization of single, black mothers

*T*he first time I saw John Singleton's *Boyz N the Hood,* I was completely swept away by the drama and the tragedy. It was like watching the last act of

Hamlet or *Titus Andronicus* for the first time. When I left the theater, I was crying for all the dead black men in my family.

In the neighborhood in Brooklyn where I live, I began to see *Boyz N the Hood* T-shirts instead of the "Stop the Violence" T-shirts of the months before. Unlike *New Jack City*, which celebrated violence with all the abandon of the old cowboy movies, *Boyz N the Hood* really seemed to try to take a critical stance toward violence. It could even be seen as a valid symbolic response to the then-recent beating of Rodney King by the Los Angeles Police Department. Moreover, through the popularity of this film, space for the acknowledgment of the alarming rates of black male homicide and incarceration grew in the dominant discourse.

But then, a black single mother brought the demonization of black single mothers in the film to my attention. In a second viewing of *Boyz N the Hood*, what made me most uneasy about the portrayal of these single black mothers was how little we're told about them, how we, as viewers, are encouraged, on the basis of crucial visual cues, to come to stereotypical conclusions about these women. We never find out what Tre's mother does for a living, whether or not Dougbboy's mother works, is on welfare, or has ever been married, or anything whatsoever about the single black mother whose babies run in the street.

I began to think about some other alarming trends in relation to the new black films:

First, black women filmmakers, not to mention black feminist film criticism, were becoming unimaginable.[1]

Second, the focus on violence against black men in particular only serves to further mystify the plight of women and girls in black communities. It's as though their condition were somehow subsidiary and derivative. As usual, it is the people who control the guns (and the phalluses) who bog the limelight.

Before *Boyz N the Hood*, there were two kinds of black female characters in film—whores and good girls. Following "race" film conventions set in the days of *Cabin in the Sky* and *Stormy Weather*, these women were all portrayed as lightweight (and more often than not, light-skinned) cartoon characters. The peak of this trend is Robin Givens's recent performance in *A Rage in Harlem*, where she plays the ebony femme fatale.

In *Boyz N the Hood*, however, a third kind of black female character appears. I call her the Shahrazad Ali nightmare: single black mothers who are white-identified and drink espresso (the Buppie version), or who . . . allow their children to run in the streets while they offer blow jobs in exchange for drugs (the underclass version).

Shahrazad Ali, in case you've forgotten, was the big hit of the summer of 1990 with her book, *The Blackman's Guide to Understanding the Blackwoman*.[2] This book offered its target reader—the black man—insight into the secret workings of the black female mind. Yet, despite Ali's insistence that the book was "the culmination of many years of study, observation and research," it was almost impossible to deduce what her sources were from reading it.

She never refers to a single text, other than the Bible, even in passing, much less by title or author or in a footnote. Although we might well expect such an author to rely heavily upon personal experience, testimony, and observation, she never uses the first person singular. You know as little about Ali when you finish the book as you did when you picked it up.

And she is no journalist either. She never describes the communities she's visited and observed or points out relevant items in the news. From this book, you would never know that Jesse Jackson was narrowly defeated in the race for the Democratic nomination for president, that Spike Lee made movies, or that playwright August Wilson wins Pulitzer Prizes. Nor would you know that the highways and byways of our major cities are flooded with the homeless—man, woman, and child—because of a depraved economic sensibility that values wealth and ostentatious consumption in all races and both genders over decency to the poor.

There isn't a glimmer of contemporary culture or society, just a vague yet insuperable cloud called the "problem with black women." Although she calls the black woman "nearly psychotic" and liberally resorts to all sorts of pseudo-psychological terminology to describe the black woman's affliction (which often sounds a lot like chronic depression), she doesn't refer to a single case study or even an interview with a friend. Her style is declamatory. For 180 pages, she insists upon the shortcomings of the black woman by the sheer force of argument. In the process, she becomes an omniscient narrator with a vengeance—as though she was gifted with the power to read all black women's minds.

If mistaken for "real life" instead of symbolic representation, I am afraid that a movie like *Boyz N the Hood* engages in the same brand of opaque cultural analysis. Its formula is simple and straightforward. The boys who don't have fathers fail. The boys who do have fathers succeed. And the success of such a movie at the box office reflects its power to confirm hegemonic family values.

Spike Lee's *Jungle Fever,* although a much more complicated film, made me even more uncomfortable for much the same reason. Especially in the context of symbolic representations, gender and race have no essential, irreducible meanings, only the ones we assign them to get from "here" to "there." But neither John Singleton nor Spike Lee is aware of how gender and race are socially and culturally constructed. And whereas Singleton is highly effective in naturalizing his black postnationalist essentialism in *Boyz N the Hood*, Lee is less successful at the same project when he takes on interracial sex.

Jungle Fever is not as easy to decode as *Boyz N the Hood*. At the narrative level, the film tells three interrelated stories. In the first and most important of these, a black male architect, Flipper Purify (Wesley Snipes) is married to Drew (Lonette McKee), a buyer at Bloomingdale's. Their pre-adolescent daughter attends a public school in Harlem, and the family lives in a brownstone on Strivers Row, one of two middle-class blocks in the middle of the worst section of Harlem.

At the architectural firm where he works, Flipper becomes sexually involved with Angie Tucci (Annabella Sciorra), a white temporary secretary who lives with her father and brothers in Bensonhurst. Working late evenings, in a series of extremely brief scenes—one never gets the impression that they either know or really like each other—Angie and Flipper end up having sex on Flipper's drawing board.

In the outdoor night scene that follows, Flipper tells his best friend, Cyrus (Spike Lee), a high school teacher, that he is "cheating on Drew" with a white woman. "You got the fever—the both of yous!" Cyrus responds, meaning "Jungle fever." Jungle fever turns out to be a condition in which blacks and whites (Asians, Native Americans, and Latinos appear to be both immune to the disease and irrelevant to the narrative) become intimately involved because of their curiosity about racial difference (perish the thought) rather than for love.

From this moment on, the film treats Angie's and Flipper's jungle fever much like a crime. In two dramatic parallel scenes, Drew evicts Flipper from their Harlem apartment, and Angie's father beats her up and throws her out of the house in Bensonhurst. Flipper is even forced out of his white architectural firm. Self-described "outcasts" in their own communities, Angie and Flipper take an apartment together. When it doesn't work out (and there was never any possibility that it would), Flipper goes back to Drew, and Angie goes back to her family.

The film's second story concerns Flipper's crack-addict brother, Gator (Sam Jackson), and his relationship to their mother, a housewife, and father, The Good Doctor Reverend Purify, a fanatical born-again Christian who forbids Gator to enter the house. Yet, Gator is always at the door seeking money for crack from his mother (played by Ruby Dee). The eery *mise en scène* of the parents' home—the mausoleum decor, the constant playing of Mahalia Jackson records, even the frightened sexually repressed demeanor of the reverend's wife—hint strongly that Gator's addiction was caused by the reverend's criminally bad fathering.

The third story revolves around Paulie (John Turturro), Angie's boyfriend, who lives with his father (Anthony Quinn) and runs a candy store in Bensonhurst that also serves as a hangout for a group of Italian-American men. These men are extremely vocal about their racial attitudes.

They hate blacks, we come to understand, partly because of their own fear that as Italians they don't look as white as they should. Their envy of whiteness and blondeness is viewed as an integral part of their loathing of blackness. But their hatred of blackness doesn't preclude their sexual interest in black women. In one of the most striking lines of the film, one of them says, "You know colored women, . . . You put a saddle on them and ride them into the sunset."

From the beginning, it is clear that Paulie is uncomfortable with the virulent, expressive racism of his clientele and is interested in Orin Goode (Tyra Ferrell), a black woman who comes into the store to ask him to order the *New York Times* and to encourage him to apply to Brooklyn College. Although Paulie receives a cursory beating from his friends while on his way to visit Orin, he gives as good as he gets. And when he arrives at Orin's door, the implication is that he's finally been successful in throwing off the burden of his father's restrictive view of marriage and family.

But what this film is really about is the threat of a female or aberrant sexuality to traditional family values. The film begins with a series of shots that establish The Cosby Show family–type locale of a middle-class urban environment in the early morning. The camera tracks a little boy on a bike delivering newspapers. After a close-up of a rolled copy of the *New York Times* being thrown onto the sidewalk in front of the house, the next shot zooms up and into the house. Reminiscent of the more impressive opening shot of *Psycho*, this shot takes us directly into Drew and Flipper's bedroom where they are having sexual intercourse. Drew's screams get progressively louder as she begins to shout, "Don't wake the baby!" The camera cuts to their daughter Ming's bedroom, where Ming sits up in bed, her eyes wide open, and slowly smiles.

Later, when father, mother, and daughter are having breakfast together, Ming asks, "Why is Daddy always hurting Mommy?" When Drew explains that they were making love, Ming says she was only testing to see whether or not they would tell the truth. Flipper then walks Ming to school. On the street, Ming's and Flipper's expensive, neat attire is juxtaposed with the garbage and graffiti, the drug addicts and abandoned buildings.

This short sequence of shots, which goes from Drew's and Flipper's bedroom to Ming's bedroom to the kitchen and then to the streets of Harlem, can be viewed as a preview of the film's double agenda on race and sexuality. On the one hand, we are supposed to read Drew's cries during sexual intercourse as idiosyncratic, Ming's mock curiosity about it as cute, and Drew's forthrightness in her explanation as progressive. But, on the other hand, there is a problem being subtly (and perhaps unconsciously) delineated: the little black girl who already knows too much through her premature entry into the mysteries of sexuality.

From the outset, the daughter is triangulated into the sexuality of the parents. The way in which heterosexual phallic (married) sex is problematized in this film is better understood in light of the history of oral sex as a crime, even for heterosexual married couples, in some states. In *Jungle Fever*, oral sex emerges again and again not only as a code for "gay" sexuality (which comes up only once in *Jungle Fever* in the black female war council scene), but also for the rest of the vast range of illicit sexual practices and psychosocial developments beyond the pale of compulsory heterosexuality, in which such perverse passions as interracial sex and drug addiction are included.

In another walk to school later in the film, Flipper and Ming run head-on into Vivian (Halle Berry), Gator's crack addict girlfriend (who looks like a grown-up version of Ming), who tells Flipper, "I'll suck your dick good for $5 . . . $3!" A startled Flipper turns to Ming (she's a girl, right?) and shakes her, shouting, "Don't you ever do anything like that!"

The studied phallocentricism of the key scenes in the film (both the opening and closing scenes, which mirror one another, as well as Flipper's first seduction of Angie), which stands against the ongoing threat of oral sex (inexplicably coupled throughout the film with crack addiction), seems too palpable to ignore. Not only is Flipper deeply threatened by the prospect of dominant female sexuality—Angie's, as well as Drew's, Vivian's, and his daughter Ming's—but the yawning threat of female sexuality somehow also becomes, within the film's larger narrative, responsible for the devastation and the insularity of ghettos, both Italian and black America.

Later in the film, when Flipper finds Gator in the dark, teeming Taj Mahal—a mythical crack factory supposedly located in Harlem on 145th Street and Convent Avenue (actually there's a very old and famous Baptist Church on that corner)—Flipper calls Vivian a whore. Vivian responds by yelling, "Eat my pussy!" This confrontation becomes yet another pretext for Flipper to be afraid his daughter will grow up to be like Vivian. After all, Ming already knows too much about sex.

Meanwhile, a crucial visual strategy in the film, undergirding the theme of uncontrolled female sexuality, is Lee's instrumentalization of skin color and lighting effects. In a technique borrowed from the noir tradition, many of the scenes were filmed at night, the strong lighting increasing the play of light and dark. As the film progresses, the shadows around both Flipper and Angie grow more and more dense and obfuscating.

Annabella Sciorra, Lonette McKee, and Wesley Snipes, despite their noteworthy individual talents, were all apparently cast for hair color and complexion: Sciorra because she's a dark-skinned white woman; McKee because she's a light-skinned black woman (visually, the racial difference between Sciorra and McKee is nill); and Snipes because he is dark. The striking visual contrast of dark and light skin is worthy of a Benetton ad.

In the film itself, Snipes is often dressed in strong bright colors—persimmon, red, or purple (an unusual palette for a man represented as so middle-class and dull)—whereas almost everybody else who appears with him, especially the women, wears black, presumably to further heighten the color contrasts. As Flipper's relationship with Angie progresses, its deterioration is signaled not so much through dialogue as by the way his face grows darker and is increasingly cast in menacing shadows. In some of their later scenes together, only his teeth and the whites of his eyes are visible. And sometimes, he is merely a black silhouette.

Revealingly, Lee's meticulous attention to visual effects isn't supported by correspondences in plot, dialogue, or characterization. As the film progresses, Drew, Flipper, and Angie become slick aestheticized surfaces, too slippery to get a handle on. The strongest characters in this film are Vivian, who epitomizes the negative threat of out-of-control sexuality and passion, and Gator, the crack addict who, nevertheless, comes across as straightforward and successful in his manipulation of the entire family system.

When Reverend Purify murders Gator in a veritable Oedipalfest, the patriarchy is the loser. His killing of Gator only serves to confirm the symbolic death of the father in African-American discourse and his descent into both madness and spiritual condemnation. Lee's ambivalence here regarding traditional family values is noteworthy.

Boyz N the Hood and *Jungle Fever*, in fact, demonize black female sexuality as a threat to black male heterosexual identity, and yet both films are extremely appealing and seductive. *Boyz N the Hood*, at the narrative level, and *Jungle Fever*, at the visual level, successfully employ mass cultural codes to entertain us, so that it becomes possible, as a black feminist viewer, to enjoy one's own symbolic decimation. The only possible corrective here, it seems to me, has to come from theoretical analysis. Whose theory this will be is, of course, much more problematic to decide.

NOTES

1. "Boyz in the (Holly)Wood," a cover article in the *New York Times Magazine*, Sunday, July 14, 1991, illustrates the invisibility of black women filmmakers.
2. Shahrazad Ali, The *Blackman's Guide to Understanding the Blackwoman* (Philadelphia, Pa.: Civilized Publications, 1989).

PART FIVE

Media and the Global Order

CHAPTER 14 Perspectives on Development

14.1 DANIEL LERNER

Modernizing Styles of Life: A Theory

After World War II, many American researchers began to examine other cultures, and the Third World was an area rich in research possibilities. Many of these countries had been colonized by dominant Western nations; many others had limited exposure to Western thought. In both areas, the economy was usually bifurcated, with a small group of elites controlling the wealth of the nation and the poor being regarded as "primitive" or "backward." Many of the researchers who focused on these areas of the world brought with them an overwhelmingly "developmentalist" bias that promoted the theory of *modernization.*

One leading proponent of this theory was Daniel Lerner, a professor at the Massachusetts Institute of Technology. He wrote what is considered one of the most rational arguments and complete methodologies for modernization, *The Passing of Traditional Society: Modernizing the Middle East* (Free Press, 1966), from which the following selection has been taken.

Lerner, along with many other influential scholars of the time, viewed mass media as the means by which people of the Third World could be influenced. He reasoned that if the people could become literate and if they could benefit from the relatively low-cost technology of radio and the impact of film and television, then they could be made aware of their problems and inspired to take action to do something about them.

Modernization came to be viewed by critical scholars as a decidedly ethnocentric idea promoted by the West to force capitalist ideology upon disempowered people, who would then be forced to adopt Western values and products. Modernization theory is still used today, though it has become increasingly suspect as an agent of change that brings with it Western cultural and ideological assumptions and goals.

Key Concept: modernization and development

Modernization . . . is the unifying principle in this study of the varied Middle East. The term is imposed by recent history. Earlier one spoke of Europeanization, to denote the common elements underlying French influence in Syria-Lebanon and British influence in Egypt and Jordan. More recently, following a century of educational and missionary activity, Americanization became a specific force and the common stimuli of the Atlantic civilization came to be called Westernization. Since World War II, the continuing search for new ways has been coupled with repudiation of the Western aegis. Soviet and other modernizing models, as illustrated by India and Turkey, have become visible in the area. Any label that today localizes the process is bound to be parochial. For Middle Easterners more than ever want the modern package, but reject the label "made in U.S.A." . . . We speak, nowadays, of modernization.

Whether from East or West, modernization poses the same basic challenge—the infusion of "a rationalist and positivist spirit" against which, scholars seem agreed, "Islam is absolutely defenseless." The phasing and modality of the process have changed, however, in the past decade. Where Europeanization once penetrated only the upper level of Middle East society, affecting mainly leisure-class fashions, modernization today diffuses among a wider population and touches public institutions as well as private aspirations with its disquieting "positivist spirit" Central to this change is the shift in modes of communicating ideas and attitudes—for spreading among a large public vivid images of its own New Ways is what modernization distinctly does. Not the class media of books and travel, but the mass media of tabloids, radio and movies, are now the dominant modes. Today's Middle East "chaos" is largely due to the shift of modernist inspiration from the discreet discourse of a few in Oxford colleges and Paris salons to the broadcast exhortations among the multitudes by the mass media.

This historic shift stimulated the inquiry begun in 1950. . . . The role of new messages in the Middle East "transition" raised a breviary of empirical questions: who was changing? from what to what? how fast? with what effects? While the great debate over Permanence *versus* Change often obliges the Middle Easterner to declare himself philosophically on such questions, we investigate them here in a more limited sense. We focus on the personal mean-

Daniel Lerner

THE MOBILITY MULTIPLIER: MASS MEDIA

The historic increase of psychic mobility begins with the expansion of physical travel. Historians conventionally date the modern era from the Age of Exploration. Every Western schoolboy knows the names of Cabot, Columbus, Cortez and is dimly aware that they "opened new worlds." This was an initial phase in the modern expansion of human communication. Gradually the technical means of transporting live bodies improved and physical displacement became an experience lived through by millions of plain folk earlier bounden to some ancestral spot. Geographical mobility became, in this phase, the usual vehicle of social mobility. It remained for a later time to make vivid that each mobile soma of the earlier epoch housed a psyche, and to reconstruct transatlantic history in terms of psychic mobility. It is the contemporary historian who now distinctively perceives the mass immigration into America as a traumatic process of psychic encounter with the new and strange.[1] We accent the contemporaneity of the psychic dimension, because the moral injunction to "look shining at new styles of architecture" is something new in the world.[2]

The expansion of psychic mobility means that more people now command greater skill in imagining themselves as strange persons in strange situations, places and times than did people in any previous historical epoch. In our time, indeed, the spread of empathy around the world is accelerating. The earlier increase of physical experience through transportation has been multiplied by the spread of *mediated* experience through mass communication. A generation before Columbus sailed to the New World, Gutenberg activated his printing press. The technical history of the popular arts suggests the sequence. The typical literary form of the modern epoch, the novel, is a conveyance of disciplined empathy. Where the poet once specialized in self-expression, the modern novelist reports his sustained imagination of the lives of others.[3] The process is carried further in the movies and in . . . television dramas. These have peopled the daily world of their audience with sustained, even intimate, experience of the lives of others. [Many television programs] bring us friends we never met, but whose joys and sorrows we intensely "share." The media create for us what has aptly been called "the world of the daytime serial."[4]

Radio, film and television climax the evolution set into motion by Gutenberg. The mass media opened to the large masses of mankind the infinite *vicarious* universe. Many more millions of persons in the world were to be affected directly, and perhaps more profoundly, by the communication media than by the transportation agencies. By obviating the physical displacement of travel, the media accented the psychic displacement of vicarious experience. For the imaginary universe not only involves more people, but it involves them in a different order of experience. There is a world of difference, we know, between "armchair travel" and actually "being there." What is the difference?

Physical experience of a new environment affronts the sensibility with new perceptions in their complex "natural" setting. The traveler in a strange land perceives simultaneously climate and clothing, body builds and skin textures, gait and speech, feeding and hygiene, work and play—in short, the ensemble of manners and morals that make a "way of life." A usual consequence for the traveler is that the "pattern of culture" among the strangers becomes confused, diverging from his prior stereotype of it and from his preferred model of reality.

Vicarious experience occurs in quite different conditions. Instead of the complexities that attend a "natural" environment, mediated experience exhibits the simplicity of "artificial" settings contrived by the creative communicator. Thus, while the traveler is apt to become bewildered by the profusion of strange sights and sounds, the receiver of communications is likely to be enjoying a composed and orchestrated version of the new reality. He has the benefit of more facile perception of the new experience as a "whole," with the concomitant advantage (which is sometimes illusory) of facile comprehension. The stimuli of perception, which shape understanding, have been simplified.

The simplification of stimuli, however, is accomplished at a certain cost. The displaced traveler's great pragmatic advantage is that he must take responsive action toward the stimuli presented by the new environment. However painful this may be—as when, to take a simple case, he has lost his way and must ask directions in a language of which his mastery is uncertain—overt action does help to discharge the traveler's interior tensions. But the passive audience for mediated communications has no such discharge channel; the radio-listener's personal response to new stimuli remains confined to his own interior. The inhibition of overt active response is a learned behavior and a difficult one. It was common, in the early days of movies, for persons strained beyond endurance to throw themselves or some object at the screen to stop the villain from strangling the heroine. Even the old media hands among the youngsters of today will sometimes, at a particularly agonizing moment in the television show, hide their faces.

Thus the mass media, by simplifying *perception* (what we "see") while greatly complicating *response* (what we "do"), have been great teachers of interior manipulation. They disciplined Western man in those empathic skills which spell modernity. They also portrayed for him the roles he might confront and elucidated the opinions he might need. Their continuing spread in our century is performing a similar function on a world scale. The Middle East already shows the marks of this historic encounter. As a young bureaucrat in Iran put it: "The movies are like a teacher to us, who tells us what to do and what not." The global network of mass media has already recruited enough new participants in all corners of the earth to make "the opinions of mankind" a real factor instead of a fine phrase in the arena of world politics. There now exists, and its scope accelerates at an extraordinary pace, a genuine "world public opinion." This has happened because millions of people, who never left their native heath, now are learning to imagine how life is organized in different lands and under different codes than their own. That this signifies a net increase in human imaginativeness, so construed, is the proposition under consideration.

A second proposition of this large historical order derives from the observation that modern media systems have flourished only in societies that are modern by other tests. That is, the media spread psychic mobility most efficiently among peoples who have achieved in some measure the antecedent conditions of geographic and social mobility. The converse of this proposition is also true: no modern society functions efficiently without a developed system of mass media. Our historical forays indicate that the conditions which define modernity form an interlocking "system." They grow conjointly, in the normal situation, or they become stunted severally.

It seems clear that people who live together in a common polity will develop patterned ways of distributing *information* along with other commodities. It is less obvious that these information flows will interact with the distribution of power, wealth, status at so many points as to form a system—and, moreover, a system so tightly interwoven that institutional variation in one sector will be accompanied by regular and determinate variation in the other sectors. Yet, just this degree of interaction between communication and social systems is what our historical exploration suggests.

We differentiated two historical systems of public communication, Oral and Media, according to the paradigm: Who says what to whom and how? On these four variables of source, content, audience, channel the ideal types differ as follows:

	Media Systems	*Oral Systems*
Channel	Broadcast (mediated)	Personal (face-to-face)
Audience	Heterogeneous (mass)	Primary (groups)
Content	Descriptive (news)	Prescriptive (rules)
Source	Professional (skill)	Hierarchical (status)

In media systems, the main flow of public information is operated by a corps of professional communicators, selected according to skill criteria, whose job it is to transmit mainly descriptive messages ("news") through impersonal media (print, radio, film) to relatively undifferentiated mass audiences. In oral systems, public information usually emanates from sources authorized to speak by their place in the social hierarchy, i.e., by status rather than skill criteria. Its contents are typically prescriptive rather than descriptive; news is less salient than "rules" which specify correct behavior toward imminent events directly involving the larger population, such as tax collections and labor drafts. (Oral and media systems also differ sharply in recreational content, as we shall see, but we here focus on informational content.) Even these prescriptive messages are normally transmitted via face-to-face oral channels (or via such point-to-point equivalents as letters) to the primary groups of kinship, worship, work and play.

Naturally, few societies in the world today give a perfect fit to either of these idealized sets of paired comparisons. America closely approximates the model of a media system, but people also speak to each other on public issues and the personal influence of the "opinion leader" is strong.[5] Conversely, Saudi

Arabia corresponds to the oral system but operates its radio transmitters at Jidda. As we move around the world, subjecting our ideal types to empirical data, various elements in the patterns begin to shift. Most countries are in some phase of transition from one system to the other.

But two observations appear to hold for all countries, regardless of continent, culture, or creed. First the *direction* of change is always from oral to media system (no known case exhibiting change in the reverse direction). Secondly, the *degree* of change toward media system appears to correlate significantly with changes in other key sectors of the social system. If these observations are correct, then we are dealing with a "secular trend" of social change that is global in scope. What we have been calling the Western model of modernization is operating on a global scale. Moreover, since this means that other important changes must regularly accompany the development of a media system, there is some point in the frequent references to a "world communication revolution" We here consider the more moderate proposition that a communication system is both index and agent of change in a total social system. This avoids the genetic problem of causality, about which we can only speculate, in order to stress correlational hypotheses which can be tested. On this view, once the modernizing process is started, chicken and egg in fact "cause" each other to develop.

To formulate the hypothesis in a manner suitable for testing, we selected indices of three principal sectors—socioeconomic, cultural, political—which could be compared in oral systems and media systems. The "profiles" were as follows:

Sector	Media Systems	Oral Systems
Socioeconomic	urban	rural
Cultural	literate	illiterate
Political	electoral	designative

To sharpen the differences, these profiles are stated in dichotomous fashion. The dogmatic appearance of this formulation should trouble no one, for we test them empirically as continuous variables on which differences are calibrated. Just as there is no perfect media system so there is no perfectly urban, literate, electoral society. Our model is probabilistic, our measures are distributive, and our test of fit is correlational.

Our procedure was to construct a matrix containing data on urbanization, literacy, voting and media participation. We handled these as indices of public participation in the four "sectors" as a whole, by expressing our data as the proportion of total population possessing each attribute. Thus, we defined *urbanization* as the proportion living in cities over 50,000; *literacy* as the proportion able to read in one language; *media participation* as the proportion buying newspapers, owning radios, and attending cinenmas (all three items being integrated into a single index number); *electoral participation* as the proportion actually voting in national elections (obtained by averaging results for the five most recent elections). Participation in these four sectors, so defined, was taken to represent participation in the social system as a whole. Recall that the participant style of modern society, as contrasted with the isolate lifeways of traditional society, hinges on the *frequency* of participation by individuals. . . .

Media Participation Items	*Correlation with Literacy*
Daily newspaper circulation	.75
Number of radio receivers	.74
Cinema seating capacity	.61

It is obvious that newspaper circulation should correlate better with literacy than does movie attendance, the enjoyment of which does not require literacy. The high correlation of radio receivers leads, for explanation, in another direction. Whereas building cinemas (in which *imported* feature films are shown) requires no modern technology, the mass production of radio receivers does require a fairly high level of industrialization.

We subsume industrialization under our index of urbanization. This is a key variable in our "system," for it is with urbanization that the modernizing process historically has begun in Western societies. Our next task, having shown that literacy and media participation are highly correlated, was to establish their interdependence with urbanism. For the historical literature on this point, while allocating great influence to the growth of cities, is not clear on several important questions: if urbanization is a necessary condition of modernization (meaning that certain other changes can occur only in cities), then what are these other changes that regularly occurred in any society when urbanization occurred? If urbanization is necessary to start modernization, how much of it is necessary (what is the "critical minimum")? Is there a point at which modernization, once started, can sustain itself without much or any further urbanization (is there a "critical optimum" for urbanization)?

We formulated these questions, for testing, in three specific hypotheses: (1) that critical limits, minimum and optimum, can be established for urbanization within which literacy will increase directly as urban population grows in all countries; (2) that countries which have not reached the minimum limit of urbanization will also be predominantly illiterate; (3) that countries which have exceeded the optimum limit of urbanization will also be predominantly literate. To test these hypotheses, we classified all 73 countries according to the data on literacy provided by UNESCO. We then found the mean urbanization for all the countries in each literacy group, as reported below.

Countries (N = 73)	*Literacy*	*Urbanization*
22	Over 80%	28.0%
4	61–80	29.2
12	41–60	25.0
13	21–40	17.0
22	Under 20	7.4

Thus in all 22 countries less than 20% literate the mean proportion of population living in cities over 50,000 is only 7.4%. The "critical minimum" of urbanization appears to be between 7–17% of total population, for convenience one may say 10%. Only after a country reaches 10% of urbanization does its literacy rate begin to rise significantly. Thereafter urbanization and literacy increase together in a direct (monotonic) relationship, until they reach 25%, which appears to be the "critical optimum" of urbanization. Beyond this literacy continues to rise independently of the growth of cities. The surplus of 1.2% of urbanization in the second row is either insignificant, with only four countries, or else confirms the analysis. Between these limits of 10–25%, our findings indicate, the growth of cities and of literacy are closely interdependent.

Having now established high pairwise correlations between urbanization-literacy and literacy-media participation, with critical optima for joint growth in each pair, we are in a position to suggest an interpretation in terms of historical phasing. The secular evolution of a participant society appears to involve a regular sequence of three phases. Urbanization comes first, for cities alone have developed the complex of skills and resources which characterize the modern industrial economy. Within this urban matrix develop both of the attributes which distinguish the next two phases—literacy and media growth. There is a close reciprocal relationship between these, for the literate develop the media which in turn spread literacy. But, historically, literacy performs the key function in the second phase. The capacity to read, at first acquired by relatively few people, equips them to perform the varied tasks required in the modernizing society. Not until the third phase, when the elaborate technology of industrial development is fairly well advanced, does a society begin to produce newspapers, radio networks, and motion pictures on a massive scale. This, in turn, accelerates the spread of literacy. Out of this interaction develop those institutions of participation (e.g., voting) which we find in all advanced modern societies. For countries in transition today, these high correlations suggest that literacy and media participation may be considered as a supply-and-demand reciprocal in a communication market whose locus, at least in its historical inception, can only be urban. . . .

The first phase, then, is *urbanization*. It is the transfer of population from scattered hinterlands to urban centers that stimulates the needs and provides the conditions needed for "take-off" toward widespread participation. Only cities require a largely literate population to function properly—for the organization of urban life assumes enough literacy to read labels, sign checks, ride subways. A population of illiterates might learn that they are not to smoke and spit in the subway, or that Express trains run on the local tracks between 5 and 7 P.M. But trial-and-error can be a wasteful societal procedure. The primitive social function of literacy, as of all skills, is to reduce waste of human effort. Its higher function is to train the skilled labor force with which cities develop the industrial complex that produces commodities for cash customers, including newspapers and radios and movies for media consumers. Cities produce the machine tools of modernization. Accordingly, increases of urbanization tend in every society to multiply national increases in literacy and media participation. By drawing people from their rural communities, cities create the demand for impersonal communication. By promoting literacy and media, cities supply this demand. Once the basic industrial plant is in operation, the development of a participant society passes into a subsequent phase. When voluntary urbanization exceeds 25%, thereby assuring the conditions of modern production, further urbanization no longer automatically guarantees equivalent increases in consumption. The need then shifts to modernizing the conditions which govern consumption.

Of this second phase, *literacy* is both the index and agent. To spread consumption of urban products beyond the city limits, literacy is an efficient instrument. The great symbol of this phase is the Sears-Roebuck catalogue. The mail-order house replaces the peddler only when enough people can read catalogues and write letters. In this sense literacy is also the basic skill required for operation of a media system. Only the literate produce the media contents which mainly the literate consume. Hence, once societies are about 25% urbanized, the highest correlation of media consumption is with literacy. We shall soon describe more fully how literacy operates as the pivotal agent in the transition to a fully participant society. Here we wish to suggest that by the time this second phase gets well under way, a different social system is in operation than that which governed behavior in a society that was under 10% urban and under 40% (roughly, less than half) literate. For, when most people in a society have become literate, they tend to generate all sorts of new desires and to develop the means of satisfying them. . . .

If modernization is the transition to participant society, then the direction of change in public communication is toward a constantly expanding opinion arena. The significant mode of participating, in any network of human communication, is by sharing a common interest in the messages it transmits—i.e., by having opinions about the matters which concern other participants. (Nonparticipation, conversely, consists of neither knowing nor caring about the messages relayed through a given network.) In a large public network, such as that of a nation, perfect participation is impossible—and perhaps undesirable. A network would hardly be manageable in which all citizens attended to all messages and expressed opinions on all public questions. There are determinate limits—maxima as well as minima—to the degree of participation appropriate for particular networks. The modernizing tendency is toward networks that can handle maximum participation, and concurrently to develop the participants needed to man these networks.

NOTES

1. Oscar Handlin, *The Uprooted* (1952).
2. W. H. Auden, "Petition."
3. J. W. Beach, *The Twentieth Century Novel* (1932).
4. P. F. Lazarsfeld and F. N. Stanton, *Radio Research, 1942–43* (1944).
5. Elihu Katz and P. F. Lazarsfeld, *Personal Influence* (1955).

Communication and Development: The Passing of the Dominant Paradigm

By the time Everett M. Rogers edited *Communication and Development: Critical Perspectives* (Sage Publications, 1976), from which the following selection is taken, modernization had been criticized for the Western bias that it assumed. In the following selection, Rogers critiques modernization, but he also explores many of the emerging pathways to development that were being explored throughout the 1970s. He discusses his work, and that of others, on the use of *diffusion studies* to better understand how new media were adopted within the specific cultural contexts in changing societies.

The following selection effectively summarizes a shift in communication research that saw a revolution in a *paradigm,* or a way of thinking about a problem. Throughout the 1970s the field of development studies began to explore different methods, theories, and approaches toward understanding the role of media in changing societies. Some of those changes were precipitated by a growing tension articulated by people in the Third World and nonaligned nations in the wake of a new world information order.

Rogers is currently a professor in and chair of the Department of Communication and Journalism at the University of New Mexico. He is a prolific writer, and he has published many significant works in the areas of diffusion research, cultural change, and comparative international studies. Some of his books are *The Media Revolution in America and in Western Europe,* coedited with Frances Balle (Ablex, 1985); *Communication Technology; The New Media in Society* (Free Press, 1986); and *A History of Communication Study: A Biographical Approach* (Free Press, 1994).

Key Concept: diffusion and social change

THE DOMINANT PARADIGM OF DEVELOPMENT[1]

Through the late 1960s, a dominant paradigm ruled intellectual definitions and discussions of development and guided national development programs. This concept of development grew out of certain historical events, such as the Industrial Revolution in Europe and the United States, the colonial experience in Latin America, Africa, and Asia, the quantitative empiricism of North American social science, and capitalistic economic/political philosophy. Implicit in the ruling paradigm were numerous assumptions which were generally thought to be valid, or at least were not widely questioned, until about the 1970s.

Definitions of development centered around the criterion of the rate of economic growth. The level of national development at any given point in time was the gross national product (GNP) or, when divided by the total population in a nation, per capita income. Although there was a certain amount of intellectual discomfort with per capita income as the main index of development, especially among noneconomists, alternative measures and definitions of development had relatively few proponents. . . .

CRITICISMS OF THE DOMINANT PARADIGM OF DEVELOPMENT

In short, the old paradigm implied that poverty was equivalent to underdevelopment. And the obvious way for less developed countries to develop was for them to become more like the developed countries.[2]

It was less obvious that the industrially advanced nations largely controlled the "rules of the game" of development. That most of the scholars writing about development were Westerners. That balances of payment and momentary exchange rates were largely determined in New York, London, and Washington. And the international technical assistance programs sponsored by the rich nations, unfortunately, made the recipients even more dependent on the donors. These gradual lessons took some time to emerge and to sink into intellectual thought.

Intellectual Ethnocentrism

Theoretical writings about modernization in this period after World War II generally followed an "individual-blame" logic and may have been overly narrow and ethnocentric in a cultural sense. Examples are the works of Walt Rostow (1961), Everett Hagen (1962), and David McClelland (1961), all drawing more or less on the earlier writings of Max Weber. The leading theorists were Westerners, and there often was a rather inadequate data base to support their conceptualizations. Portes (1973) criticized this Western and person-blame bias: "There is, I believe, a profoundly ethnocentric undercurrent in characterizations of modern men in underdeveloped countries. An invariably positive description obviously has something to do with similarity of these individuals with the self-images and values of researchers." Many economists insisted that their discipline consisted of a universally valid body of theory, applicable to both. One might ask rhetorically how different economic theory would be if Adam Smith had been Chinese or a Sikh. "Economic theorists, more than other social scientists, have long been disposed to arrive at general propositions and then postulate them as valid for every time, place, and culture" (Myrdal, 1968: 16).

After reviewing the history and nature of the dominant paradigm and contrasting it with the reality of Asian development, Inayatullah (1975, 1976) concludes: "The Western development theory . . . is not an adequate intellectual framework . . . as it suffers from an overemphasis on the role of factors internal to Asian societies as causes of underdevelopment to the exclusion of external factors."

Continuing underdevelopment was attributed to "traditional" ways of thinking and acting of the mass of individuals in developing nations. The route to modernization was to transform the people, to implant new values and beliefs.

The dominant paradigm sought to explain the transition from traditional to modern societies. In the 1950s, the traditional systems were the nations of Latin America, Africa, and Asia. All were relatively poor, with GNPs averaging about one-fifth or less those of the developed nations of Europe and North America. Almost all were former colonies (the African and Asian nations more recently so), and most were still highly dependent on the developed nations for trade, capital, technology, and, in many cases, for their national language, dress, institutions, and other cultural items. It seemed that the developing nations were less able to control their environment and were more likely to be influenced by unexpected perturbations in their surroundings. In these several respects, the developing countries seemed to be somehow "inferior" to the developed nations, but of course with the hoped-for potential of catching up in their overall development. The developed nations of the West were taken as the ideal toward which the developing states should aspire.[3] The development of traditional societies into modern ones was a contemporary intellectual extension of social Darwinian evolution.

Redefining the Causes of Underdevelopment

Western models of development assumed that the main causes of underdevelopment lay within the underdeveloped nation rather than external to it. The causes were thought to be (1) of an individual-blame nature[4] (peasants were traditional, fatalistic, and generally unresponsive to technological innovation) and/or (2) of a social-structural nature within the nation (for example, a tangled government bureaucracy, a top-heavy land tenure system, and so on). Western intellectual models of development, and Euro-American technical assistance programs based on such models, were less likely to recognize the importance of external constraints on a nation's development: international terms of trade, the economic imperialism of international corporations, and the vulnerability and dependence of the recipients of technical assistance programs. The dominant paradigm put the blame for underdevelopment on the developing nations rather than on the developed countries, or even jointly on both parties.

During the 1950s and 1960s, this assumption of blame-attribution was widely accepted not only in Euro-America, but also by most government leaders and by many social scientists in Latin America, Africa, and Asia. Many of the latter were educated in the United States or Europe, or at least their teachers and professors had been. And the power elites of developing countries were often coopted to the "within-blame" assumption by international technical assistance agencies or by multinational corporations.

International power in the 1950 to 1970 era was concentrated in the hands of the United States, and this helped lead international efforts in the development field to follow a within-blame causal attribution and to reinforce it as an assumption. As the U.S. corner on world power began to crack in the 1970s (at least, in the UN General Assembly), so did faith in the dominant paradigm of development. The "oil blackmail" of Euro-America following the Yom Kippur War in 1973 not only redistributed millions of dollars from developed to certain developing countries, but it dramatically demonstrated that developing countries could redefine the social situation of international finance. . . .

ALTERNATIVE PATHWAYS TO DEVELOPMENT

In the very late 1960s and the 1970s, several world events combined with the intellectual critiques just described and began to crack the prior credibility of the dominant paradigm.

1. The ecological disgust with environmental pollution in the developed nations led to questioning whether they were, after all, such ideal models for development. Pollution problems and overpopulation pressures on available resources helped create doubts about whether unending economic growth was possible or desirable, and whether high technology was the most appropriate engine for development.

2. The world oil crisis demonstrated that certain developing countries could make their own rules of the international game and produced some suddenly rich developing nations. Their escape from national poverty, even though in part at the expense of other developed countries, was a lesson to their neighbors in Latin America, Asia, and Africa. No longer were these nations willing to accept prior assumptions that the causes of underdevelopment were mainly internal.

3. The sudden opening of international relations with the People's Republic of China allowed the rest of the world to learn details of her pathway to development. Here was one of the poorest countries, and the largest, that in two decades had created a miracle of modernization. A public health and family planning system that was envied by the richest nations. Well-fed and clothed citizens. Increasing equality. An enviable status for women. And all this was accomplished with very little foreign assistance and presumably without

much capitalistic competition. China, and to a lesser extent Cuba, Tanzania, and Chile (in the early 1970s), suggested that there must be alternatives to the dominant paradigm.

4. Finally, and perhaps most convincing of all, was the discouraging realization that development was not going very well in the developing countries that had closely followed the paradigm. However one might measure development in most of the nations of Latin America, Africa, and Asia in the past 25 years, not much had occurred. Instead, most "development" efforts have brought further stagnation, a greater concentration of income and power, high unemployment, and food shortages in these nations. If these past development programs represented any kind of test of the intellectual paradigm on which they were based, the model has been found rather seriously wanting.

Elements in the New Development

From these events grew the conclusion that *there are many alternative pathways to development*. While their exact combination would be somewhat different in every nation, some of the main elements in this newer conception began to emerge.

1. *The equality of distribution of information, socioeconomic benefits, and so forth.* This new emphasis in development led to the realization that villagers and urban poor should be the priority audience for development programs and, more generally, that the closing of socioeconomic gaps by bringing up the lagging sectors was a priority task in many nations.

2. *Popular participation in self-development planning and execution, usually accompanied by the decentralization of certain of these activities to the village level.* Development came to be less a mere function of what national governments did *to* villagers, although it was recognized that perhaps some government assistance was necessary even in local self-development. An example is the "group planning of births" at the village level in the People's Republic of China, where the villagers decide how many babies they should have each year and who should have them. Another illustration of decentralized development was occurring in Tanzania, where social mobilization activities by the political party, the army, and by radio listening groups help provide mass motivation for local participation in development activities. As President Julius K. Nyerere stated: "If development is to benefit the people, the people must participate in considering, planning, and implementing their development plans" (in Tanganyika African National Union, 1971). People cannot *be* developed; they can only develop themselves. And this realization was demonstrated not only in communist and socialist nations, but also in such capitalistic settings as Korea and Taiwan.

3. *Self-reliance and independence in development, with an emphasis upon the potential of local resources.* Mao Tse-tung's conception of national self-development in China is an illustration of this viewpoint, including the rejection of foreign aid (after some years of such assistance from Russia), as well as the decentralization of certain types of development to the village level (as mentioned previously). Not only may international and binational technical assis-

tance be rejected, but so too are most external models of development—leading to a viewpoint that every nation, and perhaps each village, may develop in its own way. If this occurs, of course, standardized indexes of the rate of development become inappropriate and largely irrelevant.

4. *Integration of traditional with modern systems, so that modernization is a syncretization of old and new ideas, with the exact mixture somewhat different in each locale.* The integration of Chinese medicine with Western scientific medicine in contemporary China is an example of this approach to development. Acupuncture and antibiotics mix quite well in the people's minds as shown by this experience. Such attempts to overcome the "empty vessels fallacy" remind us that tradition is really yesterday's modernity. Until the 1970s, development thinking implied that traditional institutions would have to be entirely replaced by their modern counterparts. Belatedly, it was recognized that these traditional forms could contribute directly to development. "African countries should not imitate the patterns of development of the industrialized countries, but adopt development patterns suited to African indigenous traditional and cultural patterns" (Omo-Fadaka, 1974).

By the mid-1970s it seemed safe to conclude that the dominant paradigm had "passed," at least as the main model for development in Latin America, Africa, and Asia. Of course, it would still be followed enthusiastically in some nations, but even then with certain important modifications. The Chinese model, or at least particular components, had been (and were being) adopted elsewhere when nations were willing to forego certain advantages of liberal democracy for the tighter government control that they thought to be necessary to maintain nationhood over tribal, religious, or regional factions. While Cambodia, Vietnam, and perhaps Tanzania were influenced by the Chinese route to development, they seem far from very exact replicas. So multiple and varied models of development were not in style.

What Is Development?

Out of the various criticisms of the dominant paradigm of development grew a questioning of the concept of development from one that had centered on materialistic, economic growth to a definition that implied such other valued ends as social advancement, equality, and freedom. These valued qualities should be determined by the people themselves through a widely participatory process. . . . Development is change toward patterns of society that allow better realization of human values, that allow a society greater control over its environment and over its own political destiny, and that enables its individuals to gain increased control over themselves (Inayatullah, 1967: 101).

We summarize these newer conceptions of development by defining development as *a widely participatory process of social change in a society, intended to bring about both social and material advancement (including greater equality, freedom, and other valued qualities) for the majority of the people through their gaining greater control over their environment* (Rogers, 1975b).[5]

Thus the concept of development has been expanded and made much more flexible, and at the same time more humanitarian, in its implications. . . .

CRITICISMS OF COMMUNICATION IN DEVELOPMENT

By the late 1960s and the 1970s a number of critical evaluations were being made of the mass communication role in development. Some scholars, especially in Latin America, perceived the mass media in their nations as an extension of exploitive relationships with U.S.-based multinational corporations, especially through the advertising of commercial products. Further, questions were asked about the frequent patterns of elite ownership and control of mass media institutions in Latin America and the influence of such ownership on the media content. The 1965–1975 decade saw a rising number of military dictatorships in Latin America, Africa, and Asia, and these governments stressed the media's propaganda role, decreasing the public's trust in mass communication.

Communication researchers also began to question some of their prior assumptions, becoming especially critical of earlier inattention to (1) the content of the mass media, (2) the need for social-structural changes in addition to communication if development were to occur, and (3) the shortcomings of the classical diffusion-of-innovations viewpoint which had become an important explanation of microlevel development.

Inattention to Media Content

[M]ass media exposure on the part of individuals in developing nations [is] highly correlated with their modernization, as expressed by their exhibiting modern attitudes and behavior. This seemed logical because the mass media were thought to carry generally pro-development messages (Rogers with Svenning, 1969).

However, a strange anomaly was encountered. When individuals in developing nations who had adopted an innovation like a weed spray, a new crop variety, or family planning, were asked the sources/channels through which they had learned about the new idea, *the mass media were almost never reported.* Interpersonal channels with peers totally predominated in diffusing the innovation. A possible explanation of this anomaly seemed to lie in the contents of the media messages, which investigation showed seldom to carry specific messages about the innovation (such as what it is, where to obtain it and at what cost, and how to use it), even though there was much content promoting national development in a general sense (such as news of a new highway being constructed, appointment of a new minister of agriculture, and so on). So when the media content was analyzed it was found to contain very little attention to the technological innovations that were diffusing; they spread most frequently through interpersonal communication (1) from government development workers to their clients and (2) among peers in the mass audience. . . .

Need for Structural Change As Well As Communication

Even in the days of the dominant paradigm, it was realized that the contribution of mass communication to development was often limited by the social structure, by the unavailability of resource inputs, and the like. There was much more, of course, to development than just communication and information. But there was at least some hope that by raising the public's aspirations for modernization, pressure was created toward changing some of the limiting factors on development.

By the 1970s, it was becoming apparent that the social-structural restraints on development were often unyielding to the indirect influences of the media or even to more direct intervention. Under these conditions, it was realized that mass communication's role in development might be much more diminished than previously thought. And communication research was designed to determine just how limiting the structure might be on the development effects of mass communication. Illustrative of such researches is Grunig's (1971) investigation among Colombian farmers; he concluded that "communication is a complementary factor to modernization and development . . . it can have little effect unless structural changes come first to initiate the development process." Such studies helped to modify the previously enthusiastic statements by communication scholars about the power of the media.

Diffusion of Innovations and Development

One of the most frequent types of communication research in developing nations dealt with the diffusion of innovations. . . . In such research, an idea perceived as new by the receiver—an innovation—is traced as it spreads through a system (Rogers with Shoemaker, 1971). The innovation is usually a technological idea, and thus one can see that past diffusion research fits well with the dominant paradigm's focus on technology and on its top-down communication to the public.

During the 1960s, there was a tremendous increase in the number of diffusion studies in developing countries; these researches were especially concerned with the spread of agricultural innovations and of family planning methods. In fact, there were about 500 family planning diffusion studies in India alone (Rogers, 1973). Many of them left much to be desired in scientific rigor or in the originality of their design.

A number of criticisms of the assumptions and directions of diffusion research appeared in the 1970s: Marceau (1972), Grunig (1971), Golding (1974), Havens (1972), and Beltrán (1975), as well as the articles by Díaz Bordenave and Röling et al. . . . These critiques centered on the pro-innovation bias of such research and on the propensity for diffusion to widen the socioeconomic gaps in a rural audience. Out of such frank criticism came a number of modifications in the classical diffusion model and in the research designs utilized (such as more field experiments and network analysis), and these newer approaches are now being tried (Rogers, 1973, 1976).

After a tour of 20 U.S. communication research centers, Nordenstreng (1968) criticized North American scholars for their "hyperscience," which he explains as due to the fact that "American communication research has grown up in an atmosphere of behaviorism and operationalism, which has made it correct in technical methodology but poor in conceptual productivity." This comment on communication research in the United States may also apply to diffusion research. Such inquiry often sided unduly with the source "against" the receiver, perhaps a reflection of the one-way linear model of communication and of the mechanistic/atomistic components approach of much communication research.

NOTES

1. The following section is adapted from Rogers (1975b).
2. Karl Marx in *Das Kapital* stated: "the country that is more developed industrially only shows, to the less developed, the image of its own future." Lerner (1967: 115) stated: "Indeed, the Western model is virtually an inevitable baseline for Asian development planning because there is no *other* model which can serve this purpose." This predominance of the Western paradigm of development was probably correct at the time of Lerner's writing.
3. An assumption criticized by Portes (1973): "Modernity as a consequence of Western structural transformations may have little to do with, or be in fact detrimental to, causes of development in Third world nations."
4. Caplan and Nelson (1973) argue that social scientists are more likely to accept an individual-blame definition of a social problem that they investigate than a system-blame definition. For instance, unemployment and poverty are considered to be due to laziness, not to the unavailability of work and to blocked opportunities.
5. Note how my thinking has changed as to the definition of development in the past seven years: "*Development* is a type of social change in which new ideas are introduced into a social system in order to produce higher per capita incomes and levels of living through more modern production methods and improved social organization" (Rogers with Svenning, 1969).

REFERENCES

BELTRAN S., L. R. (1975) "Research ideologies in conflict." J. of Communication 25: 187–193.

CAPLAN, N. and S. D. NELSON (1973) "On being useful: the nature and consequences of psychological research on social problems." Amer. Psychologist 28: 199–211.

GOLDING, P. (1974) "Media role in national development: critique of a theoretical orthodoxy." J. of Communication 24: 39–53.

GRUNIG, J. E. (1971) "Communication and the economic decision-making processes of Colombian peasants." Econ. Development & Cultural Change 18: 580–597.

HAGEN, E. (1962) On the Theory of Social Change. Urbana: Univ. of Illinois Press.

HAVENS, A. E. (1972) "Methodological issues in the study of development." Sociologia Ruralis 12: 252–272.

INAYATULLAH (1976) "Western, Asian, or global model of development," in W. Schramm and D. Lerner (eds.) Communication and Change in the Developing Countries: Ten Years After. Honolulu: Univ. of Hawaii/East-West Center Press.

____ (1967) "Toward a non-Western model of development," in D. Lerner and W. Schramm (eds.) Communication and Change in the Developing Countries. Honolulu: Univ. of Hawaii/East-West Center Press.

McCLELLAND, D. C. (1961) The Achieving Society. New York: Van Nostrand.

MARCEAU, F. J. (1972) "Communication and development: a reconsideration." Public Opinion Q. 36: 235–245.

MYRDAL, G. (1968) Asian Drama. New York: Pantheon.

NORDENSTRENG, K. (1968) "Communication research in the United States: a critical perspective." Gazette 14: 207–216.

OMO-FADAKA, J. (1974) "Develop your own way." Development Forum 2.

PORTES, A. (1973) "The factorial structure of modernity: empirical replications and a critique." Amer. J. of Sociology 79: 15–44.

ROGERS, E. M. (1976) "Where we are in understanding the diffusion of innovations," in W. Schramm and D. Lerner (eds.) Communication and Change in the Developing Countries: Ten Years After. Honolulu: Univ. of Hawaii/East-West Center Press.

____ (1975b) "The anthropology of modernization and the modernization of anthropology." Reviews in Anthropology 2: 345–358.

____ (1973) Communication Stategies for Family Planning. New York: Free Press.

____ with F. F. SHOEMAKER (1971) Communication of Innovations: A Cross-Cultural Approach. New York: Free Press.

ROGERS, E. M., with L. SVENNING (1969) Modernization Among Peasants: The Impact of Communications. New York: Holt, Rinehart & Winston.

ROSTOW, W. W. (1961) The Stages of Economic Growth. New York: Cambridge Univ. Press.

Totems and Technologies

Development studies have given way to a wide range of approaches and subjects. The following selection contains one contemporary approach to understanding international social change within the context of development. Majid Tehranian, a professor at the University of Hawaii at Manoa, evaluates social change as a result of advanced technologies of information and communication in the following selection from *Technologies of Power: Information Machines and Democratic Prospects* (Ablex, 1990). He explores the work of many theorists from interdisciplinary backgrounds to better understand the breadth of issues for a world that is increasingly tied together by information and communication technologies.

Tehranian creates his argument by drawing from the themes within development research, but he proposes an alternative to the presupposed traditional trajectory of power relations among countries. This creation of cultural transformation suggests an agenda for future research that acknowledges the individual and shared histories of nations and their social practices. Tehranian does not apologize for what he sees as the myopic views of early developmentalists, nor does he criticize any group of researchers for the ways in which their work has been influenced. Rather, he demonstrates a positive approach to understanding complex international social relations indicating that it is possible to learn from past studies to address current and future problems. He maintains that the "mythology" that has influenced cultures and comparative studies is a powerful determinant of future research directions.

Key Concept: social change and democracy

*T*otems and technologies seem worlds apart—as far apart as the so-called "primitive" and "advanced" societies.[1] Yet, if we look carefully at the history of communication technologies, we may discern an interesting connection between the rise of certain technologies and the emergence of certain communication elites and social systems. Totemism is a primitive religious belief that systematically associates groups of persons with species of animals (occasionally plants or inanimate objects) and a certain element of social organization (Freud, 1919; Malinovski, 1927; Levi-Strauss, 1966). Communication technologies, from the invention of writing to informatics, also seem to have occasioned social, political, and cultural formations peculiar to their own biases (Innis, 1950, 1951). As a form of identity fetishism, totemism has occasioned belief in the magic of certain totemic objects, plants, or animals as representatives of tribal power. Has technological fetishism similarly led to idolatrous beliefs in the power and magic of certain communication technologies as signs of superiority of certain social systems?

The celebration of the Age of Information in recent years in both scholarly and popular literature calls for a critical reexamination of the concept's underlying myths and realities. Has the advanced capitalist world really entered a new historical stage known as the "post-industrial information society"? Are the new information technologies creating new possibilities of "technological leapfrogging" for the less developed countries? Can the global spread of the new technologies narrow the information gaps among and within nations? Will they bring about world integration on the basis of a universal secular-scientific civilization? Or will they exacerbate the existing inequalities and lead to a cultural backlash against the onslaught of modernization? Will they foster democratic equity and participation or totalitarian efficiency and tyranny? . . .

INFORMATION OR INFOGLUT SOCIETY?

The explosion of a great diversity of information technologies and their diffusion around the world during the past two decades have given rise to hopes for accelerating global development and democratization. However, what some liberal theorists have considered as the dawn of a new postindustrial, information society, Marxist theorists have generally viewed as the increasing commodification and privatization of information in the worldwide expansion of monopoly capitalism. By contrast, a third and emerging school of thought, to be labeled here "communitarian," considers the same processes as an example of the dual effects of information technologies—the harbinger of new possibilities for increasing levels of participatory democracy as well as new possible threats to individual freedom, social and information equality, and cultural autonomy and identity.

The liberal theorists have taken their cue largely from a tradition of research focusing on the technologically-propelled changes of social structure. The transition from natural sources of energy (muscle power, wind, water) to the steam engine and internal combustion clearly marks the beginnings of the First Industrial Revolution. The liberal theorists have considered the new information society as the harbinger of a Second Industrial Revolution, characterized by the application of information technologies to production, distribution, and consumption processes, transforming thereby the old industrial social and economic structures, eliminating the need for routine and repetitive jobs, providing greater opportunities for leisure and cultural creativity, and breaking down sociocultural differences and inequalities. Others in the liberal school of thought are urging the developing countries, which missed out on the First Industrial Revolution, to make efforts to bridge the widening gap between themselves and the more technologically advanced by "leapfrogging" in order to take part in this Second Industrial Revolution (Olsen, 1986).

The literature of "information society" is vast and expanding, but the origins of the concept date back to Colin Clarke's celebrated analysis (Clarke, 1940) which said that, due to sectoral differences in productivity and the increasing demand for social services (health, education, recreation, consulting, etc.), the labor force in the industrial societies will move increasingly from manufacturing to service sectors. This observation has been born out by the historical trends, elaborated upon later by Fritz Machlup (1962, 1980–84), Daniel Bell (1973), and Marc Porat (1977). While Machlup has focused on the production and distribution of knowledge as a key to the understanding of the new economic structures and processes, Bell provides a broader historical view to suggest a new stage theory of development, a movement from agrarian to industrial and information societies. Porat examines these transitions in terms of the U.S. economy where massive statistical evidence suggests a clear shift from predominantly agricultural to manufacturing, service, and information occupations and employment. To quote Porat: "In Stage I (1860–1906), the largest group in the labor force was agricultural. By the turn of the century, industrial occupations began to grow rapidly, and became predominant during Stage II (1906–1954). In the current period, Stage III, information occupations comprise the largest group" (Porat, 1978, p. 7).

The theories of "information society" have also given rise to a pop sociology serving as a new ideology to legitimate global capitalism. Alvin Toffler (1970, 1980) and John Naisbett (1982) have provided perhaps the most daring of such popular visions of "information society," focusing particularly on the democratization effects of the new information technologies. While Toffler is somewhat ambivalent about the prospects such a society might hold for democracy and human happiness, Naisbitt is unabashedly enthusiastic. The corporate world of telecommunication and computer industries have, in turn, found these concepts congenial to their own interests and views. It is not surprising, therefore, that Toffler and Naisbitt have been adopted as corporate futurologists while attaining public fame and fortune as best-selling authors and business consultants.

Theories of information society have thus rapidly evolved from simple statistical observations—demonstrating a shift in occupations from agriculture to industry and services—to a neo-evolutionary theory of historical development. In their simplicity and sweep, these theories bear a striking resemblance to their 18-century antecedent—the Idea of Progress. The fundamental assumptions are the same: inevitability, linearity, universality, and technological determinism. Information society is presumed to be an inevitable stage in a universal pattern of progressive evolution from industrial to postindustrial society—propelled by the invention and diffusion of the new information technologies.

In contrast to the liberal theorists, however, the Marxist critics of "information society" and its corporate futurologists have generally pointed to the rising tide of dualism at national and global levels, creating islands of riches and information abundance in a global ocean of poverty and information scarcity (Schiller, 1981, 1985; Mosco, 1982; Slack & Fejes, 1987). They have suggested that the new technologies have generally widened the existing gaps, mainly through the privatization, concentration, and exploitation of information resources by the transnational corporations (TNCs). To avoid increasing dependence and vulnerability, they have argued that the developing world is well-advised to pursue a strategy of dissociation, national self-sufficiency, and collective self-reliance.

The two schools clearly represent the increasing stratification of the world into centers of wealth, power, and information against the peripheries of poverty, dependency, and revolt. But the communication technologies that have contributed to this stratification have also created a global interdependence whose future depends vitally on cooperation rather than confrontation. Furthermore, international trade and cooperation in the field of information—perhaps more than any other field—depends on a clear understanding of the nature of this unique "commodity" and its role in the historical transformations of our own era. The following critical questions might therefore be well worth considering:

- Does the increasing abundance of raw data also mean increasing levels of *information* (contextualized data), *knowledge* (contextualized information), and *wisdom* (contextualized knowledge)?
- Or, conversely, is the explosion in the sources and varieties of information leading to information overload, future shock, and intellectual confusion?
- Are the technological and socioeconomic advances of the information age creating greater information equality or information gaps and dualisms between the information rich and poor?
- Does the phenomenal growth in channel capacity, brought about by the introduction of cable television, direct broadcasting satellite (DBS), teletext, videotex, and fiber optics imply greater political freedom and participation, cultural pluralism, and enrichment *or* centralization, political surveillance, cultural domination, and impoverishment?
- Are the processes of automation, implied by the application of robotics and computer-integrated manufacturing, computer-assisted design and manufacturing (CIM-CAD-CAM), leading to greater leisure and cultural creativity, *or* increasing levels of structural unemployment and waste of human resources?
- Will the worldwide extension of the new technologies lead to the diffusion of a universal, modern, scientific, and technological civilization, *or* cultural backlash against the onslaught of modernization?

A more balanced view of the possible impact of information technologies on society than those offered by liberal and Marxist theorists would have to begin perhaps with a critique of the concept of "information society" itself. I will present here the beginnings of such a critique in terms of three fundamental points:

First, in a profound sense, all human societies may be considered to have been "information" societies. No human society can be, in fact, conceived without a system of signs, meanings, and communication however "primitive"—

that vitally binds it together. Peter Berger (1967, p. 22ff) has put the central argument of this position rather poignantly:

> The most important function of society is nomization. The anthropological presupposition for this is a human craving for meaning that appears to have the force of instinct. Men are congenitally compelled to impose a meaningful order upon reality. This order, however, presupposes the social enterprise of ordering world construction. To be separated from society exposes the individual to a multiplicity of dangers with which he is unable to cope by himself, in the extreme case to the danger of immanent extinction. Separation from society also inflicts unbearable psychological tensions upon the individual, tensions that are grounded in the most anthropological fact of sociality. The ultimate danger of such separation, however, is the danger of meaninglessness. This danger is the nightmare par excellence, in which the individual is submerged in a world of disorder, senselessness and madness. Reality and identity are malignantly transformed into meaningless figures of horror. To be in society is to be 'sane' precisely in the sense of being shielded from the ultimate 'insanity' of such anomic terror. Anomie is unbearable to the point where the individual may seek death in preference to it. Conversely, existence within a nomic world may be sought at the cost of all sorts of sacrifice and suffering—and even at the cost of life itself, if the individual believes that this ultimate sacrifice has nomic significance.

Second, to proclaim the dawn of a new "information society" as the unique hallmark of our own age is to confuse information with commodification of information. In the advanced capitalist societies, information has been increasingly commodified to provide an expanding infostructure (i.e., information infrastructure) of online information networks and transborder news, data, sound, and images. This suggests the historical development of capitalism from its earliest stages of primitive accumulation within the national boundaries (national capitalism), to the expansion of national capital to the colonies (international capitalism), and increasingly towards a global capitalist system (transnational capitalism) in which production and distribution decisions are made on the basis of the strategic interests of the global corporations. To arrive at the presently emerging transnational capitalist stage, there is a vital need for a fully global transportation and information infrastructure. The new information technologies are clearly providing that infostructure, while creating the conditions for a new international division of labor.

Under international capitalism, the world division of labor relegated the production of raw materials to the peripheries, while manufacturing was concentrated at the centers of industrial production. With the rise of land, labor, and residual costs (including the costs of environmental protection imposed by the new antipollution measures in the industrial countries), manufacturing (the so-called sunset industries) has increasingly moved from the centers to the peripheries. Such peripheries as the southern states in the United States and the new industrializing countries (the so-called NICS, including Brazil, Argentina, Mexico, South Korea, Taiwan, India, Singapore, Malaysia, and the Philippines) have been the main beneficiaries of this trend. Their textile, steel, and automobile industries have thus shown considerable growth in exports during the last two decades. In the meantime, the sunrise industries (including telecommunication, computer, aerospace, and weapons industries) and the services associated with them (investment banking, value-added networks, electronic publishing, etc.) have shown remarkable growth in the advanced capitalist countries at the expense of the manufacturing activities.

Porat's four-sector workforce aggregation bears out this argument rather dramatically in the case of the United States. U.S. manufacturing takes a downward turn in 1945, precisely at the moment that the United States assumes the role of a dominant superpower in world affairs. Subsequent to that, U.S. manufacturing industries began to invest massively abroad wherever economic conditions proved more favorable (i.e., lower land, labor, and residual costs) and political conditions more secure (in allied or client states). The Marshall Plan in Europe and Point Four in the Third World were, in fact, efforts towards the reconstruction of war-torn economies as well as conduits for the encouragement of American investment abroad. They succeeded particularly well in Western Europe and in a number of other U.S. client states in Africa, Asia, and Latin America, where U.S. corporations became a dominant force in the national economies. A commensurate rise in the services and information sectors during the same period suggests not only a rise of demand for the activities (as Colin Clarke had predicted) but also the transformation of the United States from an exporter of mainly manufactured goods to an exporter of primarily banking, insurance, shipping, high technology, and information services. . . .

TECHNOCRATIC VS. COMMUNITARIAN SOCIETY

. . . [O]ur own Age of Technology clearly exhibits two contradictory tendencies—here identified as "technocratic" and "communitarian" societies. The technocratic society has been led by the cybernetic revolution and it is developing further by an accelerating technological revolution in robotics and computer-integrated manufacturing (CIM). The convergence of telecommunications and computers has led to the creation of databases and networks that serve as the infostructure of the new Technocratic Society. The progressive introduction of ISDN will only increase the level of sophistication of existing networks into a simultaneous transmission of sound, vision, and data linking global and local networks. At present, the new technologies serve primarily the purposes of the highly centralized, global, and national technocracies such as the giant transnational corporations and the national military and civilian bureaucracies. They also serve a new communication elite which we call "the technologues." This elite is acting as the custodians and managers of the large bureaucratic machines that dominate our world today. The preponderance of the engineers, programmers, and efficiency managers has in turn resulted in the dominance of a new cultural paradigm that puts technology above ideology, means over ends, and programming efficiency over spontaneity and participation.

The "Technological System," as Jacques Ellul (1983) calls this social order, has also bred its own institutions of research and instruction outside of the traditional liberal arts universities. The R & D establishments such as the Bell Labs, Rand Corporation, Arthur D. Little, or Battle Memorial Institute (all in the United States) serve the defense and corporate sectors without much of the moral and material constraints of traditional universities. Numerous "corporate universities" have also emerged as degree-granting institutions to overtake the tasks of training in the industrial arts without the constraints of teaching the liberal arts. In the United States, these alternative institutions of higher training and applied, industrial research spend over twice as much as the traditional institutions of higher education.[2]

The Technocratic Society is first and foremost a global system. It is characterized by an international communication regime of information networking indispensable to the operation of its global transportation, banking, finance, and marketing activities. This global information network connects the corporate and government headquarters with their respective localized branches in a vast and complex network of centralized nodes of decision making. It provides services in airline reservation, electronic fund transfers, remote sensing and intelligence, marketing, advertising, transborder news and data flows, and so on (Dordick, Bradley, & Manus, 1981; Canley & Ganley, 1982). The Information Society discourages, however, spontaneity and participation by its routinized systems of communication and control, innovation and production, reduction of decisions to their technical component, and fragmentation and delegation of decision-making powers to the technocratic elites (Galbraith, 1978; Kumar, 1978; Ellul, 1983).

Are we embarking upon a new, seventh age of human communication, a posttechnocratic Age of Communitarian Democracy, that could reap the benefits of information technologies without their dulling and enslaving effects? The distinction made here between "technocratic" and "communitarian" societies entertains some measure of cautious optimism on this question. In the debate outlined above between the liberal and Marxist theorists, I am taking a middle ground by granting to the former that some fundamental changes are occurring in the technological and social structures of what might be considered a "hyperindustrial" information society, but the sum total of these changes has not as yet manifested itself in the capitalist political and economic institutions. It is hypothesized, however, that the potentials for fundamental cultural, political, and economic changes are ever growing and will no doubt manifest themselves sooner or later. These changes could be observed particularly in the cultural spheres, but a variety of "green" political movements in Western Europe and the United States have also made their impact on the ecological and nuclear issues. In the socialist and Third World countries, the same set of antitechnocratic sentiments are expressing themselves in movements calling for political decentralization and participation as well as self-reliant development.[3]

A "communitarian society" is, of course, a far more difficult entity to define.[4] There are clearly no historical precedents for it. With the possible exception of modern democracies, all human societies in the past have been based primarily on coercive rather than communicative methods of rule. The idea represents therefore merely a potential—a hope. But this is a hope that is not altogether utopian; it is a historically-grounded hope. Its central concept—communication—suggests an interactive process sharply in contrast to what goes on in the mass communication systems of the world today. It further suggests "communication" against "coercion" as a procedure for discursive will formation for developing genuine "consensus" rather than manufacturing "consent." The new interactive technologies of communication are making this more and more possible. Direct democracy as distinct from representative democracy appears therefore as a viable alternative or a complementary institution. Moreover, the centralized and bureaucratic institutions of both capitalism and communism have produced such a degree of economic exploitation, political alienation, and cultural depersonalization that each system currently faces its own particular brand of legitimation crises (witness Poland alongside the advanced capitalist societies).

But history does not move in a new direction simply because of the presence of some new technological or social possibilities; it takes human consciousness and will to reshape institutions. Such movements as the Green Party in Germany, the Solidarity Movement in Poland, and the Sarvodaya Movement in Sri Lanka suggest that the ideals of a "communitarian" democracy have spread worldwide.[5] These ideals call for peaceful, cooperative, and antitechnocratic strategies of social change, including nuclear and general disarmament, conservation and ecological balance, decentralization and devolution of power, direct democracy, soft and intermediate technologies, smallness, self-reliance and self-management, cultural pluralism and identity, community media, and an economic growth based on intrinsic human needs rather than extrinsic appetites artificially induced by market or bureaucratic forces.

These ideals represent human aspirations against a disturbing situation—replete with the conflicts of a nuclear race, enormous and widening inequalities among and within nations, and cultural homogenization and depersonalization. If these ideals fail to materialize, we might face serious political problems and tragedies. The rise of a variety of dogmatic and fundamentalist movements around the world, in both developed and developing countries, are currently giving vent to the frustrations of the common people against an incomprehensible and unjust world system. If these movements continue to gain momentum, they could once again turn the world into an arena of uncompromising racial, religious, and political prejudices and conflicts.[6]

An "escape from freedom" (Fromm, 1963) and a regression to the sanctity and security of tribal solidarity thus seems to be as likely an outcome of our own age of transition as the realization of its great democratic potentialities. The new information technologies thus present a double-edged sword. On the one hand, they can eliminate the routine and repetitive tasks in production and administration, create greater leisure for cultural and political pluralism, facilitate access and participation in a new direct, electronic democracy, foster open learning systems through tele-education, and extend a variety of other social services (telemedicine, teleshopping, telebanking, telelibrary, etc.) to the remotest and most deprived sectors of the population. But on the other hand, they can also serve as instruments of a new totalitarian hegemony by reinforcing the surveillance powers of the state, expanding the gap between the information-rich and-poor, creating unemployment and underemployment through automation and robotics, and fostering excessive reliance on high technology in the problems of human conflict. The outcome clearly depends not on our stars but on our choices.

In a provocative article, Anthony Smith (1984) calls for a cultural transformation to match the technological upheavals of recent decades. "The advent of computer intelligence," he argues (p. 25), "certainly drives us towards a new attempt to define ourselves as cultural beings operating in time and space. It obliges us to grasp some definition of human totality in order to locate the self. . . . We have today to find a way to be defined as something other than particularly sensitive computers. It seems to me that this wholeness must lie somewhere in the historical sense, the sense of our own interconnections in time and space, in the shadow of which the computer's intelligence is but a copy, a representation, an intelligent picture, a piece of reality, but still object rather than subject." This means nothing less than a recapturing of the human spirit and agency in the face of the technical and organizational monstrosity of technocratic societies.

CONCLUSION

The current debate on "information society" represents a recurrent pattern in the history of major technological breakthroughs. The second Industrial Revolution, as the First, has found its celebrants among those who tend to assume technological determinist views of history. They tend therefore to underestimate the institutional fetters that stand in the way of spreading the full social benefits of the new technologies. They are the technological optimists. At the other extreme, however, we have the technological pessimists—the Luddites.

It would be salutary to remind ourselves that modern societies have proved themselves as prone to the powers of magic and myth as their so-called primitive counterparts. Modern political myths have operated as powerfully as any technology to bring about untold human tragedies in this century. Modern technologies have only put mightier means at the disposal of those myths. Such myths as the "white man's burden" in imperial Europe, "manifest destiny" in imperial America, "Aryan supremacy in imperial Germany, "historical mission of the proletariat" in the imperial Soviet Union, the "chosen people" in an expansionist Israel, and the "Islamic empire" in the fundamentalist movements of the Muslim world provide telling examples. These myths have combined the eschatological promises of a religious zeal with the mundane, political hopes of this world—worldly gain. This tonic has proved enormously powerful both in developed and developing countries. Political religions as well as religious politics fuse temporal and spiritual authorities into a single state apparatus.

The deification of the state on the basis of extremist secular or religious ideologies emanates from a single, inexorable source of power in modern society—the totalization of the means of social control: in production under the auspices of state or corporate capitalism, in surveillance under the authority of totalitarian ideologies, in culture under the auspices of mass communication, and in ecology under the awesome power of modern technologies. But technologies have no will of their own; they are developed by society in response to human needs as defined by our cultural values and institutional arrangements. They produce some intended but also many unintended consequences. They amplify certain power configurations but also set into motion certain powerful countercultural and antisystemic forces. They can be thus understood and tamed only through a reconstruction of our human traditions of civility.

But the new information technologies possess an additional trait that was lacking from most other technologies of the past. They feed on a renewable, self-regenerative, and exponentially-growing resource. The more information we give, the more information we have. Information feeds on information and thus grows at an accelerating rate. But that is also a mixed blessing. The cultural backlash against "information overload" has led, in many parts of the world, to powerful social movements representing escapes from information. These movements recoil from complexity and call for simpler models and choices in facing reality. Since the current information revolution is global in scope, the backlash is also of global dimensions. And since the gaps in information largely correspond to gaps in income and power, we may anticipate a new populist revolt that falls back on the certitudes of the past to face the uncertainties of the future.

NOTES

1. This is a revised version of an article originally published in *InterMedia*, 14(3), May 1986.
2. See the recent report published by Princeton University Press on "the Corporate Universities."
3. For early accounts of the counterculture movement, see Roszek (1969, 1972). For its further developments, see Toffler (1970, 1980); Naisbitt (1982); Ferguson (1981). For the Green Movement, See Capra (1984).
4. See Voge (1983, 1985) for similar distinctions and views.
5. For the Green Movements, see Capra (1984). For the Sarvodaya Movement, see Ariyaratne (1986).
6. For the Islamic fundamentalist movements, see Mortimer (1982) and Tehranian (1980a & b). For the Christian fundamentalist movements, see Armstrong (1979).

REFERENCES

Ariyaratne, A. T. (1986). Learning in Sarvodaya. In Thomas & Ploman (Eds.), *Learning and development: A global perspective.* Toronto: Ontario Institute Studies in Edun.

Armstrong, B. (1979). *The electronic church.* Nashville: Thomas Nelson.

Bell, D. (1978). *The cultural contradictions of capitalism.* New York: Basic Books.

Berger, P. L. (1967). *The sacred canapy: Elements of a sociological theory of religion.* Garden City, NY: Doubleday & Co.

Capra, F., & Spretnak, C. (1984). *Green politics: The global promise.* New York: E. P. Dutton.

Clarke, C. (1940). *The conditions of economic progress.* London: Macmillan.

Dordick, H. S., Bradley, H. G., & Namus, B. (1981). *The emerging network marketplace.* Norwood, NJ: Ablex.

Ellul, J. (1983). *The technological system.* New York: Continuum.

Ferguson, M. (1981). *The Aquarian conspiracy: Personal and social transformation in the 1980s.* Los Angeles & New York: J. P. Tarcher.

Fromm, E. (1963). *Escape from freedom.* New York: Harper & Row.

Galbraith, J. K. (1978). *The new industrial state* (3rd rev. ed.). Boston: Houghton Mifflin.

Ganley, O. H., & Ganley, G. D. (1982). *To inform or to control: The new communications network.* New York: McGraw-Hill.

Innis, H. (1950). *Empire and communications.* Toronto: University of Toronto Press.

Innis, H. (1951). *The bias of communication.* Toronto: University of Toronto Press.

Kumar, K. (1978). *Prophecy and progress: The sociology of industrial and post-industrial society.* New York: Penguin.

Levi-Strauss, C. (1966). *The savage mind.* London: Weidenfeld and Nicholson.

Machlup, F. (1962). *The production and distribution of knowledge in the United States.* Princeton, NJ: Princeton University Press.

Machlup, F. (1980–1984). *Knowledge: Its creation, distribution and economic significance* (vols. 1–3). Princeton University Press.

Malinovsky, S. (1927). *Sex and repression in savage societies.* London: Kegan Paul.

Mortimer, E. (1982). *Faith and power: The politics of Islam.* New York: Vintage Books.

Mosco, V. (1982). *Pushbutton fantasies: Critical perspectives on videotex and information technology.* Norwood, NJ: Ablex.

Naisbitt, J. (1982). *Megatrends: Ten new directions transforming our lives.* New York: Warner Books.

Olsen, R. J. (1986). The digital pacific—Evolution or revolution? In D. J. Wedemeyer & A. Pennings (Eds.), *Pacific Telecommunication Conference 86 Proceedings* (pp. 22–24). Honolulu: Pacific Telecommunication Council.

Porat, M. (1977). *The information economy.* Washington, D.C.: U.S. Office of Telecommunications.

Roszak, T. (1969). *The making of the counter-culture.* New York: Anchor Books.

Roszak, T. (1972). *Where the wasteland ends.* Garden City, NY: Doubleday.

Schiller, H. I. (1981). *Who knows: Information in the age of Fortune 500.* Norwood, NJ: Ablex.

Schiller, H. (1985). *Information and the crisis economy.* Norwood, NJ: Ablex.

Slack, J. D., & Ferjes, F. (Eds.). (1987). *The ideology of the information age.* Norwood, NJ: Ablex.

Smith, A. (1984, November). The self and post-industrial society. *Intermedia, 12,* p. 6.

Tehranian, M. (1980a). The curse of modernity: The dialectics of communications and modernization. *International Social Science Journal, 32*(2).

Tehranian, M. (1980b, Spring). Communication and revolution in Iran: The passing of a paradigm. *Iranian Studies, 13,* 1–4.

Toffler, A. (1970). *Future shock.* New York: Bantam Books.

Toffler, A. (1980). *The third wave.* New York: Bantam Books.

Voge, J. (1983). From information society to communication society. *Pacific Telecommunication Conference 83 Proceedings.* Honolulu: Pacific Telecommunication Conference.

Voge, J. (1985). *Crise, Information et Communications dan l'economie des Etats-Unis.* Unpublished manuscript.

CHAPTER 15 Cultural Imperialism and National Identity

15.1 CEES J. HAMELINK

Cultural Autonomy Threatened

Cees J. Hamelink is a professor of international communication at the University of Amsterdam. His work is part of a wider, critical response to the implications of development theory. Hamelink's recent research has focused on issues concerning human rights and global communication. He has published numerous articles and books on international communication, including *The Politics of World Communication: A Human Rights Perspective* (Sage Publications, 1994).

The following selection is excerpted from Hamelink's book *Cultural Autonomy in Global Communications: Planning National Information Policy* (Longman, 1983). For Hamelink, as for other critical scholars of international communication, development theory acts as an ideological legitimation of the contemporary domination of the so-called Third World by the industrial states and the transnational corporations of the First World. Critical scholars argue that just as the economic aspects of development theory assign less developed nations a subordinate niche in the world

356

Chapter 15
Cultural
Imperialism
and National
Identity

economic order, the cultural dimensions of development theory also assign those nations a subordinate niche in the *world information order*. Though the former European colonies have gained political independence, they are still caught up in economic and cultural dependency on Europe and the United States. The critical approach to international communication views global mass media as key institutions of this new world imperialist system.

For Hamelink it is essential that less developed nations gain economic and cultural autonomy—i.e., that they become less dependent on the industrialized nations of the United States and Europe and become instead more equal participants in the global system.

Key Concept: cultural synchronization

*E*very type of human society is characterized by the necessity to adapt to its environment. For this adaptation human beings develop a series of direct and indirect relations with their environment. The indirect relations constitute the cultural system of a society. This system comprises three types of adaptive relations:

- Instrumental: the instruments (techniques) human beings develop and apply
- Symbolic: the symbols with which human beings communicate
- Social: the patterns of social interaction which people create to carry out the varied tasks of life.

The development of these adaptive relations is an inherent aspect of every society's struggle to survive. Crucial for survival will be the adequacy of a culture system vis-à-vis the environment in which a society finds itself. Different climatic conditions, for example, demand different ways of adapting to them (i.e., different types of food, shelter, and clothing).

The adequacy of the cultural system can best be decided on by the members of the society who face directly the problems of survival and adaptation. They are in the best position to strike the balance between a society's environment and its material and immaterial resources. Critical for a society's chances of survival are the internal capacity and external freedom to develop its cultural system autonomously. Cultural autonomy is fundamental to the independent and full development of every society.

Since environments in which societies have developed have always been diverse, we are confronted in human history with a great variety of cultural systems. Today, however, we see the rapid disappearance of the rich variety of techniques, symbols, and social patterns developed under conditions of relative autonomy.

A quick review of my own experiences of the international scene amply illustrates this point.

- In a Mexican village the traditional ritual dance precedes a soccer match, but the performance features a gigantic Coca-Cola bottle.
- In Singapore, a band dressed in traditional Malay costume offers a heart-breaking imitation of Fats Domino.
- In Saudi Arabia, the television station performs only one local cultural function—the call for the Moslem prayer. Five times a day, North American cops and robbers yield to the traditional muezzin.
- The incredibly rich local musical tradition of many Third World countries is rapidly disappearing under the onslaught of dawn-to-dusk North American pop music.
- For starving children in the Brazilian city of Recife, to have a Barbie doll seems more important than having food.
- In Senegal, a mobile video unit intended to produce popular programs in the village stands idle; the producers of local programs prefer the expensive studio modeled after Western standards.
- In South Africa, skin cream is available that lightens a black complexion. Advertising suggests that black cannot be the ideal of beauty.
- For the poorest of people of Latin America, advertising is an important source of information. North American agencies tell them that the good life is the life of the average consumer in the U.S. Venezuelan housewives are encouraged to identify their happiness with possessing a refrigerator or dishwasher. Advertisements advise the worker in Bogota to escape from the daily routine by means of a U.S.-made Ford or a U.S. airline.
- Nigeria announces a Western color television system when the cost of a black and white set would absorb the annual income of an average farmer.
- On the Indonesian isle of Bali, performers of traditional Ramayana ballet increasingly adapt their presentations to the taste and comprehension of Western tourists.
- U.S. television entertainment fills in larger portions of air time in many countries. Moreover, local programs are produced according to U.S. formats. Even small television networks in poor countries unquestioningly follow the Western example of broadcasting as many hours as possible. Some try to fill 6 to 10 hours daily. Such a practice then pushes these networks into the open arms of Theo Kojak and Starsky and Hutch. Where the production of an authentic local program may cost $1000, the local station owner may import North American culture for less than $500.
- In Central America, school children read in their U.S.-produced textbooks that the Indians living in lands with large gold deposits did not realize its value until the Spaniards told them. In gratitude, the Spaniards taught them reading, writing, and belief in God. The Indians began to work for the Spaniards voluntarily.
- Many broadcasts from All India Radio are loyal copies of BBC models. The most important Indian newspapers could have been edited in Eng-

358

*Chapter 15
Cultural
Imperialism
and National
Identity*

land. The Indian film industry followed the Hollywood path by becoming caught up in the Western preference for sex and violence.

- In its gigantic advertising campaign, IBM assures Navajo Indians that their cultural identity can be effectively protected if they use IBM typewriters equipped with the Navajo alphabet.
- In Algeria, the influence of the French language continues to be so strong that the daily *El Moudjahid* sells ten times more copies of the French than the Algerian edition.
- The millions of copies of Latin American women's magazines disseminate the North American ideal of the efficient, well-dressed, nonpolitical housewife and homemanager.
- In many Third World countries, babies die because imported milk powder replaces efficient and cheap breast-feeding.

This summary is only a selection of the images that thoughtful people in the Third World are increasingly confronting. These observations reflect a trend of cultural awareness that has been well documented in a series of studies. Admittedly, we need more research on precisely *how* the process of cultural "imports" affects the receivers in the long term, especially with respect to cultural norms and behavior.

One conclusion still seems unanimously shared: the impressive variety of the world's cultural systems is waning due to a process of "cultural synchronization" that is without historic precedent. It appears that public recognition of cultural diversity is kept alive only on the folkloric level when traditional ceremonies, flags, and dress adorn international gatherings.

Throughout history, cultures have always influenced one another. The richest cultural traditions emerged at the actual meeting point of markedly different cultural patterns, such as the Sudan, Athens, the Indus Valley, and Mexico. The result of such confrontations, as in the case of African and Arab traditions, was an enriched—not destroyed—culture.

With few exceptions, the cultural history of humankind is not characterized by one-way traffic in cultural confrontation. To be sure, there have been notable and decisive exceptions, as is clear from the destruction of the Aztec and Inca cultures or the Brahmin kingdom of Champa.

But the more general characteristic is that cultural systems either maintain their integrity or develop a more pluralistic and richer pattern. For example, in the process of a two-way exchange, dominant nations with more primitive cultural systems may adopt the more refined systems of the nations they conquer. One illustration is that of Germanic kings who tried to convey classical Roman culture to their people after seizing power in the western Roman empire.

Moreover, in the interaction between "high" and "low" cultures, the latter is often far from passive. In many instances, the bearers of the low culture will actively and selectively adopt only certain cultural traits from the other culture. Some Indian tribes incorporated the Spaniards' use of horses; others, like the sedentary Pueblo Indians, did not.

In many cases, even the great empires of history have allowed dominated peoples their own cultural systems. Often this was a conscious strategy for the maintenance of their position of power. Such a procedure is evident in European colonial history, where the distance between the exclusively Western culture and the indigenous culture is kept as wide as possible.

In the second half of the twentieth century, a destructive process that differs significantly from the historical examples given above threatens the diversity of cultural systems. Never before has the synchronization with one particular cultural pattern been of such global dimensions and so comprehensive. Never before has the process of cultural influence proceeded so subtly, without any blood being shed and with the receiving culture thinking it had sought such cultural influence. It is remarkable that this process should happen exactly when technological development seems to facilitate optimal possibilities for mutual cultural exchange. Modern communications technology is offered to the world with the suggestion that the expression of cultural diversity is now definitely guaranteed. In reality, however, all the evidence indicates that centrally controlled technology has become the instrument through which diversity is being destroyed and replaced by a single global culture.

In international relations the preservation of cultural identity is increasingly a decisive issue. Cultural influence is now a central aspect of the military, political, and economic expansion of the Western industrial states; analysis of cultural penetration provides an essential key to understanding the mechanisms of the international metropolis-satellite structure. "The fundamental metropolis-satellite structure has remained the same throughout, but the basis of metropolitan monopoly has changed over the centuries."[1] This observation by André Frank accurately reflects the experience of many developing countries in the past half century. In the period of colonialism, the dependent satellites were kept under metropolitan control by political and military measures. After the formal recognition of their political independence, political-military coercion became the exception rather than the rule, with some notorious exceptions, such as Guatemala (1954), the Dominican Republic (1965), and Vietnam.

For many nations of Africa, Asia, and Latin America, the postcolonial period cannot be labeled independent, because of the effective maintenance of the dependency structure by such economic tools as loans, aid, investments, and trade conditions. In addition to this economic element, in the second half of this century there is a growing importance of yet another—and in the long run stronger—basis of the metropolis-satellite structure: the mechanism of cultural synchronization.

In the international literature, this phenomenon is usually described as cultural imperialism. I give preference to the concept of cultural synchronization, which is more precise for my purposes. In my view, cultural imperialism is the most frequent, but not exclusive, form in which cultural synchronization occurs. Cultural synchronization can take place without imperialistic relations constituting the prime causal factor or even without any overt imperialistic relations. The latter is illustrated by the adoption in the Soviet mass media of so many Western symbols and production formats.

Exogenous influence may be imposed on the receiving cultural systems or it may be actively invited by them. It is important to stress that even in the latter case, the synchronization with a foreign cultural system will very profoundly affect a society's long-term independent development.

360

*Chapter 15
Cultural
Imperialism
and National
Identity*

The process of cultural synchronization implies that a particular type of cultural development in the metropolitan country is persuasively communicated to the receiving countries. Cultural synchronization implies that the traffic of cultural products goes massively in one direction and has basically a synchronic mode. The metropolis offers the model with which the receiving parties synchronize. The whole process of local social inventiveness and cultural creativity is thrown into confusion or is definitely destroyed. Unique dimensions in the spectrum of human values, which have evolved over centuries, rapidly disappear.

If cultural autonomy is defined as a society's capacity to decide on the allocation of its own resources for adequate adaptation to its environment, then cultural synchronization is a massive threat to that autonomy. Global cultural synchronization locates decisions regarding the allocation of resources extraterritorially. Exogenously developed techniques, symbols, and social patterns are introduced more on the basis of the interests and needs of the metropolis than on the needs and environment of the host country. The indiscriminate adoption of foreign technology can obviously produce profound cultural effects. For example, agricultural mechanization has influenced decisively the allocation of labor resources and, in turn, the pattern of life of large parts of the labor force.

Most striking—and central to the concern of this study—is the *scale* on which the cultural systems of Third World "satellite" countries have over the past three decades adopted techniques, symbols, and social patterns from the highly industrialized metropolitan countries. The transfer of culture from metropolis to satellite is historically not a new phenomenon; but since the 1950s, it takes place in an unprecedentedly large manner. The 1950s were the years of significant transnational expansion of capitalist economies and decisive transnationalization of industrial production.[2] The agents of the metropolitan economy, specifically the transnational corporations, are introducing throughout the world a revolution in commercial thinking: the world should be seen as one economic unit.[3]

The transnational firm no longer recognizes the validity of the autonomous national state or national culture. Consequently, as Jacques Maisonrouge, IBM president of the European division, states: the basic conflict of this new period is "between the search for global optimization of resources and the independence of nation-states."[4] Transnational firms consider national boundaries politically, economically, and culturally obsolete and unable to define business requirements or consumer trends. The world is one marketplace and the world customer is essential for that market. World market and world customer demand an optimal synchronization of cultural values so that authentic national characteristics do not jeopardize the unit of the transnational system.

The satellite countries therefore are incorporated in the transnational system by the persuasive marketing of cultural values that legitimize metropolitan interests. The concept of development, for example, is marketed in its equation with the concept of modernization. The developed nation is the modern nation that achieves the per capita income and the rate of mechanization and urbanization of the advanced industrial state.

In this move toward strengthening the cultural basis for the international dependency structure, the communication industrial complex is a vital element. The international flow of communications has, in fact, become the main carrier of transnational cultural synchronization.

Cultural synchronization and its function in the maintenance of the metropolis-satellite structure cannot be understood without knowledge of the role of the ruling class in the satellite countries. The class of internal colonialists is the crucial link between foreign interests and the exploited masses. A notorious example is the traditional elite of Latin American society—wealthy families who own the national newspaper chains and benefit greatly from alliance with the transnational corporations.

A classic example of the relation between a local elite controlling the media and transnational communication interests is the situation faced by Allende in Chile when he was elected in 1974. A major part of Chilean magazine publishing was dominated by the Edwards family, who also owned the influential and widely circulated newspaper *El Mercurio* and had exclusive rights for the AP, Reuters, and Agence France Presse news agencies. Edwards was president of the Inter American Press Association; the president of the Edwards group was at the same time president of IBEC (International Basic Economy Corporation). "Through this stock company, numerous national firms were controlled by North American investors, the majority of whom belonged to the Rockefeller group."[5]

The national elite provides the nationalist legitimization of the dependency system, the local marketing knowledge, and the "native" capital, which represents in many dependent countries an increasing share of industrial investment. Nationally dominant classes are the convenient intermediaries for the global spreading of a profit-oriented mercantilistic and consumer culture.

One must be aware that cultural influence through the communications industry does not always occur in a direct way. Many people in Third World countries are scarcely touched by the modern electronic and print media. Television, newspaper, films, and books are still inaccessible to millions of people in Africa, Asia, and Latin America. It is the urban elite and middle class who are most exposed to the North American influence on the local communication industry. If the ruling elite accept the imported social models, however, their action will certainly be decisive for the economic and cultural environment of the rest of the population.

Historically, industrialization has transcended the national borders and become global. In this transnationalization, the configuration of cultural values is inevitably mediated on a global scale, becoming the cultural basis in dependent countries for reproducing the modes of production, distribution, exchange, and consumption of the metropolis. As part of this global marketing system, the cultural commodities manufactured in the metropolis—films, television series, pop music—are massively exported to be reproduced, distributed, exchanged, and consumed in the satellite countries, thus competing with indigenous cultural values and cultural forms of expression.

In the process of transnationalization, the public media are the major cultural institutions mediating the values inherent in industrialization. Their mode of mediation is generally synchronic. This means that in most social systems the public transmission of information and entertainment is guided by a concern to create a consensus regarding societal goals and their underlying

362

*Chapter 15
Cultural
Imperialism
and National
Identity*

values. This synchronization is made operative on a global scale by the transnational communications industry, which concomitantly with the transnational industrial expansion of past decades as extended the production and distribution of its goods and services from national to international markets.

Two factors are of vital importance in this process. On the one hand, in a number of branches of the communication industry, production for the home market remains the principal objective. Consider the examples of the international news agencies UPI and AP. Their most important market (between 60 percent and 70 percent of total revenues) is the public media in the United States; the production and distribution of their international product is thus guided primarily by the logic of the local national market.

On the other hand, some products of the communications industry, such as many of the television series, cannot hope to cover production costs with revenues from the home market alone. Costs for an average one-hour television drama ... amount roughly to $400,000. Sales to television stations in the United States cover 75 percent of these costs, so that export becomes an evident necessity. Thus, a mass product has to be manufactured that has a sufficiently universal appearance to be salable anywhere in the world.

With the global expansion of the communication industry, television and film production companies, news agencies, advertising firms, and publishing houses have become transnational corporations of impressive scope. In their strategy of diversification, many industrial corporations have adopted communication as a profitable investment. Between 10 and 15 percent of the largest corporations in the world have considerable interests in the international communication trade.

Increasing concentration of economic power has developed, just as in other branches of industrial activity; 75 percent of today's international communication market is controlled by some 80 transnational corporations. These corporations introduce value patterns which are native to the metropolis but which have no relation to the genuine social needs of the receiving countries. One analyst notes that in Latin America, the foreign-dominated radio and television systems carry values that are alien to the real needs of these societies. Creation of social myths and false heroes and overemphasis on entertainment and violence are all instruments of alienation and cultural disorientation.[6]

Studies by the Finnish researchers Kaarel Nordenstreng and Tapio Varis indicate that entertainment is heavily represented in the one-way traffic of television programs in the world, which leads to a global spreading of cultural values that pervade the soap opera and crime series produced in the metropolitan nations.[10] The industrial corporations, however, provide more than just television programs; they also graciously entertain the world with films, records, cassettes, women's magazines, and children's comics. Illustrative examples of the last come from the Walt Disney Corporation. Although it is claimed that the characters in the comic strips are nonpolitical, a closer analysis shows that the fantasy world of Disney has a strong political orientation.[8]

Although the international communications flow tends to consist mainly of entertainment products, the role of international news in transferring values should not be underestimated. The selection of news by the few large international news agencies undoubtedly reflects the values of metropolitan countries.

Most developing countries are dependent on this choice for their information on events outside their country. They receive international news as well as news about themselves via the news centers in New York, Paris, or London. "In the absence of a national news agency in Thailand, India receives only the American or British version of events in that country. How that keeps Thailand and India from understanding each other more deeply and readily is for those who know how to judge."[9]

The transnational communication-industrial complex is apparently characterized by an impressive variety of structures and contents; in fact, however, there is great uniformity. Both organizational structure and product are North American. Evidently the United Kingdom and France are also important exporters of media institutional patterns and products. The United Kingdom and France are subcenters of the North American communications industry, because their organizational structure and their media contents follow North American models (although there are French and British peculiarities that played an important role in the synchronization process occurring between these metropolitan subcenters and their own satellite countries). Moreover, in the Third World there are media exporters of some scope, such as Egypt and Mexico, although their own programming content is basically an adaptation of North American examples. Even the socialist countries are following the North American lead in many respects, despite the relatively infrequent flow of communications between East and West.

Of the various reasons for North American domination, the most important is economic. The enormous size of the media market in the United States of America has made it possible to develop very large communications corporations. Ready access to finance capital, technology, and marketing channels have also been important factors in the rapid creation of operations on a large scale. Such a strong national base has facilitated the expansion into the international market. The active colloboration between the communications industry and North American political, financial, and military circles has further strengthened such international expansion. This combination of economic and political factors has made it possible for corporations based in the United States not only to exploit technological possibilities but also to determine the popular media formats. Thus, the communications industry in the United States was always one step ahead of the rest of the world, especially in the critical period after World War II. Other countries could be offered a ready-made model with prices so low that competition was excluded.[10] . . .

THE CENTRAL THREAT TO CULTURAL AUTONOMY: CULTURAL SYNCHRONIZATION

. . . The cultural system of a society is here seen as the totality of instrumental, symbolic, and social adaptive relations which have evolved so that the society can create a truly human existence within the variety of the world's environments. The autonomy of people in their cultural development, that is, the

364

*Chapter 15
Cultural
Imperialism
and National
Identity*

ability of people to respond according to their own best intuitions, is crucial in establishing an adequate cultural system.

Few, if any, cultures have developed as completely isolated phenomena; part of adaptive cultural growth is selective borrowing and exchange. In recent decades, however, there has arisen a process best described as cultural synchronization which threatens, as never before, the delicate balance of adaptive cultural relations in many parts of the world. Cultural synchronization implies that the decisions regarding the cultural development in a given country are made in accordance with the interests and needs of a powerful central nation and imposed with subtle but devastating effectiveness without regard for the adaptive necessities of the dependent nation.

The principal agents of cultural synchronization today are the transnational corporations, largely based in the United States, which are developing a global investment and marketing strategy. The transnational corporations which are most directly involved with the cultural component of this global expansion are the international communications firms.

REFERENCES

1. A G. Frank, *Capitalism and Underdevelopment in Latin America,* rev. ed., Baltimore, Penguin, 1971, p. 177.

2. Robin Murray, "The Internationalization of Capital and the Nation State," in H. Radice (ed.), *International Firms and Modern Imperialism,* Baltimore, Penguin, 1975, p. 128.

3. Richard Barnet and Ronald Muller, *Global Reach,* New York, Simon and Schuster, 1974, p. 18.

4. In an address to the American Foreign Service Association, Washington, D.C., 29 May 1969.

5. Armand Mattelart, "Mass media and the Socialist Revolution: The Experience of Chile," in George Gerbner et al. (eds.), *Communication Technology and Social Policy,* New York, Wiley, 1973, pp. 425–440.

6. Marco Ordonez, *Los problemas estructuarles de la comunicacion colectiva,* Quito, CIESPAL, 1974, p. 6.

7. *Televisiontraffic: a One-Way Street?,* Paris, UNESCO, 1974.

8. Ariel Dorfman and Armand Mattelart, *How to Read Donald Duck,* New York, International General, 1975.

9. A. Mitra, "Information Imbalance," paper presented at ILET Conference, Mexico, 1976.

10. Jeremy Tunstall, *the Media are American,* New York, Columbia University Press, 1977.

15.2 ALI MOHAMMADI

Cultural Imperialism and Cultural Identity

The work of Ali Mohammadi is part of a recent shift in critical scholarship of international communication toward a focus on the construction of national-cultural identities in the former European colonies of Africa, Asia, and the Americas. From this perspective, mass media, along with other cultural forms such as literature, do not operate in any simple or unidirectional way to impose cultural domination. Mass media and popular culture are caught up in conflicts over cultural tradition and national independence. For example, in *The Empire Writes Back* (Routledge, 1989), Bill Ashcroft, Gareth Griffiths, and Helen Tifflin show that writers in postcolonial societies do not simply adopt European literary forms and styles. Rather, they *adapt* them to the complex and contradictory problems of expressing their own cultural situation, in particular the problem of resisting European domination.

In the following selection from "Cultural Imperialism and Cultural Identity," in John Downing, Ali Mohammadi, and Annabelle Sreberny-Mohammadi, eds., *Questioning the Media: A Critical Introduction,* 2d ed. (Sage Publications, 1995), Mohammadi argues that global media today are controlled by a narrow set of powerful economic and political interests and are enmeshed within a new imperialist order. However, in the case of the Iranian revolution, resistance to the U.S.-supported dictatorship of the Shah was fermented through the use of alternative, "small" media: cheaply produced and widely distributed cassette recordings of religious leaders. These recordings helped cultivate a powerful sense of Muslim identity and solidarity among many otherwise diverse segments of the Iranian population, which, according to Mohammadi, played a large part in the overthrow of the Shah's regime.

Mohammadi teaches and conducts his research at Nottingham Trent University in England. He and Annabelle Srebreny-Mohammadi have written more extensively on postcolonialism and the Iranian situation in *Small Media, Big Revolution: Communications, Culture, and the Iranian Revolution* (University of Minnesota Press, 1994).

Key Concept: alternative media and the struggle over cultural identity

INTERNATIONAL POWERS AND NATIONAL CULTURES: AN UNEVEN CONTEXT

One description of the world we live in it "postimperialist." Much of world history from 1945 has centered on the struggles of subjugated peoples to extricate themselves from the European empires of the nineteenth century and to create the newly independent nations of Africa, the Middle East, and Asia. But despite the demise of political imperialism, the economic dominance of the West has meant that many nations of the Third World find themselves still tied in very complex ways to the dynamics of Western industrial societies. Hence these Third World nations find it very difficult to pursue their own definitions of, and paths to, independent development. These new ties are different from the older ties of imperialism. The new kinds of ties are often referred to as ties of *dependency*, and "cultural imperialism" has been analyzed as one major form of dependency. The purpose of this [selection] is to analyze this new cultural imperialism and to show the vitally important role that communications technologies and flows of cultural products have in keeping planetary ties of dependency alive.

This process will be illustrated through a detailed examination of one Third World country, Iran. Although at the turn of the twentieth century the British and the Russians competed for influence in Iran, and the United States played a major role in Iranian affairs, helping to reinstate the shah in 1953, Iran was never directly colonized. Iran tried very deliberately to use communications for a particular development strategy, one strongly supported by the West, but found that the costs were greater than the benefits. This is a case study with powerful implications for other Third World nations and for mainstream—noncritical—communications analysis.

WHAT IS IMPERIALISM?

The essence of imperialism is domination by one nation over another. That relationship might be direct or indirect, and might be based on a mixture of military, political, and economic controls. There have been many different forms of imperial relations throughout world history, from the Greek and Roman empires to the Persian, Moghul, Chinese, Ottoman, and many others. But the forms of empire that have had the greatest impact on our contemporary world are the European, American, and Japanese forms of empire that prevailed through the nineteenth century into the twentieth century. Even European domination went through various stages. There were relationships that were more purely economic or "mercantilist," as in the early Portuguese empire, where the European power essentially extracted the resources it required, whether gold or ivory or slaves, from the dominated territory. Often such relations required military conquest on the outset and a continued military presence to enforce the economic exploitation.

By the end of the nineteenth century, a few form of relation had been developed that was based on the formal conquest, annexation, and administration of territories by the imperial powers. As Hobsbawm (1989) summarizes the process:

> Between 1880 and 1914 . . . most of the world outside Europe and the Americas was formally partitioned into territories under the formal rule or informal political domination of one or the other of a handful of states: mainly Great Britain, France, Germany, Italy, the Netherlands, Belgium, the USA and Japan. (p. 57)

About one-quarter of the globe's land surface was distributed or redistributed among a half dozen states, ushering in the age of imperialism based on colonial rule. This form of direct political and administrative domination helped to create a truly planetary capitalist economy in which economic transactions and flows of goods, capital, and people now penetrated into the most remote regions. The world was fundamentally divided into strong and weak, advanced and backward areas (Hobsbawm, 1989).

There were many different reactions to and consequences of imperialism, both within the "mother" power, such as movements for democracy, for socialism, and for women's rights, and also within the Third World, where revolution—as in Mexico between 1910 and 1920 or in China toward the end of the nineteenth century—or growing anticolonial movements for liberation—as in India—began to develop. Since 1945, the "postwar world" has been defined by these struggles against imperial domination and the success of independence movements in the creation of "new," independent political nations in Africa, Asia, and the Middle East. Thus, for example, India freed itself from the British in 1947, Indonesia liberated itself from the Dutch in 1960, Zaire was freed from Belgian domination in 1960, and Algeria became independent from the French in 1962 (Harris, 1987).

This process of political independence might appear to be the end of the story, but in fact it is only the start of a new global dynamic that we might label the process of *cultural imperialism* or *cultural dependency*. When the colonial powers packed their bags and removed their nationals from administrative positions directly running the government and the economy, that was not the end of their influence. Often they left behind a European language, as the "lingua franca" of the country's new governing classes. They left behind European values and attitudes, including religion, ways of organizing public life, styles of politics, forms of education, and professional training, clothing styles, and many other cultural habits, none of which had existed prior to colonial domination. All of these phenomena continued to have effects long after the formal, direct, political rule of the colonies was ended, and have created a new kind of model of domination called *neocolonialism*. In turn, neocolonialism has sparked new kinds of struggles to eradicate this enduring cultural influence in the Third World. Let us look at the constitution of this Third World and then examine how cultural issues came to be such a central focus in current international politics. . . .

CULTURAL IDENTITY IN THE THIRD WORLD

It was the independence movements in the developing world that made many people aware of the cultural dimensions of colonial domination. Many leaders in the Third World have paid serious and continuing attention to the issue of cultural freedom. For example, one of Gandhi's major concerns while he led India's independence movement was how to create an independent national identity that could united the Indian people, who were scattered over 750,000 villages and spoke many different languages. Concerned about how to foster national unity in the face of the legacy of British cultural domination, Gandhi once proclaimed:

> I do not want my house to be walled on all sides and my windows to be stuffed. I want the culture of all lands to be blown about my house as freely as possible but I refuse to be blown off my feet by any one of them. (quoted in Hamelink, 1983, p. 26)

In a major echo of Gandhi's concern, at a key 1973 meeting of the heads of states of the nonaligned nations there was a formal joint declaration that the activities of imperialism were not limited to the economic and political domains, but encompassed social and cultural areas as well, imposing a foreign ideological domination on the peoples of developing world. Many Third World nations were becoming aware of the superiority of the advanced world, in communications technologies but also in communications software, the news, entertainment, and other cultural products that the technologies transmitted, and that, as a result, their own national cultures and identities had become threatened (Harris, 1987).

It is not very hard to recognize that the continuance of Western dominance over Third World nations, even after their formal independence, was based partly on advanced technologies, including communication technologies. But it was also based on an ideology, accepted in many parts of the Third World, that there was only one path to economic development, which was to emulate the process of development of Western industrial capitalist societies.

In the 1960s, when certain Third World nations did not appear to be developing economically as fast as they had been expected to, Western analysts began to develop models and theories of development and to explain the "blockages" to development that they thought prevented Third World countries from developing like Western ones. . . .

What was valuable in the traditional culture was defined, effectively, as anything that did not impede the growth of Western capitalist endeavors; what had to change culturally was anything that interfered with this process. . . .

To begin to draw attention to some of these issues, it is instructive to examine a major Middle Eastern nation at the heart of the U.S. and Western oil-related strategy in the region, namely, Iran. . . . Iran is . . . an instructive case study because it was never directly colonized, so an examination of the impact of Western culture in Iran shows vividly how neocolonial subordination and cultural inferiority can be fostered from a distance, without the elaborate machinery of colonial rule.

Iran is located on the southern border of Central Asia and stretches south to the Persian Gulf. It borders Turkey to the northwest and Afghanistan and Pakistan to the east. In 1994 it had a population of more than 60 million. From a geopolitical viewpoint, the strategic location of Iran between East and West is very crucial. Iran's political system up to 1979 was monarchical dictatorship, but then, 2,500 years of kingship were terminated by the Iranian revolution under the leadership of the Ayatollah Khomeini.

Media and Development in Iran

Through a close look at the process of development in Iran we can see a clear pattern of dependent economic development that was centrally based on the export of crude oil and raw materials, with expansion linked to foreign investment. This economic dependence provided the basis for political and military dependence in both technological and human expertise. In the 1970s businessmen from all over the world waited in Tehran hotels to clinch multimillion-dollar deals of all kinds. Slowly, too, the media in Iran tried to convince people of the benefits of modernity and created new needs that consumer durables could satisfy.

Prior to World War II, Iran did not have a national broadcasting system. Iran's first radio transmitter went on the air in 1940. Radio programs were limited to evening broadcasts that consisted of the national anthem, major messages from government, news, and some Persian and Western music. In the early days of radio, loudspeakers and radio receivers were hooked up in various parts of Tehran, the capital, and people were very excited by this unprecedented form of communication. When the national anthem was played, people would rise and stand still. This was one of the first modern symbols of Iranian nationhood, broadcast over electronic media imported from the advanced world. Slowly, radio was used to maintain political control, to spread the ideological rhetoric of modernization, and to prepare Iranians for the neocolonial relationship that would strengthen after World War II.

In 1959, the last shah of Iran was persuaded by an imaginative urban entrepreneur to allow the establishment of commercial television. The entrepreneur was the son of a rich businessman whose wealth was based on importing Pepsi Cola from the United States. This first television station was allowed to operate tax free for five years while it developed commercial television and promoted the expansion of a consumer market, as in the United States. The family who controlled the television monopoly also controlled the importation of most television receivers, prossessing the franchise of RCA products in Iran.

Television became a multiplier of Western and consumption values. These were overtly displayed in advertisements for new consumer products and were also embedded in the depiction of Western lifestyles carried by American films and television series such as *I Love Lucy* and *Bonanza*. Private television supported the monarchy's strategy of capitalist development. After

370

*Chapter 15
Cultural
Imperialism
and National
Identity*

some studies were undertaken, and worried that the Baha'i religious sect was monopolizing television, the shah decided to take over private television and transform it into a government-financed and -operated service. In 1966 National Iranian Television started broadcasting (its first message was from the shah, of course), and among the first test week's programming was the broadcast of the shah's birthday celebration. Soon radio was amalgamated with television to create National Iranian Radio and Television (NIRT). Consumerism was still encouraged through advertising, but, more important, NIRT tried to foster support for the regime through the glorification of the monarchy and support for modernization, maintaining the state ideology. Every royal activity was broadcast, and the glorious history of 2,500 years of Persian monarchy was celebrated wherever possible, but the media also propagated the idea that the shah's major concern was to modernize Iran along the lines of the countries of Western Europe; television nightly news began with images of dams and new buildings, the physical symbols of development.

Radio and television wee given substantial government budgets, so that coverage expanded rapidly. From 2 television transmitters in 1966, the number rose to 88 by 1974, and coverage increased from 2.1 million people to 15 million of both urban and rural populations, more than half the country; radio coverage was almost universal (Mohammadi, 1976). By the mid-1970s, NIRT had became the second-largest broadcasting network in Asia, after NHK of Japan. Thus most of the nation was connected through broadcasting, linking small villages with major urban centers and creating a novel national audience.

Yet, at the same time, literacy levels remained low, particularly for women, and there were not enough primary schools to accommodate all children of school age. Publishing and the press were strictly censored, so there was little choice among the dull daily newspapers, which thus had very low circulations. One commentator noted that "if Iran continues on its present path, it will be the first nation in the world to have nationally spread television before a nationally spread press." Thus Iran seemed to leap over the stage of literacy and print development, moving almost directly from a traditional oral culture to an electronic one.

Even a brief glance at Iranian mass media in the mid-1970s would have indicated that the broadcast or published materials were not designed to preserve national culture or to raise the level of public education. Rather, they promoted the alluring manifestation of Western culture, with little consideration of the urgent needs and demands of Iranian society; they did little more than amuse and entertain their audience. One international study made in 1975 revealed that of 11 developing countries studied, NIRT had one of the highest levels of imported television programming, including Western feature films—78% of all television content—and broadcast the lowest proportion of serious programs—only 22% of total broadcast time. Typical imported programs were *Baretta, Star Trek, Marcus Welby, MD, Tarzan,* and the soap opera *Days of Our Lives.* When homemade programs were aired they became extremely popular, but much domestic programming was rather anemic because of actual and self-censorship. The prevailing policy seemed to disregard the cultural implications of importing so much Western media content, which carried Western lifestyles, gender roles, consumption values, and so on. And whereas, for many developing countries, the economic argument that it is much cheaper to buy foreign programming than to produce your own had some justification, NIRT's large budgets did not support such an argument. It seemed to be safer for the regime to allow a lot of Western entertainment to be imported than allow possibly critical homemade programs to appear (Motamed-Nejad, 1976).

The rapid expansion of broadcasting was a central element of the shah's ambitious development project, as he tried to use the communications media to help bring about the change from a traditional to a modern society. But it failed because the modernization process did not go far enough; indeed, the strategy has been described as "pseudo-modernization," a desire for the superficial style of modernity without the deeper structural changes that true development requires. For example, the government, through the mass media, talked about modernization but failed to provide adequate and coherent national health care or education. It spent millions in developing NIRT, but failed to electrify large areas, so many rural people ran their televisions and lighting from small portable generators. It talked about improving working conditions, but would not allow labor unions to operate. It established many universities, but would not allow the free exchange of ideas or free access to written materials. Iranian writers, artists, and broadcasters all had to fit in with the prevailing rhetoric of modernization, and no criticism was allowed. The security system of SAVAK (the shah's secret police) was waiting for any oppositional voices to be raised. Severe political repression thus blocked popular participation and discussion of social needs, the heart of political development.

Those in the educated middle class felt frustrated about the lack of political participation and the lack of cultural freedom, which allowed importation of American television but blocked the production of good, critical, indigenous programs. They felt frustrated as the political concerns of the state interfered in the legal system, the educational system, and the broadcasting system, undermining professional practices and independence. They felt the pinch of rampant inflation in the 1970s, with house and car prices rocketing, and watched as foreign "experts" were favored over Iranians with comparable skills.

The traditional middle classes, particularly the bazaar merchants and the clergy, were threatened by this Westernized mode of development. The economic position of the bazaaris was being undermined by large multinational corporations and agribusiness, and the social authority of the clergy was threatened by secular education and the media. They were also horrified at the effects Western values were having on the fabric of Iranian society. For example, the system of dating and marriage shown in the imported Western programming was totally in contradiction with the Islamic tradition of marriage, in which parents play a very significant role in selecting a suitable spouses and dating of any sort without the presence of a relative is not allowed. Khomeini had been speaking out since the 1940s about the negative impact of Western values, and warned that the media were propaganda vehicles for Western imperialists who were trying to undermine Iran. Some religious authorities publicly denounced watching television, and others declared that having a television was a sinful act. The city of Qum, which is the equivalent of the Vatican for Iranian Shi'ite Muslims, actually banned television during the shah's reign.

372

Chapter 15
Cultural
Imperialism
and National
Identity

From 1976, helped by Jimmy Carter's human rights policy, both the secular opposition and the religious opposition began to use a variety of small media to voice their objections to the regime. Professional groups such as lawyers and writers wrote "open letters" to the shah, demanding an end to regime intervention in the process of law and greater freedom of expression. The religious opposition also began to mobilize, and developed a communications system quite independent from the big media of the state to politicize the people. The leaders used the national network of mosques and bazaars to preach their Islamic identity against the dependent Westernization of the shah. When Khomeini left his isolated placed of exile in a small village in Iraq for the outskirts of Paris in 1977, he became the focus of much Western media attention. Also, the religious network transmitted his speeches across the international telephone lines to Tehran, and within hours thousands of audiocassettes of his voice were available on the streets of the capital and were carried to other cities and villages for all to hear—a new international electronic pulpit, In a still very oral culture, where the clergy have great social authority and are used to addressing ordinary people at the mosques, this was very powerful (Sreberny-Mohammadi & Mohammadi, 1994).

A popular movement against the shah began to grow, and when demonstrators were killed through regime violence, the Islamic mourning pattern of the seventh and fortieth days gave the demonstrations a religious rhythm. Gradually, political groups—communist, socialist, nationalist, democratic—banned by the regime resurfaced and countless photocopied leaflets began to circulate, setting out analyses, making political demands, organizing demonstrations. Thus certain small media, particularly audiocassettes and leaflets, were used very effectively in the Iranian popular mobilization. . . . These small media are interesting because they are so easily reproduced, making it extremely difficult for any regime to block their circulation. When the military tried to maintain order and took over NIRT in November 1978, the personnel went on strike, so for three months radio and television were run by the military while the professionals produced underground newspapers debunking the regime news.

Thus a combination of religious authority and small media mobilized some of the largest demonstrations in recent history, bringing together modern and traditional groups united in hostility to the pattern of Westernized development of the shah, combining a mixture of economic discontents, political frustrations, and cultural concerns into a single slogan, "Down with the shah." In January 1979, the shah left "on holiday," never to return, and in February, the Ayatollah Khomeini established the Islamic Republic of Iran.

CONCLUSION

The communication and development model failed to understand the historically different cultural contexts of Third World societies; as applied to Iran, it served to bring the West into Iranian living rooms and allowed Iranians to compare themselves with Westerners, exacerbating existing economic, political, and cultural frustrations. The model failed to pay attention to political development or less quantifiable aspirations such as equality, justice, freedom, identity, and even happiness. In the context of Iran, the communications and development process seemed to suggest that Western patterns of life and attitudes were the only ones of value, to be imitated by Iranians, and that indigenous Iranian culture had little to offer. The process created not only great gaps of wealth between urban elites and the rural poor but also a deep sense of cultural inferiority, which the clergy effectively used to mobilize people against the regime.

Frantz Fanon (1967) presents a vivid image of the effects of Western cultural products on the people of the Third World:

> Young people have at their disposition leisure occupations designed for the youth of capitalist countries: detective novels, penny-in-the-slot machines, sexy photographs, pornographic literature, films banned to those under sixteen, and above all alcohol. In the West the family circle, the effects of education and the relatively high standard of living of the working classes provide a more or less efficient protection against the harmful action of these pastimes. But in an African country, where mental development is uneven, where the violent collision of two worlds has considerably shaken old traditions and thrown the universe of the perceptions out of focus, the impressionability and sensibility of the young Africans are at the mercy of the various assaults made upon them by the very nature of Western culture. (pp. 157–158)

Although written about a different cultural context, these words could also be applied to Iran. The development strategy in Iran was undermining the very basis of cultural identity and the traditional values of Iranian society. The rapid change from small-scale self-sufficiency to commodity production for the markets, the neglect of channels for political participation, and the blocking of self-expression and indigenous cultural development undermined the harmony and tranquility of cultural life. The process of development, by definition, upsets the pattern of life that went before, but in the West that process went hand in hand with the basic values and cultural patterns of those societies. In Iran, as in much of the developing world, development was replaced by a mimetic Westernization, a copying of the superficial elements of the modern West without the fundamental political and social changes required. Economic dependency, as in the spread of montage industries, which merely assemble consumer technologies developed elsewhere (thus not helping an independent economic sector to grow), was supported by cultural dependency, in which mass media broadcast news and cultural entertainment programs more attuned to the markets of industrial nations or regime needs than the cultural habits of the Iranian people.

Iran is a unique example of a Third World country that implemented the communication and development model to accelerate the process of modernization, and the model failed dramatically. Communications can help people find new norms and harmony in a period of transition, but in the Iranian case, the effect was totally the reverse.

374

*Chapter 15
Cultural
Imperialism
and National
Identity*

The Iranian experience makes us question the powerful media/powerful effects model of communication. The shah could control all the media, but he could not produce political legitimacy. And Iranians could watch a lot of American programming and still prefer their own values. Thus both the communications and development model—which suggested that media could play such an important, positive, role in economic and political development—*and* the cultural imperialism model—which said that media were carriers of Western values that would swamp Third World cultures—are too one-dimensional, as the Iranian movement has shown.

The rhetoric of revolution included slogans against Westernization, consumerism, and the idea of self-determination, expressed in the slogan of "Not East, nor West, only Islam." The tragedy of Iran is that although cultural identity may be an important appeal against the forces of Westernization, it alone does not guarantee broader progressive social values such as freedom and justice, which were fundamental demands of the popular movement. Also, many felt that their religious identity was their cultural identity, not anticipating the rigid fundamentalism that ensued; currently, many Iranians are concerned that their traditional Iranian culture and its music and dance are being suppressed. Many have been killed or imprisoned, and many others have left Iran. The Islamic Republic has thus bitterly disappointed many hopes, and has inherited many of the old problems that the shah did not solve. Analyzing the global context in which Iranian modernization and then popular resistance took place helps to explain the deep dilemmas of political, economic, and cultural development that confront Third World nations.

REFERENCES

Fannon, F. (1967) *The wretched of the earth.* Middlesex: Penguin.

Hamelink, C. J. (1983) *Finance and information.* Norwood, NJ: Ablex.

Hobsbawm, E. (1989). *Age of empire.* New York: Vintage.

Mohammadi, A. (1976). *Development-support communication and instructional learning centers for rural areas in Iran.* Unpublished doctoral dissertation, Columbia University.

Motamed-Nejad, K. (1976). *Communication and Westernization.* Tehran: College of Mass Communication.

Sreberny-Mohammadi, A., & Mohammadi, A. (1994). *Small media, big revolution: Communications, culture and the Iranian revolution.* Minneapolis: University of Minnesota.

1.2 From Kurt Lang and Gladys Engel Lang, "The Mass Media and Voting," in Eugene Burdick and Arthur J. Brodbeck, eds., *American Voting Behavior* (Free Press, 1959). Copyright © 1959 by The Free Press. Reprinted by permission of The Free Press, a division of Simon & Schuster.

2.1 From Harold D. Lasswell, "The Structure and Function of Communication in Society," in Lyman Bryson, ed., *The Communication of Ideas* (Institute for Religious & Social Studies, 1948), pp. 37–48, 51. Copyright © 1948 by The Louis Finkelstein Institute for Religious & Social Studies–Jewish Theological Seminary of America. Reprinted by permission.

2.2 From Hadley Cantril, *The Invasion from Mars: A Study in the Psychology of Panic* (Harper Torchbooks, 1940), pp. 3, 47, 55–63, 190–205. Copyright © 1940; renewed 1968 by Princeton University Press. Reprinted by permission. Some notes omitted.

2.3 From Elihu Katz, "The Two-Step Flow of Communication: An Up-to-Date Report on an Hypothesis," *Public Opinion Quarterly*, vol. 21, no. 1 (Spring 1957), pp. 61–62, 65–77. Copyright © 1957 by University of Chicago Press. Reprinted by permission. Some notes omitted.

2.4 From Albert Bandura, Dorothea Ross, and Sheila A. Ross, "Imitation of Film-Mediated Aggressive Models," *Journal of Abnormal and Social Psychology*, vol. 66, no. 1 (January 1963), pp. 3–5, 7–11. Copyright © 1963 by The American Psychological Association. Reprinted by permission. Notes omitted.

3.1 From Charles R. Wright, *Mass Communication: A Sociological Perspective,* 3rd ed. (Random House, 1986). Copyright © 1986 by Random House. Reprinted by permission.

3.2 From Elihu Katz, Jay G. Blumler, and Michael Gurevitch, "Utilization of Mass Communication by the Individual," in Jay G. Blumler and Elihu Katz, eds., *The Uses of Mass Communications* (Sage Publications, 1974), pp. 19–32. Copyright © 1974 by Sage Publications, Inc. Reprinted by permission.

4.1 From Maxwell E. McCombs and Donald L. Shaw, "The Agenda-Setting Function of Mass Media," *Public Opinion Quarterly*, vol. 36, no. 1 (Spring 1972), pp. 176–182, 184–187. Copyright © 1972 by University of Chicago Press. Reprinted by permission.

4.2 From Kathleen Hall Jamieson, *Packaging the Presidency: A History and Criticism of Presidential Campaign Advertising,* 2d ed. (Oxford University Press, 1992), pp. 485–492. Copyright © 1992 by Oxford University Press. Reprinted by permission. Notes omitted.

4.3 From Roderick P. Hart, *Seducing America: How Television Charms the Modern Voter* (Oxford University Press, 1994). Copyright © 1994 by Oxford University Press, Inc. Reprinted by permission.

5.1 From George Gerbner, Larry Gross, Michael Morgan, and Nancy Signorielli, "The 'Mainstreaming' of America: Violence Profile No. 11," *Journal of Communication*, vol. 30, no. 3 (1980), pp. 10–29. Copyright © 1980 by George Gerbner. Reprinted by permission. Some notes omitted.

5.2 From Michael Morgan, "Television and Democracy," in Ian Angus and Sut Jhally, eds., *Cultural Politics in Contemporary America* (Routledge, 1989). Copyright © 1989 by Routledge, Chapman and Hall, Inc. Reprinted by permission of the publisher. Notes omitted.

6.1 From Marshall McLuhan, *Understanding Media: The Extensions of Man,* 2d ed. (Signet, 1964), pp. vii–ix, 19–35. Copyright © 1964 by Marshall McLuhan. Reprinted by permission.

6.2 From Neil Postman, *Amusing Ourselves to Death: Public Discourse in the Age of Show Business* (Penguin, 1985), pp. 83–98. Copyright © 1985 by Neil Postman. Reprinted by permission of Viking Penguin, a division of Penguin Books USA, Inc. Notes omitted.

6.3 From Joshua Meyrowitz, *No Sense of Place: The Impact of Electronic Media on Social Behavior* (Oxford University Press, 1985), pp. 131–149, 353. Copyright © 1985 by Oxford University Press. Reprinted by permission. Some notes and references omitted.

7.1 From Norbert Wiener, *The* Human *Use of Human Beings: Cybernetics and Society* (Houghton Mifflin, 1950). Copyright © 1950 by Norbert Wiener. Copyright renewed 1977 by Margaret Wiener. Reprinted by permission of Houghton Mifflin Company. All rights reserved.

7.2 From Claude E. Shannon and Warren Weaver, *The Mathematical Theory of Communication* (University of Illinois Press, 1964). Copyright © 1964 by the Board of Trustees of the University of Illinois. Reprinted by permission of the authors and University of Illinois Press. Some notes omitted.

7.3 From Michael Heim, *The Metaphysics of Virtual Reality* (Oxford University Press, 1993), pp. 13–17, 19–22. Copyright © 1993 by Michael Heim. Reprinted by permission of Oxford University Press, Inc.

8.1 From Herbert I. Schiller, *The Mind Managers* (Beacon Press, 1973), pp. 1, 3–5, 8–23, 192–193. Copyright © 1973 by Herbert I. Schiller. Reprinted by permission of Beacon Press.

8.2 From Edward S. Herman and Noam Chomsky, *Manufacturing Consent: The Political Economy of the Mass Media* (Pantheon Books, 1988). Copyright © 1988 by Edward S. Herman and Noam Chomsky. Reprinted by permission of Pantheon Books, a division of Random House, Inc. Some notes omitted.

8.3 From Martin A. Lee and Norman Solomon, *Unreliable Sources: A Guide to Detecting Bias in News Media* (Carol Publishing Group, 1990), pp. 59, 68–78, 80–84. Copyright © 1990 by Martin A. Lee and Norman Solomon. Reprinted by permission.

9.1 From Stuart Ewen, *Captains of Consciousness: Advertising and the Social Roots of the Consumer Culture* (McGraw-Hill, 1976), pp. 23–37, 41–48. Copyright © 1976 by Stuart Ewen. Reprinted by permission.

9.2 From Dallas W. Smythe, *Dependency Road: Communications, Capitalism, Consciousness, and Canada* (Ablex, 1981). Copyright © 1981 by Dallas W. Smythe. Reprinted by permission.

9.3 From Sut Jhally, "Image-Based Culture: Advertising and Popular Culture," *The World and I* (July 1990), pp. 507–519. Copyright © 1990 by *The World and I.* Reprinted by permission of *The World and I,* a publication of *The Washington Times Corporation.*

10.1 From James W. Carey, *Communication as Culture: Essays on Media and Society* (Unwin Hyman, 1989), pp. 14–23, 25–34. Copyright © 1989 by Unwin Hyman. Reprinted by permission. Notes omitted.

10.2 From Dick Hebdige, *Subculture: The Meaning of Style* (Routledge, 1979), pp. 5–17, 169, 172–174, 176–177. Copyright © 1979 by Dick Hebdige. Reprinted by permission. Notes omitted.

11.1 From Stanley Aronowitz, "Working Class Culture in the Electronic Age," in Ian Angus and Sut Jhally, eds., *Cultural Politics in Contemporary America* (Routledge,

1989). Copyright © 1989 by Routledge, Chapman and Hall, Inc. Reprinted by permission of the publisher.

11.2 From John Nguyet Erni, *Unstable Frontiers: Technomedicine and the Cultural Politics of "Curing" AIDS* (University of Minnesota Press, 1994), pp. 34–67. Copyright © 1994 by the Regents of the University of Minnesota. Reprinted by permission. Notes omitted.

12.1 From Molly Haskell, *From Reverence to Rape: The Treatment of Women in the Movies* (Holt, Rinehart & Winston, 1974). Copyright © 1973, 1974, 1987 by Molly Haskell. Reprinted by permission of Georges Borchardt, Inc., for the author.

12.2 From Annette Kuhn, "Lawless Seeing," in *The Power of the Image: Essays on Representation and Sexuality* (Routledge & Kegan Paul, 1985). Copyright © 1985 by Annette Kuhn. Reprinted by permission. Notes omitted.

12.3 From Elayne Rapping, *Media-tions: Forays into the Culture and Gender Wars* (South End Press, 1994), pp. 27–37. Copyright © 1994 by Elayne Rapping. Reprinted by permission of South End Press, 116 Saint Botolph Street, Boston, MA 02115.

13.1 From J. Fred MacDonald, *Blacks and White TV: African Americans in Television Since 1948*, 2d ed. (Nelson-Hall, 1992), pp. 59–71. Copyright © 1992 by J. Fred MacDonald. Reprinted by permission.

13.2 From Michael Eric Dyson, *Reflecting Black: African-American Cultural Criticism* (University of Minnesota Press, 1993), pp. 3–15. Copyright © 1993 by the Regents of the University of Minnesota. Reprinted by permission.

13.3 From Michele Wallace, "*Boyz N the Hood* and *Jungle Fever*," in Gina Dent, ed., *Black Popular Culture* (Bay Press, 1992). Copyright © 1992 by The Dia Center for the Arts. Reprinted by permission.

14.1 From Daniel Lerner, *The Passing of Traditional Society: Modernizing the Middle East* (Free Press, 1958), pp. 43–75. Copyright © 1958 by The Free Press. Reprinted by permission of The Free Press, a division of Simon & Schuster. Some notes omitted.

14.2 From Everett M. Rogers, "Communication and Development: The Passing of the Dominant Paradigm," in Everett M. Rogers, ed., *Communication and Development: Critical Perspectives* (Sage Publications, 1976). Copyright © 1976 by Sage Publications, Inc. Reprinted by permission.

14.3 From Majid Tehranian, *Technologies of Power: Information Machines and Democratic Prospects* (Ablex, 1990). Copyright © 1990 by Ablex Publishing Corporation. Reprinted by permission.

15.1 From Cees J. Hamelink, *Cultural Automony in Global Communications: Planning National Information Policy* (Longman, 1983). Copyright © 1983 by Longman, Inc. Reprinted by permission. Some notes omitted.

15.2 From Ali Mohammadi, "Cultural Imperialism and Cultural Identity," in John Downing, Ali Mohammadi, and Annabelle Sreberny-Mohammadi, eds., *Questioning the Media: A Critical Introduction*, 2d ed. (Sage Publications, 1995), pp. 363–377. Copyright © 1995 by Sage Publications, Inc. Reprinted by permission.

Index